COMPANY LAW

AUSTRALIA
Law Book Co.
Sydney

CANADA and USA
Carswell
Toronto

HONG KONG
Sweet & Maxwell Asia

NEW ZEALAND
Brookers
Wellington

SINGAPORE and MALAYSIA
Sweet & Maxwell Asia
Singapore and Kuala Lumpur

GREENS CONCISE SCOTS LAW

COMPANY LAW

by

Nicholas J.M. Grier, M.A., LL.B., W.S., Solicitor
Lecturer in Law, Napier University, Edinburgh

EDINBURGH
W. GREEN/Sweet & Maxwell
2002

Published in 2002 by W. Green & Son Ltd
21 Alva Street
Edinburgh EH2 4PS

Typeset by Interactive Sciences Ltd, Gloucester
Printed in Great Britain by Creative Print and Design
(wales), Ebbw Vale

No natural forests were destroyed to make this product;
only farmed timber was used and replanted

A CIP catalogue record for this book is available from
the British Library.

ISBN 0 414 014 960
© W. Green and Son Ltd 2002

PREFACE

This book is written at a testing time for company law. Not only are there proposals in the U.K. for a proposed new statute for companies, at present in draft form attached to the Government's White Paper, but there is an Enterprise Bill in the wings which may abolish, in the long run, much of the law and practice relating to receiverships, and a Corporate Responsibility Bill which aims to protect the interest of that amorphous group, stakeholders. At an international level, the recent scandals in the USA, such as Enron, Worldcom, and Tyco, not to mention the problems affecting Andersens, have shown the need for company laws and accounting rules that encourage fair dealing, the straightforward presentation of accounts and proper corporate governance. In the long run, anything else is counterproductive. There is also a growing awareness that in the field of commerce, compliance with the letter of the law is no longer sufficient: compliance with the spirit of the law, particularly when it comes to matters such as disclosure and transparency, as well as the need to act in good faith, is becoming more important.

At the same time, however, that flimsy rag, the corporate veil, still acts to divide the company from its managers and owners, and still permits directors and members to walk away from their companies' debts or negligence in the overall interest of encouraging commerce. The law accordingly to face both ways: it has to encourage fail dealing but not deter business.

Where does Scots law fit into this? The actual Scottishness of company law in Scotland is minimal. The Scottish rules on insolvency are different from those in England, as are the rules on floating charges and receivers. But in most other respects the law is much the same. There are Scottish versions of, for example, *Foss v. Harbottle* but it seems pointless in a book of this size referring to them when any practitioner would nowadays refer to the better known English case. In writing this book I have tried to emphasise the commercial nature of company law and to present appropriate cases and legislation from either side of the border. In so doing, it is hard not to be aware of each country's deficiencies. The worst example of this is in the law relating to receiverships and charges. In Scotland, at least until *Sharp v. Thomson*, the law on receivership was relatively clear albeit unsophisticated—but at least you knew what it was. A charge was either fixed or it wasn't, and unsecured creditors knew where they stood. *Sharp v. Thomson*, of course, however humane in its judgment, has done the law no favours.

By contrast, English law, with its ceaseless quest for ever greater flexibility, particularly to benefit the secured creditor, has sometimes made it very difficult to know if a charge is fixed or not, if it ranks ahead of some other charge, or if it is even registrable—it is no wonder that the Enterprise Bill, proposing the demise of administrative receivers, was drafted. The two national approaches could not be further apart, and yet what ultimately matters is that the law should be effective, easily comprehensible, cheap to operate and fair to all participants. Easy to say: hard to put into practice.

Suggested reading

At the end of most chapters I have included some suggested reading, but some chapters are about matters that are entirely procedural and clear cut and so there are very few relevant published articles about those matters. These matters are often well covered in company secretarial manuals, such as those published by CCH. The White Paper on company law is available from the DTI website (http://www/dti.gov.uk/whitepaper) and is well worth frequent reference.

   I have included many references to the most readable of the many books on company law, Davies' *Gower's Principles of Modern Company Law*. Although this is not necessarily the most technical of the books on company law, it has the great virtue of approachability. Readers requiring a more detailed approach should consult Palmer's *Company Law*, magisterially edited as regards Scottish matters by David Bennet W.S.; while for day to day practical matters, Tolleys has much to recommend it.

The readership of this book

This book will, it is hoped, be of use to practitioners, accountants, businessmen, students, and anyone else involved in the practice or study of company law. It is not as detailed as a company secretary manual, nor does it cover subjects in quite such depth as the great authorities on company law referred to above. But it is to be hoped that it will provide an overview, a commentary and an explanation of most of the important practical and theoretical matters arising in company law.

Acknowledgements

I have been encouraged in the writing of this book by my editors. Neil McKinlay and Luisa Deas, by the always good advice of Josephine Bisacre of Napier University, by other colleagues and friends at the Schools of Law at both Napier University and the University of Edinburgh, and by the kind of forbearance of my wife, Jean, who put up with my many hours spent writing this book. Any errors and omissions are of course my own responsibility.

Dedication

This book is dedicated to the memory of my late uncle, Francis Martin, who trained as a lawyer in Edinburgh but practised for many years in the Far East. He was a respected and sensitive translator of modern Thai literature and a meticulous legal draftsman, with particular skills in trademark law and company law. This is but a small mark of my gratitude towards him for many kindnesses.

Nicholas Grier
Napier University
October 2002

CONTENTS

Preface v
Table of U.K. Cases xi
Table of Statutes xxi
Table of Statutory Instruments xxxiii
List of Abbreviations xxxv

1. Introduction 1
2. The Corporate Veil 20
3. Company Incorporation 36
4. The Memorandum and Articles of Association 56
5. Securities 71
6. Capital Maintenance 92
7. Dividends and Accounts 116
8. Directors I: Appointment, Dismissal and Disqualification . 140
9. Directors II: Rights, Duties, Liabilities and Other Obligations 161
10. Company Secretary and Auditor 185
11. Minority Protection and DTI Investigations 196
12. Insider Dealing 222
13. Meetings and Resolutions 235
14. Takeovers and Mergers 250
15. Charges and Receivership 261
16. Winding Up 283
17. Administration and Company Voluntary Arrangements ... 303

Index 311

TABLE OF CASES

A & BC CHEWING GUM Ltd, Re; *sub nom*. Topps Chewing Gum Inc v. Coakley
[1975] 1 W.L.R. 579; [1975] 1 All E.R. 1017 .... 4.24
ADT Ltd v. Binder Hamlyn [1996] B.C.C. 808 ....10.18
A Company (No. 005287 of 1985), Re [1986] 1 W.L.R. 281; [1986] 2 All E.R.
253 .... 11.16, 11.28
A Company (No. 005009 of 1987) ex p. Copp, Re (1988) 4 B.C.C. 424; [1989]
B.C.L.C. 13 .... 8.13
A Company (No. 000789 of 1987) ex p. Shooter, Re [1990] B.C.L.C. 384 ....11.23
—— (No. 000709 of 1992), Re. *See* O'Neill v. Phillips
—— (No. 0032314 of 1992), Re. *See* Duckwari plc (No. 1), Re
—— (No. 004803 of 1996), Re. *See* Secretary of State for Trade and Industry
v. Taylor
Abbey Leisure, Re; *sub nom*. Virdi v. Abbey Leisure [1990] B.C.C. 60; [1990]
B.C.L.C. 342 ....16.18
Aberdeen Combworks Ltd, Petrs (1902) 10 S.L.T. 210 ....13.13
Aberdeen Railway Co. v. Blaikie Bros (1854) 1 Macq. 461 .... 9.05
Acatos and Hutcheson plc v. Watson [1995] B.C.C. 446; [1995] 1 B.C.L.C.
218 .... 6.23
Adam & Partners Ltd, Re. *See* IRC v. Adams and Partners Ltd
Adams v. Cape Industries plc [1990] Ch. 433; [1990] 2 W.L.R. 657; [1991] 1 All
E.R. 929 .... 2.14, 2.17
Advocate (H.M.) v. Mackie, 1994 J.C. 132; 1995 S.L.T. 110; 1994 S.C.C.R. 277 ...12.23
Advocate (Lord) v. Royal Bank of Scotland, 1977 S.C. 155; 1978 S.L.T. 38 ....15.37
Aerators Ltd v. Tollitt [1902] 2 Ch. 319 .... 3.08
Agnew v. IRC. *See* Brumark Investments Ltd, Re
Airlines Airspares Ltd v. Handley Page Ltd [1970] Ch. 193; [1970] 2 W.L.R.
163; [1970] 1 All E.R. 29 ....15.29
Allied Carpets Group plc v. Nethercott [2001] B.C.C. 81 .... 7.25
Amaron Ltd, Re (No. 1). *See* Secretary of State for Trade and Industry v.
Lubrani (No. 1)
Anderson v. Hogg, 2000 S.L.T. 634 ....11.13
Andrew v. Kounnis Freeman [1999] 2 B.C.L.C. 641; [2000] Lloyd's Rep. P.N.
263 ....10.18
Anglo-Austrian Printing and Publishing Union (No. 3), Re Sub Nom: Bra-
bourne v Anglo-Austrian Printing and Publishing Union [1895] 2 Ch.
891 .... 9.44, 15.33
Arab Bank plc v. Mercantile Holdings Ltd [1994] Ch. 71; [1994] 2 W.L.R. 307;
[1994] 1 B.C.L.C. 330 .... 6.16
Arctic Engineering Ltd, Re [1986] 1 W.L.R. 686; [1986] 2 All E.R. 346; [1986]
B.C.L.C. 253 (not in citator) 8.26
Armour v. Mycroft, Ptns, 1983 S.L.T. 453 ....15.37
—— v. Thyssen Edelstahlwerke [1991] 2 A.C. 339, [1990] 3 W.L.R. 810, [1990]
3 All E.R. 481, 1990 S.L.T. 891, [1991] B.C.L.C. 28, 1990 B.C.C. 925 ...... 15.13,
16.32

Armour Hick Northern Ltd v. Whitehouse [1980] 1 W.L.R. 1520; [1980] 3 All
    E.R. 833 .... 6.18
Ash & Newman Ltd v. Creative Devices Research Ltd [1991] B.C.L.C. 403 ......15.29
Ashbury Railway Carriage and Iron Co. Ltd v. Riche (1875) L.R. 7 HL 653 ...... 4.05
Association of Certified Public Accountants of Britain v. Secretary of State for
    Trade and Industry [1998] 1 W.L.R. 164; [1997] B.C.C. 736; [1997] 2
    B.C.L.C. 307 .... 3.06
Astec (BSR) plc, Re [1999] B.C.C. 59; [1998] 2 B.C.L.C. 556 .. 4.21, 11.32, 11.34, 14.06
Atlas Wright (Europe) Ltd v. Wright. *See* Wright v. Atlas Wright (Europe)
    Ltd
Aveling Barford Ltd v. Perion Ltd [1989] B.C.L.C. 626; [1989] P.C.C. 370 ..... 7.24,
                                                                                                           9.13

BABY MOON (UK) LTD, RE [1985] P.C.C. 103 .... 3.04
Bahia and San Francisco Railway Co. Ltd, Re (1868) L.R. 3 Q.B. 584 ... 5.20, 5.27
Baltic Real Estate Ltd (No. 2), Re [1992] B.C.C. 629; [1993] B.C.L.C. 498; [1993]
    B.C.L.C. 503 ....11.27
Bairstow v. Queens Moat Houses plc [2000] B.C.C. 1025; [2000] 1 B.C.L.C.
    549 .... 7.25
Baku Consolidated Oilfields Ltd, Re [1993] B.C.C. 653; [1994] 2 B.C.L.C.
    173 .... 5.20
Bamford v. Bamford [1970] Ch. 212; [1969] 2 W.L.R. 1107; [1969] 1 All E.R.
    969 .... 9.10, 9.13
Barclays Bank plc v. British and Commonwealth Holdings Ltd [1996] 1
    W.L.R. 1; [1996] 1 All E.R. 381; [1996] 1 B.C.L.C. 1 .... 6.13
Barings plc v. Coopers and Lybrand [1997] B.C.C. 498; [1997] 1 B.C.L.C. 427 ...10.18
—— (No. 6), Re. *See* Secretary of State for Trade and Industry v. Baker (No.
    6)
Barlow v. Polly Peck International Finance Ltd. *See* Polly Peck International
    Plc (Jn Administration) (No. 4), Re
Barrett v. Duckett [1995] B.C.C. 362; [1995] 1 B.C.L.C. 243 reversing [1993]
    B.C.C. 778; [1995] 1 B.C.L.C. 73 ....11.13
Barron v. Potter [1914] 1 Ch. 895; 83 L.J. Ch. 646 .... 8.01
Barton Manufacturing Co Ltd, Re [1998] B.C.C. 827; [1999] 1 B.C.L.C. 740 ......16.28
Bell Houses Ltd v. City Wall Properties Ltd (No. 1) [1966] 2 Q.B. 656; [1966]
    2 W.L.R. 1323; [1966] 2 All E.R. 674 .... 4.05
Belmont Finance Corp. v. Williams Furniture Ltd (No. 2) [1980] 1 All E.R.
    393 .... 6.18
Biba Group Ltd v. Biba Boutique [1980] R.P.C. 413 .... 3.08
Bird Precision Bellows Ltd, Re [1986] Ch. 658; [1986] 2 W.L.R. 158 ... 11.25, 11.33
Bishopsgate Investment Management Ltd (in liquidation) v. Ian Maxwell
    (No. 1) [1994] 1 All E.R. 261, [1993] B.C.L.C. 1282 .... 9.09
Bloomenthal v. Ford [1897] A.C. 156 .... 5.20, 5.27
Blum v. OCP Repartition SA (1988) 4 B.C.C. 771; [1988] B.C.L.C. 170; [1988]
    F.L.R. 229 .... 2.09
Bonus Breaks Ltd, Re [1991] B.C.C. 546 .... 3.06, 9.49
Borland's Trs v. Steel Bros & Co. Ltd [1901] 1 Ch. 279 .... 5.02
Boston Deep Sea Fishing Co. Ltd v. Ansell (1888) L.R. 39 Ch. D. 339 .... 9.07
Bottrill v. Secretary of State for Trade and Industry. *See* Secretary of State for
    Trade and Industry v. Bottrill
Brady v. Brady [1989] A.C. 755; [1988] 2 W.L.R. 1308; reversing (1987) 3 B.C.C.
    535; [1988] B.C.L.C. 20 .... 6.18, 6.19
Bratton Seymour Service Co. Ltd v. Oxborough [1992] B.C.C. 471; [1992]
    B.C.L.C. 693 .... 4.21
Breckland Group Holdings Ltd v. London and Suffolk Properties (1988) 4
    B.C.C. 542; [1989] B.C.L.C. 100 .... 4.21
Brenfield Squash Racquets Club Ltd, Re [1996] 2 B.C.L.C. 384 ....11.23

Brian D. Pierson (Contractors) Ltd, Re; *sub nom.* Penn v. Pierson [1999] B.C.C.
26; [2001] 1 B.C.L.C. 275 .... 9.48
Brown v. British Abrasive Wheel Co. Ltd [1919] 1 Ch. 290 .... 4.23
Brumark Investments Ltd, Re; *sub nom.* Inland Revenue Commissioner v.
Agnew; Agnew v. IRC [2001] UKPC 28; [2001] 2 A.C. 710; [2001] 3 W.L.R.
454 ....15.07
Bugle Press Limited, Re; *sub nom.* Houses & Estates Ltd, Re; HC Treby's
Application [1961] Ch. 270; [1960] 3 W.L.R. 956 ....14.13
Bushell v. Faith [1970] A.C. 1099; [1970] 2 W.L.R. 272 .... 4.21, 13.04

C. Evans Ltd v. Spritebrand Ltd [1985] 1 W.L.R. 317; [1985] 2 All E.R. 415 ...... 9.34
CS Holidays Ltd, Re. *See* Secretary of State for Trade and Industry v. Tay-
lor
Cameron v. Glenmorangie Distillery Co. Ltd (1896) 23 R. 1092 .... 6.44
Caparo Industries plc v. Dickman Touche Ross [1990] 2 A.C. 605; [1990] 2
W.L.R. 358; [1990] 1 All E.R. 568 ....10.18
Cargo Agency Ltd, Re [1992] B.C.C. 388; [1992] B.C.L.C. 686 .... 8.33
Charterhouse Investment Trust Ltd v. Tempest Diesels Ltd [1985] W.L.
312033 .... 6.13
Chartmore Ltd, Re [1990] B.C.L.C. 673 .... 8.33
City Equitable Fire Insurance Co Ltd, Re [1925] Ch. 407; [1924] All E.R. Rep.
485 .... 9.14
Cohen v. Selby [2002] B.C.C. 82; [2001] 1 B.C.L.C. 176 .... 9.17
Cook v. Deeks [1916] 1 A.C. 554 .... 9.13, 11.11
Copp v. D'Jan. *See* D'Jan of London Ltd, Re
Coulthard v. Russell [1998] B.C.C. 359; [1998] 1 B.C.L.C. 143 ....10.17
Craven Insurance Co. Ltd, Re [1968] 1 W.L.R. 675; [1968] 1 All E.R. 1140 ....16.17
Creasey v. Breachwood Motors Ltd [1992] B.C.C. 638; [1993] B.C.L.C. 480 .... 2.13,
                                                                                                            2.20, 2.29
Cumana Ltd, Re [1986] B.C.L.C. 430 ....11.30
Cumbrian Newspapers Group Ltd v. Cumberland and Westmorland Herald
and Printing Co. Ltd [1987] Ch. 1; [1986] 3 W.L.R. 26; [1986] B.C.L.C.
286 .... 4.23
Cunninghame v. Walkingshaw Oil Co. Ltd (1886) 14 R. 87 ....16.17

DHN Food Distributors Ltd v. Tower Hamlets LBC [1976] 1 W.L.R. 852;
[1976] 3 All E.R. 462 .... 2.17
DKG Contractors Ltd, Re [1990] B.C.C. 903 ....16.28
Daido Asia Japan Co. Ltd v. Rothen, unreported, Chancery 1997, July 24,
2001 .... 9.35
Daimler Co. Ltd v. Continental Tyre and Rubber Co. (Great Britain) Ltd
[1916] 2 A.C. 307 .... 2.15
Daniels v. Daniels [1978] Ch. 406; [1978] 2 W.L.R. 73 ....11.11
Data Express Ltd, Re, *The Times*, April 27, 1987 .... 5.19
Dawson International plc v. Coats Paton plc, 1988 S.L.T. 854 .... 9.11
Dawson Print Group Ltd, Re (1987) 3 B.C.C. 322; [1987] B.C.L.C. 601 .... 8.30
Director General of Fair Trading v. Pioneer Concrete (UK) Ltd; *sub nom.*
Supply of Ready Mixed Concrete (No. 2), Re [1995] 1 A.C. 456; [1994] 3
W.L.R. 1249 .... 2.27
D'Jan of London Ltd, Re; *sub nom.* Copp v. D'Jan [1993] B.C.C. 646; [1994] 1
B.C.L.C. 561 .... 7.25, 9.15, 9.16, 9.43
Dorchester Finance Co Ltd v. Stebbing [1989] B.C.L.C. 498 .... 9.15
Duckwari Plc v. Offerventure Ltd (No.1). *See* Duckwari plc (No. 1), Re
—— v. Offerventure Ltd (No. 2). *See* Duckwari plc (No. 2), Re
—— (No. 1), Re; *sub nom.* Duckwari Plc v. Offerventure Ltd (No.1); A
Company (No. 0032314 of 1992), Re [1995] B.C.C. 89; [1997] 2 B.C.L.C.
713 .... 9.25

Duckwari plc (No. 2), Re; *sub nom*. Duckwari Plc v. Offerventure Ltd (No. 2)
[1999] Ch. 253; [1998] 3 W.L.R. 913; *The Times*, May 18, 1998 .... 9.25
Dunlop Pneumatic Tyre Co. Ltd v. Dunlop Motor Co. Ltd, 1907 S.C. (HL)
15 .... 3.08

EDC v. UNITED KINGDOM [1998] B.C.C. 370, ECHR 8.29, 8.36
Ebrahimi v. Westbourne Galleries Ltd [1973] A.C. 360, [1972] 2 All E.R.
492 .... 11.34, 16.18
Edwards v. Halliwell [1950] 2 All E.R. 1064; [1950] W.N. 537 .... 11.09
Electra Private Equity Partners v. KPMG Peat Marwick [2000] B.C.C. 368;
[2001] 1 B.C.L.C. 589 .... 10.18
Eley v. Positive Government Security Life Assurance Co Ltd (1875) L.R. 1 Ex.
D. 20 .... 4.21
Elgindata Ltd, Re [1991] B.C.L.C. 959 .... 11.32
Equitable Life Assn. v. Hyman [2002] 1 A.C. 408; [2000] 3 W.L.R. 529; [2000]
3 All E.R. 961 .... 4.21
Erlanger v. New Sombrero Phosphate Co. Ltd (1878) 3 App. Cas. 1218 .... 3.39
Ewing v. Buttercup Margarine Co. Ltd [1917] 2 Ch. 1; (1917) 34 R.P.C. 232 .... 3.08
Exchange Banking Co. (Flitcroft's Case), Re (1882) 21 Ch. D. 519 .... 7.25

FG (FILMS) LTD, RE [1953] 1 W.L.R. 483; [1953] 1 All E.R. 615 .... 2.16
Fahey Developments Ltd, Re. *See* Lowe v. Fahey
Firestone Tyre & Rubber Co. Ltd v. Lewellin [1957] 1 W.L.R. 464; [1957] 1 All
E.R. 561; affirming [1956] 1 W.L.R. 352; [1956] 1 All E.R. 693 .... 2.19
Forth Wines Ltd, Petrs, 1993 S.L.T. 170 .... 6.10
Foss v. Harbottle (1843) 2 Hare 461 .. 11.03, 11.04, 11.05, 11.07, 11.13, 11.14, 11.38
Freeman & Lockyer v. Buckhurst Park Properties (Mangal) Ltd [1964] 2 Q.B.
480; [1964] 2 W.L.R. 618 .... 8.06
Freevale Ltd v. Metrostore Ltd [1984] Ch. 199; [1984] 2 W.L.R. 496; [1984] 1
All E.R. 495 .... 15.29
Fulham Football Ltd v. Cabra Estates plc [1992] B.C.C. 863; [1994] 1 B.C.L.C.
363 .... 9.11

GALOO LTD v. BRIGHT GRAHAME MURRAY [1994] 1 W.L.R. 1360; [1994] 1 All
E.R. 16; [1994] B.C.L.C. 319 .... 9.45, 10.19
Gencor ACP Ltd v. Dalby [2000] 2 B.C.L.C. 734; [2001] W.T.L.R. 825 .... 9.08
German Date Coffee Co. Ltd, Re (1882) 20 Ch. D. 169; 46 L.T. 327 ..... 4.05, 16.18
Gibson Davies Ltd, Re [1995] B.C.C. 11 .... 8.33
Gilford Motor Co. Ltd v. Horne [1933] Ch. 935 .... 2.14
Grampian RC v. Drill Stem (Inspection Services) Ltd (in receivership), 1994
SCLR 36 .... 15.37
Greenhalgh v. Arderne Cinemas Ltd [1951] Ch. 286; [1950] 2 All E.R. 1120 ...... 4.23
Grosvenor Press plc [1985] 1 W.L.R. 980; [1985] P.C.C. 260 .... 6.07
Guinness plc v. Ward and Saunders [1990] 2 A.C. 663; [1990] 2 W.L.R. 324;
[1990] 1 All E.R. 652 .... 8.01

HC TREYS'S APPLICATION. *See* Bugle Press Limited, Re
H.R. Harmer Ltd, Re [1959] 1 W.L.R. 62; [1958] 3 All E.R. 689 .... 11.29
Haematite Steel Co. Ltd [1901] 2 Ch. 746 .... 6.07
Halls v. David. *See* Produce Marketing Consortium (In Liquidation) (No.1),
Re
Harold Holdsworth & Co. (Wakefield) Ltd v. Caddies [1955] 1 W.L.R. 352;
[1955] 1 All E.R. 725 .... 8.06
Heald v. O'Connor [1971] 1 W.L.R. 497; [1971] 2 All E.R. 1105 .... 6.16
Hickman v. Kent and Romney Marsh Sheepbreeders Assn. [1915] 1 Ch. 881 ... 4.21
Hogg v. Cramphorn [1967] Ch. 254; [1966] 3 W.L.R. 995 .... 9.10
Holders Investment Trust Ltd, Re [1971] 1 W.L.R. 583; [1971] 2 All E.R. 289 .... 6.11
Hong Kong and China Gas Co Ltd v. Glen [1914] 1 Ch. 527 .... 5.16

Houldsworth v. Yorkshire Woolcombers Association Ltd. *See* Illingworth v. Houldsworth

House of Fraser v. ACGE Investments Ltd [1987] A.C. 387; [1987] 2 W.L.R. 1083 .... 6.07

Houses & Estates Ltd, Re. *See* Bugle Press Limited, Re

Howard Smith Ltd v. Ampol Petroleum Ltd [1974] A.C. 821; [1974] 2 W.L.R. 689 .... 9.10

Hunt v. Edge & Ellison Trustees Ltd; *sub nom.* Torvale Group Ltd, Re [2000] B.C.C. 626; [1999] 2 B.C.L.C. 605 .... 9.26

Hydrodan (Corby) Ltd, Re [1994] B.C.C. 161; [1994] 2 B.C.L.C. 180 .... 8.13

ILLINGWORTH V. HOULDSWORTH; *sub nom.* Houldsworth v. Yorkshire Wool-combers Association Ltd; Yorkshire Woolcombers Association Ltd, Re [1903] 2 Ch. 284 ....15.16

Imperial Hotel (Aberdeen) Ltd v. Vaux Breweries Ltd, 1978 S.C. 86; 1978 S.L.T. 113 ....15.28

Independent Pension Trustee Ltd v. Law Construction Co Ltd, 1997 S.L.T. 1105 ....15.28

Industrial Development Consultants Ltd v. Cooley [1972] 1 W.L.R. 443; [1972] 2 All E.R. 162 .... 9.08

IRC v. Adams and Partners Ltd; *sub nom.* Adam & Partners Ltd, Re [2000] B.C.C. 513; [1999] 2 B.C.L.C. 730 ....17.09

—— v. Agnew. *See* Brumark Investments Ltd, Re

JENICE LTD v. DAN [1994] B.C.C. 43; [1993] B.C.L.C. 1349 .... 2.09

Jesner v. Jarrad Properties Ltd, 1993 S.C. 34; 1994 S.L.T. 83; [1993] B.C.L.C. 1032 ....16.18

Jones v. Lipman [1962] 1 W.L.R. 832; [1962] 1 All E.R. 442 .... 2.14

Jupiter House Investments (Cambridge) Ltd [1985] 1 W.L.R. 975; (1985) 82 L.S.G. 2817 .... 6.07

KINGSTON COTTON MILL (NO. 2), RE [1896] 2 Ch. 279 ....10.17

Konamaneni v. Rolls Royce Industrial Power (India) Ltd [2002] 1 W.L.R. 1269; [2002] 1 All E.R. 979; [2002] 1 All E.R. (Comm) 532; [2002] 1 B.C.L.C. 336 ....11.13

Knight v. Frost [1999] B.C.C. 819; [1999] 1 B.C.L.C. 364 ....11.13

Kuwait Asia Bank E.C. v. National Mutual Life Nominees Ltd [1991] 1 A.C. 187; [1990] 3 W.L.R. 297; [1990] B.C.L.C. 868 .... 8.13

LAFFERTY CONSTRUCTION LTD v. McCOMBE, 1994 S.L.T. 858 ....16.25

Laing v. Gowans (1902) 10 S.L.T. 461 (OH) 16.08

Lander v. Premier Pict Petroleum Ltd, 1997 S.L.T. 1361; [1998] B.C.C. 248 ... 9.20

Lee v. Lee's Air Farming Ltd [1961] A.C. 12; [1960] 3 W.L.R. 758 .... 2.02

Legal Costs Negotiators Ltd, Re [1999] B.C.C. 547; [1999] 2 B.C.L.C. 171 .....11.27

Lindop v. Stewart Noble & Sons Ltd; *sub nom.* Lindop v. Stuart Noble & Sons Ltd, 1999 S.C.L.R. 889; [2000] B.C.C. 747 ....15.30

—— v. Stuart Noble & Sons Ltd. *See* Lindop v. Stewart Noble & Sons Ltd

Liquidator of West Mercia Safetywear Ltd v. Dodd; *sub nom.* West Mercia Safetywear (In Liquidation) v. Dodd (1988) 4 B.C.C. 30; [1988] B.C.L.C. 250 .... 9.34

Lithgow Factoring Ltd (t/a Inver Salmon) v. Nordvik Salmon Farms Ltd, 1999 S.L.T. 106; 1998 S.C.L.R. 496 ....15.36

Lloyd Cheyham & Co. Ltd v. Littlejohn & Co [1987] B.C.L.C. 303; [1986] P.C.C. 389 .... 7.05

Lo-Line Electric Motors Ltd, Re [1988] Ch. 477; [1988] 3 W.L.R. 26 .... 8.30

Loch v. John Blackwood Ltd [1924] A.C. 783; [1924] All E.R. Rep. 200 ....16.18

London School of Electronics Ltd, Re [1986] Ch. 211; [1985] 3 W.L.R. 474 ...11.26

Lowe v. Fahey; *sub nom.* Fahey Developments Ltd, Re [1996] B.C.C. 320;
  [1996] 1 B.C.L.C. 262 ....11.13
Lubbe v. Cape Industries plc [2000] 4 All E.R. 268 .... 2.29

MACAURA V. NORTHERN ASSURANCE COMPANY LTD [1925] A.C. 619 .... 2.03
Macleod v. Alexander Sutherland Ltd, 1977 S.L.T. (Notes) 44 ....15.29
Maxwell v. Department of Trade and Industry [1974] Q.B. 523; [1974] 2
  W.L.R. 338 ....11.44
Medforth v. Blake [2000] Ch. 86; [1999] 3 W.L.R. 922; [1999] B.C.C. 771 ....15.28
Micro Leisure Ltd v. County Properties and Developments Ltd, 1999 S.L.T.
  1428; [2000] B.C.C. 872; *The Times,* January 12, 2000, (OH) 9.25
Mitchell and Hobbs (UK) Ltd v. Mill [1996] 2 B.C.L.C. 102 .... 8.01, 8.06
Moorgate Metals Ltd, Re [1995] B.C.C. 143; [1995] 1 B.C.L.C. 503 .... 8.34
Morphites v. Bernasconi [2001] 2 B.C.L.C. 1 .... 9.45
Morris v. Banque Arabe Internationale d'Investissement SA (No. 2) [2002]
  B.C.C. 407; [2001] 1 B.C.L.C. 263 .... 9.45
Mubarak v. Mubarak [2000] W.L. 1720346 .... 2.24
Multinational Gas and Petrochemical Co Ltd v. Multinational Gas and Pet-
  rochemical Services Ltd [1983] Ch. 258; [1983] 3 W.L.R. 492; [1983] 2 All
  E.R. 563 .... 9.34

NATIONAL WESTMINSTER BANK PLC V. IRC [1995] 1 A.C. 119; [1994] 3 W.L.R.
  159; [1994] 2 B.C.L.C. 239 .... 5.09
Neptune (Vehicle Washing Equipment) Ltd v. Fitzgerald [1996] Ch. 274;
  [1995] 3 W.L.R. 108; [1995] 3 All E.R. 811; [1995] B.C.C. 474; [1995] 1
  B.C.L.C. 352 .... 3.23, 8.01, 9.23
—— v. —— (No. 2), Re [1995] B.C.C. 1000 .... 9.28
New Bullas Trading Ltd [1994] B.C.C. 36; [1994] 1 B.C.L.C. 485 ....15.07
New Cedos Engineering Co., Re [1994] 1 B.C.L.C. 797 .... 5.19
New Technology Systems Ltd, Re; *sub nom.* Official Receiver v. Prior [1997]
  B.C.C. 810 .... 8.29
Newhart Developments Ltd v. Co-operative Commercial Bank Ltd [1978]
  Q.B. 814; [1978] 2 W.L.R. 636 ....15.28
Nicoll v. Steelpress (Supplies) Ltd, 1992 S.C. 119; 1993 S.L.T. 533 ..... 15.19, 16.25
Nordic Oil Services v. Berman, 1993 S.L.T. 1164 .... 9.34
Norfolk House plc (in receivership) v. Repsol Petroleum Ltd, 1992 S.L.T.
  235 ....15.34
North-West Transportation Co. v. Beatty (1887) 12 App.Cases. 589 .... 9.13
Northern Engineering Industries, Re [1993] B.C.C. 267; [1993] B.C.L.C.
  1151 .... 6.08
Norwest Holst Ltd v. Secretary of State for Trade [1978] Ch. 201; [1978] 3
  W.L.R. 73 ....11.43

O'NEILL V. PHILLIPS; *sub nom.* A Company (No. 000709 of 1992), Re; Pectel Ltd,
  Re [1999] 1 W.L.R. 1092; [1999] 2 All E.R. 961 .... 11.03, 11.34, 11.37
Official Receiver v. Brady [1999] B.C.C. 258 .... 8.25
—— v. Nixon. *See* Tasbian (No. 3) Ltd, Re
—— v. Prior. *See* New Technology Systems Ltd, Re
Ord v. Belhaven Pubs Ltd [1998] B.C.C. 607; [1998] 2 B.C.L.C. 447 .... 2.13, 2.20, 2.21

PANORAMA DEVELOPMENTS LTD V. FIDELIS FURNISHING FABRICS LTD [1971] 2
  Q.B. 711; [1971] 3 W.L.R. 440 ....10.04
Park House Properties Ltd, Re; *sub nom.* Secretary of State for Trade and
  Industry v. Carter [1998] B.C.C. 847; [1997] 2 B.C.L.C. 530 .... 8.24
Parlett v. Guppys (Bridport) Ltd [1996] B.C.C. 299; [1996] 2 B.C.L.C. 34 ...... 6.22
Patrick and Lyon Ltd, Re [1933] Ch. 786 ....16.28
Pavlides v. Jensen [1956] Ch. 565; [1956] 3 W.L.R. 224 ....11.11

Pectel Ltd, Re. *See* O'Neill v. Phillips
Pender v. Lushington (1877) L.R. 6 Ch. D. 70 ....11.10
Penn v. Pierson. *See* Brian D. Pierson (Contractors) Ltd, Re
Percival v. Wright [1902] 2 Ch. 421 .... 9.37
Pergamon Press Ltd, Re [1971] Ch. 388; [1970] 3 W.L.R. 792 ....11.44
Pettie v. Thomson Pettie Tube Products Ltd, 2001 S.C. 431; 2001 S.L.T. 473 ......11.31
Plaut v. Steiner (1989) 5 B.C.C. 352 .... 6.18
Platt v. Platt [1999] 2 B.C.L.C. 745 .... 9.38
Polly Peck International Plc (Jn Administration) (No. 4), Re; *sub nom.* Barlow
    v. Polly Peck International Finance Ltd [1996] 2 All E.R. 433; [1996]
    B.C.C. 486 .... 2.14
Polly Peck International plc (No. 3), Re; *sub nom.* Secretary of State for Trade
    and Industry v. Ellis (No.2) [1993] B.C.C. 890; [1994] 1 B.C.L.C. 574 ..... 8.29
Popely v. Planarrive Ltd, [1997] 1 B.C.L.C. 8; *The Times*, April 24, 1996 .... 5.19
Pow Services Ltd v. Clare [1995] 2 B.C.L.C. 435 .... 8.16
Precision Dippings (Marketing) Ltd [1986] Ch. 447; [1985] 3 W.L.R. 812 ...... 7.24
Produce Marketing Consortium (In Liquidation)(No.1), Re; *sub nom.* Halls v.
    David [1989] 1 W.L.R. 745; [1989] 3 All E.R. 1; (1989) 5 B.C.C. 399; [1989]
    B.C.L.C. 513 .... 9.43, 9.48, 16.28

QUAYLE MUNRO LTD, Petrs, 1992 S.C. 24; 1993 S.L.T. 723; [1994] 1 B.C.L.C.
    410 .... 6.07
Quin & Axtens Ltd v. Salmon; *sub nom.* Salmon v. Quin & Axtens Ltd [1909]
    A.C. 442 .... 4.21, 11.08

R. V. BROCKLEY [1994] B.C.C. 131; [1994] 1 B.C.L.C. 606 .... 8.27
——— v. Cole [1998] B.C.C. 87; [1998] 2 B.C.L.C. 234 .... 3.06, 9.49
——— v. Georgiou (1988) 4 B.C.C. 472; (1988) 87 Cr. App. R. 207 .... 8.26
——— v. Goodman [1993] 2 All E.R. 789; [1992] B.C.C. 625; [1994] 1 B.C.L.C.
    349 .... 8.26, 12.06
——— v. Great Western Trains Co Ltd, Att.-Gen. Ref. No. 2 of 1999 [2000] Q.B.
    796; [2000] 3 W.L.R. 195; [2000] 3 All E.R. 182; [2001] B.C.C. 210 .... 2.25
——— v. Kite and OLL Ltd, unreported, December 8, 1994 .... 2.25
——— v. McCredie [2000] 2 B.C.L.C. 438 .... 3.06
——— v. Panel on Takeovers and Mergers, ex p. Datafin [1987] Q.B. 815; [1987]
    2 W.L.R. 699 ....14.04
——— v. ———, ex p. Fayed plc [1992] B.C.C. 524; [1992] B.C.L.C. 938 ....14.04
——— v. ———, ex p. Guinness plc [1990] 1 Q.B. 146; [1989] 2 W.L.R. 863 ....14.04
——— v. Registrar of Companies, ex p. Att.-Gen. [1991] B.C.L.C. 476 .... 3.04
R. A. Noble (Clothing) Ltd [1983] B.C.L.C. 273 .... 11.19, 11.27
R. Gaffney and Son Ltd v. Davidson, 1996 S.L.T. (Sh.Ct) 36 .... 15.19, 16.25
R. Rollco Screw and Rivet Co Ltd, [1999] 2 Cr. App. R. (S.) 436; [1999] I.R.L.R.
    439; *The Times*, April 29, 1999 .... 9.36
Rankin v. Meek, 1995 S.L.T. 526 ....16.25
Ransomes plc, Re; *sub nom.* Ransomes Plc v. Winpar Holdings Ltd; Winpar
    Holdings Ltd v. Ransomes Plc [2000] B.C.C. 455; [1999] 2 B.C.L.C. 591 ..... 6.11
——— v. Winpar Holdings Ltd. *See* Ransomes plc, Re
Ratners Group plc, Re (1988) 4 B.C.C. 293; [1988] B.C.L.C. 685 .... 6.09
Rafsanjan Pistachio Producers Ltd v. Reiss [1990] B.C.C. 730; [1990] B.C.L.C.
    352 .... 2.08
Red Label Fashions Ltd, Re [1999] B.C.C. 308 .... 8.12
Regal Cinemas (Hastings) Ltd v. Gulliver [1967] 2 A.C. 134 (Note); [1942] 1
    All E.R. 378 .... 9.07
Rolled Steel Products (Holdings) Ltd v. British Steel Corporation [1986] Ch.
    246; [1985] 2 W.L.R. 908 .... 4.18

Royal Bank of Scotland v. Sandstone Properties Ltd [1998] 2 B.C.L.C. 429 .... 5.27
Royal British Bank v. Turquand (1856) 6 EI & BI 327; 5 E & B 248 .... 4.18
Russell v. Northern Bank Development Corp. Ltd [1992] 1 W.L.R. 588; [1992]
    3 All E.R. 161 .... 4.24

St PIRAN LTD, RE [1981] 1 W.L.R. 1300; [1981] 3 All E.R. 270 ....14.06
Salmon v. Quin & Axtens Ltd. *See* Quin & Axtens Ltd v. Salmon
Salomon v. A. Salomon & Co. Ltd (1887) A.C. 22 .... 2.01, 2.21
Saltdean Estate Co Ltd, Re [1968] 1 W.L.R. 1844; [1968] 3 All E.R. 829 .... 6.10
Sasea Finance Ltd v. KPMG [2000] 1 All E.R. 676; [2000] B.C.C. 989; [2000] 1
    B.C.L.C. 236 ....10.19
Saul Harrison & Sons plc, Re [1994] B.C.C. 475; [1995] 1 B.C.L.C. 14 ..... 11.33, 11.34
Saunders v. United Kingdom [1997] B.C.C. 872; [1998] 1 B.C.L.C. 362; (1997)
    23 E.H.R.R. 313 .... 8.36, 11.44
Scottish Insurance Corp Ltd v. Wilsons & Clyde Coal Co Ltd; *sub nom.*
    Wilsons & Clyde Coal Co Ltd, Petrs [1949] A.C. 462; [1949] 1 All E.R.
    1068; 1949 S.C. (H.L.) 90 .... 6.08
Secretary of State for Trade and Industry v. Baker (No. 5) [1999] 1 B.C.L.C.
    262 .... 8.31
—— v. —— (No.6); *sub nom.* Barings Plc (No. 6), Re [2001] B.C.C. 273; [2000]
    1 B.C.L.C. 523 affirming [1999] 1 B.C.L.C. 433 .... 8.30
—— v. Bottrill; *sub nom.* Bottrill v. Secretary of State for Trade and Industry
    [2000] 1 All E.R. 915; [1999] B.C.C. 177 .... 2.02
—— v. Carter. *See* Park House Properties Ltd, Re
—— v. Croshaw, unreported, 1999 .... 8.10
—— v. Deverell [2001] Ch. 340; [2000] 2 W.L.R. 907; [2000] 2 All E.R. 365;
    [2000] B.C.C. 1057; [2000] 2 B.C.L.C. 133 .... 8.13, 8.25
—— v. Ellis (No.2). *See* Polly Peck International plc (No. 3), Re
—— v. Griffiths. *See* Westmid Packaging Services Ltd (No. 2), Re
—— v. Hasta International Ltd, 1998 S.L.T. 73 ....16.20
—— v. Jones [1999] B.C.C. 336 .... 8.12
—— v. Laing [1996] 2 B.C.L.C. 324 .... 8.31
—— v. Lubrani (No. 1); *sub nom.* Amaron Ltd, Re (No. 1) [1997] 2 B.C.L.C.
    115 .... 8.31
—— v. McCormick [1998] 2 B.C.L.C. 18 ....11.44
—— v. Rosenfield [1999] B.C.C. 413 .... 8.33
—— v. Taylor; *sub nom.* CS Holidays Ltd, Re; A Company (No. 004803 of
    1996), Re [1997] 1 W.L.R. 407; [1997] 1 B.C.L.C. 341 .... 8.35
Sevenoaks Stationers (Retail) Ltd [1991] Ch. 164; [1990] 3 W.L.R. 1165; [1991]
    B.C.L.C. 325 .... 8.32
Shanks v. Central Regional Council, 1988 S.L.T. 212 ....15.28
Sharp v. Thomson; *sub nom.* Sharp v. Woolwich Building Society, 1997 S.C.
    (H.L.) 66; 1997 S.L.T. 636; 1997 S.C.L.R. 328; [1998] B.C.C. 115; [1997] 1
    B.C.L.C. 603 .... 1.27, 15.10, 15.38
—— v. Woolwich Building Society. *See* Sharp v. Thomson
Sheffield Corporation v. Barclay [1905] A.C. 392 .... 5.20, 5.27
Shuttleworth v. Cox Bros & Co. Ltd [1927] 2 K.B. 9 .... 4.21
Smith and Fawcett Ltd, Re [1942] Ch. 304 .... 5.27
Smith, Stone and Knight Ltd v. Birmingham Corp. [1939] 4 All E.R. 116 ..... 2.19
Snelling v. John G Snelling Ltd [1973] Q.B. 87; [1972] 2 W.L.R. 588; [1972] 1 All
    E.R. 79 .... 4.24
Southard & Co. Ltd, Re [1979] 1 W.L.R. 1198; [1979] 3 All E.R. 556 .... 2.18
Southern Foundries (1926) Ltd v. Shirlaw [1940] A.C. 701 .... 4.21
Standard Chartered Bank v. Pakistan National Shipping Corporation (No. 2)
    [2000] 1 All E.R. (Comm) 1; [2000] 1 Lloyd's Rep. 218 .... 9.35
—— v. Walker [1982] 1 W.L.R. 1410; [1982] 3 All E.R. 938 .... 15.28, 15.33
Stuart Eves (in liquidation) v. Smiths Gore, 1993 S.L.T. 1274 ....16.25

Supply of Ready Mixed Concrete (No. 2), Re. *See* Director General of Fair
   Trading v. Pioneer Concrete (UK) Ltd

TASBIAN (NO. 3) LTD, RE; *sub nom.* Official Receiver v. Nixon [1992] B.C.C. 358;
   [1993] B.C.L.C. 297 .... 8.13
Tesco Supermarkets Ltd v. Nattrass [1972] A.C. 153; [1971] 2 W.L.R. 1166 ... 2.27
Thomas Brinsmead & Sons Ltd, Re [1897] 1 Ch. 45 ....16.18
Thundercrest Ltd, Re [1994] B.C.C. 857; [1995] 1 B.C.L.C. 117 .... 5.19
Torvale Group Ltd, Re. *See* Hunt v. Edge & Ellison Trustees Ltd
Topps Chewing Gum Inc v. Coakley. *See* A & BC Chewing Gum Ltd, Re
Tottenham Hotspur plc, Re [1994] B.C.C. 681 ....11.32
Trustor AB v. Smallbone (No. 3) [2001] 1 W.L.R. 1177; [2001] 3 All E.R. 987 ...... 9.35
Tudor Grange Holdings Ltd v. Citibank NA [1992] Ch. 53; [1991] 3 W.L.R.
   750; [1991] B.C.L.C. 1009 ....15.28

VALE SEWING MACHINES V. ROBB, 1997 S.C.L.R. 797; 1997 G.W.D. 11–480 ....16.32
Virdi v. Abbey Leisure. *See* Abbey Leisure, Re

WEIR V. REES, 1991 S.L.T. 345 ....11.39
West Mercia Safetywear (In Liquidation) v. Dodd. *See* Liquidator of West
   Mercia Safetywear Ltd v. Dodd
Westmid Packaging Services Ltd (No. 2), Re; *sub nom.* Secretary of State for
   Trade and Industry v. Griffiths [1998] 2 All E.R. 124; [1998] B.C.C. 836;
   [1998] 2 B.C.L.C. 646 .... 8.30
Williams v. Natural Life Health Foods Ltd [1998] 1 W.L.R. 830; [1998] 2 All
   E.R. 577 .... 9.34
Wilson v. Wilson 1999 S.L.T. 249; 1998 S.C.L.R. 1103 .... 2.24
Wilsons & Clyde Coal Co Ltd, Petrs. *See* Scottish Insurance Corp Ltd v.
   Wilsons & Clyde Coal Co Ltd
Winpar Holdings Ltd v. Ransomes Plc. *See* Ransomes plc, Re
Wright v. Atlas Wright (Europe) Ltd; *sub nom.* Atlas Wright (Europe) Ltd v.
   Wright [1999] B.C.C. 163; [1999] 2 B.C.L.C. 301; *The Times*, February 3,
   1999 .... 9.23
Wright, Layman and Umney Ltd v. Wright (1949) 66 R.P.C. 149, CA 3.08
Woolfson v. Glasgow Corp. *See* Woolfson v. Strathclyde RC
—— v. Strathclyde RC; *sub nom.* Woolfson v. Glasgow Corp., 1978 S.C. (H.L.)
   90; 1978 S.L.T. 159 .... 2.17
Wragg Ltd, Re [1897] 1 Ch. 796 .... 5.16

YENIDJE TOBACCO CO. LTD, RE [1916] 2 Ch. 426 ....16.18
Yorkshire Woolcombers Association Ltd, Re. *See* Illingworth v. Houlds-
   worth
Yukong Line of Korea Ltd v. Rendsburg Investments Corp. of Liberia (No. 2)
   [1998] 1 W.L.R. 294; [1998] 4 All E.R. 82 .... 2.21

TABLE OF STATUTES

1720 Bubble Act (c. 28) 1.02
1835 Statutory Declarations Act (5
      & 6 Will. 4, c. 62) 3.03
1844 Joint Stock Companies Act (7
      & 8 Vict. c. 110) 1.02
1856 Joint Stock Companies Act
      (19& 20 Vict. c. 47) 1.02
1862 Companies Act (25 & 26
      Vict. c. 89) 2.01, 2.03
      s.16 .... 5.02
1890 Partnership Act (53 & 54
      Vict. c. 39) 1.19
      s.1 .... 1.19
      s.4(2) 1.20
      s.9 .... 1.20
      s.20 .... 1.20
1907 Limited Partnership Act (7
      Edw. 7, c. 24) 1.24
1922 Workers Compensation Act
      (c. ??) 2.03
1928 Agricultural Credits Act (18
      & 19 Geo. 5, c. 43) 15.06
1939 Trading with the Enemy Act
      (2 & 3 Geo. 6, c. 89) 2.15
1948 Companies Act (c. 38)
      s.210 ....11.03
1958 Companies Act (c. 72) 6.18
1961 Companies (Floating Charg-
      es) (Scotland) Act (9 &
      10 Eliz. 2, c. 46) 15.09
1965 Monopolies and Mergers Act
      (c. 50) 14.07
1972 Companies (Floating Charges
      and Receivers) (Scot-
      land) Act (c. 67) 15.09
      European Communities Act
      (c. 68)
      s.9 .... 4.07
1973 Fair Trading Act (c. 41) 14.07
      s.74 ....14.08
      s.75 ....14.08
      s.75G-K 14.07
      s.137(5) 14.07

1973 Prescription and Limitation
      (Scotland) Act (c. 52)
      s.6 .... 7.23
1976 Damages (Scotland) Act (c.
      13) 16.33
      Fatal Accidents Act (c.
      30) 16.33
      Race Relations Act (c. 74) 3.05
1980 Companies Act (c. 25) 11.03
      Limitation Act (c. 58)
      s.5 .... 7.23
1982 Insurance Companies Act (c.
      50) 8.26
1985 Companies Act (c. 6) 1.07, 1.12,
                        2.05, 3.03, 3.23, 3.25,
                        6.01, 7.27, 8.36,
                        11.03, 15.11
      s.1(1) 3.04
      s.1(3) 3.09
      s.1(3A) 1.14
      s.3A 4.08
      s.4 .... 4.03, 4.15
      s.5 .... 6.06, 6.23
      s.8(2) 4.21
      s.9 .... 4.21, 5.03
      s.10 .... 3.01
      s.12 .... 3.03
      s.14 ....4.21, 5.02, 11.34
      s.16 .... 6.13
      s.22 ....3.37, 5.09, 5.19
      s.23(1) 4.03
      s.24 .... 1.14, 2.05
      s.25 ....10.07
      s.25(1) 3.05
      s.25(2) 10.07
      s.26(1)(d) 3.05
      s.26(1)(e) 3.05
      s.26(2)(a) 3.05
      s.27 ....10.07
      s.28 .... 8.01
      s.28(1) 3.06
      s.28(2)(a) 3.06
      s.28(6) 3.07
      s.28(7) 3.07

1985   Companies Act—*cont.*
       s.29 ....10.07
       s.30 .... 3.05
       s.32(1) 3.06
       s.32(6) 3.07
       s.33(1) 3.07
       s.33(2) 3.07
       ss.35–35B 1.14
       s.35 .... 4.06, 8.02
       s.35(1) 4.13, 4.15
       s.35(2) 4.14, 11.07
       s.35(3) 4.15, 9.13
       s.35A 4.06, 8.02, 13.17
       s.35A(1) 4.18
       s.35A(2)(a) 4.18
       s.35A(2)(b) 4.18
       s.35A(2)(c) 4.18
       s.35B 4.06, 4.19, 8.02, 10.04,
                                          13.17
       s.36C 1.14
       s.42 .... 1.14
       ss.43–47 .... 3.30
       ss.43–48 .... 3.12, 3.30
       s.43(1)(a) 3.30
       s.43(2) 3.30
       s.43(2)(e)(ii) 3.30
       s.43(3)(b) 3.30
       s.43(3)(c) 3.30
       s.43(3)(2)(e)(ii) 3.30
       s.43(5) 3.30
       s.44 .... 3.30
       s.45 .... 3.30
       s.45(2) 3.30
       s.46 .... 3.30
       ss.49–50 .... 3.31
       s.49 .... 4.03
       s.49(2) 3.31
       s.49(3) 3.31, 3.33
       s.49(5) 3.31
       s.49(6) 3.31
       s.49(8)(a) 3.31
       s.49(8)(b)(i) 3.31
       s.49(8)(b)(ii) 3.31
       s.50 .... 3.31
       ss.51–52 .... 3.32
       s.51(1) 3.32
       s.51(2) 3.32
       s.51(3)(a) 3.32
       s.51(3)(b) 3.32
       s.52 .... 3.32
       ss.53–55 .... 3.33
       s.53(1) 10.07
       s.53(1)(a) 3.33
       s.53(2) 3.33
       s.54 .... 6.23
       s.54(2) 3.33
       s.54(5)(6) 3.33

1985   Companies Act—*cont.*
       s.55 .... 3.33
       s.80 .... 3.37, 5.15
       s.80(1) 5.12
       s.80(2)(a) 5.12
       s.80(2)(b) 5.12
       s.80(4) 5.12
       s.80(4)(a) 5.12
       s.80(4)(b) 5.12
       s.80(6) 5.12
       s.80A 5.12, 13.27
       s.80A(2) 5.12
       s.81 .... 5.13
       ss.83–85 .... 2.12
       s.88 .... 3.37
       s.89 .... 2.12, 3.37, 5.14
       s.89(4) 5.15
       s.90(6) 5.14
       s.91 .... 5.15
       s.92 .... 2.12
       s.92(1) 5.14
       s.92(2) 5.14
       s.93 .... 5.15
       s.94(3) 5.15
       s.94(4) 5.15
       s.94(5)(a) 5.15
       s.94(5)(b) 5.15
       s.96(1) 5.15
       s.96(2) 5.15
       s.97(3) 5.16
       s.99(2) 5.17
       s.99(3) 5.17
       s.100 .... 5.16
       s.101 .... 5.17
       s.102(1) 5.17
       s.102(2) 5.17
       s.102(5) 5.17
       s.102(6) 5.17
       s.103 .... 5.17
       s.103(1)(b) 5.17
       s.103(1)(c) 5.17
       s.103(3) 5.17
       s.103(4) 5.17
       s.103(5) 5.17
       s.103(6) 5.17
       s.104 .... 5.18
       s.104(4)(a) 5.18
       s.104(4)(c) 5.18
       s.104(4)(d) 5.18
       s.104(6) 5.18
       s.105 .... 5.17
       s.107 .... 5.17
       s.108 .... 5.17
       s.110 .... 5.17
       s.112 .... 5.17
       s.117 .... 2.07
       s.117(3) 3.12

1985 Companies Act—*cont.*
s.117(8) 3.12
s.118 .... 3.11, 5.11
s.121 ....3.30, 3.37, 4.03, 5.11
s.121(2)(a) 6.05
s.121(2)(c) 6.05
s.121(2)(e) 6.05
s.122 ....6.05, 13.24
s.123 .... 6.05
s.125 .... 4.23, 5.02
s.125(2)(b) 13.26
s.130(2) 6.44
ss.131–134 .... 6.44
s.131 .... 6.44
s.132 .... 6.45
ss.135–141 .... 6.06, 6.07
s.135 .... 7.03, 7.11
s.135(1) 6.10, 6.11
s.135(2) 6.10
s.136(3) 6.11
s.136(5)(a) 6.11
s.136(5)(b) 6.11
s.136(6) 6.11
s.137 .... 6.12
s.137(2)(a) 6.11
s.137(2)(b) 6.12
s.139(4) 6.12
s.142 ......4.06, 6.43, 8.03, 13.11
s.143(1) 6.23
s.143(3) 6.23
s.143(3)(d) 6.23
s.144 .... 3.25, 6.23
s.146 .... 5.31
s.146(2)(b) 6.24
s.146(3)(a) 6.24
s.146(3)(b) 6.24
s.146(4) 6.24
s.148 .... 6.24
s.151(1) 6.16
s.151(2) 6.16
s.151(3) 6.16
s.152(1) 6.13
s.152(2) 7.01
s.152(3) 6.16
s.153 .... 6.14, 6.18
s.153(1) 6.14, 6.17
s.153(2) 6.14, 6.17
s.153(3)(a) 6.14
s.153(3)(b) 6.14
s.153(3)(c) 6.14
s.153(3)(d) 6.14
s.153(3)(e) 6.14
s.153(3)(f) 6.14
s.153(4)(a) 6.15
s.153(4)(b) 6.15
s.153(4)(c) 6.15

1985 Companies Act—*cont.*
s.153(4)(d) 6.15
s.154(1) 6.15
s.154(2) 6.15
ss.155–158 .... 6.14
s.155(1) 6.20
s.155(2) 6.20
s.155(3) 6.20
s.155(4) 6.20
s.155(5) 6.20
s.155(6) 6.20
s.155(6A) 6.20
s.156 .... 6.20
s.156(4) 6.21
s.156(7) 6.21
s.157 .... 6.20
s.157(2) 6.21
s.158(2) 6.22
s.158(4) 6.22
ss.159–181 .... 6.14, 6.23
s.159(2) 5.06
s.159(3) 5.06, 6.26
s.160(1)(a) 6.33
s.160(2) 6.33, 6.34, 6.44
s.160(3) 5.06
s.160(4) 6.26, 6.35
s.162(3) 6.27
s.163(1) 6.28
s.163(2) 6.28
s.164(5) 6.28, 6.40
s.164(6) 6.28
s.165 .... 6.28, 6.31
s.166(2) 6.29
s.166(3) 6.29
s.166(4) 6.29
s.166(6) 6.29
s.167 .... 6.30
s.169(1) 6.32
s.169(4) 6.32
s.170(1) 6.35
s.170(2) 6.36
s.170(4) 6.04, 6.36
ss.171–175 .... 6.06
s.171 .... 6.33
s.171(1) 6.37
s.171(3) 6.37
s.171(4) 6.38
s.171(5) 6.38
s.171(6) 6.38, 6.39
s.172(5) 6.38
s.172(6) 6.38
s.173 .... 6.40
s.173(1) 6.40
s.173(3)(a) 6.40, 8.03
s.173(3)(b) 6.40
s.174(1) 6.40, 6.41
s.174(4) 6.40

1985 Companies Act—*cont.*
s.175 .... 6.40
s.175(4) 6.40
s.177 .... 6.41
s.178(2) 6.42
s.178(3) 6.42
s.178(5) 6.42
s.185 .... 5.20
s.186(1)(b) 5.20
s.199(2)(b) 5.29
ss.202–209 .... 5.29
s.209 .... 5.29
s.212 .... 5.29
s.221 .... 7.44
s.221(1) 7.27
s.221(2) 7.27
s.221(5) 7.27
s.222(5) 7.27
s.223(2) 7.30
s.223(3) 7.31
s.224(a) 7.31
s.224(2) 3.04, 7.30
s.224(3) 7.30
s.224(3A) 7.30
s.224(4) 7.30
s.225 .... 3.04, 7.31
s.225(4) 7.31
s.225(4)(b) 7.31
s.225(6) 7.31
s.226 .... 7.44
s.226(1) 7.28
s.226(2) 7.28, 7.29
s.227 .... 7.45
s.228 .... 7.45
s.228(3) 7.45
s.229(2) 7.45
s.229(3)(a) 7.45
s.229(3)(b) 7.45
s.229(3)(c) 7.45
s.229(4) 7.45
s.232 .... 8.17
s.233(1) 7.35
s.233(2) 7.35
s.233(4) 7.35
s.234 .... 7.35
s.234A(1) 7.35
s.234A(3) 7.35
s.235(2) 7.32
s.236(1) 7.32
s.236(3) 7.32, 7.35
s.237(1)(a) 7.32
s.237(1)(b) 7.32
s.237(2) 7.33
s.237(3) 7.33
s.237(4) 7.33
s.238 .... 7.35
s.241 .... 7.19, 7.36

1985 Companies Act—*cont.*
s.242 .... 7.36, 8.03
s.242(2) 7.37
s.242A 7.37
s.244 .... 8.26
s.244(1)(a) 7.36
s.244(1)(b) 7.36
s.244(2)(a) 7.36
s.244(2)(b) 7.36
s.245 .... 7.49
s.245A 7.49
s.245B 7.49
s.246 .... 7.44
s.247(3) 7.40, 7.41, 17.10
s.247A 7.42
s.249(3) 7.46
s.249A 7.19
s.249A(1) 7.44
s.249A2 .... 7.34
s.249A(3) 7.34
s.249A(3)(b) 7.44
s.249A(3A) 7.34, 7.43
s.249A3(a) 7.44
s.249A4 .... 7.34, 7.43
s.249AA 7.48
s.249AA(5)–(7) 7.48
s.249B(1) 7.43
s.249B(1B) 7.43, 7.47
s.249B(1C) 7.43, 7.47
s.249B(2) 7.43, 7.44
s.249B(4)(a) 7.44
s.249B(4)(b) 7.44
s.249B(4)(c) 7.44
s.249C 7.34
s.250 .... 3.24
s.251(1) 7.40
s.252 .... 7.35
s.252(1) 13.27
s.252(3) 7.19
s.253 .... 7.35
s.253(2) 13.28
s.254(1) 7.38
s.254(2) 7.38
s.254(3) 7.38
s.258 .... 3.26
s.258(4)(a) 3.26
s.258(4)(b) 3.26
s.259(1) 3.26
s.262(3) 7.04
ss.263–265 .... 7.19, 7.24
s.263 .... 7.02
s.263(1) 7.09
s.263(2)(a) 7.02
s.263(2)(b) 7.02
s.263(2)(c) 7.02
s.263(2)(d) 7.02
s.263(3) 7.01, 7.03

1985 Companies Act—*cont.*
s.264(1) 6.07, 7.21
s.264(1)(a) 6.04
s.264(3) 7.22
s.264(4) 7.22, 7.47
s.265 .... 7.22
s.266(1)(a) 7.22
s.266(1)(b) 7.22
s.269(1) 7.16
s.269(2) 7.17
s.269(2)(a) 7.18
s.269(2)(b) 7.18
s.270(2) 7.33
s.270(3) 7.19
s.270(4)(a) 7.21
s.270(4)(b) 7.20
s.271(4) 7.33
s.272(4) 7.21
s.273(3) 7.20
s.273(4) 7.20
s.273(5) 7.20
s.273(6) 7.21, 7.21
s.275(1) 7.05, 7.06
s.275(2) 7.07
s.275(3) 7.08
s.275(5) 7.07
s.275(6) 7.07
s.275(6)(a) 7.07
s.276 .... 7.14
s.277 .... 7.24
s.277(1) 2.12, 7.19, 7.24
s.277(2) 7.24
s.282 .... 3.14
s.283(2) 3.03, 3.23, 10.03
s.283(4) 3.23
s.283(4)(a) 10.03
s.283(4)(b) 8.15, 10.03
s.286 .... 3.14
s.286(1) 10.03
s.288(1) 8.18
s.288(2) 8.18, 8.22
s.291 .... 8.15
s.291(1) 8.15
s.291(3) 8.15
s.292 .... 8.16
s.292(1) 3.14
s.293 ....3.14, 8.01, 8.15, 8.22
s.293(2) 3.01
s.293(5) 13.14
s.303 .....8.21, 8.23, 9.12, 11.02,
                                13.01, 13.14
s.304(1) 8.23
s.304(2) 8.23
s.304(3) 8.23
s.304(4) 8.23
s.308 .... 8.03
s.309 .... 9.36

1985 Companies Act—*cont.*
s.310 ....9.13, 9.14, 10.19
s.311 .... 9.19
s.312 .... 8.17, 9.20
s.314 .... 9.21
s.317 ....3.23, 8.20, 9.23
s.318 .... 8.17, 9.23
s.319 .... 8.17, 9.23
s.319(2) 9.24
s.319(6) 9.23
s.320 ....3.37, 9.25, 11.14
s.322(2) 9.25
s.322(2)(c) 9.25
s.322A 4.17, 9.26, 11.07
s.322A(3)(a) 4.17
s.322A(3)(b) 4.17
s.322A(5)(a) 4.17
s.322A(5)(b) 4.17
s.322A(5)(c) 4.17
s.322A(5)(d) 4.17
s.322B 1.14
s.322B(1) 3.23, 9.27
s.322B(2) 3.23
s.322B(6) 3.23
s.323 ....8.17, 9.28, 11.48
s.324 ....5.20, 8.19, 11.48
s.325 .... 5.20, 8.19
s.327 ....5.20, 8.17, 8.19
s.328 .... 5.20, 8.19
s.329 .... 5.20, 8.19
s.300 .... 8.04
s.330(1) 9.29
s.330(3) 9.29
s.331(3) 9.29
s.331(6) 3.25, 9.29
s.331(7) 9.30
s.332 .... 9.29
s.333 .... 9.30
s.334 .... 9.29
s.335(1) 9.30
s.335(2) 9.30
s.336(a) 9.30
s.336(b) 9.30
s.337(1) 9.30
s.337(3) 9.30
s.338 .... 9.31
s.338(4) 9.31
s.338(6) 9.31
s.338A(1) 10.07
s.341 .... 9.29
s.341(1)(a) 9.29
s.341(1)(b) 9.29
s.341(2) 9.29
s.341(2)(c) 11.41
s.346(4) 9.33
s.347B(4) 9.33
s.347C(1) 9.33

1985   Companies Act—*cont.*
          s.347F(2) 9.33
          s.347F(3) 9.33
          s.349 .... 2.08
          s.352A 1.14, 3.23, 5.19
          s.353 .... 5.19
          s.354 .... 5.19
          s.356 .... 5.19
          s.359 .... 5.19
          s.360 .... 5.19
          s.361 .... 5.19
          s.366 ....13.06
          s.366(1) 13.07
          s.366(2) 13.07
          s.366(3)(a) 13.07
          s.366A 13.27
          s.366A(1) 13.07
          s.366A(3) 13.07, 13.28
          s.366A(3A) 13.07
          s.367 ....13.07
          s.368 .... 8.03
          s.368(2) 13.08
          s.368(4) 13.08
          s.368(6) 13.09
          s.369 ....13.07
          s.369(1)(b) 13.12
          s.369(1)(b)(i) 13.12
          s.369(1)(b)(ii) 13.12
          s.369(2)(b)(i) 13.12
          s.369(4) 13.12, 13.27
          s.369(4A)–(4G) 13.07
          s.370(4) 13.17
          s.370(5) 13.17
          s.370A 3.23
          s.371 ....13.07
          s.372 ....13.13
          s.372(1) 13.18
          s.372(2)(c) 13.18
          s.372(3) 13.13
          s.372(5) 13.13
          s.373(1)(a) 13.18
          s.373(1)(b) 13.18
          s.373(2) 13.18
          s.375 ....13.18
          s.376(1) 13.15
          s.376(2) 13.15
          s.377(1)(a) 13.15
          s.377(1)(b) 13.15
          s.377(2) 13.15
          s.377(3) 13.15
          s.378(1) 13.13
          s.378(2) 13.13, 13.25
          s.378(3) 13.27
          s.379A 13.27
          s.379A(2)(a) 13.27
          s.379A(2)(b) 13.27
          s.379A(2A) 13.27

1985   Companies Act—*cont.*
          s.379A(2B) 13.28
          s.379A(2C) 13.28
          s.379A(3) 13.28
          s.380 ....13.23
          s.380(1) 13.26, 13.28
          s.380(4) 13.30
          s.380(4)(a) 13.25
          s.380(4)(b) 13.26
          s.380(4)(bb) 13.27
          s.381A(1) 13.29
          s.381A(6) 13.28
          s.381A(7) 13.29
          s.381B 13.29
          s.381B(4) 13.29
          s.382 .... 8.01
          s.382(B) 3.23
          s.385(2) 10.08
          s.385(3) 10.08
          s.385(4) 10.08
          s.386 ....13.27
          s.388(3)(a) 13.14
          s.388(3)(b) 13.14
          s.388(8) 13.09
          s.390A 10.12
          s.390B 10.12
          s.391(1) 10.13
          s.391(2) 10.13
          s.391(3) 10.13
          s.391(4) 10.13
          s.391A 10.13
          s.391A(1)(a) 13.14
          s.391A(1)(b) 13.14
          s.391A(3) 10.13
          s.391A(4) 10.13
          s.391A(5) 10.13
          s.391A(6) 10.13
          s.392 ....10.14
          s.392A(1) 10.14
          ss.392A(2)–(8) 10.14
          s.392A(2) 13.10
          s.392A(5) 13.10
          s.393(1) 13.28
          s.393(4) 10.14
          s.393(5) 10.14
          s.394(1) 10.15
          s.394(2) 10.15
          s.394(3) 10.15
          s.394(5) 10.15
          s.394(6) 10.15
          s.394(7) 10.15
          s.394A 10.16
          s.409 ....15.11
          s.410(2) 15.14
          s.410(4) 15.12
          s.410(4)(c)(i) 5.30
          s.410(5)(b) 15.11

1985 Companies Act—*cont.*
s.411(1) 15.12
s.411(2) 15.12
s.412 ....15.13
s.413 ....15.13
s.414 ....15.13
s.415(1) 15.13
s.418 ....15.16
s.420 ....15.14
ss.421–423 ....15.15
s.421(2)(b) 11.41
s.423(2) 11.22
s.425 ....6.14, 7.12, 14.01,
                     16.35, 17.03
s.425(1) 14.16
s.425(2) 14.16, 14.17
s.425(3) 14.17
s.426(2) 14.17
s.426(4) 14.17
s.427 ....14.18
s.428(1) 14.12
s.429(1) 14.13
s.429(3) 14.13
s.429(4) 14.13
s.430(2) 14.14
s.430(5) 14.14
s.430(13) 14.14
s.430A 14.14
s.430A(4) 14.14
s.430b(2) 14.14
s.430C(1) 14.13
s.431(1) 9.29
s.431(2)(a) 11.41, 11.46
s.431(2)(b) 11.46
s.431(3) 11.41
s.431(4) 11.41
s.432(1) 11.41, 11.43
s.432(2) 11.42, 11.43
s.432(2A) 11.42
s.432(3) 11.43
s.434 .... 9.39
s.434(5A) 8.36, 11.44
s.434(5B) 8.36, 11.44
s.435(2) 14.16
s.436 .... 9.39
s.437(2) 11.45
s.438 ....11.45
s.441 ....11.45
s.442 ....11.46
s.442(3) 11.46
s.442(3A) 11.46
s.444 ....11.46
s.446 ....11.48
s.447 ....11.49
s.447(8) 11.49
s.447(8A) 11.49
s.447(8B) 11.49

1985 Companies Act—*cont.*
s.448 ....11.49
s.452(1) 11.43
s.452(1A) 11.44
ss.454–457 .... 5.29, 11.47
s.458 ....8.26, 9.45
s.459 ......4.23, 5.02, 6.06, 6.23,
            7.12, 9.15, 11.03, 11.13,
            11.15, 11.20, 11.30, 11.32,
            11.33, 11.34, 11.35, 11.36,
                     11.37, 11.38
s.459(2) 11.20
s.460 .... 11.22, 11.45
s.461 ....11.13, 11.17, 11.23
s.462(5) 15.10
s.464(4)(a) 15.07, 15.18
s.464(4)(b) 15.18
s.464(4)(c) 15.18
s.464(5) 15.18
s.652A 16.35
s.680(1)(A) 1.14
s.690A 1.14
s.690B 1.14
s.711A 4.06
s.713 ....8.26
s.716 .... 1.20
s.727 ......7.25, 9.13, 9.17, 9.43,
                                 10.19
s.736 .... 3.25
s.736(1) 3.25
s.736(1)(a) 3.25
s.736(1)(b) 3.25
s.736(1)(c) 3.25
s.741(1) 8.01, 8.12, 8.16
s.741(2) 8.13
s.741(3) 1.14
Sched. 1 .... 1.14
Sched. 4 ....1.15, 7.19, 7.29
paras 4.34(3) and (3A) 6.04
para. 12(a) 7.04
para. 36A 7.05, 7.08
para. 89 .... 7.05
Pt II 7.04
Sched. 4A 1.14, 7.47
Sched. 5 .... 1.15
Sched. 6
Pt I 8.17
Pt III 10.04
Sched. 7 .... 7.35
Sched. 8 .... 7.40
para. 2 .... 7.40
para. 3 .... 7.40
para. 4 .... 7.40
para. 5 .... 7.41
Sched. 8A 7.40
Scheds 11–14 .... 1.14
Sched. 13 .... 8.19

1985   Companies Act—*cont.*
       Pt I, para. 2 .... 8.19
       para. 4(a) 8.19
       para. 4(b) 8.19
       Sched. 15 .... 1.14
       Sched. 15A 14.11
       Pt 1 ....13.29
       Sched. 15A1(a) 8.23
       Sched. 19 ....11.20
       Sched. 21A 1.14
       Sched. 21B 1.14
       Sched. 24 .... 2.28
       Pt VI 1.15
       Pt X 2.12
       Pt XII 15.16
       Pt XIV 11.40
       Pt XXIII 3.28
       Business   Names   Act   (c.
          7) 1.12
       s.4 .... 3.05
       s.5 .... 3.05
       Company Securities (Insider
          Dealing) Act (c. 8) 1.15
       Bankruptcy (Scotland) Act (c.
          66) 16.25
       s.37 ....16.25
1986   Company Directors Disquali-
          fication Act (c. 46) 1.07,
               1.12, 2.05, 2.11, 7.25,
               8.01, 8.04, 8.15, 8.22,
               9.15, 9.48, 12.06
       s.1 .... 8.25
       s.1A 8.25
       s.2 .... 8.26
       s.3 ....1.07, 8.26, 8.27
       s.3(2) 8.26
       s.3(5) 8.27
       s.4 .... 8.26
       s.4(1)(b) 8.26
       s.5 .... 8.27
       s.5(5) 8.27
       s.6 ....8.25, 8.28
       s.6(2) 8.28
       s.6(3C) 8.28
       s.6(4) 8.28
       s.7 ....16.29
       s.7(1) 8.29
       s.7(2) 8.29
       s.7(2A) 8.29
       s.7(3) 8.29
       s.8(1) 8.29
       s.8(2A) 8.29
       s.8A 8.25
       s.10 .... 8.27
       s.11 ....8.15, 8.27
       s.12 .... 8.27
       s.13 .... 8.34

1986   Company Directors Disquali-
          fication Act—*cont.*
       s.14 .... 8.25
       s.15 ....2.11, 8.34
       s.15(2) 8.15
       s.17 .... 8.33
       s.22(5) 8.13
       s.441 ....11.45
       Sched. 1 .... 7.27
       Financial   Services   Act   (c.
          60) 1.12, 5.26, 7.43, 14.04
       s.48(2)(i) 12.22
       s.150 .... 5.26
       ss.177–178 ....12.19
       s.177(3) 12.19
       s.177(4) 12.19
       s.177(6) 12.19
       s.177(6A) 12.19
       s.177(7) 12.19
       s.177(8) 12.19
       s.177(11) 12.19
       s.178 ....12.19
       s.178(2) 12.19
       s.178(3) 12.19
       Pt IV 1.15, 5.10, 5.26
       Insolvency Act 1.12, 9.15
       ss.1–7 .... 6.14
       s.1 .... 8.03
       s.1(3) 17.09
       s.2(2) 17.09
       s.2(3) 17.09
       s.3(1) 17.09
       s.3(2) 17.09
       s.4 ....17.09
       s.4(3) 17.09
       s.4(4) 17.09
       s.4(5) 17.09
       s.5(2) 17.09
       s.5(3) 17.09
       s.6 ....17.09
       s.7 ....17.09
       s.8(3) 17.03
       s.8(4) 17.03
       s.9 ....17.03
       s.9(2) 17.04
       s.9(4) 17.04
       s.10 ....17.04
       s.11 ....17.05
       s.12 ....17.05
       s.14(1) 16.19, 17.05
       s.15 ....17.05
       s.17(2) 17.05
       s.17(3) 17.05
       s.19(4) 17.06
       s.19(6) 17.06
       s.22 ....9.39, 17.06
       s.23 ....17.05

1986 Insolvency Act—*cont.*

s.23(1) 17.05
s.23(2) 17.05
s.24(2) 17.05
s.24(4) 17.05
s.24(5) 17.05
s.27 ....17.05
s.29(2)(a) 15.06
s.41 .... 8.26
s.42(1) 16.19
ss.50–71 ....15.25
s.52 ....15.25
s.52(1)(a) 15.25
s.52(1)(b) 15.25
s.52(1)(c) 15.25
s.52(1)(d) 15.25
s.52(2) 15.26
s.53(1) 15.26
s.53(5) 15.26
s.53(6)(a) 1526
s.53(6)(b) 15.26
s.53(7) 15.26
s.54 ....15.26
s.55(2) 16.19
s.55(3)(a) 15.37
s.57(1) 15.29
s.57(1A) 15.30
s.57(2) 15.29, 15.30
s.57(2A) 15.30
s.57(3) 15.29, 15.31
s.57(4) 15.29
s.57(5) 15.30
s.59 .... 15.08, 15.27
s.60 ....15.32
s.60(2) 15.32
s.65(1)(a) 15.26
s.65(1)(b) 15.26
s.66 ....9.39, 15.27, 15.33
s.67 .... 15.27, 15.33
s.67(2) 15.27
s.67(4) 15.27
s.67(5) 15.27
s.68 ....15.27
s.72 ....15.34
s.74(2)(f) 7.23
s.75 ....16.19
s.76 .... 2.12, 16.19
s.76(1)(a) 6.40
s.76(2)(a) 16.19
s.76(2)(b) 16.19
s.77 ....16.19
s.79(1) 16.19
s.84(1)(a) 16.07
s.84(1)(b) 16.07
s.84(1)(c) 13.26, 16.07
s.84(3) 16.07
s.85(1) 16.07

1986 Insolvency Act—*cont.*

s.86 ....16.07
s.87(1) 16.07
s.87(2) 16.07
s.88 ....16.07
s.89 .... 8.03
s.89(1) 16.07
s.89(2)(a) 16.07
s.89(4) 16.07
s.89(5) 16.07
s.91(1) 16.10
s.91(2) 16.10
s.94(1) 16.10
s.94(3) 16.10
s.96 ....16.07
s.98 ....16.11
s.99(1) 16.11
s.99(2) 16.11
s.100(1) 16.12
s.100(2) 16.12
s.100(3) 16.12
s.101(1) 16.12
s.101(2) 16.12
s.101(3) 16.12
s.103 ....16.12
s.105 ....16.13
s.107 ....16.10
s.109 .... 16.07, 16.12
s.109(1) 16.10
s.110 ....6.14, 14.15, 17.08
s.110(1) 16.14
s.110(3)(a) 16.14
s.110(3)(b) 16.14
s.111 ....16.14
s.114 ....16.08
s.115 ....16.08
s.117 ....16.16
s.120 ....16.15
s.122 ....6.20, 6.40, 16.17
s.122(1)(a) 16.16
s.122(1)(b) 16.16
s.122(1)(d) 16.16
s.122(1)(e) 1.14, 16.16
s.122(1)(f) 16.16, 16.17,
                                            16.20
s.122(1)(g) 8.21, 11.38,
                                  16.16, 16.20
s.122(2) 16.16
s.123 .... 15.21, 16.25
s.123(1) 16.17
s.123(1)(a) 16.17
s.123(1)(b) 16.17
s.123(1)(c) 16.17
s.123(1)(e) 16.17
s.123(2) 16.17
s.124(1) 16.19
s.124(2)(a) 16.20

1986   Insolvency Act—*cont.*
        s.124(2)(b) 16.20
        s.124(3) 16.20
        s.124A 11.45, 16.18, 16.20,
                                        17.07
        s.124A(1) 16.19
        s.124(4)(a) 16.19
        s.125(1) 16.17, 16.21
        s.125(2) 8.21, 11.38, 16.18,
                                        16.21
        s.126 ....16.21
        s.127 ....16.21
        s.129(1) 16.21
        s.129(2) 16.21
        s.130(1) 16.21
        s.130(2) 16.21
        s.131 ....16.22
        s.133 ....16.22
        s.134 ....16.22
        s.135 ....16.21
        s.138 ....16.22
        s.139 ....16.22
        s.140 ....16.22
        s.142 ....16.22
        s.144 ....16.23
        s.145 ....16.23
        s.148 ....16.23
        s.149 ....16.23
        s.157 .... 9.39
        s.165 .... 16.10, 16.13
        s.167 ....16.13
        s.170 .... 8.26, 16.23
        s.185 ....16.25
        s.195 ....16.17
        s.201 ....16.09
        s.204 ....16.24
        s.206–211 .... 9.39, 9.41
        s.208 .... 9.39
        ss.212–216 ......1.09, 1.22, 1.25,
                                  2.10, 8.24
        ss.212–217 .... 9.41
        s.212 ....2.10, 8.04, 9.43, 9.44,
                            10.01,15.33, 16.28
        s.213 ....2.10, 5.02, 8.04, 8.27,
                    9.15, 9.43, 9.45, 16.19, 16.28
        s.214 ....2.10, 8.04, 8.27, 9.15,
                    9.43, 9.46, 9.48, 16.19, 16.28
        s.214(1) 9.46
        s.214(2) 9.46
        s.214(3) 9.46
        s.214(4) 9.15, 9.47
        s.216 ......2.10, 3.06, 8.04, 16.28
        s.216(3) 9.49
        s.216(3)(c) 9.49
        s.217 .... 2.10, 3.06
        s.217(2) 9.49
        s.218–219 .... 9.39

1986   Insolvency Act—*cont.*
        s.218 .... 7.25
        s.233 ....17.05
        s.238 ....16.25
        s.239 ....16.25
        ss.242–245 ....16.05
        s.242 .... 16.25, 17.04
        s.242(4)(a) 16.25
        s.242(4)(b) 16.25
        s.242(4)(c) 16.25
        s.243 ....15.19, 16.25, 17.04
        s.243(2)(a) 15.19, 16.25
        s.243(2)(b) 15.19, 16.25
        s.243(2)(c) 15.19, 16.25
        s.243(2)(d) 15.19, 16.25
        s.243(4) 16.25
        s.243(5) 15.19
        s.244 ....16.25
        s.245 ....17.04
        s.245(2)(a) 15.22, 16.25
        s.245(2)(b) 15.22, 16.25
        s.245(2)(c) 15.22, 16.25
        s.245(3)(a) 15.21, 16.25
        s.245(3)(c) 15.21, 16.25
        s.245(4)(a) 15.21
        s.245(4)(b) 15.21
        s.245(5) 15.21, 16.25
        s.245(4)(a) 16.25
        s.245(4)(b) 16.25
        s.246 ....16.31
        s.249 .... 15.21, 16.25
        s.291(3) 8.22
        s.386 .... 15.08, 16.30
        s.386(1) 15.31
        ss.423–425 ....16.29
        s.423 .... 2.21
        s.425 .... 14.15, 17.08
        s.426 ....16.31
        s.435 .... 15.21, 16.25
        s.651(1) 16.33
        s.651(5) 16.33
        s.652 ....16.34
        s.653 ....16.35
        s.654 ....16.36
        s.656 ....16.36
        s.657 ....16.36
        Pt II 7.31
        Sched. 1 ....17.05
        Sched. 1.21 ....16.19
        Sched. 2 ....15.27
        Sched. 2.21 ....16.19
        Sched. 4, Pt I 16.10, 16.23
        Pt II 16.10, 16.23
        Pt III 16.10, 16.23
        Sched. 6 .....15.08, 15.31, 16.30
        Sched. A1 ....17.10
        para. 6 ....17.10

1986 Insolvency Act—*cont.*
    para. 7 ....17.10
    para. 8(1) 17.10
    para. 8(6) 17.10
    para. 8(8) 17.10
    para. 11 ....17.10
    paras 12–14 ....17.11
    para. 18 ....17.11
    para. 24 ....17.11
    para. 25 ....17.11
    paras 29–31 ....17.11
    para. 32 ....17.10
1987 Companies Act
    s.317 .... 9.07
1989 Companies Act (c. 40) 1.12,
    4.07, 4.12, 4.16, 4.18,
    11.03
    s.112 .... 4.16
    s.112(3) 4.16
    s.112(4) 4.16
1990 Law Reform (Miscellaneous
    Provisions) (Scotland)
    Act (c. 40)
    s.14 ....16.19
1992 Trade Union and Labour Re-
    lations (Consolidation)
    Act (c. 52) 7.43
1993 Criminal Justice Act (c.
    36) 12.08, 12.12, 12.18
    s.52(1) 12.07
    s.52(2)(a) 12.07
    s.52(2)(b) 12.07, 12.21
    s.52(3) 12.07
    s.53 ....12.20
    s.53(1)(a) 12.21
    s.53(1)(b) 12.21
    s.53(1)(c) 12.21
    s.53(2) 12.21
    s.53(3)(a) 12.21
    s.53(3)(b) 12.21
    s.53(6) 12.21
    s.55 ....12.13
    s.56(1) 12.08

1993 Criminal Justice Act—*cont.*
    s.56(2) 12.16
    s.57(1) 12.09
    s.57(2) 12.10
    s.58(1) 12.12
    s.58(2) 12.12
    s.58(3) 12.12
    s.59 ....12.15
    s.60(1) 12.14, 12.17
    s.62 ....12.23
    s.62(1)(b) 12.23
    Pt V 1.12, 1.15
    Sched. 1 .... 12.20, 12.22
    para. 1 ....12.22
    Sched. 2 ....12.11
1998 Late Payment of Commercial
    Debts (Interest) Act (c.
    20) 16.17
2000 Financial Services and Mar-
    kets Act (c. 8) 1.12, 14.02
    s.118(2)(a) 12.26
    s.118(2)(b) 12.26
    s.118(2)(c) 12.26
    s.118(5) 12.26
    s.119 ....12.26
    s.120(4) 12.26
    s.123 ....12.26
    s.129 ....12.26
    s.132–136 ....12.26
    s.137 ....12.26
    s.206(3) 12.26
    s.367 ....17.07
    Pt VI 5.10
    Pt VIII 9.28, 12.26
    Limited Liability Partnership
    Act (c. 12) 1.08, 1.21, 1.22
    Insolvency Act (c. 39) 8.25,
    17.10
    s.14 ....16.31
2001 Abolition of Poindings and
    Warrant Sales Act (asp
    1) 16.24

TABLE OF STATUTORY INSTRUMENTS

1972 Mortgaging of Aircraft Order
(S.I. 1972 No. 1268) 15.12

1981 Company and Business
Names Regulations (S.I.
1981 No. 1685) 3.05

1985 Companies (Tables A to F)
Regulations (S.I. 1985
No. 805) 4.02
Table A 4.21, 8.21
reg. 27 .... 8.06
reg. 38 ....13.13
reg. 39 ....13.13
regs 40–63 ....13.17
reg. 46 ....13.18
reg. 50 ....13.18
reg. 60 ....13.13
reg. 61A 13.13
regs 65–69 .... 8.11
reg. 70 .... 1.25, 9.01
reg. 72 ....13.22
reg. 81 .... 8.15, 8.22
reg. 82 .... 8.17
reg. 83 .... 8.17
reg. 84 .... 8.06
regs 88–89 ....13.21
reg. 92 .... 8.15, 13.21
reg. 93 ....13.21
reg. 94 ....8.21, 9.07, 13.21
reg. 95 ....13.21
reg. 96 ....13.21
reg. 70 .... 8.01
reg. 105 .... 7.23
reg. 109 .... 7.27
reg. 117 ....13.26

1986 Insolvency (Scotland) Rules
(S.I. 1986 No. 1915) 15.25
rr. 4.1–82 ....16.21
r. 4.12(2A) 16.22
r. 4.15 ....16.23
r. 4.18 ....16.21
r. 4.19 ....16.21

1986 Insolvency (Scotland) Rules
—*cont.*
r. 4.22 ....16.23
r. 4.66 ....16.30
r. 4.67 ....16.30
rr. 4.78–82 .... 9.49
r. 4.80 .... 3.06
r. 4.81 .... 3.06
r. 4.82 .... 3.06
r. 7.12(1) 17.09
r. 7.12(2) 17.09

1993 Companies Accounts (Regulations) (S.I. 1993 No.
1820) 7.38

1994 Insider Dealing (Securities
and Regulated Markets)
Order (S.I. 1994 No.
187) 1.15

1995 Police (Scotland) Amendment Regulations (S.I.
1995 No. 137) 1.15

Companies Act (Disclosure
of Remuneration for
Non-audit Work) Regu-
lations (S.I. 1991 No.
2128) 10.12

Public Offer of Securities
Regulations (S.I. 1995
No. 1537) 1.15, 3.15, 5.10,
5.25
reg. 7 .... 5.13
reg. 7(2) 5.25
reg. 8(3) 5.25
reg. 9 .... 5.25
reg. 10 .... 5.25
reg. 11 .... 5.25
reg. 13 .... 5.25
reg. 14 ....2.12, 5.25
reg. 15 .... 5.25

ABBREVIATIONS

CA 1985	Companies Act 1985
CDDA 1986	Company Directors Disqualifications Act 1986
FSA 1986	Financial Services Act 1986
FSMA 2000	Financial Services and Markets Act 2000
IA 1986	Insolvency Act 1986
RIE	Recognised investment exchange

CHAPTER 1

INTRODUCTION

MAJOR FEATURES OF COMPANIES

A company's existence

At the heart of company law is a major premise: that the law **1.01**
recognises the creation of an artificial legal person, called a registered
company, which is a freestanding legal personality, separate from those
who own it (the members) and those who manage it (the officers, and in
particular the directors) and which only comes into existence on registration. The registered company is entirely intangible, its existence
symbolised by a paper certificate of incorporation. Although without a
physical existence, it can do most things that a human being can do,
especially trade, own property, pay taxes, or act as a servant or
employer, but it cannot, for example, commit certain crimes, such as
rape, nor enter into certain civil contracts, such as an ante-nuptial
agreement.

The minor premise is this: that the form of a company is more
important than the substance. Provided the requisite paperwork has been
prepared properly, the fee duly paid and the certificate of registration
issued, a company will exist. Although, as we shall see later, the courts
will occasionally look behind the apparent legal personality of the
company to investigate the conduct of a company's directors, on
the whole, irrespective of the motives, the actions and the behaviour of
the directors, the members or the company's employees, the company
will remain in existence and alone will remain responsible for its own
liabilities and retain its own assets.

Incorporation

Companies only exist because Parliament allows them to. Until 1844 **1.02**
companies as we know them scarcely existed, and did so either because
a monarch had granted a charter of incorporation, as with the Honour-
able East India Company, or because Parliament granted a charter of
incorporation, as the Scots Parliament did on the incorporation of the
Bank of Scotland in 1695. Other, unincorporated companies did exist,

with a rather uncertain legal identity, and with a form of trading in shares, mostly through coffee shops which doubled as the first stock exchanges. Company law was slow to develop in the United Kingdom, mainly because of the ill effects of the South Sea Bubble, the name given to a speculative fever that seized the country in 1720, and in which many lost fortunes[1-2] through folly and chicanery. The Bubble Act 1720 was passed to limit the possibilities of future bubbles, but had the equal effect of frustrating commerce. Later, however Gladstone saw that business was leaching to the USA and France, both of which countries had developed the idea of the joint stock company with limited liability. Gladstone[3] recognised the importance of incorporation and registration for giving substance and legitimacy to the company, and recognised the commercial significance of the benefit of limited liability. Thus were passed the Joint Stock Companies Acts 1844 and 1856.

Inherent in the idea of *incorporation* is a document that sets out the terms of the corporation by way of a constitution or a charter: in a company this is nowadays provided by the memorandum and articles of association.[4] These were derived from partnership agreements which set out the rights and duties of the individual partners. A further part of incorporation is the idea of public accessibility to its incorporation documents.[5] There are plenty of unincorporated associations which have their own internal bylaws, constitutions or charters,[6] but these documents are not generally available to those who are not members of that association. A partnership is an unincorporated association, but the terms of any partnership agreement are privy to the partners themselves. This book does not deal with unincorporated associations, though it will

---

[1-2] The South Sea Company was set up to trade in the South Seas, but was hampered by the fact that the Spanish, who controlled the area, refused permission for such trade to take place. This fact was carefully concealed from the credulous investors. When the company's share price reached its highest point, the promoters of the company, who had artfully talked up the share price, smartly sold their shares and fled to France. "Bubbles" were not restricted to Britain: contemporaneously, the French had their own disastrous Mississippi bubble, engineered by the Scots financier John Law of Laurieston, and in 2001 there was a mini-bubble in technology companies ("dot.com" companies) caused by investors speculating in a new and untried market without considering the true underlying value of the businesses they were investing in. The Wall Street Crash of 1929 was another example.

[3] Admirers of Gladstone may inspect his statue in Coates Crescent in Edinburgh. Gladstone was at one stage MP for Midlothian. His grandparents are buried in the old Leith cemetery.

[4] See Chap. 4.

[5] Such accessibility was until recently not in practice very realistic, but now that the Register of Companies is on line it is actually now easier than ever before to access the relevant documents. The problem remains, however, that the documents are not easily intelligible to those untrained in company law.

[6] Typical unincorporated associations with charters or constitutions include kirk sessions, clubs, amateur dramatic societies and so on.

deal with the distinctions between companies, partnerships and limited liability partnerships.

Registration requires the setting up of a register, or authorised list, **1.03** controlled by a registrar who ensures that registration is granted only on the fulfilment of certain conditions, namely the correct documentation and the payment of a fee. Once a company is registered, it is placed on the register and that company's details may be accessed either in person at the Register of Companies[7] or on-line by anyone who wishes to do so.

Limited liability

Gladstone's third change was the introduction of *limited liability*. **1.04** This a characteristic of many companies, but not all.[8] What this means is that the liability of the *members*[9] is limited, not that the company's liability is limited. In a company limited by shares, the limit of a shareholder's liability is the amount required to pay up the full nominal value of each of his shares. So in the case of a company whose shares have a nominal value[10] of 50 pence, and provided he has paid the whole 50 pence for each share that he owns, the shareholder will have no further liability to the company, even if asked to pay more by the directors or by the company's liquidator. His liability to the company is therefore limited to the nominal value of the share. He is only obliged to pay more if he agrees to do so.[11] If the shareholder chooses for the time being to pay only some of the nominal value of each 50 pence share, say to the extent of 20 pence only, he could be required at a later date by the directors or the liquidator to pay the balance of 30 pence on each share; but again, once he has paid the remaining 30 pence per share, he has no further liability to his company except where he agrees to accept such liability. Even if the company's debts are substantial, the

---

[7] In Castle Terrace, in Edinburgh: there is an outstation in Glasgow. The main English Register of Companies is in Cardiff, but there is an outstation in London. Northern Ireland has its own Register in Belfast.

[8] For example, it is possible to register an unlimited company. Such companies are discussed further in Chap. 3.

[9] "Members" is a global term that includes shareholders. A shareholder only exists in a company if that company has shares, but some companies, in particular guarantee companies, do not often have shares, and cannot therefore have shareholders. The owners of a guarantee company are therefore known as members, and a shareholder is automatically a member.

[10] The "nominal value" of a share is the imaginary value given to a share purely for the purpose of enabling the full liability of the shareholder to be extinguished by payment. The nominal value bears no relation to the market value of a share, and only exists as part of an accounting convention. See also Chap. 5.

[11] This might arise where there is a premium payable on the shares when they are issued. The market price for a newly issued share may sometimes be much greater than the nominal value. The difference between the market price and the nominal value is the premium and reflects the desirability of the share.

shareholder's liability still remains limited to the extent of the nominal value of each share that he owns.[12]

In the case of a guarantee company, the amount required by way of the guarantee will be stated in the company's memorandum, and if the company requires funds for whatever reason specified in the memorandum (commonly on insolvent liquidation), each member will have to pay up to the predetermined amount specified in the guarantee. Once that is paid, the member has no further liability to the company.

1.05 The advantage of the limitation on liability is that investors know exactly how much they will lose if the company loses all its money. There is a predetermined cap on their loss, but no limit to the amount of money they might gain. This makes investors more likely to invest.

The promotion of commerce

1.06 Not only are investors willing to invest, but entrepreneurs are more willing to set up businesses. This in turn creates employment and creates wealth, out of which taxes may be paid, so that the country benefits as well. A country that did not permit the existence of limited liability companies would find that its best entrepreneurs would flee to countries with a more sympathetic commercial regime. A country that did not have limited liability companies would have no risk-takers and no-one would have the incentive to try out new commercial ideas. Over a period of time the country would stagnate and become impoverished relative to other countries. Limited liability also allows investors to pool their wealth together for very large projects. In the nineteenth century, many railways and canals were built by companies because only they could harness the savings of a large number of investors and raise the capital to carry out huge and risky undertakings at limited commercial risk to the investors.

It is also a great deal easier to ascertain the financial state of a company, as disclosed by its audited accounts, than the financial state of a partnership, whose partners may not actually have the wealth they say they have. If you wanted to be sure a partnership was truly viable, you might need to see statements of assets and liabilities for every single partner—a laborious and time-consuming activity. Accordingly limited companies find it easier to raise funds from lenders or other investors than do partnerships or other trading bodies.

The disclosure principle

1.07 The price of limited liability is the requirement for a limited company to disclose its accounts and other information to the general public at the Registrar of Companies. Every limited company must do this, but

---

[12] In some countries, share capital is seen as an anachronism and it is possible to have shares with no nominal value. These are known as no-par value shares, and will be discussed further in Chap. 5.

unlimited companies, whose members are personally liable for their companies' debts, do not need to publish their accounts.[13] There are sanctions for failure to publish the required documentation, and directors' persistent failure to lodge accounts, annual returns, etc., is possible grounds for disqualification under the Company Directors Disqualification Act 1986.[14] Publication of the accounts enables potential investors and creditors to have some idea whether or not the company is safe to invest in, or to do business with, and even if investors or creditors choose to do so, it is always open to them to safeguard themselves by checking the company's financial state before investing in it or trading with it. However, there are ways of disguising a company's true financial state and it is unwise to place too much reliance on the published accounts, private companies do not need to publish full details of their accounts: for example, small companies need to disclose an annual list of shareholders, registered charges, new issues of shares and much other information that will be useful to investors, creditors and the public generally. (Company accounts are dealt with in greater detail in Chapter 7.)

By contrast, sole traders and partnerships do not have to disclose anything, except to the Inland Revenue and Customs and Excise, and their affairs may be as secret as they wish. But equally, sole traders are personally liable for all their business debts, and partners are jointly and severally personally liable for the debts of their partnership.

The maintenance of professional standards

Historically, certain professions, particularly accountants, doctors and **1.08** solicitors, were not allowed to incorporate, because it was feared that limiting their liability might lead to a lapse in professional standards; or to put it another way, being personally liable for their mistakes would concentrate partners' minds on doing a proper job. However the increasing costs of professional liability insurance and the ever higher costs of negligence claims resulted in the passing of the Limited Liability Partnership Act 2000. Since April 2001 limited liability partnerships have been available in the United Kingdom and it is anticipated that many professional firms will adopt this new corporate form. Further details of limited liability partnerships are given shortly.

The danger of fraud

Precisely because limited liability offers investors and directors the **1.09** opportunity to walk away from insolvent companies, leaving creditors and employees unpaid, the law has to be vigilant to ensure that the opportunities for taking unfair or fraudulent advantage of limited liability and a company's separate legal personality are restricted. Under

---

[13] Companies Act 1985, s.254.
[14] Company Directors Disqualification Act 1986, s.3.

certain circumstances directors may be found personally liable for the debts of their insolvent companies,[15] and even when a company is solvent, there are occasions both under common law and statute when directors or others will be liable if abuse the corporate form.[16] The law has to find a balance between encouraging commerce while preventing sharp or dishonest practice, and that balance is not always easily found. Registration of a company and regular lodging of annual accounts are no guarantee that a company is operating honestly.

The opportunities for personal wealth creation

1.10 It is perfectly possible to make a great deal of money as a sole trader, perhaps as an artist, an advocate or a computer consultant. Partners in a successful firm can be wealthy too. But for what might be vulgarly called "serious money" there are few better ways than by starting as a entrepreneur, with a private limited company, expanding to became a public limited company, and finally having your own company floated on the London Stock Exchange. At that point, assuming your company's shares are desirable enough and you run the company successfully enough, you may sell some of your own shares, thereby releasing a great deal of cash, or retain your own shares while the share price climbs, the dividends flow in and your own personal status as a director of a listed company rises. Having your company listed on the London Stock Exchange is not in every respect satisfactory, but it does provide unrivalled opportunities for wealth creation.

The universality of the limited liability company

1.11 The limited liability company has proved one of the most effective economic developments in commerce in the last 200 years. It is probably as significant as double entry book-keeping or the introduction of universally accepted systems of weights and measurements. Limited liability companies are now to be found all over the developed world, and while they may differ in detail from country to country, they all share a system of registration, with directors in charge and members owning the shares. Some countries have more investor-friendly rules than others, while others have minimal disclosure requirements. To some extent there is a market in company law jurisdictions: some states in the USA (and Delaware in particular) have set themselves out to attract high quality business by the excellence of their company legislation and the skills of their commercial judges; those states attract significant income from the number of companies that choose to register there and pay fees to the state for doing so. Dubious off-shore tax havens permit companies to be set up with minimal information being

---

[15] Insolvency Act 1986, ss. 212–216. (Hereafter referred to as IA 1986.)
[16] See Chap. 2.

revealed to anyone. Such companies often attract the attention of political despots, money-launderers and drug-dealers. Other countries, such as New Zealand, are trying to encourage their economies by having very investor– and entrepreneur-friendly company legislation. Former Communist countries are generally adopting either German or American models of company legislation. China, in its pursuit of Socialism with Chinese characteristics, has sent experts round the world to garner the best features of company law internationally for their own company laws. Increasingly we shall see company law become more and more similar throughout the developed world, as capital follows legal jurisdictions with which it feels comfortable. The principles of corporate governance, which include transparency, accountability and an adherence to generally agreed standards of best practice, are also gradually being adopted internationally, and those countries which do not choose to follow these principles may in the long run be starved of capital since investors will not be confident that their capital is being properly used.

United Kingdom company legislation

In the United Kingdom the main legislation applicable to companies is the Companies Act 1985 ("CA 1985") as amended by the Companies Act 1989 and various other statutory instruments since then. Most current published editions of the CA 1985 will already incorporate the changes since 1985. Much of the Companies Act 1989 was not in fact implemented, despite the Act being passed, because of opposition to its changes, particularly in respect of the registration of charges. **1.12**

Other significant legislation applicable to companies comprises the Insolvency Act 1986 ("IA 1986"), which has substantial parts dedicated to Scottish procedure; the Company Directors Disqualification Act 1986 ("CDDA 1986"); the Criminal Justice Act 1993, Part V, which deals with insider dealing; the Financial Services Act 1986 and the Financial Services and Markets Act 2000, both of which deal with the issue of securities to the public and the authority given to those who issue them; and the Business Names Act 1986. At the time of writing there are moves afoot to introduce a new Companies Bill, but it is likely that the introduction of a new bill will take a great deal of consultation. There is a general awareness that much needs to be done to improve the current company legislation in the United Kingdom, and an enormous exercise was undertaken by the Department of Trade and Industry (DTI), culminating in the Company Law Review Steering Group's document *Modern Company Law for a Competitive Economy—the Final Report*[17] which was enthusiastically received by Margaret Becket, then Minister for Trade and Industry. Many of the Steering Group's recommendations have been accepted by the White Paper with its draft Companies Bill. A

---

[17] DTI July 2001.

major feature of the proposed bill is to make life simpler for private companies which form the bulk of companies in the United Kingdom: the aim is to strip out unnecessary bureaucratic requirements, such as unnecessary annual general meetings (AGMs) and complicated capital maintenance rules, in order to encourage commerce and not let form-filling stand in the way of trade.

1.13   One of the difficulties bedevilling any company legislation is that Parliamentary draftsmen have to cope with conflicting demands. One demand is that the legislation should be very easy to understand and user-friendly, so that the layman can understand what he needs to do to set up and run a company. Such an approach will not always do justice to the complexity of some of the issues. Another demand is that the legislation should aim for elegant succinctness and brevity. The problem with this is that if the text is too condensed, matters may be omitted and it may be difficult for even experts to understand. A third demand is that the legislation should somehow magically resolve the often conflicting policy issues that can be found in some areas of company law, financial assistance being a good example. On a human level, Parliamentary draftsmen are often working under great pressure, with little reward and less thanks, with insufficient time for revision, and with constant sniping from academics, judges and politicians. With all these pressures, it is not surprising if in the past some company legislation has not always been drafted as well as it might have been, and if sometimes the temptation to leave matters as they stand, however unsatisfactory, is better than drafting new legislation which might in its own right prove just as problematic as the familiar old legislation. However, the aim of the new Companies Bill is to remedy some of these past faults and to have legislation that is flexible and responsive to future business needs.

European legislation

1.14   The United Kingdom has an admirable record in introducing European company legislation and in taking steps to follow the rules encouraging the harmonisation of the law relating to companies throughout Europe. The United Kingdom has not adopted all the company proposals emanating from Europe but where Directives have been approved, the United Kingdom has taken steps to bring in legislation to bring them into force.

To date the following European company law Directives have been implemented:

- First Directive (68/151). This simplified the *ultra vires* rules[18];

---

[18] See Chap. 4.

- Second Directive (77/91). This dealt with public limited companies,[19] the net asset rule applicable to dividends of public companies,[20] and the rules relating to the raising of capital[21];
- Third Directive (78/855). This relates to mergers[22];
- Fourth Directive (78/660). This dealt with the standardisation of the lay-out of accounts and the accounting disclosure rules applicable to small and medium sized companies[23];
- Sixth Directive (82/891). This deals with scission (also known as demergers) of public limited companies into smaller companies[24];
- Seventh Directive (83/349). This deals with the consolidation of company accounts[25];
- Eighth Directive (84/345). This deals with auditors' qualifications[26];
- Eleventh Directive (89/248). This deals with branches of foreign companies[27];
- Twelfth Directive (89/667). This deals with single-member companies.[28]

Certain draft Directives have not been passed by the European Parlia- **1.15** ment. These include the draft Fifth Directive, which the United Kingdom would not accept because of the requirement to have worker participation in management of companies above a certain size. It would also have had specific duties relating to directors and auditors. The draft Ninth Directive concerned corporate groups, especially in the context of inter-group liability on insolvency. Drawn from a German model, it has not been very effective even in Germany and has since been withdrawn. The draft Tenth Directive on cross-border mergers had too many provisions for employee protection for the United Kingdom's taste and it has been withdrawn too. The draft Thirteenth Directive on takeovers, after 12 years' patient planning, was dramatically rejected in June 2001 by one vote by the European Parliament after intensive lobbying by German politicians, mainly on protectionist grounds and because the provisions, which were in many ways similar to the United Kingdom's City

---

[19] Implemented in CA 1985, ss. 35–35B, 36C and 42. See Chap. 3.
[20] See Chap. 6.
[21] See Chap. 5.
[22] Implemented in CA 1985, Sched. 15. See Chap. 14.
[23] *ibid.,* Pt VII, Scheds 4 and 5. See Chap. 7.
[24] *ibid.,* Sched. 1.
[25] *ibid.,* Pt VII, Sched.4A.
[26] *ibid.,* Pt II, Scheds 11–14.
[27] *ibid.,* ss. 690A, 690B and Scheds 21A and 21B.
[28] *ibid.,* ss. 1(3A), 24, 322B, 352A, 680(1)(A), 741(3) and IA 1986, s.122(1)(e).

Code on Takeovers and Mergers,[29] might have led to an increase in
takeover activity in Europe which might in turn have led to job losses.[30]
A proposed draft Fourteenth Directive on cross-border migration of
companies has not been taken further.

Directives that apply to companies in the United Kingdom, without
being company law Directives, include the following:

- Admission to Listing (79/279). This deals with the rules relating
  to the admission of companies to the Official List of the (now)
  London Stock Exchange[31];
- Listing Particulars (80/390). This deals with the information
  required to be given to the London Stock Exchange by companies wishing to be admitted to that Exchange[32];
- Continuing Disclosure (82/121). This deals with the requirement
  to update the information provided to the London Stock
  Exchange by listed companies[33];
- Mutual Recognition of Listing Particulars (87/345). A company
  admitted to one stock exchange in Europe may be admitted to
  any other stock exchange anywhere else in Europe[34];
- Disclosure of Major Shareholdings (88/627). This enables companies to find out who is building up substantial shareholdings in
  listed companies[35];
- Insider Dealing (89/852). This replaced the former Insider Dealing (Company Securities) Act 1985[36];
- Directive on Prospectuses (1995/137). This lays down minimum
  requirements for the information required to be published in
  prospectuses[37];
- Mutual Recognition of Prospectuses. A prospectus recognised
  under the rules of one country may be recognised in another
  country.[38]

---

[29] The U.K. was not entirely convinced of the merits of the draft Thirteenth Directive
because it effectively added little to the City Code and indeed might have introduced an
extra legalistic impediment, by way of appeal to the courts, to the operation of takeovers.

[30] There is some truth in this suggestion: it is a rare takeover that does not involve job
losses.

[31] Implemented in Financial Services Act 1986, Pt IV. (Hereafter referred to as FSA
1986.)

[32] Implemented in FSA 1986, Pt IV.

[33] *ibid.*, Pt IV.

[34] *ibid.,* and the Listing Rules.

[35] CA 1985, Pt VI.

[36] Implemented by Criminal Justice Act 1993, Pt V, and S.I. 1994 No. 187.

[37] Implemented by S.I. 1995 No. 137.

[38] Implemented by S.I. 1995 No. 1537, also known as the Public Offer of Securities
Regulations 1995.

Regulations that are applicable to company law in the United King- **1.16** dom include EC Regulation 2137/85 on European Economic Interest Groupings, which are non-profit making cross-border ventures in such fields as research and development, and EC Merger Control Regulation No. 4064/89, which enables the European Commission to investigate very large EC mergers for competition issues. Regulation 1346/2000 deals with cross-border insolvencies.

One particular regulation, which has been 30 years in the making, is the regulation for the European Company Statute, (to be known by its Latin name *Societas Europaea* ("SE")) which will allow for the existence of pan-European companies without specific national identity, and based collectively in Europe or part of Europe. It is thought that with a common currency, the Euro, in existence, there will be opportunities for economies of scale with companies that are not tied to any country, and for projects that straddle frontiers. It should save having to have separate national subsidiaries. There is some doubt as to the extent of the demand for such companies, and further doubt as to how and where the companies are going to be taxed and have their place of residence or seat. A particular feature of an SE is that there must be regular reports to and consultation with a body that represents its workers' interests. If the management and the representative body cannot agree, then a set of standard principles, attached to the related Directive on Worker Involvement, will apply.

The legislation for this Regulation and the related Directive is expected to come into force on October 8, 2004.

The aim of much of the European law, at least for public companies **1.17** and listed companies, is to have "a level playing field" for all such companies and on the whole to reduce artificial and national barriers to commerce. This commendable objective is generally welcomed in EC countries until individual national and sometimes protectionist interests are significantly threatened, or some rule is introduced which runs contrary to a nation's culture. For example, the United Kingdom has a horror of employee participation, whereas Germany and France are hostile to foreign takeovers because of the threat to employment and the national interest. By having a level playing field it is hoped that countries within the EC will not vie with each other for the laxity of their corporate law.

COMPARISON WITH OTHER FORMS OF TRADING ORGANISATION

Sole traders

A sole trader is a person running a business on his own account. He **1.18** is responsible for his entire losses, but equally he keeps all the profits himself and need not disclose his accounts to anyone save the Inland Revenue and the Customs and Excise (assuming he is VAT-registered).

It can be a precarious existence, dependent on the sole trader's continued good health, and there may be no-one with whom to share the responsibility of running the business. One option for sole traders nowadays is to incorporate as a single member private limited company, which combines all the benefit of limited liability and the separate legal personality of the company with the total independence of running a business alone, not subject to any "boss" or other interference. Many small businesses, such as self-employed tradesmen, small shopkeepers, artists, musicians, freelance journalists and consultants are sole traders.

Partnerships

1.19   A partnership is defined in the Partnership Act 1890 as two or more persons carrying on a business with a view of profit.[39] The business does not necessarily have to be profitable, but it should intend to make a profit; and the business carried on by the partners must have something in common, so that a business of a seamstress and a tree surgeon would not be a partnership, but a partnership of a plumber and a joiner might be.

The principal advantages of partnerships are as follows:

- Partnerships are easy to set up. No paperwork is needed, although a partnership agreement is desirable as it puts beyond doubt the partners' rights towards and duties to each other. If there is no partnership agreement, the Partnership Act 1890 imposes a series of standard assumptions which are deemed to apply unless there is agreement to the contrary; for example, in the absence of agreement otherwise, each partner has a right of management, and the partners share their profits and losses equally.
- A partnership need not disclose its accounts to anyone other than the Inland Revenue and the Customs and Excise. This means that a partnership's employees will not be able to find out how much the partners are earning.

1.20   The principal disadvantages of partnerships are as follows:

- Partners are jointly and severally personally liable for the partnership's debts.[40] This means that any creditor may sue the partnership, and all the partners personally, for a debt owed to him by the partnership. The creditor may even try to extract his debt from the wealthiest partner, leaving it up to that unfortunate partner to reclaim from the other partners the sums he has had to

[39] Partnership Act 1890, s.1.
[40] Partnership Act 1890 s.9.

pay on their behalf.[41] Partners put their own personal wealth at risk in their business.

- Partnerships are not supposed to have more than 20 partners. If they do the partners are required to incorporate,[42] and if they fail to do so, the partnership cannot enforce any contracts. This does not apply in the case of most professional partnerships, such as doctors, accountants and lawyers, and in any event the rule is increasingly seen as anachronistic. At the time of writing partnership law is being reviewed by the Law Commissions and one proposal is that this rule be removed.

- In practice in Scotland partnerships may only borrow against the value of the partnership's heritable assets, and cannot, unlike a company, borrow against the value of the partnership's moveable assets unless they go through the inconvenience of assigning those assets to the lender or physically delivering them to the lender. A company may grant a floating charge and may raise funds thereby with greater ease than a partnership.

- A partnership is only as strong as its weakest partner. When a partner in the course of his partnership business enters into a contract he binds the whole partnership, and the partners are supposed to have trust in each other and be confident of each other's abilities. Such trust may not always be whole-heartedly given. In any large firm of partners, there is commonly at least one partner whom the other partners regard with some disfavour, and who has a reputation for signing letters and deeds on behalf of the partnership where other, more prudent partners, would not. Such a partner may be a liability as far as the partnership as a whole is concerned, unless he has some redeeming feature such as being good at bringing in clients.

Features of partnerships that are neither advantageous nor disadvantageous include:

- Partnerships in Scotland have a legal personality separate from their partners. This enables partnerships to sue in their own name, and equally to be sued, though it is good practice to include all the names of the partners—and to refer to their successors—the partners acting as trustees for the partnership. When partnerships own heritage, the partners again themselves act as trustees for the partnership in the titles.[43] The fact that a partnership has a separate legal personality in practice makes very little difference, because the partners are still jointly and

---

[41] Partnership Act 1890, s.4(2).

[42] CA 1985, s.716.

[43] Partnership Act 1890, s.20.

severally liable for the partnership debts. Partnerships in Scotland (but not in England) may act collectively as directors or company secretaries.[44-45] In Scotland, it is possible for a partner to be a debtor or a creditor of his own partnership, but this is conceptually impossible in England. In England partnerships do not have a separate legal personality, but court rules have been specially adapted to allow partnerships to sue and be sued in the normal manner. One of the proposed amendments to partnership law is that English law should follow Scots law in giving partnerships a separate legal personality.

- Partnerships are supposed to reconstitute themselves every time a partner dies or retires. But in a partnership, such as some of the large accounting or legal partnerships, with a continuous turnover of partners, it is clearly unrealistic to keep reconstituting the partnership. Accordingly most partnership agreements are carefully drafted to permit the partnership to remain in existence despite the death or retiral of partners. It is sometimes said that perpetual succession is one of the advantages of companies, but equally some firms of solicitors, such as Dundas and Wilson C.S. have been operating happily since the mid-eighteenth century without difficulty.

Limited liability partnerships

1.21   Limited liability partnerships were introduced by the Limited Liability Partnership Act 2000, which came into force on April 1, 2001. They combine some of the features of partnerships with the some of the features of companies. Slightly confusingly the "partners" in a limited liability partnership are called members.

Limited liability partnerships have some of the rights of partnerships, such as equal treatment of members (subject to agreement to the contrary), privacy of internal arrangements (again, usually drawn up in an agreement which is not disclosed to non-members) and the tax treatment of partnerships (this meaning that the members are treated as self-employed).

1.22   In the same manner as a limited company, a limited liability partnership has to be registered with the Registrar of Companies and comply with the disclosure requirements under the Limited Liability Partnership Act 2000; it must publish its accounts for all to see; it has the benefit of limited liability, so that the partnership's liability to its creditors generally is limited to the amount of capital in the partnership; it may grant

---

[44-45] Although this is permissible it is not generally a good idea: a firm of solicitors, if asked to act as a company secretary for a client's firm, will generally use an in-house limited company owned collectively by the firm to act as the company secretary. This means that if the company secretarial work done is not done well, at least it will be the in-house that will be initially responsible rather than the firm's partners individually.

Introduction

15

floating charges; and its members will not generally be liable to creditors except on the same terms as directors are liable to creditors.[46]

It is anticipated that, in the near future, some professional firms will convert to limited liability partnerships. In order to comply with professional requirements imposed by such bodies as the Institute of Chartered Accountants in Scotland and the Law Society of Scotland, firms of accountants and solicitors will still need to be insured against losses arising through their own negligence or other cause. A limited liability partnership's capital may also be used to pay its losses, though after that fund has been exhausted, a creditor, if still not satisfied, will have no further satisfaction from the limited liability partnership which will then go into liquidation—but without the members, on the whole, being personally liable for the limited liability partnership's losses beyond what they have agreed to pay. If however the members are found to have breached their fiduciary duties, or otherwise acted in a manner prejudicial to creditors and others in terms of the amended rules applicable to company directors under the IA 1986, sections 212 to 216, the members may be liable to reimburse the limited liability partnership for such sums as the court deems appropriate. These reimbursed sums could then be used to help repay the creditors.

The individual membership interests in a limited liability partnership **1.23** may not be traded in the same manner as a share. Accordingly limited liability partnerships may have trouble attracting large amounts of capital. The main drawback, as far as existing partnerships are concerned, to the conversion to limited liability partnership status is the requirement to disclose accounts.

Limited partnerships

These are not to be confused with limited liability partnerships, and **1.24** are regulated by the Limited Partnership Act 1907. There is a special registrar for limited partnerships.

Limited partnerships are not very common, though they exist in the agricultural community. In a limited partnership, there are two types of partner, the limited partner and the general partner. The limited partner puts capital into the business and is entitled to draw interest from his investment. He may take no part in the management whatsoever, but he is protected to the extent that if the limited partnership's business goes into liquidation, he only loses the capital he has invested and no more. The other partner, known as the general partner, also puts capital (if he wishes) into the limited partnership, but is personally liable for the limited partnership's losses. On the other hand he has all the rights of management. Occasions where limited partnerships are commonly used arise when a landowner sets up a limited partnership with himself as the limited partner, drawing an income, and the general partner is the farmer

---

[46] See Chaps 2 and 9.

who does the work, takes the decisions and bears all the risk but equally keeps much of the profits.[47] On some occasions the limited partners will be parents in a farm-owning family and the general partners will be their children. There may be more than one limited partner and more than one general partner.

Registered companies

1.25   The main advantages of a limited liability company are as follows:

- A company has a legal personality separate from its members and its managers. Its members and its managers are not normally responsible for its debts unless the company is unlimited.
- The members do not have to bother themselves with the minutiae of managing the company. In general they delegate that power to the directors,[48] instead expecting to receive dividends, capital appreciation in the value of their shares, voting rights for certain major matters (including dismissing directors) and such other rights as are available to the members under the company's constitution.
- Publication of the accounts is advantageous if the accounts show that the company is prospering, as creditors will then be prepared to deal with the company and investors to invest. On the other hand, if the company is not prospering, creditors and investors may feel less inclined to deal with or invest in the company.
- Companies may borrow large sums in a hurry if necessary because they can with relative ease grant security over their moveable assets by the use of a floating charge. This enables companies to take advantage of commercial opportunities.
- A successful company may ultimately be able to float its securities on a recognised investment exchange such as the London Stock Exchange. If all goes well and the floated securities are seen to be desirable, the shareholders may make a great deal of money.
- A company may endure for a very long time and be able to retain its assets indefinitely even though the members and the managers may change from time to time.
- Holding companies may set up subsidiaries through which to trade in new ventures. Providing the holding companies have not

---

[47] This is particularly the case where the general partner would otherwise be a tenant with protected agricultural tenancy rights. As these rights depress the value of the land and are generally unwelcome to landowners, a common ploy for a landowner is not have an agricultural lease but to insist on the tenant being the general partner in a limited partnership—thus defeating the kindly purpose of the agricultural tenancy legislation.

[48] See reg. 70 of Table A.

guaranteed their subsidiaries' debts, holding companies may enjoy all the benefits of their investments in the subsidiaries but avoid all the liabilities of those subsidiaries if the subsidiaries turn out to be unsuccessful.

- Some people enjoy the kudos of being a director of a company.

The disadvantages of being a company are as follows:

- Some directors much resent the requirement to publish the company's accounts thereby allowing competitors to find out too much about their company.
- There are incorporation costs and continual compliance costs, such as auditing and the provision of legal advice, which do not arise in some other forms of trading venture;
- It is difficult to withdraw capital from a company except by following certain complicated rules or selling shares, assuming, that is, that the articles permit sale and that there is a willing buyer for the shares—which may not always be the case.
- Directors may believe that they will not normally be responsible for their companies' debts, but it is very common for commercial lenders to insist on personal guarantees by the directors for their companies' borrowings. On certain other occasions, particularly in the context of insolvency, directors may be responsible for their company's losses.[49]

1.26 Features of companies that are neither advantageous nor disadvantageous:

- Perpetual existence is often said to be an advantage of companies, but in practice it makes very little difference. So many companies change so much over so many years, even though the name may remain the same, that it is of little consequence.
- Taxation may sometimes favour incorporation or partnership (or limited liability partnership) according to the prevailing taxation rules. At the moment it is broadly neutral, but historically there have been times when it has been noticeably advantageous not to incorporate.

Scots Law and Company Law

1.27 Gladstone ensured that the nationality of a company should be included in its memorandum of association, and it is not, at least at present,

---

[49] IA 1986, ss. 212–216.

possible to change that nationality. This means that a Scottish-registered company remains a Scottish-registered company even if its business is all over the world. Company law in Scotland has been strongly influenced by the greater commercial world of England, and while Scots law copes adequately with most areas of company law, one area that is noticeably unsatisfactory, and has long been recognised as such, is the law relating to floating charges and receiverships.[50] This will be explored in more detail in Chapter 15. A second area is the problem of cross-border insolvency.

Finally it may be regrettable but it is no surprise that even major businesses in Scotland, such as construction companies, insurance companies and banks, often conduct their corporate business using English law, because inevitably so many more of the participants know English law, it is the dominant legal system, and incoming businesses are unlikely to feel drawn to an unfamiliar and in some respects (as noted above) unsatisfactory legal system. To take account of the increasing dominance of English law, this book will frequently refer to English law. While technically many English cases may not be binding on Scots law, it is clearly pointless for a small island to have widely diverging commercial/legal practice depending which side of the Tweed one may happen to be,[51] and consequently much regard is paid to English cases. This book will follow this precept.

COMPANY LAW AND JURISPRUDENCE

1.28 Company law is very unsatisfactory from a jurisprudential point of view. There is a certain amount of academic literature devoted to establishing what exactly in law a share is—to which the general answer is that it is a species of moveable property *sui generis,* which is hardly very informative and begs the question of whether it actually matters what in law a share is provided it works in practice. Although there is a certain amount of discussion about the moral issues in connection with the corporate veil, particularly in the context of victims of the company's negligence and the potential liabilities of directors, company law does not greatly lend itself to philosophic issues. Company law is about the regulation of power within a company, and it is about the proper use of money within a company. Even the current stakeholder debate ultimately may be reduced to the essential point about money: is the money a company deals with purely for the shareholders to play with, or should any wider considerations apply? Company law is predominantly a

---

[50] As may be seen in the controversy arising from the case of *Sharp v. Thomson,* 1997 S.C. (HL) 66, 1997 S.L.T. 636.

[51] At the time of writing it looks as though there will be a particular difficulty with regard to proposed new systems of registration of charges in England and Scotland because of the different approach to property laws.

pragmatic set of laws to help businesses make money fairly. It presupposes capitalistic instincts and it is no surprise that former Socialist countries had no company law. Company law is not a deep law, replete with significance for the rights of mankind: it is down to earth, commercial, pragmatic and is ultimately about helping businesses work more effectively.

Further Reading

Davies, *Gower's Principles of Modern Company Law* (6th ed., Sweet and Maxwell, 1997), Chaps 1–4

Davies, *Introduction to Company Law* (2002 Oxford University Press), Chap. 1

Farrar and Hannigan, *Farrar's Company Law* (4th ed., Butterworths, 1998), Chaps 1–8

For information on the White Paper and on forthcoming U.K. legislation on company law, see: www.dti.gov.uk/companiesbill

For information on European Directives, etc., on company law, see: Europa.eu.int/eur-lex/en/lif/reg/en_register_1710/html

CHAPTER 2

THE CORPORATE VEIL

THE IMAGINARY BARRIER

The separate legal identity of the company

2.01 Chapter 1 outlined the various commercial effects of the concept of limited liability and the advantages, relative to other forms of trading organisation, of the registered company. This chapter analyses the legal effects of the separate legal personality of the company.

The general principle of the separate legal personality rule is that a company is separate from those who own the company (the members), those who direct it (its directors), and those who are employed by it (its employees). The seminal case in all these discussions is the well-known case of *Salomon v. A. Salomon & Co. Ltd*[1]:

> Mr Salomon owned a bootmaking business. He was also the majority shareholder and managing director of a limited company, A. Salomon & Co. Ltd, to which he sold his business for the high but not fraudulent price of £39,000. The company could not pay the entire purchase price itself, so in his capacity as managing director Salomon arranged that the outstanding balance of the purchase price be treated as an unpaid debt, though recorded as debentures, repayable to himself personally by the company, and secured over the company's assets.[2] After various vicissitudes, and the appointment of a receiver,[3] the company went into liquidation. The unsecured creditors found that there was nothing left over for them following repayment of the debentures. The unhappy unsecured creditors persuaded the liquidator to raise an action against

---

[1] (1887) A.C. 22.

[2] In effect he had a mortgage over the company's assets, so that if the loan was not repaid, he had a prior right to the secured assets ahead of any other creditors and would thereby get his money back.

[3] The receiver was appointed by a Mr Broderip, who had bought the debentures from Salomon, to recover the assets secured by the debentures, and used the funds realised therefrom to discharge the debentures.

Salomon personally, (i) to have the debentures in favour of himself rescinded on the grounds of fraud, and (ii) to have the contract for the sale of the business to the company rescinded. But the House of Lords held that as a matter of statutory interpretation, Salomon had complied with all the requirements of the Companies Act 1862, that there was no evidence of fraud and that it was perfectly legitimate for Salomon to contract personally with his company both in respect of the debentures and in respect of the sale of his business to the company. The creditors were well aware that they had been dealing with a limited company, not Salomon personally; and if they chose to deal with a company, they had to be aware of the risks of doing so. Salomon was not therefore personally liable to those creditors.

The important issues to be drawn from this are that (i) Salomon and his company were two separate legal personalities who were free to contract with each other, and (ii) that in the absence of fraud there was nothing wrong with Salomon being a secured creditor of his own company even though he had been in a position, through his managing directorship and his controlling shareholding, to make the company enter into a contract with himself.

This same principle was followed in *Lee v. Lee's Air Farming Ltd*[4]: **2.02**

Mr Lee set up an aerial crop-spraying company in New Zealand with himself as the majority shareholder and governing director. His wife had a small shareholding. Following the proper procedures, he, as the main shareholder, caused the company to pass a resolution appointing himself the chief (and indeed only) pilot of the company. A contract of employment was signed, and his wages as company pilot were duly entered into the company's books. He later was killed while aerial crop-spraying, and the question arose as to whether or not his widow was entitled to a state pension, under the (New Zealand) Workers Compensation Act 1922, because of his death during the course of his employment. The New Zealand government asserted that as governing director and controller of the company he was precluded from being a servant of his company. The Privy Council disagreed, and held that it was acceptable for Lee's company to contract with Lee personally to be employed as the company's chief pilot; and therefore his widow was entitled to her pension.

The question of a majority shareholder also being an employee (and thereby entitled to normal employee rights on redundancy) was recently revisited in *Secretary of State for Trade and Industry v. Bottrill*[5] where

---

[4] [1961] A.C. 12.
[5] [1999] B.C.C. 177.

the Court of Appeal ruled, in an employment case, that even if the employee is the majority shareholder, he is still entitled to be treated as an employee if he has an employment contract and paid tax and national insurance as if he were an employee—thus affirming the principle of the *Lee* case above.

2.03   However, the separate legal personality of the company can work to a person's disadvantage too, as can be seen in the case of *Macaura v. Northern Assurance Company Ltd*[6]:

> Macaura grew timber on his farm in Northern Ireland. The Government encouraged the growing of timber for use as pit props in mining, and to hold up trench walls in the event of another war. As part of the Government's encouragement for timber growing, a tax liability could be avoided by transferring the ownership of the growing timber, at the appropriate stage, to a limited company. Macaura duly did this, but neglected to insure the timber, now owned by the company, in the name of the company, instead putting the insurance in his own name. The timber mysteriously caught fire, and on its destruction, he (and not his company) claimed the value of the timber from the insurers. The insurers successfully resisted the claim on the grounds that he had no insurable interest in the timber.

These three familiar cases establish the separate legal identity of the company, with the first two cases ultimately turning on the statutory interpretation of the Companies Act 1862 and the Workers Compensation Act 1922.

The corporate veil

2.04   The corporate veil is the term given to the imaginary barrier that separates the company from those who direct it (the directors) and from those who own it (the members). On the whole this barrier prevents the directors and/or members being liable for the company's acts and omissions, but occasionally, the veil is said to be lifted or pierced,[7] on which occasion the directors and/or members may be found liable for the company's acts and omissions, or alternatively, the members (particularly if they are a holding company) may be able to have a benefit, attributable to the company, made available to themselves.

There are two main grounds for lifting the veil, the first being where statute so requires it, and the second being where the courts have permitted it (under common law).

---

[6] [1925] C. 619.

[7] Despite one or two efforts to suggest a difference between these two verbs, there is little difference in practice, and the word "lift" will be used hereafter.

Lifting the veil under statute

There are a number of occasions under CA 1985, IA 1986 and **2.05** the CDDA 1986 where this arises. The following is a list of some of the better known occasions.

Public limited companies ("plcs") trading with only one shareholder—Companies Act 1985, section 24

Although it is an unlikely occurrence, if a plc drops below the **2.06** required two members, without converting itself into a single member private limited company, the one remaining member will be jointly and severally liable for the plc's debts after a period of six months commencing from the date that there was only one member, unless (as would be surprising) that member is genuinely unaware that he is the sole member.

The purpose of this rule is to force plcs to convert to private limited companies under these circumstances.

Absence of a section 117 trading certificate

When a plc is incorporated as a plc (as opposed to incorporating **2.07** initially as a private limited company and converting itself into a plc), if the directors start trading without having obtained a section 117 trading certificate,[8] following the provision to the Registrar of Companies of certain forms and a statutory declaration,[9] the directors will be jointly and severally liable, together with the company, for any unpaid debts of the company if they have failed to obtain the required certificate within 21 days of being called upon to do so.

This is in practice extremely rare, and exists primarily as an inducement to directors to ensure that plcs genuinely have sufficient capital to start trading.

Inaccurate company name under Companies Act 1985, section 349

A company is required to put its correct company name on all **2.08** negotiable instruments (such as cheques, promissory notes and bills of exchange). In particular the word "limited", assuming the company is limited, must be included. Failure to do so makes the officer[10] of the company who signed the negotiable instrument liable.

> *Rafsanjan Pistachio Producers Ltd v. Reiss*[11]
> Mrs Reiss was director of her company, Firegreen Ltd, which owned money to Rafsanjan. She agreed to pay the outstanding debt

---

[8] This corresponds to CA 1985, s.117.
[9] See para. 3.12.
[10] An officer is any director, company secretary or auditor of the company.
[11] [1990] B.C.C. 730.

by means of five post-dated cheques, drawn in US dollars, on the company account. Because the company's bank did not have proper cheques for the company, the bank supplied special cheques with which to pay the debt. The cheques were printed with the company's registered number but not with its name on them. Mrs Reiss wrote the five cheques on the company account, inserting her own name as drawer, but not the company name. The first three cheques cleared. The latter two were dishonoured by the bank. Rafsanjan sued Mrs Reiss personally under CA 1985, s.349; as the company's name was omitted, she was personally liable as a director of her company. Had she had the name "Firegreen Ltd" printed or written on her cheques, and had she signed the cheques "Mrs Reiss, for and on behalf of Firegreen Ltd" or "Mrs Reiss, Managing director, Firegreen Ltd" or by other means included the proper company name she would not have been liable.

2.09   The idea behind the rule is that creditors need to be forewarned if they are dealing with a company (in theory riskier than a personally liable individual) and so the proper company name must be included. The rule is strictly applied. In *Blum v. OCP Repartition SA*,[12] Blum omitted to include the word "limited" at the end of his company's name on its cheques: Blum became liable for his company's cheques on his company's liquidation. The simple insertion of the one word would have saved him. However a simple spelling mistake may be permissible, provided no doubt as to the company's identity arises.[13]

Liability on the insolvency of the company under Insolvency Act 1986, sections 212–216

2.10   This topic is dealt with in greater detail in Chapter 16, but in essence, where a company has become insolvent, a liquidator is entitled to look at the behaviour of the directors in the period leading up to the insolvency of the company. The liquidator may apply to the court for an order to make a director compensate the company for any breach of his duty, fiduciary, statutory or otherwise, to the company, in that period,[14] for fraudulent trading (this applies to members as well)[15] and for wrongful trading[16] which is where a director continues to accept credit or accept supplies when he knows or ought to have known that the company was not in a position to honour its obligations, and failed to take all steps that he ought to have done to minimise the loss to the creditors. In addition, if a company is put into insolvent liquidation and

---

[12] [1988] BCLC 170, [1988] F.L.R. 229.
[13] A company called "Primekeen Ltd" was misspelt as "Primkeen Ltd": *Jenice Ltd v. Dan* [1993] BCLC 1349.
[14] IA 1986, s.212.
[15] IA 1986, s.213.
[16] IA 1986, s.214.

a new company is created with a very similar name, usually in the same line of business and with the same personnel, the directors will be jointly and severally liable for the debts of the new company if the new company's name is virtually the same as the old company's now prohibited name, and consent has not been granted by the courts for the use of the prohibited name or a name very similar to it.[17]

Liability under the Company Directors Disqualification Act 1986

If a director has been disqualified from acting as a director for any **2.11** reason, and if he does then act as a director of a company despite being disqualified, he will be jointly and severally liable, together with the company for which he was acting, for the debts of that company.[18]

Less well known statutory occasions for personal liability

These include the personal liability for directors who make unjusti- **2.12** fied statutory declarations about the company's continued solvency following a payment out of capital on redemption or repurchase of shares[19]; for directors, jointly and severally with the company, where the requirement to offer pre-emption rights under CA 1985, section 89 has been ignored by the directors and the deprived members have suffered loss[20]; for directors where they allot shares although the minimum subscription has not been received by the company[21]; for directors under various parts of CA 1985 Part X (enforcement of fair dealing by directors) which require the directors personally to indemnify the company for any loss, or account to the company for any profit, arising out of their improper actions[22]; providing inaccurate information in a prospectus thereby causing loss to a person relying on that prospectus[23]; for members if they receive an unlawful distribution of profits and know it[24]; and various other occasions dealt with later in Chapter 9.

There are also occasions under tax statutes, customs and excise rules, prevention of terrorism laws and money-laundering rules which enable the courts to pierce any corporate veils behind which funds may be lurking; but such matters are beyond the ambit of this book.

Lifting the veil under common law

Lifting the veil under statute is relatively easy to do. Would that the **2.13** same could be said of the common law. Under the common law, the

---

[17] IA 1986, ss.216, 217. This is also known as "phoenix trading". See also Chap. 16.
[18] CDDA 1986, s.15. See also Chap. 8.
[19] IA 1986, s.76 (this also applies to previous shareholders).
[20] CA 1985, s.92.
[21] CA 1985, ss.83–85.
[22] This is discussed in greater detail in Chap. 9.
[23] Public Offer of Securities Regulations (S.I. 1995 No. 1537), reg. 14.
[24] CA 1985, s.277(1).

cases collectively suggest that on some occasions the courts may be prepared to lift the veil, but that on the whole they are very reluctant to do so. Most commentators struggle to find any coherent body or theme of law running through the common law decisions.[25] It is unfortunate that there is no coherent policy on this matter because it makes it difficult for a lawyer to advise directors or members when they may be personally liable for their company's acts and omissions, or equally whether clients may be able to seek redress against a company's directors or members who may have taken too much advantage of their company's separate legal identity. The very uncertainty of the law every year encourages a few hardy litigants to see if directors or holding companies may be made personally liable for the acts of their companies or subsidiaries; and once in a while, temporarily, they may succeed[26] though on the whole they are unlikely to be successful.[27]

One way of looking at the common law cases is to look at certain general categories, even though they overlap to some extent.

Evasion of responsibilities

2.14   In *Gilford Motor Co. Ltd v. Horne*[28] a salesman who had been dismissed by his former employers, and who had had a covenant in his employment contract preventing him from soliciting his former clients after leaving his employers, deliberately solicited his former clients through the medium of a company set up by his wife and a former employee. When an injunction was duly obtained to prevent him soliciting his former clients, he claimed that he personally was not soliciting the clients, even if his company was, and that the original covenant did not therefore apply. The Court of Appeal rejected his specious argument, and ruled that the covenant applied both to him and to his wife's company. The abuse of the corporate form to evade a previous obligation is therefore unacceptable.[29] However, it would appear permissible for a company to arrange its future corporate affairs in such a manner as to minimise its future responsibilities.[30]

---

[25] For further reading on this topic, see Sealy, *Cases and Materials in Company Law* (7th ed., Butterworths, 2001), p. 57, f. 20.

[26] *Creasey v. Breachwood Motors Ltd* [1992] B.C.C. 638, now overruled by *Ord v. Belhaven Pubs Ltd* [1998] 2 BCLC 447, CA; but notwithstanding the subsequent overruling six years later, in the meantime Creasey won his case, mainly because his opponent chose not to appeal.

[27] The issue of directors' personal responsibility to creditors and victims of their negligence will be addressed in Chap. 9.

[28] (1933) C.A. 935.

[29] See also *Jones v. Lipman* [1962] 1 All E.R. 442, [1962] 1 W.L.R. 832, for the operation of the same principle.

[30] *Adams v. Cape Industries plc* [1990] Ch. 433, [1991] 1 All E.R. 929 (CA); *Re Polly Peck International plc* [1996] 2 All E.R. 433.

Political reality or public policy

In *Daimler Co. Ltd v. Continental Tyre and Rubber Co. (Great* **2.15**
Britain) Ltd[31] which took place during World War I, Daimler was
admittedly due to pay Continental a large sum of money. Daimler
successfully contended that the courts should look behind the registration of Continental to see Continental's underlying predominantly German ownership and management and that Continental should be treated
as having "enemy character". If it had enemy character the debt ceased.
As far as a company is concerned enemy character could be established
by looking at who controlled it, in this case Germans; and thus Continental was not able to claim its debt.

As a cynical aside, during the First World War anti-German feeling
ran high, and in London and elsewhere the homes of people with
German names or German sympathisers had their windows smashed. It
is unrealistic to think that the highest court in the land would at that
perilous time have found in favour of Continental.[32] Nowadays were
such an issue to arise, the Trading with the Enemy Act 1939 would
ensure that the debt would not need to be paid.

Public policy also applies in some of the tax cases, such as *Re FG* **2.16**
(Films) Ltd[33] where a film company was set up in the United Kingdom
in order to take advantage of certain tax breaks, even though the entire
ownership and control was American. The courts lifted the corporate
veil to see the true ownership and thereby deprived the company of its
tax breaks. Much tax legislation is now artfully worded to catch artful
tax-avoiding movement of funds round companies, their members or
companies within a group.

The demise of the group entity theory

In *DHN Food Distributors Ltd v. Tower Hamlets London Borough* **2.17**
Council[34] the Court of Appeal established that a group of companies
including DHN was so closely intertwined that it would have required
a simple transfer of the legal title of a piece of land from one company
within the group to another to enable certain compensation payments to
be paid by the Council to DHN. Technically the paperwork was missing,
but as it could so very easily have been effected, the compensation
ought to be paid.

This case established what is known as the "group entity theory"
which presupposes that a group of companies all closely connected may
be presumed to be one greater whole, known as a group entity. In this
case there was no suggestion of fraud or deceit involved, and, on the

---

[31] [1916] 2 A.C. 307.
[32] The Court of Appeal was willing, however, to find in favour of Continental.
[33] [1953] 1 W.L.R. 483, [1953] 1 All E.R. 615: the courts refused to allow the company
the benefits it sought to obtain.
[34] [1976] 1 W.L.R. 852, 3 All E.R. 462.

face of it, it would have been unjust to deprive the business as a whole
of the compensation otherwise due had the appropriate paperwork been
in place. Under these circumstances it probably was reasonable to have
ordered the compensation to be paid. Nonetheless later courts were
clearly unimpressed by this decision. The Scottish courts very noticeably failed to follow the *DHN* decision in the case of *Woolfson v.
Strathclyde Regional Council*,[35] a case in some respects similar to *DHN*,
but one in which the courts held that in principle companies should be
treated as separate within a group, and that the corporate veil should
only be lifted where special circumstances exist indicating that it is a
"mere façade concealing the true facts".[36] The decision of the *Woolfson*
case was referred to with approval in the case of *Adams v. Cape
Industries plc*[37] and the *DHN* decision, while not explicitly overruled,
was politely disparaged by being said to depend on the statutory provisions for compensation and on being expressed "somewhat broadly".

2.18 As far as subsidiaries are concerned, the position is well expressed in
Lord Templeman's famous words in *Re Southard & Co. Ltd*[38]:

> "A parent company may spawn a number of subsidiary com-
> panies, all controlled directly or indirectly by the shareholders of
> the parent company. If one of the subsidiary companies, to change
> the metaphor, turns out to be the runt of the litter, and declines into
> insolvency to the dismay of the creditors, the parent company and
> the other subsidiary companies may prosper to the joy of the
> shareholders without any liability for the debts of the insolvent
> subsidiary."

Agency

2.19 Historically the courts have sometimes tried to lift the corporate veil
by saying that the company was acting as an agent for its members, thus
making the members liable for the company's actions, and in particular
a holding company liable for its subsidiaries acting as the holding
company's agents. Although this approach was favoured in a few cases
such as *Firestone Tyre and Rubber Co. Ltd v. Lewellyn*[39] and *Smith,
Stone and Knight Ltd v. Birmingham Corp.*,[40] it does not appear to have
found much favour since the *Woolfson* case.

---

[35] 1978 S.C. (HL) 90, 1978 S.L.T. 159.
[36] See Lord Keith of Kinkel's speech at p. 96 (or for S.L.T., p. 161).
[37] [1990] Ch. 433, [1991] 1 All E.R. 929, CA.
[38] [1979] 3 All E.R. 556 at 565, [1979] 1 W.L.R. 1198 at 1208.
[39] [1956] 1 All E.R. 693, [1956] 1 W.L.R. 352, aff'd [1957] 1 All E.R. 561, [1957] 1
     W.L.R. 464, HL.
[40] [1939] 4 All E.R. 116.

Hard cases make bad law

In *Creasey v. Breachwood Motors Ltd*[41] Creasey obtained a worthless **2.20** judgement against his former employer. The company that formerly employed him had blatantly removed all its assets to another company with similar members and directors, leaving in the employing company only the potential liability to Creasey. When Creasey tried to enforce payment from his former employing company, he found that he could not in practice enforce the judgment and that the employing company had already been removed from the Register of Companies.[42] He successfully sought permission to transfer his claim to the second company in order to have someone to sue and in the interests of justice. Nonetheless, this decision of a lower court was very deliberately overruled in *Ord v. Belhaven Pubs Ltd*[43] where the courts refused the plaintiff's request to transfer a claim from one company to another on the grounds (i) that there had been no evidence of impropriety and (ii) that the plaintiff had had ample opportunity to make his claim against the original company and delayed in doing so; in this case the Court of Appeal also made it very clear, and in a surprisingly irritable manner, that *Creasey* was wrongly decided.

Alternative remedies

There is no doubt that Creasey was entitled to damages arising from **2.21** his employer's breach of his contract. However when the employer then transferred its assets to another company, the employer still in theory could have been sued. In an ideal world and according to the judgment in *Ord*, Creasey should have raised an action against his employer, and on finding that it was not worth suing, petitioned for the liquidation of the employer. The liquidator could then have raised an action against the recipient of the employer's funds, (*i.e.* the second company) under IA 1986, section 423[44] in order to have the divested assets restored to the employer and then made available to Creasey and any other creditors.

A similar issue arose in *Yukong Lines of Korea Ltd v. Rendsburg Investments Corp. of Liberia (No. 2)*[45] where the director of Rendsburg, realising that penalty clauses would come into play as a result of the late arrival of his company's ship carrying the plaintiff's cargo to the port of destination, abstracted a substantial sum of Rendsburg's money, paid it to a company controlled by the director personally, and then smartly

---

[41] [1993] BCLC 480.

[42] It is arguable that he should have protected his position by means of a *Mareva* injunction or freezing order to prevent the employer's assets being removed, but it possibly did not occur to him that his employers would use the stratagem they did.

[43] [1998] 2 BCLC 447, CA.

[44] This is not applicable in Scotland, but the same result might be obtained by a petition under the *nobile officium*.

[45] [1998] 1 W.L.R. 294.

disappeared with the abstracted funds. Although the circumstantial evidence was not to the director's advantage, it was not, in Toulson J.'s view, sufficient to displace the normal rule under *Salomon*, and the plaintiffs were not permitted to raise an action against the rogue director personally, even though Rendsburg by now had minimal assets. What the plaintiffs were expected to do, and the main reason why the judge would not grant the plaintiffs their request, was to have the defendant company wound up and again, as in *Ord*, obtain an order under IA 1986, section 423, for the liquidator to seek the abstracted funds.

2.22   The problem with all this is practical: it is easy for the courts to say that the liquidator must trace the abstracted funds, but by the time a liquidator has been appointed and found his way through the company's accounts, the abstracted funds will have long since disappeared into the banking system, no doubt laundered through some unscrupulous off-shore bank. The creditor thus has to pay the costs of petitioning the courts for the liquidation of the defendant and of tracing the funds, which are likely to still be under the control of the rogue director, who of course will be taking every advantage of foreign banking secrecy laws and any other methods of avoiding payment. And there may be other creditors who will wish to share in any sums that the liquidator recovers.

On the other hand, the plaintiffs in this case could have taken more steps to protect themselves. The plaintiffs might have obtained a bond from the defendants to make good any loss arising from the freight-carrying; there could have been personal guarantees from the director and security over his own property and the defendant's property.

2.23   And finally there is always the commercial point: Yukong was not obliged to deal with Rendsburg: if you deal with a company you must expect from time to time that companies will take unfair advantage of their position, and it is up to those who deal with such companies to be on their guard.

Problematic areas

2.24   What happens to property that is owned by a company, and the company is owned by a husband and wife who are divorcing each other? Can the company's assets be divided in half? Can the courts look behind the company to distribute the company's assets between husband and wife? In *Wilson v. Wilson*[46] Lord Marnoch deliberately said that the separate legal persona of a company could not be interfered with even in the interests of dividing up matrimonial assets, and in the English case of *Mubarak v. Mubarak*[47] Bodey J. felt unable to look behind the corporate veil of a company owned by a husband and in which a husband was sheltering assets in order to prevent his wife obtaining

---

[46] 1999 S.L.T. 249.
[47] 2000 W.L. 1720346.

them. Bodey J. was in the difficult position of having to decide whether the plaintiff wife should have a higher right to the company's assets than the company's creditors; and in the end he decided that she did not, even though there was a strong suspicion that the husband was deliberately building up creditors (some of which were other companies with which he was connected) in order to make it difficult for his wife to get at his company's assets. In practice the courts could make an order requiring the husband to pay such sums to his wife as might force him to sell some of his shares and use the proceeds to pay his wife; but nonetheless in principle the wife could not have the corporate veil lifted in the interests of a matrimonial settlement.

Criminal matters

One of the most difficult areas of company law is that of the criminal **2.25** responsibility of companies, and their directors, for certain crimes. There is not normally any difficulty with strict liability crimes, where the prosecution need not prove that anyone within the company actually had the *mens rea* to commit a crime: it is enough that the crime was committed. Examples of such crimes are pollution offences. The company is publicly embarrassed, fined, and sometimes mends its ways.

The situation is more difficult with crimes of recklessness. Few employees deliberately wish to cause loss of life, but some employees do cause loss of life through recklessness. The Paddington rail crash was, according to the Cullen report, partly the fault of the driver who went through a red light and predominantly the fault of senior management at Railtrack. In the Southall rail disaster, neither the automatic train protection system nor the advance warning device was working at the time of the accident, as a result of management cut-backs on safety spending. Despite these findings, neither Railtrack[48] nor Great Western Railways was prosecuted for manslaughter.[49] It was not possible to establish a "directing mind" to prosecute. Collectively both companies failed to carry out proper procedures and maintenance that might have prevented these accidents, but no one person in either of those two companies had a "directing mind" which set out to be reckless as to the consequence of his failure to attend to safety matters.[50] Accordingly, the Crown Prosecution Service declined, to public outrage, to prosecute. There was a strong feeling at the time that the company should be

---

[48] In any case, with Railtrack now in administration and being run by the Government, there is little point in prosecuting the company.

[49] *R. v. Great Western Trains Co. Ltd, Att.-Gen. Ref. No. 2 of 1999* [2001] B.C.C. 210, [2000] 3 W.L.R. 195, [2000] 3 All E.R. 182.

[50] In the celebrated Ford Pinto case in the USA, however, the manufacturers of the Ford Pinto car secretly calculated how many people would die as a result of Ford's dangerous design and set off the cost of accident claims against the anticipated profits.

prosecuted[51]—and indeed so should the directors, who, it was alleged, had been more interested in corporate profits, their own salaries and the share price than in attending to unprofitable safety matters.

2.26   The English Law Commission considered these matters[52] and a Corporate Homicide Bill for England was drafted in 2000. The Government issued a consultation paper[53] in 2000, since when nothing has happened. One proposal is that in order to prevent companies setting up complex company structures to avoid liability, the prosecution could prosecute a holding company or any other group company where those companies' management failures caused the death in question,[54-55] thus lifting the corporate veil for the benefit of the prosecution. "Management failure" arises where the management fails to maintain the health and safety of employees or others affected by the management's acts (generally customers) and management may be held responsible even if the actual death resulted from an employee's act or omission. The penalties will be fines for the company, imprisonment and fines for any convicted officers of the company, and the company may receive an order from the courts requiring the company to take remedial action for the future.

These proposals, which echo proposals in other countries, such as France, are not without their difficulties, not the least of which is the disincentive to be a director, or the opportunity for vengeful workers to "set up" the management for a conviction. The CBI, as might be imagined, was not enthusiastic. On the other hand, it might be argued that a personal responsibility by directors for sloppy procedures might considerably improve the safety record of some companies.

2.27   As regards less contentious matters involving the criminal liability of companies, probably the leading case in England is *Re Supply of Ready Mixed Concrete (No. 2)*.[56] In this case senior management had explicitly undertaken to the Restrictive Practices Court that its middle management, which had been secretly operating a cartel with other middle managers in the concrete business, would no longer operate the cartel. Middle management at RMC was duly told not to operate any more

---

[51] The Lyme Regis canoeing disaster, also known as *R. v. Kite and OLL Ltd*, unreported, December 8, 1994, was an example where a company was found guilty of manslaughter, but as the company was run and owned by Mr Kite who pleaded guilty for himself and his company, it does not serve as a very good example of the effectiveness of prosecuting a company of this crime.

[52] *Legislating the Criminal Code: Involuntary Manslaughter* (Law Commission No. 237, 1996).

[53] *Reforming the Law on Involuntary Manslaughter: The Government's Proposals*, May 2000, www.homeoffice.gov.uk.

[54-55] There are also proposals to extend this principle to other bodies, corporate or otherwise, such as partnerships, hospital trusts, etc.

[56] [1995] 1 A.C. 456.

cartels, but nevertheless disobeyed the instructions from senior management. The ensuing cartel was discovered and the company was successfully prosecuted. In vain did senior management explain that middle management had disobeyed express instructions: if the undertaking given to the court was to be meaningful it had to be adhered to, and senior management ought to monitor middle management properly so that middle management did not repeat its former offences.[57]

Scotland has not seen any recent significant reported cases on corporate criminal responsibility, but it would be unusual if the law relating to corporate criminal responsibility were to be different in Scotland. At the time of writing the Crown Office has indicated that Transco plc will be prosecuted for the culpable homicide of four workers in Grangemouth. It is likely that the same legal and policy problems will still arise as in England.

There are other, more pragmatic problems involved in fixing com- **2.28** panies and their directors with criminal responsibility. Punishing a company is difficult. A company itself cannot be imprisoned. If instead a company is fined, the ones who suffer are the innocent shareholders, and the fine needs to be enormous to make any difference at all to the profits of a large company. If the fine was very large indeed, the fine might actually put the company out of business, thus creating unemployment. Imprisoning directors who may genuinely have known nothing of the bad practices of their employees, especially if the employees have deliberately made it difficult for directors to find out their malpractice, is unfair. Furthermore, imprisoning the directors could also cause a company to collapse, as well as deterring able employees from accepting responsibilities.

These are intractable issues, and the United Kingdom is not alone in having difficulties in its jurisprudence on these matters.

There are many sections in the Companies Act 1985[58] and elsewhere which if contravened may result in the conviction of the company or its directors. These sections are mostly regulatory offences where directors may be fined or imprisoned for various failures to lodge the correct documents in time or fail to carry out undertakings required by law. This book does not venture into these criminal matters.

The moral issue

In the past it is possible to see occasions when the courts quite clearly **2.29** felt that a company has behaved badly, *Creasey* being a good example. There is also a view that victims of delicts are sometimes treated badly when companies that would otherwise be due to pay damages to the victims of their negligence deliberately or otherwise go out of business

---

[57] As a result of this decision, the case of *Tesco Supermarkets Ltd v. Nattrass* [1972] A.C. 153 would probably not now be followed.
[58] See Sched. 24.

to avoid paying any negligence claims. During 2001 South African victims of asbestos-related illnesses sued the British holding company of its defunct South African subsidiary. The subsidiary had quarried asbestos and then abandoned its factory, leaving clouds of powdery carcinogenic asbestos swirling around to be inhaled by the former employees and their families. After an immense struggle, leaving aside the question of the liability of the holding company for its subsidiary, the House of Lords held that the victims were able to have their case heard in the United Kingdom.[59] The next battle was to establish whether the holding company could be held liable for its subsidiary's actions. The point was never explored because the case was settled by the holding company's insurers. This suggests the following:

- that the victims thought they had better accept a good offer while it still was available;
- that the holding company may have thought that the victims had such a good moral case against the holding company that it was better to settle quickly than attract bad publicity;
- that the insurers for the company may have considered that the House of Lords might have ruled in favour of the victims in the light of the company's shameless lack of concern for the victims.

This case shows up very clearly the major problem with the idea of the corporate veil. There is little doubt that the dying black workers of the South African subsidiary were only marginally in a position to bargain with their employers, that the mines were not properly looked after and that environmental breaches took place. Although the holding company was legally entitled to close down its subsidiary, is it arguable that the holding company has a moral duty towards its subsidiary's employees, having enjoyed the fruits of their labours in the past; and many would think that it would be unjust to refuse the employees a remedy and abandon them to bleak deaths from asbestos-related illnesses. However, had the House of Lords ruled in favour of the employees, the United Kingdom would overnight have become a less attractive place in which to do business as holding companies became liable for their subsidiaries; furthermore liability indemnity premiums would have gone up, inflation would have gone up and business might have fled abroad.

It would have been a difficult decision: no doubt the House of Lords was very relieved not to have had to make it.

---

[59] *Lubbe v. Cape Industries plc* [2000] UKHL 41.

Further Reading

Grantham and Rickett, *Corporate Personality in the 20th Century* (Hart Publishing, 1998)

Davies, *Introduction to Company Law* (Oxford University Press, 2002), Chap. 2

Lowry and Watson, *Company Law* (Butterworths, 2001), Chap. 3

Ottolenghi "From peeping behind the corporate veil to ignoring it completely" [1990] M.L.R. 338

CHAPTER 3

COMPANY INCORPORATION

THE PRACTICALITIES OF INCORPORATION

The initial documentation

3.01   To set up a company all that is required is the completion of the Forms 10 and 12, a memorandum of association and the articles of association.

The Form 10 corresponds to Companies Act 1985 ("CA 1985"), section 10 and requires the insertion of the proposed company name; the proposed registered office (for which P.O. boxes are unacceptable) in Scotland; the agent's name and address (if used); the name and address of the company secretary (if the company secretary is a partnership, limited liability partnership or registered company its principal office or registered office, as the case may be, should be used as its address); and a list of the directors, together with information regarding the full names and previous names, their titles, their addresses[1] (directors which are companies or limited liability partnerships supply their registered office, while directors which are partnerships supply their principal office), their dates of birth,[2] their nationality, their business occupations, and their other directorships. Directors need not give all their other directorships: they need only specify the directorships of those companies of which the director has been a director in the last five years, whether still extant or struck off, but excluding within that same period any company which was or is dormant, a parent company of the company being

---

[1] It is possible for a director to apply to the Secretary of State for a Confidentiality Order if the director is at genuine risk of violence or intimidation if his address is published. The Companies (Particulars of Usual Residential Address) (Confidentiality Orders) Regulations 2002 (S.I. 2002 No. 912).

[2] The reason for the date of birth is partly because of the rule for plcs that directors may not be over the age of 70 without shareholder approval (CA 1985, s.293(2)), but also to help identify directors with the same name in the same household, as for example, father and son both called Ian Smith.

36

formed, a wholly owned subsidiary of the company being formed[3] or another subsidiary of the holding company of the company being formed.

The reason for providing such information about the directorships is **3.02** to enable investors and creditors to look up at the Registrar of Companies those other companies of which the proposed or new director is or was a director, and to see how those companies have fared. The reason for the exclusion of certain directorships is apparently to prevent directors complaining of "red tape" and the provision of unnecessary information.

The last piece of information required for the Form 10 is the completion of the box where the subscribers (the initial members who sign the memorandum of association) sign, or their agents sign on their behalf.

In a single member private limited company the same rules apply, **3.03** except that there will only be one subscriber and commonly only one director who must not be the same person as the company secretary.[4]

The Form 12 (which corresponds to CA 1985, section 12) is a somewhat pointless form requiring either a solicitor involved in the formation of the company, or one of the directors, or the company secretary to swear in terms of the Statutory Declarations Act 1835 in the presence of a notary public, commissioner for oaths in England, a Justice of the Peace or a solicitor that all the requirements of the Companies Act 1985 in respect of the incorporation of a company have been complied with.

The Forms 10 and 12, the memorandum and articles of association **3.04** are sent to the Registrar of Companies along with the fee, at present £20, and assuming all the documentation is in order, the Registrar will issue a certificate of registration. This is *prima facie* conclusive evidence that the company is properly founded, even if in fact the Registrar of Companies has recorded something incorrectly.[5] The certificate will show the company's name, the company's number, the Registrar's signature and the date of registration. A company comes into existence at midnight on the day of registration.

---

[3] It is obviously unlikely that a company in the process of formation will have a subsidiary, but the rules applicable to the Form 10 are also applicable to the Form 288(a) used for the appointment of a new director, in which case the new director might well also be a director of a subsidiary, and for the Form 366, known as the Annual Return, which requires the same information about directors.

[4] CA 1985, s.283(2).

[5] In *Re Baby Moon (UK) Ltd* (1985) 1 B.C.C. 99 a company with a registered office in Livingston in West Lothian was held to be registered in England as stated in the certificate. However, in *R. v. Registrar of Companies, ex p. Att.-Gen.* [1991] BCLC 476 the frolicsome Miss Lindi St Claire was not allowed to set up a company whose object was prostitution, it being contrary to public policy to set up a company for such a purpose (CA 1985, s.1(1)), notwithstanding that the Registrar of Companies had issued a certificate of registration.

On incorporating a company it is quite common to send in a Form 224 as well.[6] This Form deals with the accounting reference date. If no accounting reference date is specified by the use of the Form 224, a new company's first accounting reference date will be deemed to be the anniversary of the end of the month of incorporation, so that a company formed on, say, March 8, 2001 will have to make up its first accounts up to March 31, 2002. However under CA 1985, section 225 it is possible to extend the normal date for a period of up to 18 months after the date of incorporation, or indeed to shorten the period, though the company's financial year must be at least six months in duration. The common reason for doing so is to align the accounting reference date of a new company with that company's holding company or with another subsidiary. There are restrictions to prevent companies altering their accounting reference dates more than once every five years.

For the practicalities of operating a newly formed company, see the end of the chapter.

The company's name

3.05 A company may not have the same name as any other company name. The difference may only be minimal—one letter or digit—but there must be no duplication of names within the United Kingdom; and it is sensible not to have a name that is too close to an existing company in the same line of business. It is therefore common in practice for people who wish their company to have a particular name to check with company formation agents or with the officials at the Register of Companies to see if their proposed name is already being used, is too similar to an existing name, or is otherwise unsuitable. There is no virtue in having a name that leads to litigation.

The company must indicate in its name if it is limited company, or a public limited company.[7] Unlimited companies do not need to specify that they are unlimited. Certain charities may apply to dispense with the word "limited" if they are guarantee companies and/or founded under certain conditions before 1948.[8] The name that a company chooses must not be one that in the opinion of the Secretary of State for Trade and Industry is a criminal offence[9] or offensive.[10] It is also forbidden (except with the approval of the Secretary of State) for a company to have a

---

[6] The Form 224 may only be used in the first nine months of a company's existence (CA 1985, s.224(2)); thereafter the Form 225 would be used.

[7] CA 1985, s.25(1).

[8] CA 1985, s.30.

[9] CA 1985, s.26(1)(d)—as, for example, a name that would incite racial hatred in terms of the Race Relations Act 1976.

[10] CA 1985, s.26(1)(e). There do not appear to be guidelines as to what the Secretary of State will find offensive, but in practice the Registrar of Companies tends to suggest to company promoters that certain proposed names would be unlikely to be acceptable. Most take the hint.

name (either its company name or its trading name) that suggests that the company is connected in any way with the Government or any local authority[11] or any name specified in the Company and Business Names Regulations 1981.[12] These regulations restrict the use of certain words, amongst them words relating to royalty, health, nationality, insurance and higher education unless their use can be justified. Approval for any of those words needs to be sought first from the relevant body specified in the Regulations to authorise them. A company may have a trading name that is the same as its company name or different, but in either event, the name that it trades under is also subject to the requirements of the Business Names Act 1985 which lays down further rules as to the display of the proper company name and registered office at the business's place of business[13] where documents from the court or elsewhere may be served.

A company may not use a name that is the name of a previously **3.06** insolvent company. It is tempting for directors of a company either in insolvency or approaching insolvency to set up a company with a similar name, usually with the intention of confusing its creditors. This is prohibited under the phoenix trading rules for a period of five years from the date of the date of the first company's insolvent liquidation.[14] This is a strict liability offence and there is no need to prove intention to deceive.[15] In addition a director who does this will be jointly and severally liable for the debts of the new company,[16] unless the new company has taken over all or nearly all of the business of the insolvent company from the liquidator,[17] permission has been sought from the courts[18] or where there was a pre-existing company with the forbidden name which had been using that name for a year beforehand and which was not dormant.[19]

It is permissible to change a name by means of a special resolution[20] but not to a name that is otherwise forbidden. There are various rules which permit the Secretary of State to require a registered company to change its name if in his opinion it is too like an existing company's name or a name.[21] There are entrepreneurs who make it their business to incorporate companies with names of well-known businesses or individuals in the hope that those businesses or individuals will buy the

---

[11] CA 1985, s.26(2)(a).

[12] S.I. 1981 No. 1685 as amended.

[13] Business Names Act 1985, ss. 4 and 5.

[14] IA 1986, ss. 216 and 217.

[15] *R. v. Cole* [1998] 2 BCLC 235; *R. v. McCredie* [2000] 2 BCLC 235. In both cases the directors received community service orders.

[16] IA 1986, s.217.

[17] Insolvency (Scotland) Rules 1986, r.4.80.

[18] *ibid.*, r.4.81. In *Re Bonus Breaks Ltd* [1990] B.C.C. 491 the courts granted permission for the use of a forbidden name, subject to certain undertakings by the directors.

[19] *ibid.*, r.4.82.

[20] CA 1985, s.28(1).

[21] CA 1985, s.28(2)(a).

company names from them.[22] If the company disagrees with the Secretary of State the matter may be referred to court. The Secretary of State may also require a company to change its name if the name gives a misleading impression of the nature of the company's activities, such that is "likely to cause harm to the public".[23]

3.07   The fact that a company changes its name makes no difference to its obligations and rights, and existing litigation against or by the company may be continued under its old or its new name.[24] Despite the change of name, the company number never alters, which is why it is prudent in all formal documentation involving a company to include the company's registered number. The new name takes effect from the date of the new certificate.[25]

It is an offence for a private company to suggest that it is public[26] or for a public company to suggest that it is private.[27]

Passing off

3.08   Passing off is the common law term for the unauthorised use of an existing business' name. The leading case is *Ewing v. Buttercup Margarine Co. Ltd*[28] where Ewing, who operated a number of shops selling tea and margarine under the name of the Buttercup Dairy Co., successfully prevented the defendants from setting up a wholesaling business with the name "Buttercup Margarine Co. Ltd" on the grounds that it would cause confusion in the minds of Ewing's customers. By contrast in Scotland the mighty Dunlop tyre company was refused permission to prevent a small car-repairing garage in the Borders carrying on its lawful business on the grounds that there could be no possible confusion between the two companies.[29] The use of an ordinary word in a company's name does not entitle that company to the exclusive use of that word.[30] It is permissible to use your own name without fear of being

---

[22] A certain Robert Kershaw from Cheshire has registered such names as Beckham Spice Ltd and Virgin IT Ltd. However his attempt to register Daewoo Ltd was unsuccessful, following objections from Daewoo UK Ltd, the car manufacturers.

[23] CA 1985, s.32(1). *Association of Certified Public Accountants of Britain v. Secretary of State for Trade and Industry* [1997] 2 BCLC 307.

[24] CA 1985, ss.28(7), 32(6).

[25] CA 1985, s.28(6).

[26] CA 1985, s.33(1).

[27] CA 1985, s.33(2).

[28] [1917] 2 Ch. 1.

[29] *Dunlop Pneumatic Tyre Co. Ltd v. Dunlop Motor Co. Ltd,* 1907 S.C. (HL) 15. Similarly in London a firm of fast food Chinese restaurants was allowed to carry on trade under the name of McChina, much to the annoyance of McDonalds, the burger retailers (*The Independent*, November 28, 2001).

[30] *Aerators Ltd v. Tollit* [1902] 2 Ch. 319. Tollit proposed to use the words "aerator" in his company's name and it was held that the plaintiffs did not have the sole rights to such an ordinary word.

liable for an action of passing off[31] but not your nick-name.[32] Matters that the court will take into consideration in an action of passing off will be the geographical area where the passing off is taking place, the degree of similarity of the pursuer's and defender's businesses, the degree to which the pursuer has suffered loss and the balance of convenience and fairness. Where an action of passing off is successful, the pursuer will be able to prevent the defender using the challenged name, and may also be able to demand an accounting for profits or indemnity for the pursuer's losses occasioned by the defender's use of the challenged name.

TYPES OF COMPANY

In the United Kingdom there are about 1.4 million companies. There are **3.09** two main types of company. The first is the public limited company ("plc") and the second is the private company. Any company that is not a plc will be a private company.[33] In addition there are oversea companies.

The public limited company

There are many differences between plcs and private companies, but **3.10** in essence, the law relating to a plc is more demanding and more detailed than that for private companies. This is because any plc could potentially (though most in fact do not do so) offer its securities[34] to the public, and if the public is to be persuaded to invest in such a company (whether or not the company does offer its shares to the public) there must be high standards of accountability by the directors to its members and creditors, and high standards of transparency in its financial dealings.

The capital of a plc

A plc must have a minimum authorised share capital of £50,0000.[35] **3.11** The authorised share capital is the maximum number of shares that could be allotted. Many plcs in fact have authorised share capital far greater than £50,000. The company must at a minimum have allotted 50,000 £1 nominal value shares or 100,000 50 pence nominal value shares (or such other combination of shares and nominal value as equals £50,000) though the shares only have to be paid up to the extent of one quarter. This means that on becoming a plc, a plc could in theory have,

---

[31] *Wright, Layman and Unmay Ltd v. Wright* (1949) 66 R.P.C. 149, CA.
[32] *Biba Group Ltd v. Biba Boutique* [1990] R.P.C. 413.
[33] CA 1985, s.1(3).
[34] The word securities encompasses shares, debentures, warrants, options, etc.
[35] CA 1985, s.118.

say, 50,000 shares of £1 nominal value each, all paid up to the extent of
one quarter each (*i.e.* 25 pence) (plus any premium[36]), thus making a
paid up capital of £12,500. The balance (or part thereof) of £37,500
could then be called for at any time by the directors if the company
needed further funds, or could be demanded in full by the liquidator in
the event of the company's insolvency. Although it is rare nowadays for
shares to be partly paid, the point of the legislation is to provide
reassurance to creditors that the company either has £50,000 sitting as
cash (or assets) in its accounts or at least £12,500 with the promise of
the balance to come whenever needed—all of which could be used to
pay creditors' bills. In practice, £50,000 provides very little reassurance
to anyone, but the theory is that it forms a sizeable fund from which to
pay creditors.

There are also various rules relating to the capital maintenance rule,
in particular the net asset rule for dividends, which apply more closely
to plcs than to private companies. These are dealt with in Chapter 6.

*A plc, incorporated as such, must have a section 117 trading
certificate*

3.12 Nearly all plcs start off their existence as private companies, the
procedure therefor being explained later in this chapter. But some are
incorporated as plcs from the beginning, and in order to ensure that the
company has the capital it ought to have, the directors have to obtain a
section 117 trading certificate before commencing to trade. This is done
by furnishing the Registrar of Companies with a statutory declaration[37]
that the company has the capital the company says it has, together with
information about the company's preliminary expenses and any benefits
paid to promoters of the company. If the Registrar of Companies is
satisfied with the terms of the declaration he will issue the certificate. If
the directors do start trading in defiance of the statutory requirements,
and the company enters into a transaction and fails to obtain the
certificate within 21 days of being called upon to do so, the directors
will become personally jointly and severally with the company for any
loss or damage sustained by the other party to the transaction.[38] Under
the circumstances, it is much wiser to start trading as a private company
and follow the normal rules for conversion to a plc[39] in which case no
section 117 trading certificate is required.

---

[36] The premium on a share is the difference (say, 50p) between the nominal value of a
newly allotted share (say, £1.00) and the amount that you pay to the company to buy
the share (£1.50). The premiums are credited to a share premium account which is
treated like any other capital account. A premium reflects the desirability of the share
to the purchaser.

[37] CA 1985, s.117(3).

[38] CA 1985, s.117(8).

[39] CA 1985, ss. 43–48.

Non-cash consideration for shares in a plc

Because a plc is supposed genuinely to have the capital it says it has, **3.13** shares may only be offered for non-cash consideration where the non-cash consideration has been independently valued before the allotment of the shares. This is to prevent people selling assets to the plc for more shares than the assets are truly worth. This, and shares generally in a plc, are extensively dealt with in Chapter 5.

Officers of a plc

The company secretary of a plc is required to be properly qualified to **3.14** act as a company secretary.[40] The directors may not without permission from the members, by means of an ordinary resolution preceeded by special notice, be over the age of 70[41]; there must be at least two of them[42]; and they must be voted for separately.[43] There are certain extra restrictions on loans to directors of plcs. These are dealt with in greater detail in Chapters 8 and 9.

Issue of shares to the public

Despite the confusing use of the word "public" most plcs do not offer **3.15** their shares to the public. Furthermore, the use of the word "public" does not mean that a plc is owned by the State for the public benefit (as in the term "public utilities"). As far as company law is concerned, the "public" in plc means that the shares could potentially be offered to the public provided the company has been admitted to the relevant recognised investment exchange ("RIE"), the two main ones being the London Stock Exchange ("LSE") and its younger brother, the Alternative Investment Market ("AIM")[44] or, more speculatively, where a market-maker is willing to make a market in the company's securities even though the securities are not traded on a RIE. In order for a company to be admitted to the LSE it must comply with the Admission of Securities to Listing, known colloquially as the "Purple Book" which contains the requirements for any company that wishes to have its shares floated on LSE[45] or the AIM. The Purple Book is organised by the Financial Services Authority. Companies that wish to offer their shares to investors in other RIEs or elsewhere must comply with the

---

[40] CA 1985, s.286. See also Chap. 10.
[41] CA 1985, s.293.
[42] CA 1985, s.282.
[43] CA 1985, s.292(1).
[44] There used to be other, now defunct, markets, known as the Third Market and the Unlisted Securities Market. There are a very few small other REIs, the best known of which is Tradepoint plc.
[45] A company whose shares are traded on the Official List of the LSE is said to be a "listed" company.

requirements of the Public Offer of Securities Regulations 1995.[46] This is dealt with in greater detail in Chapter 5.

General meetings

3.16   A plc has to have general meetings (AGMs and where necessary EGMs) where the directors may be held accountable to the members. Private companies may sometimes dispense with these requirements. This is discussed further in Chapter 13.

Accounting requirements

3.17   Private companies are not obliged (depending on their size) to give quite as much information in their accounts as plcs. This is mainly to preserve commercial secrets. But in a plc, greater transparency in accounting is required, and for listed companies and other companies whose shares are being offered to the public through a RIE, the degree of transparency is greater still, and with much more information (at least in theory, if not always in practice) being revealed to members and creditors.

Why become a plc?

3.18   The advantages of being a plc are that:

- The minimum capital requirements give an impression of commercial credibility;
- The greater accounting and company law requirements enable investors and creditors to have a more informed view of the company;
- An ambitious director who wishes ultimately to have company's securities traded on the LSE will need to take his company from being a private company to a plc as an initial stage before admission to the Official List;
- Unsuspecting members of the general population misguidedly think that a plc is automatically bigger and more impressive than a private company, so sometimes even quite small companies convert to plcs because they think it good for their image;
- Some directors like the personal status of being a director of a plc.

Is being a plc worth the effort?

3.19   Many private companies choose not to convert to being a plc, even though they could easily do so. This is generally because the main shareholders have no intention of floating the company's securities and

---

[46] S.I. 1995 No. 1537.

thereby possibly losing control of the company, and because the greater accounting and company law requirements of being a plc are seen as onerous and intrusive.

The private limited company

There are several types of private limited company. **3.20**

The private company limited by shares

This is by far the most common type of company in the United **3.21** Kingdom. There are no minimum capital requirements, no trading certificate is needed and the capital maintenance rules are more relaxed than for plcs, as are the rules relating to the issue of shares. There are fewer rules relating to directors and company secretaries; with a little ingenuity it is possible to avoid having general meetings altogether; and if the company is small enough not too much information need be given away in the accounts. All these points will be discussed in later chapters.

The private company limited by guarantee

This is similar to a private company limited by shares except that **3.22** instead of having shares, the company's members undertake in the memorandum to pay a certain amount by way of a guarantee (commonly £1,000) in the event of the insolvency of the company. Although it used to be possible for a company limited by guarantee also to have shares (in which case it would be a company limited by guarantee and by shares) there are very few such companies nowadays. Guarantee companies by convention are much used by charities. The Inland Revenue appears to like the use of guarantee companies for such purposes. A guarantee company usually does not have shares so it cannot have shareholders. It has members instead.[47] When a member leaves he does not sign a stock transfer form. He just leaves and his name is deleted from the register of members.

The single member private limited company

A single member private company is one where there is only one **3.23** shareholder. There must also be at least one director and a company secretary—so that rather surprisingly two individuals must be involved although only one member is required.[48] If there is only one director, the company secretary may not be a company of which the single member

---

[47] Strictly speaking a shareholder will always be a member of a company, since a "member" is the global term for an owner of part of a company; but, as in a guarantee company, it would be possible to be a member without being a shareholder.
[48] CA 1985, s.283(2).

is a sole director or company secretary.[49] Single member companies are commonly used by "one man bands", sole traders who are prudently incorporating, or are the wholly owned subsidiaries of holding companies.[50] Single member companies also quite often originally start off with more than one member but eventually the other members leave and transfer their shares to the remaining, single member. If so, the company minutes must record that the company has become a single member company as from the date of the final transfer.[51]

Even though there is only one member, that member must fulfil all the requirements of normal company meetings, ideally with the company secretary present to record decisions. There must be a proper record of general meetings[52] (absurd as it may be to have a meeting of one member) and there should be minutes recording the approval of any contracts between the company and the sole member who is also a director,[53] unless the contracts are those entered into in the ordinary course of business.[54] If a minute is not kept, it does not necessarily mean that the contract is not valid *per se*,[55] but it does mean that the person founding on it will not be able to prove that he complied with other requirements of the Companies Act 1985 such as a director declaring his interest in a contract under section 317.[56]

The quorum for a single member is one member present.[57]

Other types of company

Dormant companies

3.24   These are companies that exist but undertake no activity at all. They are sometimes used to hold an asset at arm's length (using the separate legal personality of the company) or to keep a potentially desirable name which the owner of the company may be able to sell one day. Such companies need only provide minimal accounts and need not have their accounts audited.[58]

---

[49] CA 1985, s.283(4).

[50] Traditionally, a wholly owned subsidiary had 99 per cent of its shares owned by its holding company, and one per cent owned by the company secretary of the holding company, holding the shares as nominee for the holding company. This was because there used to be a requirement that every company had to have two members—the word "company" having a connotation of more than one person being present.

[51] CA 1985, s.352A.

[52] CA 1985, s.382B.

[53] CA 1985, s.322B(1).

[54] CA 1985, s.322B(2).

[55] CA 1985, s.322B(6).

[56] *Re Neptune (Vehicle Washing Equipment) Ltd* [1995] B.C.C. 474.

[57] CA 1985, s.370A.

[58] CA 1985, s.250.

Subsidiaries

A subsidiary company is one that is wholly or partly owned or **3.25** controlled by a holding company. They are commonly used by holding companies as a way of distancing the holding company from the commercial activities of the subsidiary: if the subsidiary is profitable, the holding company receives dividends and possibly management fees; if the subsidiary is unsuccessful, the holding company will not normally be responsible for its debts and may dissolve it if necessary. Subsidiaries may have subsidiaries of their own. Sometimes companies have a complex network of subsidiaries, cross-holdings and holding companies, often in an attempt to bamboozle auditors and investors. Subsidiaries may not own shares in their holding companies except when acting as a nominee.[59]

Under CA 1985, section 736 a subsidiary is a subsidiary of a holding company if the holding company

- holds a majority of the voting rights in it[60];
- is a member of and has the right to appoint or remove a majority of its board of directors,[61] or
- is a member of it and controls alone, pursuant to an agreement with the other shareholders or members,[62] a majority of the voting rights in it,[63] or
- is a subsidiary of a company which is itself a subsidiary of that holding company.[64]

These definitions of a subsidiary are significant because there are several occasions in the Companies Act 1985 where rules that apply to a plc are deemed to apply to the subsidiaries (as defined above) of those plcs.[65]

There is a second definition of subsidiary for accounting purposes.[66] **3.26** In this case the holding company is known as a "parent undertaking" and the subsidiary company as a "subsidiary undertaking". The definition is almost the same as the above, but in addition, the legislation refers to the parent undertaking's right to exercise a "dominant influence" over the subsidiary. A dominant influence is a right given under the company's memorandum or articles to influence the management of the company, or a right given under a "control contract". Control contracts are not common in the United Kingdom, being a feature of

---

[59] CA 1985, s.144.
[60] CA 1985, s.736(1)(a).
[61] CA 1985, s.736(1)(b).
[62] This would commonly be known as a "shareholders agreement".
[63] CA 1985, s.736(1)(c).
[64] CA 1985, s.736(1).
[65] For example, the prohibition on certain loans to directors in CA 1985, s.331(6).
[66] CA 1985, s.258.

German corporate law, whereby the holding company accepts responsibility for the subsidiary. Furthermore, this second definition of subsidiary carries on to the effect that where a parent undertaking in practice exercises a dominant influence which is not caught by the above rules,[67] or where the parent and the subsidiary are operated on a "unified basis"[68] the subsidiary undertaking will be deemed to be a subsidiary undertaking.

The word "undertaking" is used because that word includes not only companies, but also partnerships, limited liability partnerships and unincorporated associations.[69]

3.27　　The point of the second definition is to ensure that when companies prepare their consolidated accounts, all the accounts of peripheral businesses partly or wholly owned or controlled by the company are included within those consolidated accounts, thus presenting a more accurate picture of the enterprise's financial health.[70]

Oversea companies

3.28　　A company that wishes to do business in the United Kingdom is much more likely to be viewed favourably if it registers its presence in the United Kingdom. It can do this either by incorporating a United Kingdom subsidiary, or it may have a branch registered in the United Kingdom in terms of CA 1985, Part XXIII. A registered branch will provide the Registrar of Companies with information similar to that required by a United Kingdom registered company. The rules relating to oversea companies are known to be unstructured and require reform and the White Paper proposes to address this issue.

CONVERSION FROM ONE TYPE OF COMPANY TO ANOTHER

3.29　There are four methods of conversion which are summarised below
They are:

- private to public
- limited to unlimited
- unlimited to limited
- public to private

A public but not a private company could convert into a guarantee company.

---

[67] CA 1985, s.258(4)(a).
[68] CA 1985, s.258(4)(b).
[69] CA 1985, s.259(1).
[70] It is this provision in U.K. company accounting that would have prevented some of the off-balance sheet accounting that featured in the collapse of Enron in USA. At the time USA accounting rules in this respect were laxer than U.K. ones.

For all of the above, there are special prescribed application Forms available from the Registrar of Companies. These need to be completed by the directors/company secretary and sent to the Registrar of Companies along with all the other required documentation.

From private to public—Companies Act 1985 sections 43–48

For a private company to convert into a plc, one must follow the **3.30** procedure specified in CA 1985, sections 43–47. This requires the passing of a special resolution,[71] an increase in authorised share capital to at least £50,000 if necessary,[72] the alteration of the company's name, memorandum and articles wherever necessary to effect the change to public status,[73] a recent balance sheet[74] (confirmed by an unqualified[75] report[76] from the company's auditor) confirming that the company has the required minimum allotted share capital of at least £50,000 with each share paid up to at least one quarter plus any premium[77] and that the company's net assets are not less than the aggregate of the called up share capital and its undistributable reserves,[78] and a statutory declaration[79] from the directors in respect of the consideration[80] (properly valued[81]) for any shares issued since the balance sheet date[82] confirming that that the company's financial position has not deteriorated since that date.[83]

Assuming these requirements have been fulfilled, the Registrar of Companies will issue a certificate of re-registration of the company as a plc. This is *prima facie* conclusive evidence of the re-registration.

The main reason for such conversions are stated above in *Why become a plc?*

From limited company to unlimited—Companies Act 1985 sections 49–50

A plc may not do this[84] and neither may a company that formerly was **3.31** unlimited and subsequently became limited.[85] To enable the

---

[71] CA 1985, s.43(1)(a).
[72] CA 1985, s.121.
[73] CA 1985, s.43(2).
[74] CA 1985, s.43(3)(c). The balance sheet must not be more than seven months old (CA 1985, s.43(5)).
[75] CA 1985, s.46.
[76] CA 1985, s.43(3)(b).
[77] CA 1985, s.45(2).
[78] Such as its share premium account or capital redemption reserve.
[79] CA 1985, s.43(2)(e)(ii).
[80] CA 1985, s.45.
[81] CA 1985, s.44.
[82] CA 1985, s.44.
[83] CA 1985, s.43(3)(2)(e)(ii).
[84] CA 1985, s.49(3).
[85] CA 1985, s.49(2),(3).

re-registration to take place, all the members will need to consent to the change.[86] There needs to be a statutory declaration from the directors confirming that all the members have signed or had someone properly sign on their behalf[87] and altered memorandum[88] and articles[89] to take account of the loss of limited liability. Assuming all is in order a certificate of re-registration in the usual manner as above will be issued.[90]

The reason for conversion is generally to avoid having to publish the company's accounts while retaining the benefit of the separate legal personality of a company.

From unlimited to limited—Companies Act 1985 sections 51–52

3.32   This procedure may not be used to register an unlimited company as a plc, nor may it be used if the company previously was limited.[91] It may be used to create a company limited by shares or by guarantee. The members need to pass a special resolution,[92] alter the memorandum and articles of association to reflect the new limited liability status for the company's shares or for the members (if a guarantee company).[93] If the company is to be limited by shares, it will need to state what its new share capital is to be.[94] Assuming all is in order, a certificate of re-registration will be issued in the normal manner.[95]

The reason for this conversion is normally the desire to take advantage of the benefits of limited liability despite the requirement to disclose accounts.

From public to private—Companies Act 1985 sections 53–55

3.33   This procedure may not be used to convert a plc into an unlimited company.[96] The members must pass a special resolution[97] which will also make the necessary changes to the memorandum and articles to delete references to being a public company.[98] If shareholders holding five per cent of the nominal value of the company's issued share capital or of any class thereof, or five per cent of the members in a guarantee

---

[86] CA 1985, s.49(8)(a). Unanimous consent is required because the members are collectively becoming liable for the company's debts.
[87] CA 1985, s.49(8)(b)(i) and (ii).
[88] CA 1985, s.49(5).
[89] CA 1985, s.49(6).
[90] CA 1985, s.50.
[91] CA 1985, s.51(2).
[92] CA 1985, s.51(1).
[93] CA 1985, s.51(3)(a), (b).
[94] CA 1985, s.51(3)(a).
[95] CA 1985, s.52.
[96] CA 1985, s.49(3).
[97] CA 1985, s.53(1)(a).
[98] CA 1985, s.53(2).

company, or at least 50 members object to the conversion, they may, provided they did not previously vote in favour of the conversion, within 28 days apply to the court to object to the conversion.[99] The court may deal with the objection as it sees fit, either cancelling or confirming the order, arranging some settlement, adjourning the proceedings or requiring the objectors' shares to be bought by the company and making such changes to the memorandum and articles as may be required.[1] One reason for objection may be that once the company is private there will be no further opportunity to trade in the company's shares.

Assuming there are no objectors, or those that object are pacified, and assuming the documentation is in order, a certificate of re-registration will be issued in the normal manner.[2]

A company might wish to re-register as private because of the inconvenience and expense of complying with all the extra accounting and company law applicable to plcs. In addition certain actions, such as financial assistance, are considerably easier for private companies than for plcs, thus making private status desirable. **3.34**

THE PRACTICALITIES OF OPERATING A NEWLY FORMED COMPANY

As indicated earlier, a company is set up by sending the appropriate Forms to the Registrar of Companies and waiting for the certificate of registration. Once it has been received, the company may hold its first board meeting, on which occasion the new directors will appoint the company's bankers and auditors, issue share certificates, instruct the company secretary to complete the company books and prepare minutes, etc. If the company has been founded for a particular purpose, such as to acquire a property, the directors will record the purchase of the property in the minutes. The board may also convene an extraordinary general meeting to be held at short notice for the members to give the directors authority to allot shares in the future in terms of CA 1985 section 80 (if this is not available already in the articles, as it usually will be), and to receive subscriptions for any newly allotted shares. The members may also carry out such other activities as require shareholder approval, as opposed to board approval, such as changing the company name or altering the company's articles. There may be a slightly artificial air about these proceedings, since commonly the members and the directors are the same people, but the paperwork still has to record when they are acting as members and when as directors since the **3.35**

---

[99] CA 1985, s.54(2).
[1] CA 1985, s.54(5),(6).
[2] CA 1985, s.55.

auditors will need to be assured that all the paperwork was done properly.

Off the shelf companies

3.36   Although it is perfectly possible to prepare all one's own paperwork for a company and obtain a company very quickly from the Registrar of Companies, at a price, it is common for those who need companies in a hurry to approach either lawyers, accountants or company formation agents to ask them to prepare the paperwork to their specification or to buy from them an already prepared "off the shelf" company. This is a company which already exists, with a name, number and shareholders, directors and company secretary. These last three are commonly in-house nominee companies. On receiving the clients' instructions, it is a simple matter to change the name to the clients' choice, to transfer the shares from the nominee holders to the clients, for the nominees to resign their directorships and company secretaryship, having appointed the clients as the new directors and company secretary first by means of a board meeting. Such board meetings do not actually physically take place, but are artificial paper exercises to serve as a formal record for the company's books. The new directors and company secretary may then proceed as in the previous paragraph.

Acquisition of an existing business from the directors in their private capacity

3.37   Assuming a company has been set up and constituted by one of the methods in the above two paragraphs, the directors may decide that their company should acquire the directors' own personal business (for example, the directors in their private capacity as partners in a business might sell to the company the partnership assets, its goodwill, its capital, its book debts, etc.,). This may happen when an existing partnership decides that it wishes to incorporate in order to avoid the risk of personal liability. In this event a contract for the sale of the business, usually known as a sale and purchase agreement or a vending agreement, is drawn up between the company and the partnership and the partners as trustees for the partnership. The directors of the company will sign the contract for the company, and the partners will sign for the partnership, even though in reality they are all the same people. The company then acquires the business and as consideration may give the partners shares in the company, or perhaps will give some cash and some shares, or some shares and loan notes if the company has insufficient cash to hand. The aggregate value of the consideration will in theory equal the value of the business. It is common to have the partnership audited and valued first, not least because of capital gains tax consequences later.

If the company is going to issue shares to the former partners the company must have sufficient unissued share capital within the limits of its authorised share capital, and if it does not it may be necessary for the members at an EGM[3] to increase the authorised share capital under CA 1985, section 121. Directors will need to obtain authority from the members to allot shares under CA 1985, section 80 if such authority is not already in place. Existing shareholders may be entitled to their pre-emption rights[4] and these may need to be disapplied or waived first before the partners receive their shares. If the partners selling the business are also the directors of the company, the members need to give approval to the sale and purchase agreement under CA 1985, section 320.[5] If the sale and purchase agreement includes the transfer from the partnership to the company of heritage or other items that attract stamp duty, such as deposit accounts and book debts, the sale and purchase agreement will need to be adjudicated by the Capital Taxes Office and Stamp Duty paid to the Inland Revenue by the company. Pending adjudication, the directors may cause the company to issue the new shares to the former partners and their names will be entered in the Register of Members[6] and various other registers (depending on whether the former partners are the company's directors) and a return made to the Registrar of Companies[7] indicating the allotment of the new shares. The company secretary will issue share certificates for the new shares.

There are various practical consequences of such as sale and pur- **3.38** chase. Dispositions of heritage and leases of property will need to show the change of ownership from the partnership to the company. This may require consent from landlords. Assets formerly insured in the partnership name will need to show the company's interest instead. Vehicles will need to be registered in the company's name. Hire purchase agreements may need to be cancelled and new ones started in the company name. Outstanding liabilities[8] may need to be continued by the partnership, but the company will have to indemnify the partners for the costs arising. Equally if the partners receive any payments which should have been made to the company, they will hold those payments in trust for the company and pay them to the company as soon as convenient.

PROMOTERS

Promoters of companies were much more common at the beginning of **3.39** the twentieth century than they are now. A promoter was someone who

---

[3] If it is a private company, written resolutions could take the place of an EGM.
[4] CA 1985, s.89.
[5] This is dealt with further in Chap. 9, and refers to substantial acquisitions by and from directors and their companies.
[6] CA 1985, s.22.
[7] CA 1985, s.88.
[8] Such as non-transferrable hire-purchase obligations.

set up a company and then invited others to subscribe for shares in it. He would issue an impressive prospectus, advertising the likely profits of the company and the desirability of investment in it. If the promoter was a rogue, he would talk up the company's likely profits, and then sell his own assets to the company at an inflated price, or would hope to make his money persuading the gullible to pay for his own worthless shares by ramping the share price.

Nowadays, such frauds are harder to carry out. For shares to be offered to the public the company needs to be admitted to the relevant investment exchange or to find a market maker willing to make a market in the shares of the company. Neither of these will welcome a company whose promoters appear to be gulling the public. The Financial Services Authority is empowered under the Financial Services and Markets Act to police such activity. The financial press will expect higher standards of probity of promoters than were expected a century ago. Following the case of *Erlanger v. New Sombrero Phosphate Co. Ltd*[9] promoters must disclose any personal benefits they may be receiving from the promotion of the company.

3.40   Promoters as they used to exist do not really exist any longer, and the law continues to refer to them purely to prevent anyone trying to carry out the more disreputable practices of yesteryear. Most people employ company agents, lawyers and accountants to set up companies for them, rather than promoters; and if a company's shares are to be offered to the public, the company will approach a merchant bank to help the company do this. Investors would nowadays be very dubious of a company trying to issue its own shares without the advice and support of a reputable merchant bank. Without the backing of a merchant bank the company will have little credibility. In any event, any company seeking to have its shares listed will have to ensure that it complies with the listing rules.

Sometimes directors of a company provide their own services to the company before it is founded, and then seek to obtain shares as recompense for their labour in setting the company up. Provided there is an express contract with the company, once the company is in existence, there is no difficulty with this.

3.41   There have been no significant cases on promoters in the last 100 years and the matter is mainly of historical interest only.

PRE-INCORPORATION CONTRACTS

Sometimes a would-be director of an as yet unformed company is so keen to get this company to enter a contract that he will make the

---

[9] (1878) 3 App. Cas. 1218.

company enter into a contract even before the company has any legal existence. If this happens the would-be director becomes personally liable unless the contract says otherwise.[10] The solution is therefore to persuade directors not to sign anything until their companies are formal.

---

[10] CA 1985, s.36C.

Chapter 4

THE MEMORANDUM AND ARTICLES OF ASSOCIATION

The founding documents

4.01   Just as most partnerships have a partnership agreement, setting out the rights and duties of the partners, and just as most august institutions such as universities, colleges and charitable bodies have a charter which sets out the intentions of the founders, their aspirations for the institution's future and its rules for its governance, so do companies have their documentation to the same effect. In the United Kingdom this documentation comes in two parts, the memorandum of association and the articles of association, popularly known as the "memo and arts".

The purpose of the memorandum

4.02   The original purpose of the memorandum was to inform potential investors of the five following matters:

- The company's name
- The company's country of registration
- The objects (or purpose) for which the company was set up
- The limited liability of the members of the company (if appropriate)
- The authorised capital of the company

Memoranda of association follow the styles or examples given in the Companies (Tables A to F) Regulations,[1] Tables B to F being example memoranda and articles of association for ordinary private limited companies limited by shares, companies limited by guarantee, plcs and unlimited companies, etc. Plcs have an extra clause stating that they are public companies and guarantee companies indicate that the members' liability is limited to the extent of the guarantee.

---

[1] S.I. 1985 No. 805.

Historically companies were sometimes set up with further additional clauses. This was commonly done because the founders of such companies had strong views on how their companies were to operate, and consequently inserted extra, sometimes unalterable, clauses in the memoranda to reflect that. Sometimes one can still find extra clauses in memoranda nowadays: for example, a charity company will commonly have a clause in its memorandum to the effect that if the company no longer can carry on the activity for which it was set up,[2] the remaining funds, after payment of all creditors, must be passed to a similar but extant charity.

It is now unusual to set up companies with extra clauses in the memoranda. This is because although the founder members may believe their special extra clauses to be a good thing, a later generation may not agree; in time the extra clauses often became uncommercial and a deterrent to future investment.

All but one of the standard five clauses of the memorandum may be altered: at present only the company's nationality may not change. A company's name may be changed by special resolution[3]; the objects clause may be changed also by special resolution, subject to certain safeguards[4]; the limited liability clause may be removed if the company becomes an unlimited company[5]; and the authorised capital may be increased.[6]   **4.03**

The objects clause

Of the five clauses above, only the objects clause has caused any great difficulty. The objects clause is the clause that states the purpose for which the company has been set up. An objects clause for a fish-farming company might read as follows: **4.04**

> The objects for which this company is set up is to carry on in such place or places as the directors shall determine the business of breeding, hatching, rearing and farming of fish, fry and young fish of any description, together with all related aspects of pisciculture, including the culinary preparation of such fish and other marine creatures, the provision of angling and sporting facilities, and all other matters connected with fish generally.

This paragraph tells its readers what the company does, and it, at least in theory, both provides reassurance for the company's investors that the company is going to concentrate on fish-farming, and equally that it

---

[2] For example, a charity might be set up to campaign for a particular cause: if that cause ceases to be an issue there would be no reason to continue the charity.

[3] CA 1985, s.23(1).

[4] CA 1985, s.4.

[5] CA 1985, s.49. This is not however possible if the company was formerly a plc.

[6] CA 1985, s.121.

should restrict its activities to fish-farming and closely related activities.

4.05 Historically the law looked favourably upon investors in a company. It was considered important to protect the investors from wily directors who might make the company carry out activities which were not the purposes for which the investors had paid their capital into the company. The best-known example of this is *Re German Date Coffee Co. Ltd*[7] where a few members who objected to the company's general production of coffee from dates instead of, as the objects clause indicated, specifically using a German patent to make coffee out of dates, were successfully able to have the company wound up—despite the fact that the company was solvent and the fact that most members were indifferent to the matter of the patent. Nonetheless it was held that the few objecting members were entitled to insist on the use of a German patent, and in its absence, they were entitled to have the company wound up. In those days it was impossible to alter an objects clause, and so the obvious modern remedy of passing a special resolution to rewrite the objects clause was unavailable.[8]

This protection for investors was well intentioned (at least from the investors' point of view), and its effects linger still. When a company acts beyond the powers given to it in its objects clause, so that the company does something that strictly speaking it should not, it is said to be acting *ultra vires*.[9] If the company acts within its powers it is said to be acting *intra vires*.[10] The directors should not make the company act *ultra vires* and in theory, the directors are liable to the company for making the company act *ultra vires*. Furthermore, historically the company was not bound by its own *ultra vires* acts, and could shamelessly avoid liability for its *ultra vires* acts even if the company had entered into them knowingly.[11] Equally some creditors, equally shamelessly, might be tempted to avoid paying their bills to the company if the act for which the company rendered the bill was *ultra vires* the company.[12] This was clearly unsatisfactory.

4.06 The *ultra vires* concept relied for its validity on the deemed notice rule. This rule postulated that because a company's objects clause was available to the public at the Registrar of Companies, any person dealing with the company was deemed to be aware of the contents of that company's objects clause; and it was open to a creditor to see what a company could or could not do in terms of its objects clause. If the

---

[7] (1882) 20 Ch.D. 169; 46 L.T. 327.

[8] It is very unlikely that the courts would nowadays decide this case as they did then. Nowadays the courts would remit the matter back to the members for them to vote upon. The importance of the case is purely to show the historical background to the *ultra vires* rule.

[9] Beyond its powers.

[10] Within its powers.

[11] *Ashbury Railway Carriage and Iron Co. Ltd v. Riche* (1875) L.R. 7 HL 653.

[12] *Bell Houses Ltd v. City Wall Properties Ltd* [1966] 2 All E.R. 674.

creditor entered into a contract with a company it was thought that it was up to the creditor to check that the company was not acting *ultra vires* if it entered into that contract. The deemed notice rule depended on the unrealistic assumption that creditors (and investors too) could and would visit the Registrar of Companies and were prepared to take the trouble to inspect the objects clause—and that such people could would (a) know what an object clause was and (b) could understand it having found it. Strictly speaking this rule still operates[13] though in practice in the light of CA 1985, sections 35, 35A and 35B it is unlikely to be applied.

Reform

The law relating to objects clauses was well known as being confus- **4.07** ing, unhelpful and unpredictable, with a clear gap between commercial practising lawyers and the courts. Fortunately when the United Kingdom joined the European Community in 1972, the European Communities Act 1972, section 9 implemented Article 9 of the First Company Law Directive[14] which protected third parties who (a) were dealing in good faith with a company acting *ultra vires* and (b) were unaware that the company with which they were dealing was acting *ultra vires*. This took account of the fact that most people dealing with a company had no idea about objects clauses. The wording of this too had its problems and Companies Act 1989 the law relating to objects clauses was substantially clarified. Since that date much of the old common law has been swept away—to general rejoicing.[15]

The general commercial company clause

The first reform was that in 1989 a new section 3A was introduced to **4.08** the Companies Act 1985, allowing a company to have a wide-ranging, non-specific objects clause:

> 3A Where the company's memorandum states that the object is to carry on business as a general commercial company
>
> (a) the object of the company is to carry on any trade or business whatsoever, and
> (b) the company has the power to do all things as are incidental or conducive to the carrying on of any trade or business by it.

---

[13] There was an attempt to abolish it in CA 1985, s.711A (introduced by CA 1985, s.142) except in respect of registrable charges, but its wording was so enigmatic and the exception in respect of charges so unworkable that s.711A was never brought into force. So the deemed notice rule still technically applies.

[14] 68/151.

[15] Except amongst academic lawyers, for whom this subject used to be a fruitful source of learned articles and questions for examination papers.

The idea behind this clause was that if the company adopted an objects clause that allowed it to carry on business as a general commercial company, almost everything that a company could do would be *intra vires*. There would then be no more litigation about the *ultra vires* rule.

Company lawyers saw the virtue of section 3A and so, increasingly since 1989, companies have a primary or specific objects clause, such as the fishfarming clause above, followed by a secondary clause, stating that the company may carry on business as a general commercial company, and closely following the wording of section 3A above. Whereas historically these two clauses might have been followed by four pages of all sorts of ancillary objects and powers, there is now no need to have any thing else at all in the objects clause other than a primary and secondary objects clause. Some newly incorporated companies follow the new pattern, and many older companies are changing their objects clauses to the same effect, but it is still common to find companies with old-fashioned four-page-long objects clauses, even though there is no longer any need to have them.[16]

4.09   Despite the "user-friendliness" of the new rules, there are a few areas of doubt. One area is that of a company's giving of donations to charity or to a political party. Is the giving of a donation, or a granting of a guarantee to a holding company, conducive to the carrying out of a business? If not, a donation or a guarantee might be *ultra vires*. As there has not been a test case on this matter since section 3A was introduced, there is no solution to this issue. The best that can be said is that those members of a company who might complain about donations have found other more effective methods of raising their complaints than the expensive and unreliable method of going to the courts to test new legislation, and as for guarantees, if the subsidiary is predominantly owned by the holding company anyway, if there were any difficulties it would be easy enough to pass a special resolution to permit the granting of guarantees to the holding company.

A second area of doubt is that a general commercial company clause does give the directors a very wide degree of latitude: is it wise to let directors have such a free rein? If the directors know a great deal about fishfarming, should the objects clause be so wide that they could embark on any other activity that took their fancy? To this it might be replied that the clause does indeed give very wide latitude, but (i) again there have been no test cases, suggesting that the issue is not very important, and (ii) that there are other better ways of harnessing directors, through the articles and their service contracts, than trying to tie them down by the objects clause.

---

[16] It is true that many company lawyers still retain the four page objects clause—just to be on the safe side, and because old habits die hard. Banks often seem to like their clients' companies to have them.

A third area of doubt is that a general commercial company clause is **4.10** not suitable for a dormant company or a non-trading company. This may well be true, in which case the solution is not to have a general commercial company clause in existence until such time as the company ceases to be dormant or starts to trade, whereupon the objects clause may be altered.

What about companies that have not yet adopted the general commercial company clause?

Although many companies have adopted a general commercial com- **4.11** pany clause, many have not changed their objects clauses, or have deliberately chosen not to have a general commercial company clause. There is still then the risk that a company could refuse to honour its own *ultra vires* act as far as outsiders were concerned, or that the members might be unhappy that the directors were making the company act *ultra vires* contrary to the wishes of some of its members. There is also a further issue which is that certain companies have clauses in their memorandum or articles that say that certain activities may only take place if the members have expressly authorised them—as, for example, a loan over £100,000 may only be entered into following an ordinary resolution of the members. What would the position be if the directors defied the requirement for the ordinary resolution and made the company enter into the loan? Would the company be able to rescind the loan? Could the directors be made accountable to the company? Could the members ratify the loan? How could members object to the loan if it had already been made?

Parliament's solution

The Companies Act 1989 introduced three rules to deal with these **4.12** problems.

The first rule might be called the *over-riding statute*. This generally allows companies to do whatever they wish irrespective of the objects clause, thought members may object to this by means of the *internal policy* rule. Outsiders are still nonetheless protected by means of the third rule, the *external policy* rule.

(1) The over-riding statute. A company's capacity to carry out any act **4.13** is now no longer limited by its memorandum. Companies Act 1985, section 35(1) states:

> "The validity of an act done by a company shall not be called into question on the ground of lack of capacity by reason of anything in the company's memorandum."

This means that if a company has a specific objects clause, and carries out an act that is not permitted by that objects clause (or anything else in the memorandum), that act is not in itself invalid just because the company should not have carried it out. In other words the company cannot renounce its own act. Equally outsiders cannot renounce their responsibilities to a company where that company has acted *ultra vires* when dealing with those outsiders. In section 35(1) the word "act" was used advisedly as it covers not only contracts but gifts, guarantees and other activities.

4.14 **(2) The internal policy rule.** Section 35(1) is all very well for outsiders, reassured that the company will not renounce its contracts on the grounds of their being *ultra vires*, but the members may be unhappy that the company has acted *ultra vires*. The legislation affords the members limited protection.

Section 35(2) states:

> "A member of a company may bring proceedings to restrain the doing of an act which but for subsection (1) would be beyond the company's capacity; but no such proceedings shall lie in respect of an act to be done in fulfilment of a legal obligation arising from a previous act of the company."

This means that any member may apply to the court for an interdict[17] to prevent the directors making the company enter into a new *ultra vires* act; but no interdict would be granted if the company had already embarked upon the act, or had incurred some legal obligation to the other party to the act. It would be very unfair to the other party if, half way through the *ultra vires* act, an objecting member obtained an interdict preventing the company fulfilling its side of the bargain or completing the act—all to the other party's prejudice. So all the objecting member may do is to prevent the repetition of the same *ultra vires* acts, and prevent the directors making the company enter into new *ultra vires* acts.

4.15 However, although the remedy of the interdict may be gratifying for the objecting member, the other members may be less impressed. Indeed, it is quite likely that the other members will not have such strong feelings about the inviolability of the objects clause, and consider that the objecting member is making an unnecessary fuss. If so, the members may pass a special resolution ratifying the *ultra vires* act against which the interdict was taken,[18] and for good measure, lest any action be taken against the directors for making the company act *ultra*

---

[17] Injunction in England and Wales.
[18] CA 1985, s.35(3).

vires, the members may also pass a separate special resolution exonerating the directors personally from any liability for making the company act *ultra vires*.[19] Alternatively the members could pass a special resolution altering the objects clause to permit the *ultra vires* act against which the interdict was taken.

The purpose of the interdict remedy under CA 1985, section 35(1) is protection for members who do feel strongly about the company's adherence to the objects clause. However, the interdict will only be useful (a) where a company has a very specific objects clause and no general commercial company clause, (b) where the objecting member is sufficiently well informed of the company's activities (and indeed its objects clause) to be aware that the company is not adhering to its objects clause, (c) where the objecting member is able to obtain the interdict before the company starts the *ultra vires* act (otherwise it will be too late), and (d) where the other members are unlikely subsequently to overturn the interdict by a special resolution ratifying the *ultra vires* act or (e) to rewrite the objects clause under CA 1985, section 4. As these five requirements are hard to meet in practice, it is not surprising that there have been no cases on this issue. This suggests both that the obstacles are hard to surmount and that on the whole potential objectors are being advised that trying to obtain an interdict on this matter is probably a waste of effort and expense. However, it does mean that a large number of cases relating to a company's capacity and the *ultra vires* rule no longer have any applicability—which is no small mercy.

Charities

One area where the old *ultra vires* rule still applies as before[20] is in charities, which specifically must act within the terms of their objects clauses[21] except as regards acts of a charity company in favour of a person who did not know that the charity company was acting either beyond its capacity or its directors' powers, and had paid a proper price in connection with those acts, or did not know that the company was a charity.[22] There are also rules to protect persons who acquire property from a charity company (which should not be disposing of that property) for full consideration and without notice of any prohibition on the company's or its directors' capacity to transfer that property.[23]

4.16

---

[19] CA 1985, s.35(3). It is curious that the members must pass a special resolution to exonerate the directors from liability for making the company act *ultra vires* whereas an ordinary resolution is all that is required to exonerate the directors for a breach of fiduciary duty.

[20] That is, in the manner before the reforms introduced by the Companies Act 1989.

[21] CA 1989, s.112.

[22] CA 1989, s.112(3).

[23] CA 1989, s.112(4).

Directors acting in their own interests

4.17   A second area where the *ultra vires* rule still continues is where a company enters into a transaction with a director[24] in his personal capacity. This is because of all people directors ought to know what is *ultra vires* or *intra vires* and the company has the right under CA 1985, section 322A to make the transaction voidable at its instance. This means that the company could terminate any such transaction and demand the return of the subject matter of the transaction, and make the director account to the company for any benefit,[25] or indemnify the company for any loss,[26] unless restitution of the subject matter is impossible,[27] the company has been indemnified for any loss,[28] the rights of third parties who acquired the subject matter in good faith and for value would be prejudiced[29] or the members ratify the *ultra vires* act by ordinary or special resolution.[30]

The external policy rule

4.18   Before the reform of the *ultra vires* rule in the Companies Act 1989, a particular area of difficulty was where directors acted beyond the powers given to them in the objects clause. When objects clauses were four pages long, usually somewhere within them would be authority for the directors to carry out all necessary acts for the promotion of the company. In addition under regulation 70 of Table A, directors commonly have the power to do everything conducive to the promotion of the company. But occasionally there were companies with poorly drafted objects clauses or restrictive articles that did not give the directors all the powers they might have wished, or imposed restraints upon the directors so that they had to seek the approval of the members for certain actions, such as loans. What happened when the directors ignored those restrictions on their powers or were inquorate when they made their decisions? Were the transactions they made the company enter into valid?[31] There was also the difficult question of whether a company could be bound by the actions of its directors where those directors had breached their fiduciary duty to the company. To add further to these complications sometimes the directors would act beyond the powers given to them by the company, but the other party to the contract knew that.[32] It was recognised that the law left much to be

---

[24] Or a person connected with a director.
[25] CA 1985, s.322A(3)(a).
[26] CA 1985, s.322A(3)(b).
[27] CA 1985, s.322A(5)(a).
[28] CA 1985, s.322A(5)(b).
[29] CA 1985, s.322A(5)(c).
[30] CA 1985, s.322A(5)(d).
[31] *Royal British Bank v. Turquand* (1856) 6 El & Bl 327; 5 E & B 248.
[32] *Rolled Steel Products (Holdings) Ltd v. British Steel Corporation* [1986] Ch. 246; [1985] 2 W.L.R. 908.

desired in this area, and that third parties dealing with directors or the directors' authorisees should be protected even where those directors, or their authorisees, were strictly speaking not entitled to make the company enter into certain transactions. This resulted in CA 1985, section 35A(1):

> "In favour of a person dealing with a company in good faith, the power of the board of directors to bind the company, or authorise others to do so, shall be deemed to be free of any limitation under the company's constitution."

Although the matter is not absolutely without doubt, it is thought that this sub-section protects third parties generally, in that when they deal in good faith with a company's directors, or with other people authorised by the directors to act on the company's behalf (generally agents and employees) the third parties can assume that there is nothing in the company's memorandum or articles prohibiting the directors, or those whom they authorise, from entering into transactions[33] with those third parties. Even if there were, say, an express clause in the articles requiring a particular resolution before the directors could enter into a certain contract with a third party, the third party could assume that the directors were authorised to enter into the contract even if the directors should not in fact have done so as the particular resolution had not been passed. However, to complicate matters, "good faith" was given a special meaning for the purposes of this sub-section. First, CA 1985, section 35A(2)(b) states that a person is not to be regarded as acting in bad faith merely because he happens to know that the directors have done something that goes beyond the powers given to them in the company's constitution. So if a third party knew that, as in the example above, a particular resolution ought to have been passed before the directors entered into a contract with him, and that the directors had omitted to obtain the resolution first, he could still be said to be acting in good faith. Secondly, the third party is assumed to be acting in good faith unless the contrary can be proved.[34] So for a third party not to be acting in good faith would require him to do something suitably wicked but which has no reference to the company's constitution.[35]

Finally CA 1985, section 35B needs to be considered. This deals with **4.19** the question of how much effort a third party should take to find out whether an act is *ultra vires* or not.

> "A party to a transaction with a company is not bound to enquire as to whether it is permitted by the company's memorandum or as

---

[33] CA 1985, s.35A(2)(a) refers to "transactions or acts" thereby meaning both contracts and gratuitous acts such as gifts and guarantees.

[34] CA 1985, s.35A(2)(c).

[35] Such as, perhaps, bribing the directors or blackmailing them?

to any limitation on the board of directors to bind the company or
authorise others to do so."

From this it would appear that a third party no longer is expected to
look at the company's memorandum, to ask the company if a proposed
act is *ultra vires* the memorandum, or even to ask if there are limits on
the board of directors' powers either to make a company enter into a
transaction or authorise others (namely agents and employees) to enter
into the transaction on the company's behalf. Quite whether this sub-
section achieves anything at all is open to question, but despite it, as a
matter of prudence, third parties dealing with a company who are unsure
as to whether or not a company should be entering into a particular
transaction with the third party are well advised to see a copy of the
board minute authorising the signing of the transaction. It would be
difficult for a company to gainsay the validity of such a transaction if
there were a board minute approving it.

Do we even need an objects clause?

4.20   Much of this chapter has been devoted to the objects clause, and to
the benign intentions of Parliament in seeking both to protect third
parties who cannot be expected to know about objects clauses, and
members who may feel strongly that their companies should adhere to
their objects clauses. The 1989 legislation, while by no means ideal,
seems so far to have worked in that no-one has felt strongly enough
about objects clauses, since the new legislation was introduced, to make
a test case about them. Objects clauses are no longer as important as
once they were. There is even an argument that they should be dispensed with entirely, as is suggested in the White Paper, and as has
happened in some jurisdictions elsewhere, and it may be that in time to
come they are treated as a historical quirk of company law.

The function of the articles of association

4.21   Where the memorandum was the outward and visible face of the
company, the articles are the internal rules, predominantly for the
benefit of the members. The articles form a standing set of rules for such
matters as the procedure for directors' meetings, the right of members to
transfer shares, the right of the company to call members to pay the
unpaid capital on their shares, the practice (where not covered in statute)
of general meetings, and a host of other procedural matters. The articles
detail the relationship of the company to the members, the members to
the directors, and the company to the directors.[36] There is a standard set

---

[36] This is effectively stated in CA 1985, s.14, which is generally regarded as poorly
drafted and confusing. It is likely to be changed in any new Companies Act.

of articles, known as Table A,[37] which may be adopted as a whole,[38] but more commonly is adapted before incorporation to suit clients' requirements.[39] The common practice for articles that are not Table A in their entirety is to state that the company's articles are Table A, subject to certain amendments. The amendments are then detailed, usually by deleting certain regulations and inserting new ones that suit the clients better than the Table A regulations. Amending Table A to suit clients' requirements is perfectly acceptable providing the amendments are not contrary to statute and are not contrary to any provisions in the memorandum, in which case the memorandum's rules will prevail. Common amendments to Table A are the introduction of terms relating to classes of shares, restrictions on the transferability of shares, weighted voting,[40] defined *quora*,[41] named directors[42] and for Listed companies, the adoption of the Stock Exchange's recommended wording for the securities being listed.

It is permissible to change the articles of association at any time provided a special resolution has been passed first.[43] Unless the members can change the articles, the members have to live with the wording of the articles[44] and follow their wording[45]: extrinsic evidence, even in the case of error or oversight when drafting the articles, will not be entertained, because the articles are meant to be a public document[46] and members, creditors and others are entitled to rely on what is stated in the company's memorandum and articles of association as a complete statement of the members' rights, notwithstanding the expectation that some shareholders should adhere to certain codes of practice such as the

---

[37] See S.I. 1985 No. 805. There are other Articles specified in Tables C, D and E.

[38] If a company does not specifically draft any set of Articles of its own, Table A will be deemed to be the one that it uses and the articles will not need to be registered (CA 1985, s.8(2)).

[39] Most solicitors, accountants and company formation agents will have pre-prepared articles for most types of company, and they rarely use Table A, preferring their own versions instead. These versions are usually especially drafted to be conveniently used by small family companies, large plcs or whatever.

[40] As in *Bushell v. Faith* [1970] A.C. 1099.

[41] A quorum is the minimum number of persons required to be present to make a decision valid. It is possible to provide that a meeting is inquorate is a named individual is absent.

[42] Although naming directors in the articles is not as common as it was, namely because of the need to rewrite the articles on the death, illness or retiral of the named director, directors are occasionally still named in articles. Sometimes they used to be given certain employment rights in the articles, but a better practice is to have a separate contract of employment.

[43] CA 1985, s.9. Any change must again not be contrary to statute nor contradict the memorandum, and if it does contradict the memorandum, the memorandum prevails.

[44] If there are insufficient members to pass a special resolution to change the articles, the unhappy members' only practical option is to sell their shares if they can—not always easy in a small company.

[45] *Hickman v. Kent and Romney Marsh Sheepbreeders Assn* [1915] 1 Ch. 881; *Quin & Axtens Ltd v. Salmon* [1909] A.C. 442.

[46] *Bratton Seymour Service Co. Ltd v. Oxborough* [1992] BCLC 693.

68   *Company Law*

City Code.[47] However, directors cannot use their rights under the articles to use their discretion in certain matters to vary the company's
contractual obligations.[48] Shareholders cannot use the fact that they
have a majority (albeit not a majority sufficient to pass a special
resolution to change the articles) to override the provisions of the
articles.[49] Directors and indeed members must always be alert to the fact
that articles are inherently alterable.[50] If you wish to enforce any
provisions of the articles, you must do so in your capacity as a member,
not in some other capacity such as the company's proposed solicitor.[51]

4.22   There are proposals in the White Paper that a new draft constitution,
encompassing both the Memorandum and Articles in one document,
should replace Table A, which is now seen as out of date and
unwieldy.

Classes of shares

4.23   Sometimes the price for new shareholders' investment in a company
is that the new shareholders will insist on particular rights, such as a
right to a prior return on capital or to appoint a particular director to
represent their interests. If such rights are denied to the other shareholders, the new shareholders will insist on those rights being enshrined
in the rights attaching to a new class of shares for their benefit. Those
rights attaching to classes of shareholders will normally need to be set
out in the articles[52] and unless the class of shares is present in the
company from its incorporation, the articles as a whole will need to be
varied by a special resolution to allow for the creation of the new class
of shares.[53] Because historically some companies were very anxious to
protect the rights of classes of shareholders (sometimes putting the class

---

[47] *Re Astec (BSR) plc* [1998] 2 BCLC 556.
[48] *Equitable Life Assn v. Hyman* [2000] All E.R. 961, [2000] 3 W.L.R. 529 (HL).
[49] *Breckland Group Holdings Ltd v. London and Suffolk Properties* [1989] BCLC 100.
[50] *Shuttleworth v. Cox Bros & Co. Ltd* [1927] 2 K.B. 9; *Southern Foundries (1926) Ltd v. Shirlaw* [1940] A.C. 701.
[51] *Eley v. Positive Government Security Life Assurance Co. Ltd* (1875) 1 Ex. D. 20. Eley had drafted the company's articles and included a term stating that he was to be the company's lawyer. The company failed to appoint him, but due to poor pleadings in court, he failed to assert his right as a member to have the terms of the articles followed. On a more practical note, he failed to draw up an employment contract between the company and himself. One begins to see why the company did not appoint him.
[52] In *Cumbrian Newspapers Croup Ltd v. Cumberland and Westmorland Herald and Printing Co. Ltd* [1987] Ch. 1, [1986] 2 All E.R. 816, [1986] 3 W.L.R. 26, [1986] BCLC 286, the articles failed to spell out the different classes of shares though it was clear from an overall reading that there were meant to be two classes of share, and so by taking an overview it was established that there were two different classes of share.
[53] Business "angels", or Government agencies that invest in new and developing com-
panies, will commonly have a standard wording for the class of shares that they will
wish the company's articles to provide for them.

rights or the variation procedure in the memorandum), or failed to include provision for the variation of those rights, CA 1985, section 125 provides elaborate procedures for the variation of the rights of classes of shareholder, but nowadays, it is rare to find such complicated procedures necessary.[54] The standard procedure is that if a class of shareholders wishes to vary the rights attaching to its shares, the members of that class alone must pass an extraordinary resolution, or the holders of three quarters in nominal value of the issued shares of that class in writing consent to a written resolution, varying the rights in the desired manner, the rights will be accordingly varied. Historically in a company with a larger class and a smaller class of shares, there was a temptation for the larger class to use its greater voting power to pass special resolutions which would alter the articles to the detriment of the smaller class.[55] This was sometimes considered acceptable if the larger class could persuade the courts that the alteration was carried out *bona fide* for the benefit of the company as a whole, or that the alteration could be advantageous for the smaller class too,[56] but nowadays if the alteration smacked of oppression to the smaller class, the smaller class would use the minority protection provisions of CA 1985, section 459 to safeguard its own interests. Furthermore, nowadays, the drafting of class rights is more intelligent than it used to be. It is now common to include in the terms relating to the rights of any class of shares a right to prevent any other class of shares improving its rights relative to the rights enjoyed by the first class. Indeed the wording of the rights attaching to classes of shares is generally very careful, common rights being specification of a method of appointing directors to represent the class, a method of calculating dividends, rights to prevent unauthorised capital expenditure and rights to prevent the directors altering the business of the company in any unapproved manner.

SHAREHOLDERS AGREEMENTS

Enshrining shareholders' rights in the articles, and more rarely in the memorandum, suffers from the drawback that there is a loss of commercial confidentiality and any variation of the rights requires general meetings or written resolutions. One solution is a shareholders agreement, which is a contractual document signed by all or some of the shareholders. Common terms will include an agreement all to vote in a certain pre-arranged manner,[57] not to sell shares to outsiders and not to vote to alter the articles. If a shareholder does act contrary to the terms **4.24**

---

[54] This is generally because the more complicated the procedure, the more likely it is that it will not be followed correctly—thus leading to litigation.
[55] *Brown v. British Abrasive Wheel Co. Ltd* [1919] 1 Ch. 290.
[56] *Greenhalgh v. Arderne Cinemas Ltd* [1951] Ch. 286.
[57] *Re A & BC Chewing Gum Ltd* [1975] 1 All E.R. 1017.

of the shareholders agreement, by, say, casting his votes for a resolution in a manner contrary to the manner agreed in the shareholders agreement, the votes will still be validly cast, but the other shareholders in the shareholders agreement could sue him for breach of contract. If shareholders contract in a shareholders agreement that they will not seek repayment of their loans to a company while certain arrangements are in place, any shareholder who in defiance of the agreement seeks to sue the company for payment of his loan may be stopped from doing so by the terms of the shareholders agreement.[58]

The company whose shareholders enter into a shareholders agreement may enter the shareholders agreement if it wishes to do so, but the company itself cannot undertake not to alter its capital, because the company itself does not vote on altering its capital: it is the members who do that.[59]

4.25 One significant problem with a shareholders agreement is that it is only valid amongst the parties to it, and so if one shareholder leaves, the agreement has to be drawn up again. It is a common term of a shareholders agreement that any shareholder leaving the agreement must procure that the incomer undertakes the outgoing shareholder's obligations instead—until which the outgoing shareholder will not be released from his obligations.

Further Reading

Davies, *Gower's Principles of Modern Company Law* (6th ed., Sweet and Maxwell, 1997) Chaps 6–7
Howell "Section 35A of the Companies Act 1985 and an inquorate board: one won't do" (2002) 23(3) *Company Lawyer* 96–98

For company registration, see: www.companieshouse.gov.uk
For proposed changes to company registration, see: www.dti.gov.uk/companiesbill/whitepaper.htm

---

[58] *Snelling v. John G Snelling Ltd* [1972] 1 All E.R. 79.
[59] *Russell v. Northern Bank Development Corp. Ltd* [1992] 3 All E.R. 161.

CHAPTER 5

SECURITIES

THE DEFINITION OF A SECURITY

"Security" is a confusing term in company law, as it covers a multitude **5.01** of terms that convey a degree of ownership of a company or indebtedness of a company to a creditor. Unfortunately "security" also means a charge (a right of recourse against an asset of the company) as, for example, a standard security over a company's heritage or a charge over a company's book debts; and indeed in some respects there is common ground between the two meanings. As far as this chapter is concerned, securities means shares, debentures, warrants, options and convertibles. A *share* is a unit of ownership of a company measured in terms of an imaginary or "nominal" value, predominantly for accounting purposes in order to show the liability of the company to repay the shareholder on solvent liquidation. A *debenture* is the written acknowledgment of a debt by a company to a debenture holder, and in effect is a loan. A *warrant* is an entitlement (which usually must be paid for) to subscribe for a share usually at a certain price and at a certain date.[1] Warrants are rare in the United Kingdom for historical reasons to do with exchange controls imposed in the post-War years: in addition, warrants are a risky form of investment as they normally are made out to bearer[2] and therefore worth stealing. An *option* is a right to buy, following payment, an existing share at a predetermined price at a predetermined date. The option can then be exercised in the hope that the predetermined price is less than the actual value of the share in the market at the time of exercise of the option, so that the share, once purchased following the exercise of the option, may be immediately sold at a profit.[3] *Convertibles* are generally shares which will convert into other types of shares

---

[1] Warrants are obtained from the company itself, whereas options, as discussed below, are available from market makers in traded options.

[2] *i.e.* the person who happens to have it in his possession (legitimately or otherwise) at the time of exercising the warrant.

[3] Conversely, it is possible to have an option to sell a share at price higher than the actual market price.

71

or debentures, according to the terms of the conversion. This chapter concentrates primarily on shares.

SHARES

5.02 As far as Scots Law is concerned, a share is an item of incorporeal moveable property.[4] As with most items of property, it conveys rights and duties. It gives the owner a right to a proportion of the company's assets relative to the size and number of the shares overall, if that right were converted into cash or equivalent and subject to the company's prior repayment of all creditors. It also gives a right to a vote, if the share is a voting share, and to dividends (if declared by the directors and/or provided for in the articles). It gives the owner various other rights as specified in the company's articles (such as the right to transfer the share subject to any qualifications to that right in the articles), rights granted by the directors[5] and certain rights under statute, such as the right not to be treated in an unfairly prejudicial manner if in the minority[6] (all of which rights collectively amount to the word "interest" in the next paragraph). Of the duties, the principal duty is to pay up to the nominal value and to pay any premium if asked.[7] In limited circumstances, owning shares may cause the owner to be liable to the company[8] (all of which duties amount to "liability" in the paragraph below). In short, a share is a bundle of rights and obligations, which the shareholder is bound to accept in terms of Companies Act 1985, section 14 (hereafter "CA 1985").[9]

The classic description of a share was given by Farwell J. in *Borland's Trustee v. Borland*[10]:

> "A share is the interest of the shareholder in the company measured by a sum of money, for the purpose of liability in the first

---

[4] There have been various valiant attempts to say what a share is in English law. The general view is that it is a chose in action *sui generis*.

[5] For example, shareholders in certain banks may obtain reduced rates on insurance, gold cards, etc.

[6] CA 1985, s.459.

[7] The premium attaching to a share is the amount in excess of the nominal value which must be paid to the company in order to obtain the share. All premiums should be paid into a special capital account known as the share premium account. Sums held in the share premium account may be used for limited purposes such as paying up bonus shares or paying any premium on the redemption of debentures.

[8] For example, the fraudulent trading rules in Insolvency Act 1986, s.213 ("IA 1986") apply to the members (*i.e.* shareholders) if they have been making the company trade while insolvent and for a fraudulent purpose.

[9] s.14 is generally agreed to be an unsatisfactory wording nowadays and it is anticipated that more coherent wording will be produced in the next Companies Bill. It is to be hoped that the wording will better reflect the contractual rights of companies, directors and members to each other.

[10] [1901] 1 Ch. 279.

place, and of interest in the second, but also consisting of a series of mutual covenants entered into by all the shareholders inter se in accordance with s.16 of the Companies Act 1862 (now s.14 Companies Act 1985)."

The *sum of money* referred to above is the nominal value of a share. This bears no relation to the market value of the share but exists primarily to indicate the extent of the shareholder's liability to the company. Once the nominal value of the share is paid up, no more need be paid to the company, even in the event of the company's insolvency, unless the shareholder agrees to do so. Such is the nature of limited liability.

The *interest* has been referred to above.

The *mutual covenants* referred to above are the effectively con- **5.03** tractual rights under the memorandum and articles of association of the directors to the company and to the members, and the rights of the members to the company. If a member does not like those rights, his options are to band together with enough other members to change the memorandum and/or articles (depending on the change required) by means of a special resolution,[11] to sell his shares if he can (which may not always be possible in a small company with no market in the shares) or in extreme circumstances to give his shares away. Alternatively he may just have to live with the memorandum and articles and endure them until such time as he can persuade enough others to help him change them.

There are many types of shares, although the standard share is the ordinary share. Where a company has more than one type of share, the company will either need to be created having different types, or more properly "classes" of shares, or have to change its articles to allow for the creation of new classes of share. This will require a special resolution. Once a class of shares is created, the only persons who may alter the rights attaching to that class of shares are the members of that class itself according to the methods specified in the rights attaching to the class itself, or using the methods specified in CA 1985, section 125 if for some reason the methods of alteration are not spelt out in those rights —though nowadays class rights are usually carefully worded to avoid the somewhat impenetrable complications of section 125.[12] Commonly the price of investment in a company by an new investor will be the right of the investor to have a special class of shares which will give him rights denied to other investors, such as a right to appoint a nominee director, or to have special weighted voting rights—all of which are designed to protect his investment, and without which he would not generally be willing to invest. Having a class of shares also limits other

---

[11] CA 1985, s.9.

[12] Alteration of class rights commonly requires an extraordinary resolution by the members of the class alone.

shareholders' rights to interfere with the investor's rights. In companies where there is more than one class of share, it is common to provide in the rights attaching to the first class of shares a provision that no other class of shares may try to improve its rights relative to the first class of shares without the consent of the shareholders of that first class.

Below are shown some of the more usual types of share.

Ordinary shares

5.04   In the absence of any definitions to the contrary, the "default" share is an ordinary share, with one vote per share and a right to participate in the company's profits and to receive a return of capital on solvent liquidation. A company may nonetheless provide such further rights for ordinary shares as it chooses, such as a right to have extra votes on certain occasions or a right to arbitration in the event of a dispute.

Preference shares

5.05   These are shares that normally attract a fixed return on capital, commonly a percentage of the nominal value (as in "six per cent preference shares"). They receive this dividend, which is commonly provided for by means of an arithmetical formula specified in the articles,[13] before the ordinary shareholders receive their dividend. Since the percentage return may sometimes not be very impressive relative to the dividend the ordinary shareholders are receiving, it is possible to have a "participating preference share" which receives not only a fixed return but an additional right to participate, to an agreed extent, in the dividends that the ordinary shareholders are enjoying—thus obtaining a double benefit. Preference shares are commonly said to be cumulative.[14] Preference shares commonly have a right to receive their capital back on solvent liquidation before the ordinary shareholders receive their capital. By convention many companies' preference shares are non-voting except on such occasions as a resolution to wind up the company.

Redeemable shares

5.06   These are shares issued in the knowledge that they will be repurchased by the company at a future date, at a certain price and at the option of either the company or the shareholder as specified; and when redeemable shares are issued there must be other, non-redeemable,

---

[13] The formula will commonly refer to the level of profits made by the company and have a method of preventing the company increasing its overheads, in particular directors' salaries, in order to reduce the amount payable by way of the preferential dividend.
[14] This means that they are automatically entitled to any arrears of dividend as a prior claim on any distributable profits.

shares in issue.[15] The terms of the redemption will generally nowadays be specified in the articles,[16] and redeemable shares must be fully paid up before redemption can take place.[17] It is permissible for shares to be redeemed at a premium; the financing of this and indeed of redemption of shares generally is discussed in the next chapter. Redeemable shares are a useful way of obtaining short term finance if a company does not wish to have an outside investor involved in a company for too long: on redemption the company will buy back the investor's shares and return him his capital plus any premium if contracted to do so. Redeemable shares are also useful as a method of giving shares to motivate a temporary manager or other employee who wants a stake in his employer's business but wants to know that there will be a market for his shares eventually.

Convertible shares

These are shares that are designed to be converted either into other **5.07** types of shares or to debentures on the fulfilment of certain events. It is not unusual to have a class of shares with specified rights to convert to an ordinary share on the flotation of the company's shares on the London Stock Exchange: this is because an ordinary share is more marketable than a share with complex and unusual rights. Sometimes a share will be designed to convert into a debenture since that will protect the investor better than remaining a shareholder, since shareholders are last to be repaid (if at all) in the event of the company's liquidation.

It is possible to have shares that combine several of the features of the above shares.

ALLOTMENT OF SHARES

To borrow or to seek further capital?

When a company needs more cash it has the choice of borrowing **5.08** more money or seeking more share capital. The advantage of borrowing is that the existing shareholders' control of the company is not diluted; but instead the company may be under the thumb of the lender, who may also insist on strict rules for payment of interest on the loan and on

---

[15] CA 1985, s.159(2).
[16] CA 1985, s.160(3), the wording says "redemption of shares may take place on such terms and in such manner as may be provided by the articles" which allows for the possibility of non-disclosure of the terms; but nonetheless it is still common to state the terms in the articles.
[17] CA 1985, s.159(3).

security over the company's assets and indeed the directors' personal assets as a precondition of the loan. The advantage of seeking more share capital is that it may be cheaper to pay dividends than to pay interest. It may be possible to persuade investors to accept a lower dividend on their investment than the same amount of money could receive by way of loan interest, if those investors believe that there are opportunities for capital growth in the long run. The investors may also have the attraction of the company's flotation of its shares on the Stock Exchange if the company prospers, or of its shares being bought at a premium by someone who wishes to purchase the company. Ultimately it is a commercial decision by the potential investors and the directors.

The disadvantage, from the existing shareholders' point of view, in having further shares issued is that unless the existing shareholders are given and take up the opportunity to acquire further shares in proportion to their current shareholdings (known as the right of pre-emption) they will find that their control of the company diminishes (sometimes known as "stock-watering").

5.09   "Allotment" and "issue" have similar but different meanings. Allotment is the unconditional right to have the member's name inserted in the register of members; issue takes place the moment the member's name is inserted in the register of members.[18] The date of issue may occasionally be important for taxation purposes.[19]

The procedure for allotment

5.10   The procedure for allotment of shares in an ordinary private company, or a plc not offering its shares to the public, in essence has five main steps. These are

(1) Is the authorised share capital sufficiently large to allow for the issue of the new shares?
(2) Have the directors authority to issue the shares?
(3) Do the existing members propose to exercise their pre-emption rights?
(4) Has payment been made for the new shares, and has the consideration for the shares taken account of all the relevant rules, particularly where there is non-cash consideration?
(5) Has proper intimation of the allotment of shares been given to the Registrar of Companies and have the new members received their share certificates?

---

[18] CA 1985, s.22.
[19] *National Westminster Bank plc v. IRC* [1994] 2 BCLC 239, HL.

For plcs issuing shares to the public there are further issues to consider in addition to the above. Where a public (but non-listed) company[20] offers shares to the public, the offer must comply with the Public Offer of Securities Regulations,[21] and if the company is listed, the Financial Services Act 1986, Part IV and the Financial Services and Markets Act 2000, Part VI apply to the offer of shares to the public, and to prospectuses[22] in particular.

The authorised share capital

Before a company allots shares, the authorised capital[23] must be large **5.11** enough to permit the allotment of the new shares; and if it is not large enough, it must be increased by ordinary resolution.[24] For example, if a company has an authorised capital of £100,000 and an issued share capital[25] of £60,000, it could issue up to £40,000 worth of new shares. But if the same company wished to increase its issued share capital from £60,000 to £150,000, it would first need to increase the authorised capital from £100,000 to at least £150,000. The increase would be done by ordinary resolution under CA 1985, section 121 together with intimation to the Registrar of Companies on form 122.[26] The authorised share capital serves as a cap on the number of shares the directors may issue, and the requirement to seek the members' approval before its increase is supposed to ensure (a) that directors do not lightly increase the authorised share capital and (b) that members are aware that any further issue of shares following on the increase in authorised share

---

[20] In practice not many plcs do offer their shares to the public, and the most that do so are listed on the Official List of the London Stock Exchange. However, there are plcs whose shares are listed either on other recognised investment exchanges (*e.g.* Ofex) or for which market-makers (*i.e.* stockbrokers) will "make a market" by agreeing to act as a middleman or broker who will buy and sell securities in the companies concerned. Needless to say, non-listed securities are generally considered very speculative and not for the unwary.

[21] S.I. 1995 No. 1537.

[22] A prospectus is effectively an invitation to treat issued by the company offering more shares. Prospectuses tend to be weighty documents detailing all the information that a prudent investor could want in order to enable him to decide whether or not to invest in the company.

[23] The authorised share capital is the value of the total number of shares that could be issued by the directors. It is not permissible to issue shares in excess of the authorised share capital.

[24] CA 1985, s.121.

[25] The issued share capital is the number of shares issued by the directors multiplied by each share's nominal value. The issued share capital can never exceed the authorised share capital.

[26] This form should be accompanied by a certified copy of the ordinary resolution authorising the increase. The memorandum of association should also be altered to show the increased authorised share capital. It is good practice to send the Registrar a new copy of the memorandum showing the increase.

capital may dilute their equity.[27] Plcs must have an authorised and issued share capital of at least £50,000.[28]

The directors' authority for allotment

5.12   Directors' authority for allotment comes either from the articles or members' resolutions.[29] On incorporation a company will commonly authorise its directors to allot relevant securities for a period of no more than five years commencing from the date of incorporation of the company,[30] or will permit its directors, by ordinary resolution, to allot relevant securities for a period of no more than five years from the date of the resolution.[31] The authority may be renewed or indeed revoked where necessary. The authority (either in the articles or the resolution) must indicate the maximum number of relevant securities that may be issued[32] and in any event the aggregate of the shares already issued and to be issued must not exceed the authorised capital. "Relevant securities" in this context means shares other than subscriber shares,[33] employee share scheme shares,[34] rights to subscribe for shares[35] or rights to convert any security (such as a debenture) into a share.[36]

Private companies may dispense with the five year rule by means of elective resolution[37] under CA 1985, section 80A. This allows private companies to give the directors authority to allot securities for a period in excess of five years or indeed indefinitely, although there must still be a limit on the number of securities that the directors may issue.[38]

5.13   No private company may issue securities to the public,[39] and to attempt to do so is a criminal offence.[40] In practice this means that the directors of a private company must approach potential investors by

---

[27] There are suggestions that the authorised share capital rule is an anachronism and could be removed without loss to anyone involved in the company. (See *Modern Company Law for a Competitive Economy: Completing the Structure,* Chap. 7, the Company Law Review Steering Group, DTI.)

[28] CA 1985, s.118. However, the shares need only be paid up to the extent of one quarter of their nominal value.

[29] CA 1985, s.80(1).

[30] CA 1985, s.80(4)(a).

[31] CA 1985, s.80(4)(b).

[32] CA 1985, s.80(4) and (6).

[33] Subscriber shares are the shares given to the subscribers to the memorandum and articles of association and who sign the Form 10.

[34] CA 1985, s.80(2)(a).

[35] Effectively this means warrants.

[36] CA 1985, s.80(2)(b).

[37] See Chap. 13.

[38] CA 1985, s.80A(2).

[39] It is possible for a private company to seek outside investors, but it may only do so provided it does not contravene the terms of the Public Offer of Securities Regulations 1995, reg. 7 (S.I. 1995 No. 1537). So, for example, an offer to a restricted circle of hardy investors, or to employees, or to a group of no more than 50 persons, does not count as "an offer to the public".

[40] CA 1985, s.81.

means other than public advertisements or notices. Issuing of securities following the publication of a prospectus will be dealt with shortly.

Members' pre-emption rights

Companies Act 1985, section 89 predicates that existing members **5.14** will wish to be given the opportunity to exercise their pre-emption rights in order to maintain their equity or voting power within the company. Accordingly the directors must offer existing shareholders this opportunity, and failure to do so, except where the directors have received permission not to do so, renders the directors jointly and severally personally liable, along with the company, for any loss occasioned to the shareholders deprived of this opportunity.[41] However, if the shareholders have not objected to this deprivation within two years of the allotment, they are precluded from bringing any proceedings against the directors on this matter.[42]

On the assumption that the directors are aware of the members' pre-emption rights, and expect the members to want to exercise those rights, the procedure is that the directors write to the members explaining the rights and inviting the members to subscribe for the shares in proportion to their existing shareholdings.[43] So a member who owns 20 per cent of the equity in a company will be invited to apply for 20 per cent of the shares about to be allotted. Members are not obliged to take up their pre-emption rights in full (unless the articles say otherwise), may sell their entitlement to the new shares if they wish, or may elect not to exercise their rights. Such election may take place either by inertia (by not responding within 21 days or such greater period as may be permitted by the directors[44]) or in writing, known as a "waiver of pre-emption rights", again within the required time period.

It may be that the directors would prefer the pre-emption rights not to **5.15** be exercised. In that case, the directors must write to the members to explain why the pre-emption rights should be disapplied, and ask the members to pass a special resolution to disapply the pre-emption rights following the grant of directors' authority to allot shares under section 80 (as above) either particularly for a specific allotment[45] or for allotments generally.[46] In the latter case, it is also permissible to have the same power to disapply the pre-emption rights under the articles.[47]

---

[41] CA 1985, s.92(1).
[42] CA 1985, s.92(2).
[43] An offer of new shares, initially to existing shareholders, is known as a right issue.
[44] CA 1985, s.90(6).
[45] CA 1985, s.96(2).
[46] CA 1985, s.96(1).
[47] CA 1985, s.96(1). This particular provision enables plcs to disapply pre-emption rights, either by special resolution or under the articles, but only where the disapplication is connected with the general grant of authority under s.80 to allot shares.

Private companies, if they wish, may also disapply the pre-emption rights under their memorandum or articles of association.[48]

The pre-emption rights do not apply, however, on all occasions. Under CA 1985, section 89(4) pre-emption rights do not apply where the shares are wholly or partly paid up otherwise than in cash.[49] Preference shares[50] and employee share scheme shares,[51] not being "relevant shares", do not attract pre-emption rights, though an employee who has received shares from an employee share scheme is able to obtain pre-emption rights once the employee share scheme shares are in his possession.[52] Bonus shares and subscriber shares, not being "equity securities",[53] likewise do not attract pre-emption rights.

Since the loss of pre-emption rights, even where preference shares or employee share scheme shares are concerned, may be a significant matters for all the investors generally, it is possible to word the articles so that pre-emption rights apply even for preference shares or employee share scheme shares.[54]

Payment for the shares

5.16   Shares may not be issued at a discount.[55] The only permissible form of discount is where a company pays a commission, usually to an underwriter, for subscribing for shares, or for arranging for others to subscribe for shares, providing that no more than 10 per cent of the price for the subscribed shares is used by way of commission, and that all information about the discount is made available to investors.[56]

Although the consideration for shares will normally reflect the true value of the consideration, and be paid in cash, in private companies it would appear that provided there is no fraud a company may accept non-cash consideration even if it does not truly reflect the value of the shares[57] and there is genuine and present consideration.[58]

5.17   However, in plcs the position is different. In order to maintain the impression that plcs are relatively safe to invest in or to trade with, plcs are required to ensure that the consideration they receive for their issues

---

[48] CA 1985, s.91.

[49] That is, if an asset of some sort is transferred or services supplied to the company as consideration for the shares. Presumably even a small element of non-cash consideration would be sufficient to disapply the pre-emption rules.

[50] See CA 1985, s.94(5)(a).

[51] CA 1985, s.94(5)(b).

[52] CA 1985, s.94(4).

[53] CA 1985, s.94(3).

[54] CA 1985, s.93.

[55] CA 1985, s.100.

[56] CA 1985, s.97(3).

[57] *Re Wragg Ltd* [1897] 1 Ch. 795, CA.

[58] *Hong Kong and China Gas Co Ltd v. Glen* [1914] 1 Ch. 527. English law is very keen on present consideration: it is arguable that Scots law might be less concerned at its absence.

is justified. A plc may not in exchange for shares accept an undertaking to carry out work or perform services for any other person,[59] and if it does so, the recipient of the shares has to pay the nominal value of the shares concerned, plus any premium on the shares and any exigible interest.[60] In a plc, shares must be paid up at least to the extent of one quarter of each share's nominal value, together with payment of the premium in full.[61] In a plc, if the consideration for the shares is an undertaking to be performed more than five years after the date of the allotment, and the undertaking is not carried out within that period, the recipient of the shares must pay the full amount plus the premium and any interest.[62] If the contract for the undertaking is for a lesser period than five years and the undertaking is still not completed by the expiry of the period, the same penalty applies.[63] In a plc, where non-cash consideration is given for the allotment, the non-cash consideration must be independently valued to ensure that the company truly receives its money's worth.[64] The asset will be valued by the company's auditor or someone appointed by him as a specialist valuer[65] and who must be provided with all relevant information about the asset.[66] The valuation report must state whether or not the value ascribed to the non-cash consideration is proper, as well as detailing the method by which the valuation was carried out[67] and must state that the valuation was carried out within six months prior to the allotment.[68] The allottee is entitled to see the valuation report.[69] In a plc, where the non-cash consideration being provided is all or some of the shares in another company, the shares in that other company will not need to be independently valued, provided that the plc offers its own shares in exchange for the shares in the other company or class of shares in the other company[70] and provided the offer is made to all of the members of the other company (irrespective of whether they take up the offer) or all of the members of the class[71] of that other company. In addition there is no requirement for independent valuation of non-cash consideration in the form of all the assets and liabilities of another company which will merge with the plc

---

[59] CA 1985, s.99(2).

[60] CA 1985, s.99(3). At present the interest rate is five per cent, CA 1985, s.107.

[61] CA 1985, s.101. There are exemptions for shares in employee share schemes.

[62] CA 1985, s.102(1) and (2).

[63] CA 1985, s.102(5) and (6).

[64] CA 1985, s.103.

[65] CA 1985, s.108.

[66] CA 1985, s.110.

[67] CA 1985 s.108

[68] CA 1985, s.103(1)(b).

[69] CA 1985, s.103(1)(c).

[70] CA 1985, s.103(3). This is effectively a takeover, and in a takeover, at least in theory, the shares should be at market value anyway unless there has been some form of market manipulation.

[71] CA 1985, s.103(4).

which is offering its own shares as consideration for those assets and liabilities.[72]

In the event of contravention of the above rules, the allottee will be required to pay the proper price that should have been paid, together with any premium and interest, thus putting the burden on the allottee to ensure that the procedure is properly carried out.[73] A person who acquires shares from an allottee who has been allotted shares in contravention of the above rules is also liable unless he can prove that he acquired the shares for value and without notice of the contravention.[74]

5.18   A further issue connected with the allotment of shares arises when either (i) a plc either incorporated as such, within two years of the issue of its section 117 trading certificate, or (ii) a private company has re-registered as a plc, within two years of the date of re-registration, as the case may be, allots shares for non-cash consideration.[75] Under such circumstances, if the allottee is a subscriber to the memorandum in the case of a plc incorporated as such, or a member of the (formerly private) company at the time of re-registration, and the consideration is equal to one-tenth of the company's nominal share capital at the time, the consideration will need to be independently valued in the same manner as above.[76] In addition the terms of the agreement for the non-cash consideration must be approved by the members by ordinary resolution[77] having been circulated to the members beforehand.[78] This rule does not apply, however, where the company in the ordinary course of business acquires assets of a particular description in exchange for shares,[79] as opposed, presumably, to a deliberate allotment of shares for non-cash consideration as part of an exercise to increase the company's capital.

Intimation of allotment and registration of the new shares

5.19   Assuming all the above has been dealt with, the directors will normally convene a meeting at which the payments for the shares are approved and the company secretary or company registrar instructed to allot the shares. The Form 88(2) is usually used to intimate the allotment and the new allottees to the Registrar of Companies. If there is non-cash consideration for the shares, and that consideration attracts Stamp Duty,

---

[72] CA 1985, s.103(5).
[73] CA 1985, s.103(6) and 105.
[74] CA 1985, s.112.
[75] CA 1985, s.104.
[76] CA 1985, s.104(4)(a).
[77] CA 1985, s.104(4)(c).
[78] CA 1985, s.104(4)(d).
[79] CA 1985, s.104(6).

a copy of the contract for the transfer to the company of the consideration will need to be sent to the Stamp Office first in order for the Inland
Revenue to assess the relevant duty.[80]

When the company secretary or registrar inserts the details of the new
allotment against the new (or as the case may be, existing) shareholder's
name in the register of members, the shares are said to be issued to the
shareholder.[81] If there is an inaccuracy in the issue of shares or the
register of members, and although the register of members is *prima
facie* evidence of the ownership of shares,[82] it is open to an aggrieved
shareholder to apply to the courts for rectification of the register if the
company is unwilling to rectify it itself.[83] The register of members is
normally kept at the company's registered office but may be maintained
by a professional registrar.[84] The register must have an index if there are
more than 50 shareholders[85] and be open to inspection, free to members
and for a fee for others.[86] If the company is a single member company,
that fact must be noted on the register, along with the date of sole
membership, and any subsequent increase in membership must also be
recorded.[87] In England a trust may not be noted in the register[88] but a
trust may be registered in Scotland. In England it is possible to have a
stop notice or a stop notice placed by a creditor (or other interested
party) against a member's entry in the register of members. This
effectively prevents the transfer of the shares or payment of a dividend
without intimation to the creditor or other party. There is no such
mechanism in Scotland.

If the new allottee is a director, his interest in his shares will have to **5.20**
be intimated within five days to the company[89] and noted in a special
register of directors' interests.[90] This rule also applies to the interests in
his company of his immediate family.[91] If the company is listed the

---

[80] It is common to send a copy Form 88(2) to the Registrar of Companies to indicate that
the principal version and the contract are with the Stamp Office, and to ask the Stamp
Office to forward the stamped Form 88(2) to the Registrar once the duty has been paid.
If there is no written contract for the non-cash consideration, the necessary information
is inserted on the Form 88(3). This too must be stamped. The benefit of using a Form
88(3) is that a degree of commercial secrecy is maintained. Items that attract stamp duty
include heritage, book debts, goodwill, securities etc.
[81] CA 1985, s.22.
[82] CA 1985, s.361.
[83] CA 1985, s.359. See also *Re Data Express Ltd, The Times*, April 27, 1987; *Re
Thundercrest Ltd* [1994] B.C.C. 855; *Re New Cedos Engineering Co.* [1994] 1 BCLC
797; *Popely v. Planarrive Ltd, The Times*, April 24, 1996.
[84] CA 1985, s.353. Such as Compatashare or Lloyds Registrars.
[85] CA 1985, s.354.
[86] CA 1985, s.356.
[87] CA 1985, s.352A.
[88] CA 1985, s.360. What usually happens instead is that the first-named trustee is held to
be the nominee for the trust.
[89] CA 1985, s.324.
[90] CA 1985, s.325.
[91] CA 1985, s.327 and s.328.

same information as is included in the register of directors' and their families' interests must be intimated to the London Stock Exchange by the end of the day following the allotment.[92]

Within two months the company or its registrar must issue the share certificates for the new shares.[93] These are traditionally paper based and are signed by a director or the company secretary or their authorisee. Many investors like the reassurance of a paper certificate, but listed companies now also use CREST which is an electronic record of investors' shareholdings. Paper certificates are now usually only applicable for private and non-quoted companies. A share certificate is sufficient evidence of share-ownership.[94] When a company issues a share certificate it is personally barred from denying the validity of the share certificate,[95] and while this may be onerous for the company, most companies will insure against the risk of being tricked into issuing a share certificate when they should not have done.

5.21   CREST is used extensively as a computerised record of each investor's holding. Stockbrokers', accountants' and lawyers' firms commonly are CREST members and are thus able to deal swiftly and cheaply with allotments to their clients and transfers of shares by and to their clients.

A particular issue arising out of CREST is the fact that the individual shareholder is one step removed from the company in which he is investing. He has a beneficial interest in the share which is held for him by his CREST nominee (usually his stockbroker, lawyer or banker). There are possible issues over the extent to which it is possible to grant a charge over such a beneficial interest, or even if there is a right to speak at general meetings; these are issues which no doubt will have to be sorted out as share certificates are increasingly held electronically.

RIGHTS, BONUS AND SCRIP ISSUES

Rights issue

5.22   A rights issue is an offer to existing shareholders to subscribe for further shares in proportion to their existing holdings. It is generally done when a company needs more cash and wishes to tap its shareholder loyalty first and to enable existing shareholders to maintain their equity in the company. Rights issues are usually issued at a discount to the existing share price to take account of the dilution of the value of each

---

[92] CA 1985, s.329.

[93] CA 1985, s.185.

[94] CA 1986, s.186(1)(b). Owning the certificate does not necessarily mean that the certificate-owner is entitled to all the benefits of the underlying shares: *Re Baku Consolidated Oilfields Ltd* [1993] B.C.C. 653.

[95] *Re Bahia and San Francisco Railway Co Ltd* (1868) L.R. 3 Q.B. 584; *Bloomenthal v. Ford* [1897] A.C. 156; *Sheffield Corporation v. Barclay* [1905] A.C. 392.

share once further shares are in existence. It is also possible to sell one's entitlement to a rights issue.

Bonus issue

A bonus issue is when retained profits, or sums held in the share **5.23** premium account or capital redemption reserve, are converted into share capital. If, for example, a company had £100 by way of retained profits, it could, instead of paying that £100 to the members by way of dividends, use the £100 to create a further 100 shares of one pound nominal value each and issue these to the existing members in proportion to their existing holdings. This procedure, which only requires an ordinary resolution, enables members to gain more shares without paying stockbrokers' fees. If members wish to sell their bonus shares they may do so. Bonus issues are sometimes used to increase the number of shares a company has in order to make the shares more marketable, especially if the shares have a high value.

Scrip issue

A scrip issue is a method of paying dividends in the form of shares. **5.24** The sums that would normally be paid in cash are paid in shares instead. The articles must permit this. This practice is particularly advantageous for investors who wish to build up capital and are not needing the dividends for income. It also saves stockbrokers' fees.

PROSPECTUSES

A prospectus is a document either inviting potential investors amongst **5.25** the general public to subscribe for shares in a company seeking capital, or to buy shares from an existing shareholder. A prospectus is not an offer to the shareholder: it is an invitation to treat and when the potential shareholder completes the documentation in the prospectus and sends it to the company or its agent with his cheque, he is making an offer which the company may accept or reject as it chooses. Prospectuses are predominantly used in plcs since private companies are not allowed to offer their shares to the public. As over many years potential investors have been gulled into subscribing for shares on what turned out subsequently to be erroneous or misleading information in prospectuses,[96] prospectuses are now expected to be as honest as possible and contain all information that a reasonable investor could reasonably want. For

---

[96] Quite often it is difficult to prove that the prospectus is false, but even so the prospectus may have painted an unduly rosy picture of the company's prospects. In the long run such sharp practice will not benefit the share price. As an example of how not to draw up a prospectus see the DTI investigation of the Mirror Group floatation available at www.dti.gov.uk/cld/mirrorgroup/index/htm

public but non-listed companies offering their securities to the public, the Public Offer of Securities Regulations 1995[97] apply, but they do not apply when the offer of shares is made to small well-informed groups of investors, family members related to the founder members of the company, employees, etc., all as specified in regulation 7(2). The information that is supplied in the prospectus must be easily analysable and as comprehensible as possible.[98] There must be disclosure of all information that an investor could reasonably want in order to make an informed assessment of the present and future financial state of the company and the rights attaching to the securities offered in the prospectus.[99]

Where a company's financial situation changes during the time of the offer, the company must issue a supplementary prospectus[1] but information for which the disclosure might be contrary to public policy need not be disclosed.[2] Those who prepare the prospectus may be required to pay compensation to any person who has acquired securities to which the prospectus relates and who suffered loss as a result of inaccurate or misleading statements or omitted information in the prospectus.[3] There are exemptions from liability for compensation where the person who provided the inaccurate or misleading statement, or who omitted the omitted information, did all he could to bring the error or omission to the attention of investors, reasonably believed that the statements were true or properly omitted, reasonably relied on an expert's opinion or otherwise reasonably ought to be excused.[4]

5.26 For listed companies, very similar rules apply. Under the Financial Services Act 1986, when a listed company issues a prospectus, that prospectus must comply with what are effectively the same rules applicable to non-listed companies in terms of the requirement for transparency, compensation for erroneous, misleading or omitted information,[5] all to be found in Part IV of the Financial Services Act. For a company to be listed, it must be first admitted to the London Stock Exchange by complying with the terms of its handbook, known colloquially as the Purple Book[6] and more properly as the Admission of Securities to Listing. This is the rule book for listed companies, and while there are no direct sanctions against companies that fail to adhere to the terms of the Purple Book, other than suspension of trading in the shares, failure to adhere to the practice recommended in the Purple Book without good cause will cause doubts to arise about the company—doubts which will

---

[97] S.I. 1995 No. 1537.
[98] POSR 1995, reg. 8(3).
[99] POSR 1995, reg. 9.
[1] POSR 1995, reg. 10.
[2] POSR 1995, reg. 11.
[3] POSR 1995, regs 13, 14.
[4] POSR 1995, reg. 15.
[5] See in particular FSA, s.150.
[6] Formerly the Yellow Book.

generally affect the company's share price negatively. The Purple Book operates on the principle that listed companies should adhere to the spirit of its rules, rather than its letter: such an approach sometimes goes counter to the grain of the more buccaneering entrepreneurs.

Although there are common law rules to the same end, it is more than likely nowadays that investors would use the above statutory rules to claim compensation where they have been misled. The effect of the rules has been salutary in ensuring that transparency and fair and open practices are increasingly required in the financial industry. Although there will always be some companies tempted to beguile investors if they can possibly do so, the common practice in prospectuses and listing particulars of noting who is responsible for every single statement in those documents ensures that sharp practice is a questionable activity. No merchant bank, market maker or stockbroker will wish, in the long run, to attract a reputation for lack of integrity.

TRANSFER AND TRANSMISSION OF SHARES

Subject to the terms of the company's articles, a shareholder may **5.27** normally transfer his shares to whomever he pleases. However, many small family companies' articles impose restrictions on the transfer of shares away from the founder members, impose certain pre-emption requirements in favour of existing members or reserve to directors an unfettered right not to register the transfer of any shares to those of whom they disapprove. If the wording in the articles allows directors such discretion, then provided the directors have not acted fraudulently they will be entitled to refuse to register such transfers.[7] Nonetheless in principle procedures relating to transfer and specified in the articles must be followed. Listed companies generally do not impose restrictions on transfers since that would affect the liquidity of the shares, thus negating the point of having the shares in the market in the first place. Most share transfers attract stamp duty at the rate of half a per cent and stock transfer forms are used for this purpose. Gifts of shares do not attract stamp duty. The seller or disponer signs the stock transfer form and the recipient need only sign it if the shares are partly paid, thereby acknowledging his liability for the unpaid part of the shares. The recipient will exhibit the stamped stock transfer form to the company in order to have his name entered into the register of members.

As stated earlier, if a company is wrongfully induced to issue a share certificate following a purported transfer, the new share certificate is still *prima facie* valid[8] and an innocent third party buying in good faith from the transferee the shares represented by the share certificate is entitled to

---

[7] *Re Smith and Fawcett Ltd* [1942] Ch. 304 CA.
[8] Even when the company makes a mistake, as when shares were stated to be fully paid when in fact they were not: *Bloomenthal v. Ford* [1897] A.C. 156.

rely on it[9]; and likewise the person who is wrongfully apparently deprived of the shares by, say, the forging of his signature on a stock transfer form, is entitled to be restored to the company's register of members since he never actually loses the shares anyway, and a forged transfer is a nullity.[10] Where the issue of the share certificate has followed representations made to the company (or its registrar) and the representor then sells the shares to a third party (who then obtains the share certificate), the representor may be liable to the company or its registrar as having induced the company or its registrar to issue the share certificate, even if he acts in good faith.[11]

5.28   Transmission arises when a share moves from its original owner to someone who is looking after it but does not have true ownership. For example, a debtor does not transfer his shares to his trustee in sequestration: the shares are said to be transmitted to the trustee. The trustee may transfer the shares to somebody else.

Concert parties and disclosure of interests

5.29   A concert party is when a shareholder in a plc buys a substantial number of shares, but does it through various subsidiaries and other interests in order to disguise the true identity of the person acquiring the shares. This is because of the three per cent rule, whereby in a plc, anyone buying three per cent or more of the company's share capital (whether by transfer or allotment) is supposed to declare his acquisition as it is a "notifiable interest".[12] Since ingenious investors, seeking to build up a commanding position in a company prior to launching a takeover bid, will generally wish to disguise their actions, a common practice is to acquire 2.99 per cent of the shares and arrange for their nominees or associates to buy similar amounts on their behalf. Consequently the rules in sections 202–209 require disclosure by their nominees and associates too. Companies may well wish to know who is considering mounting a takeover bid and this is one way of flushing a predatory takeover bidder out of the bushes. Sometimes a company may wish to know the true identity of someone who owns shares in the company (whether a takeover bidder or not) and, if so, the directors may send a request under CA 1985, section 212 to the named shareholder to divulge what his interest in the shares is, and if he is a nominee for another person, who that nominee is, together with any other matters

---

[9] *Re Bahia and San Francisco Railway Co Ltd* [1868] L.R. 3 Q.B. 584.

[10] *Sheffield Corporation v. Barclay* [1905] A.C. 392.

[11] *Sheffield Corporation v. Barclay* [1905] A.C. 392; *Royal Bank of Scotland v. Sandstone Properties Ltd* [1998] 2 BCLC 429.

[12] CA 1985, s.199. There is a further rule under s.199(2)(b) for aggregate interests, whereby the same rules apply where a shareholder has overall an interest in 10 per cent of the company's share capital, albeit spread out through various types of beneficial holding. There are many exemptions for persons acquiring shares in the course of business for others, such as market-makers, or trusts, charities and so on (s.209).

which may be of relevance particularly in connection with concert parties. If the shareholder is unwilling to provide the requested information within a reasonable time, the company may apply to the court for an order under CA 1985, sections 454–457. This will enable the company to prohibit the shareholder from transferring any of his shares, receiving any of his dividends, voting, receiving any bonus issues or obtaining rights under a rights issue. This effectively renders the shares useless, except on a solvent liquidation, so there is considerable incentive to comply with the request.[13]

Charges over shares

Sometimes shareholders wish to borrow against the security of their **5.30** shares. As a practical matter this is only worthwhile, from the lender's point of view, when the shares are in a well known listed company.[14] A lender is unlikely to seek security over the relatively illiquid shares of a small private company. The borrower/shareholder may deposit the share certificates with the lender by way of semi-security for a loan,[15] but there is then a danger that the shareholder might fraudulently persuade the company to issue him with a duplicate share-certificate and then attempt to sell his shares without repaying the loan. The proper method of obtaining a charge in Scotland is for the borrower to transfer his shares to the lender by means of a stock transfer form. The lender then apparently owns the shares, but issues the borrower with a back letter whereby the lender undertakes to re-transfer the shares to the borrower on the expiry of the loan and full payment of all sums due. The back letter will also indicate what may be done with the votes, dividends and other rights attaching to the shares for the duration of the loan. If the borrower defaults, the lender merely sells the shares which are already in its name.

If a company grants a floating charge, technically the charge would cover any shares it owns. A company could also grant a charge over the dividends arising from the shares, since those are book debts and therefore registrable.[16]

---

[13] Artful concert-party goers, however, merely have a further nominee or nominees as the beneficial owners of the shares.

[14] There are mechanisms within CREST to take account of the charging/mortgaging of uncertificated shares, but the whole area of charging of uncertified shares is fraught with practical difficulties since the law has not really caught up with the idea of computerised securities. See *Registration of Security Interests: Company Charges and Property other than Land: A Consultation Paper,* Law Commission Consultation Paper No. 164, at paras 5.17–5.35.

[15] This is not a proper security as Scots law knows it, since the shares still remain in the ownership of the borrower and delivery has not therefore taken place.

[16] CA 1985, s.410(4)(c)(i).

Lien and forfeiture

5.31   It is now rare to have a lien over shares, but under Table A regulation 8 a company may have a lien over a partly paid share. If the share is not paid up as requested, the company may then arrange for the transfer of the shares to a purchaser, with the purchase price being used to defray the unpaid part of the share. Some companies have articles that allow them a lien over a member's share if the member owes any money for any reason to the company.

Forfeiture is the right of the company to insist that if a member does not pay the unpaid amount on a share the company may arrange that the shareholder forfeits his share.[17] He then loses all sums that he may already have paid on the shares and any sums, such as dividends, that he may be due. He loses all rights in the shares and the company will normally cancel the shares.[18] Forfeiture is very rare nowadays, mainly because shares are now generally fully paid.

DEBENTURES

5.32   A debenture is the written acknowledgement of a loan traditionally known in Scotland as a "bond". When a company borrows money, it may either borrow in terms of one large loan from one or a few lenders, each of whom receives a debenture in similar terms, or may borrow from many lenders all lending similar sums of money to the company and receiving what is commonly known as debenture stock. Where a company borrows from one or only a few lenders, each lender is usually in a good position to monitor the loan and its repayment, but where a company borrows from many thousands of lenders, there will need to be a system for the registration of debenture-holders, a procedure for the transfer of debentures, and a method of ensuring that debenture-holders' interests are properly looked after. The common solution to the latter problem is that the debenture-holders collectively join a trust, in terms of a debenture trust deed, supervised by a debenture trust deed trustee whose business it is to look after the interests of the debenture-holders collectively, to ensure that the debenture-holders receive their interest on their loans regularly and to ensure, on the debenture-holders' behalf, that the company complies with the terms of the debenture by, say, ensuring that the company's assets are properly insured and by insisting that there will always be funds available to repay the debentures. The trustee commonly acts as a registrar for the debenture-holders. Debentures in quoted companies may be traded in the same manner as shares and attract the same stamp duty.

---

[17] Table A, regs 18–22.
[18] A plc must re-issue or cancel the shares in three years (CA 1985. s.146). A private company is not required to do this.

Debentures may be secured, so that when the company receives the loan it grants in favour of the debenture-holder a charge over the company's assets. This must be registered in the normal manner.[19] Where there are many debenture-holders, the company issues a charge in favour of the debenture trust,[20] so that the trustee can monitor the company's adherence to the terms of the charge, and if necessary appoint a receiver (in the case of a floating charge) or enter into possession of the secured subjects (in the case of a standard security or legal mortgage) if the company defaults on its obligations. A secured debenture is generally a safer investment than an unsecured one, but equally may attract a lesser interest rate for the lenders.

Further Reading

Worthington "Shares and Shareholders: Property, Power and Entitlement, Part I" (2001) 22(9) *Company Lawyer* 258–266
Worthington "Shares and Shareholders: Property, Power and Entitlement, Part II" (2001) 22(10) *Company Lawyer* 307–314

---

[19] See Chap. 15.
[20] In England the charge would have to be in favour of the trustee as the representative of the trust.

CHAPTER 6

CAPITAL MAINTENANCE

THE CAPITAL OF A COMPANY

The theory behind capital maintenance

6.01   The theory behind capital maintenance is that shareholders' capital, and other forms of capital, are paid to the company to serve as a fund of last resort for the benefit of creditors. For that reason, the share capital is sometimes known as the "creditors' buffer", in that once all the retained profits have been used up in settling creditors' bills so far as possible, the creditors can then evacuate the fund containing the share capital. In a plc, the issued share capital of £50,000 is intended to provide some reassurance as to a company's credit-worthiness.

Given that the share capital exists for the creditors' benefit, the law has deliberately made it difficult for shareholders to withdraw their capital from the company. If there were no restrictions on withdrawal, the moment there was anything untoward with the company, astute members would promptly withdraw their capital, thus depriving the creditors of much chance of getting their money back, and leaving the less well informed investors to carry the burden of the company's losses. Accordingly if a member wishes to get his capital back from a company in which he has invested, he must either sell his shares, if there is a market for those shares, or persuade the company to buy back his shares using the particular procedures outlined in the Companies Act 1985 (CA 1985), or if the worst comes to the worst, put the company into liquidation.

6.02   The theory of capital maintenance is also extended to prevent the reduction of capital being carried out without proper checks on what is happening to the company's capital, to prevent companies providing financial assistance in any form to enable potential shareholders to acquire shares in their company[1] and to prevent companies paying dividends out of anything other than distributable profits.[2]

---

[1] Except for private companies, as will be explained shortly.
[2] Dividends are dealt with in the next chapter.

The reality of capital maintenance

While the theory is admirable, it is easily undermined. Many private **6.03** companies have an issued share capital of £100, and in theory a company could have an issued share capital of one penny. Furthermore, there is nothing to prevent a company spending all its capital reserves so that there is little left in the capital accounts with which to satisfy creditors.

The rules relating to capital maintenance, with the exception of the rules relating to dividends, are widely seen as complex and lacking commercial justification. The involvement of the court in reductions of capital, at least in private companies, is arguably an unnecessary expense, and does not significantly protect creditors. The rules relating to financial assistance are seen as bewildering. The rules relating to capital maintenance stem from a time when creditors looked much more than they do now to a company's capital for reassurance as to the company's solvency. For this reason the White Paper is suggesting that the concept of authorised capital should be abolished, and that for private companies financial assistance should be both permissible and the procedure greatly simplified. There will also be no need to go to court to reduce a private company's capital, and the process of repurchase and redemption of shares in private companies will be simplified. All this is to be welcomed because nowadays creditors are more interested in net assets, cash flow and interest cover than in share capital.

Types of capital account

There are various types of capital account. The collective nominal **6.04** value of all the issued shares in a company comprises the *issued share capital*. If subscribers paid premiums to acquire newly allotted shares, the collected premiums are paid into a *share premium account* (discussed later). A company's *capital redemption reserve* (or fund) comprises a sum of money equal in value to the nominal value of shares that are redeemed or repurchased by a company. It may be used for paying up bonus shares.[3] A company's *revaluation reserve* is the difference between the historic cost of an asset and its estimated current value. Although it is not normally considered part of a company's capital (since it represents unrealised gains) it too may be used for bonus shares.[4] A company may have other capital reserves if its articles permit. Together these various capital accounts (with the exception of the share capital) amount to the "undistributable reserves" referred to from time to time through the Act.[5]

---

[3] CA 1985, s.170(4).
[4] CA 1985, Sched. 4, paras 4.34(3) and (3A).
[5] For example, CA 1985, s.264(1)(a).

Alteration of capital

6.05   A company may increase its authorised share capital by means of an
ordinary resolution provided there is power to do so under the articles.[6]
If so, the alteration must be indicated in a revised memorandum of
association and the change intimated to the Registrar of Companies.[7]
The authorised share capital may be reduced.[8] The issued share capital
may be consolidated or subdivided[9] or converted into stock.[10]

REDUCTION OF CAPITAL

6.06 A company may nowadays reduce its capital should it need to do so. As
this potentially means that there is less money available for its creditors,
the following procedure has to be followed so that no creditors or
investors have grounds for complaint. The main method of reduction of
capital is to be found in CA 1985, sections 135–141, but a company may
also reduce its capital when a private company buys or redeems its own
shares out of capital,[11] when a company is ordered by the court to buy
back a minority shareholder's shares under the minority protection
provisions of CA 1985, section 459 or following an objection to the
company's alteration of its objects clause,[12] or when a member sur-
renders or forfeits his shares to the company.

**Reasons for reduction of capital under the Companies Act 1985
sections 135–141**

6.07   The main reasons why a company might wish to reduce its capital
are:

> (1) the nominal value of the company's share capital is greater
>   than the value of its assets;
> (2) the company may wish to be rid of a class of shareholders;
> (3) the company may have more capital than it knows what to do
>   with and wishes to return some to the members;
> (4) the company may wish to use unused funds held in a capital
>   account for some other purpose.

Of these reasons, the first is the most common, particularly in plcs,
where the full net worth rule applicable to dividends[13] prevents plcs

---

[6] CA 1985, s.121(2)(a).
[7] CA 1985, s.123.
[8] CA 1985, s.121(2)(e).
[9] CA 1985, s.122.
[10] CA 1985, s.121(2)(c).
[11] CA 1985, ss.171–175.
[12] CA 1985, s.5.
[13] CA 1985, s.264(1).

paying dividends where the net asset value of the company after payment of the dividend would be less than the aggregate of the company's share capital and undistributable reserves. By reducing the company's capital (*i.e.* effectively writing off the loss of some its assets) the company may pay dividends again. The loss must be permanent[14]; and where there is doubt as to whether it will be permanent, the court in one instance in England insisted that there be an undertaking that if the loss were made good, the recovered sums should be placed in an undistributable capital reserve,[15] but in another instance suggested that such recovered sums would not necessarily need to be placed in such a reserve provided adequate arrangements had been already made for the benefit of any creditors.[16] In *Quayle Munro Ltd, Petitioners*[17] the court permitted the petitioners to cancel the share premium account and use the funds therefrom to write off a deficit on the profit and loss account. In addition, the company undertook to place the remaining funds from the share premium account into a special reserve which would not be distributed while the company had outstanding creditors, but which could be used to repay certain preference shareholders and to write off future losses.

The second reason is less common nowadays, because of greater skill **6.08** in drafting the rights attaching to classes of shares. If the company follows the required procedure and pays the members of a class of shares exactly what they would have received in a solvent liquidation, the repaid members have no grounds for complaint, except to the extent that the shares have not provided their expected dividends for as long as might have been anticipated.

House of Fraser v. AGCE Investments Ltd [1987] A.C. 387
House of Fraser attempted to reduce the company's capital and repay AGCE, which had a class of shares which attracted a high preferential dividend. AGCE claimed that the reduction could not be done without their consent, but it was held that reduction of capital had not been stated in their class rights as an alteration of their class rights,[18] that AGCE was receiving exactly what it would have received in a solvent liquidation and that any shareholder stood the risk at any time of his investment being curtailed by the company's liquidation or reduction of capital; House of Fraser was therefore entitled to take advantage of the omission in the drafting of the class rights to reduce its capital by paying back AGCE its share capital.

---

[14] *Re Haematite Steel Co. Ltd* [1901] 2 Ch. 746 at 749 *per* Romer L.J.
[15] *Re Jupiter House Investments (Cambridge) Ltd* [1985] 1 W.L.R. 975.
[16] *Re Grosvenor Press plc* [1985] 1 W.L.R. 980.
[17] 1992 S.C. 24, 1993 S.L.T. 723, [1994] 1 BCLC 410.
[18] One presumes that this was an oversight of the part of AGCE or their advisors; alternatively it may never have occurred to anyone that reduction of capital was a possible means of removing AGCE.

Following the decision in that case, classes of shareholders normally include in the terms attaching to their class rights a provision that there is to be no reduction of capital as it affects their shares without their consent.[19]

The third reason is also uncommon though still valid. Where a company has more funds than it knows what to do with (*i.e.* over-capitalisation), it may choose to return its capital to its members. Provided the creditors, members and potential creditors or investors are content with this, and the repayment is in accordance with the articles, there should be no difficulties with this.[20]

6.09   As for the fourth reason, it is possible to reduce a capital account and use the released funds to pay for some newly acquired asset such as the goodwill of a company the petitioner had purchased.[21]

The main types of reduction of capital

6.10   Under CA 1985, section 135(2) there are three main types of reduction:

> (1) the extinction or reduction of liability on any of the company's shares in respect of capital not paid up (for example, if a company had £1.00 nominal value shares each paid up to the extent of 60 pence only, the company might extinguish the liability to pay the remaining 40 pence per share, thus making the former £1.00 nominal value shares into 60 pence nominal value shares);
>
> (2) the cancellation of any paid up capital which is lost or no longer represented by assets (for example, if a company's issued share capital is £1 million, but its net assets are only £400,000 due to various trading losses, the company could write off £600,000 of share capital);
>
> (3) the repayment of share capital in excess of the company's wants.

The legislation does not exclude other types of reduction[22] but the above are the common ones, and in practice the second is the one most used.

---

[19] Such a provision was upheld in *Re Northern Engineering Industrial Plc* [1993] B.C.C. 267.

[20] *Wilson and Clyde Coal Co. Ltd v. Scottish Insurance Corporation Ltd*, 1949 S.C. (HL) 90.

[21] In *Re Ratners Group plc* [1988] BCLC 685, the share premium account was reduced. The released funds were used to help acquire the goodwill of a company Ratners had taken over.

[22] The wording of s.135(1) states that a company "may", having followed the required procedure, reduce its capital "in any way". For example, it is possible to return capital at a premium (*Re Saltdean Estate Co. Ltd* [1968] 1 W.L.R. 1844, or to use the released funds to pay for the redemption of ordinary shares (*Forth Wines Ltd, Petrs*, 1993 S.L.T. 170).

The procedure for reduction of capital

Under CA 1985, section 135(1) it is permissible to reduce a com- **6.11**
pany's capital provided:

(1) the company's articles permit it (as regulation 34 of Table A
does);
(2) the members pass a special resolution approving the reduction[23]; and
(3) the court approves the reduction.

The role of the court is to ensure that creditors are aware of and
content with the reduction. Accordingly, where the reduction involves

(1) the diminution of liability in respect of unpaid share capital
(*i.e.* writing off the unpaid part of each share);
(2) the payment to a shareholder of any paid-up share capital;
or
(3) in any other case where the court so directs,

creditors must be given the opportunity to object to the reduction.[24] This
is done by making a list of creditors and contacting them by newspaper
advertisement, or better, by writing to each creditor or potential creditor
intimating the proposed reduction to him and indicating the date by
which any objection must be received. Since newspaper advertisements
are potentially misleading, it is permissible to dispense with advertisement except where the reduction is by means of cancelling paid up share
capital unrepresented by assets,[25] provided that all known creditors have
been paid off and those creditors whose claims are contingent or
disputed can have their claims met by sums or bonds paid into court for
the creditors' benefit.[26] The court can compel the company to set aside
funds for such claims if necessary.[27] Members might also object to the
reduction of capital, but provided their interests have been properly
taken care of and there is scrupulous adherence to their rights under the
articles, it will be difficult for them to prevent the reduction taking
place.[28]

Once the court has ordered the reduction, a minute confirming the **6.12**
reduction is sent to the Registrar of Companies who registers it and

---

[23] When there is a vote in a class of shares in respect of the resolution, the members of the
class are expected to vote with "detached altruism" as members of that class, as
opposed to voting according to any other more selfish interests arising out of their
ownership of any other shares in the company and not part of that class of shares: *Re
Holders Investment Trust Ltd* [1971] 1 W.L.R. 583, [1971] 2 All E.R. 289, Ch. Div.
[24] CA 1985, s.136(3).
[25] CA 1985, s.136(6).
[26] CA 1985, s.136(5)(a).
[27] CA 1985, s.136(5)(b).
[28] *Re Ransomes plc* [1999] 4 BCLC 591.

certifies it.[29] The memorandum of association will need to be altered.
The court may, if it chooses, demand that the company publish its
reasons for the reduction of capital and/or change its name to include,
bizarrely, the words "and reduced" after the word "limited" in its
name.[30] If in the process of reduction a plc finds that its capital is less
than £50,000, it must re-register as a private company[31] unless that
matter has already been dealt with in the court's interlocutor.

FINANCIAL ASSISTANCE

6.13 Financial assistance is broadly speaking the provision of financial help[32]
from a company, by way of gift, loan, granting security for a loan or
other means whereby a potential (or existing) shareholder is able to use
the company's (or its subsidiaries') funds, directly or indirectly, to buy
shares in the company, and that company has no net assets, or if it does
have net assets, these assets are reduced by the financial assistance to a
material extent.[33]

The law relating to financial assistance is one of the more unhappy
aspects of the capital maintenance rule. On the one hand it is prohibited
for the good reason that it is not necessarily a good use of the company's
assets for them to be applied to enable a shareholder to acquire shares
in itself; but on the other hand, if the members of a company are content
that the company's assets should be used in this way, and provided
creditors are aware of what is happening, is there any reason why it
should not be permitted? As can be imagined, the opposing policy
objectives make the drafting of the legislation problematic, and it is
widely seen that the current wording of the Act leaves much to be
desired. Financial assistance is also prohibited under the rules applicable
to the Admission of Securities to Listing[34] and the law itself is based on
the Article 23 Second Directive on Company Law.[35]

6.14 Evils that the prohibition is designed to prevent are the practice of
using the company's funds (which could be better used to pay dividends) to help investors acquire shares, with the risk that the investor
might not repay the funds, or the use of the company's assets as security
for a loan granted by a bank to an investor who uses funds borrowed

[29] CA 1985, s.137.
[30] CA 1985, s.137(2)(b) and (a).
[31] CA 1985, s.139(4).
[32] The words "financial assistance" are apparently to be given their normal commercial
meaning: *Charterhouse Investment Trust Ltd v. Tempest Diesels Ltd* [1986] BCLC 1 at
10 *per* Hoffman J. and *Barclays Bank plc v. British and Commonwealth Holdings Ltd*
[1996] 1 BCLC 1 at 40 *per* Aldous L.J.
[33] CA 1985, s.152(1). There is no clear indication as to what is meant by "material" in
these circumstances.
[34] Chap. 9; s.16.
[35] Directive 77/91.

from the bank to take over the company. Once he has the majority of the company's shares in his pocket, he arranges for the company to grant a charge over the company's assets. He then proceeds to sell off the company's assets to repay his loan. In so doing he breaks up the company (sometimes known as asset-stripping) with the separate sold off parts in total being greater in value than his loan. After repayment of the loan and the break up of the company, he should have made a profit at the expense of the collapse of the company. A third evil is the practice of giving favoured shareholders or would-be shareholders the opportunity to acquire shares in the company with minimal risk because the company would offer an indemnity to those shareholders by undertaking to reimburse any losses that the shareholders might suffer if the share price dipped below the acquisition price. In the scandal relating to the Guinness takeover of Distillers in the 1980s certain shareholders were given such indemnities as part of a concerted plan to keep the Guinness share price high (also known as a "share support scheme") so that the Guinness shares would be seen to be desirable to Distillers shareholders. This would encourage them to sell their shares to Guinness.

Financial assistance is in principle unlawful, but that rule is subject to various exceptions, the main one of which is the "whitewash" exception for private companies,[36] to be discussed shortly, and other exceptions to be found in section 153, these being the "principal purpose" exception[37] (also to be discussed shortly), the payment of lawful dividends,[38] the allotment of bonus shares,[39] a court-authorised reduction of capital,[40] the redemption or purchase of shares under CA 1985, sections 159–181,[41] a scheme of arrangement under CA 1985, section 425,[42] anything connected with a winding up in terms of the Insolvency Act 1986 (IA 1986), section 110[43] and a company voluntary arrangement under IA 1986, sections 1–7.

Further exceptions include the lending of money by a commercial **6.15** lender to a shareholder in the ordinary course of business,[44] the provision of financial assistance for an employees share scheme,[45] the provision of financial assistance to help employees and their families acquire shares in their employers' companies[46] and the making of loans to

---

[36] CA 1985, ss.155–158.
[37] CA 198, s.153(1) and (2).
[38] CA 1985, s.153(3)(a).
[39] CA 1985, s.153(3)(b).
[40] CA 1985, s.153(3)(c).
[41] CA 1985, s.153(3)(d).
[42] CA 1985, s.153(3)(e).
[43] CA 1985, s.153(3)(f).
[44] CA 1985, s.153(4)(a), this is designed to cover the situation where a bank lends money to a debtor who then chooses to use his loan to buy shares in the bank.
[45] CA 1985, s.153(4)(b).
[46] CA 1985, s.153(4)(c).

employees other than directors in order to enable those employees to buy shares in their companies or those companies' holding companies.[47] In respect of these further exceptions, where a plc provides the relevant financial assistance, the company may only provide such assistance if the company has net assets[48] which will not be reduced, or if the net assets are reduced by the assistance, the assistance may be provided out of distributable profits.[49]

A foreign subsidiary cannot be prohibited from providing financial assistance to individuals purchasing shares in its United Kingdom holding company.[50]

6.16   Financial assistance is the giving of assistance both for the acquisition of shares[51] and for the purpose of reducing or discharging any liability incurred by an acquirer of shares (or any other person)[52]: this means that it is unacceptable for the company to give or lend money to a would-be purchaser of shares, and that it would be unacceptable for a company to, say, guarantee a loan made by a bank to the purchaser to enable him to buy the shares or to indemnify a would-be purchaser for any loss arising after the acquisition of his shares.[53] If unlawful financial assistance takes place, the company is liable to a fine and the officers of the company may be imprisoned or fined.[54] It is curious that the company could be fined, thus penalising shareholders who may well have known nothing about the financial assistance anyway. As unlawful financial assistance is criminal, it means that transactions "downstream" of the financial assistance may be unenforceable even if the parties involved were unaware of the original assistance.[55] This too is seen as unsatisfactory.

The principal purpose

6.17   If a company is not a private company, and thus able to avail itself of the provisions of the whitewash procedure to be discussed shortly,[56] or

---

[47] CA 1985, s.153(4)(d).

[48] For the purposes of this part, net assets means aggregate assets less aggregate liabilities including reasonably anticipated contingent and prospective liabilities, as indicated by the company's accounting records immediately before the financial assistance is given: s.154(2).

[49] CA 1985, s.154(1). If the company provides a gift by way of assistance, there would be a reduction of net assets and so the assistance would have to provided out of distributable profits; if the company grants a charge over its assets in favour of someone lending to the purchaser of the shares, the net assets are not reduced unless the purchaser defaults on the loan.

[50] *Arab Bank plc v. Mercantile Holdings Ltd* [1994] 1 BCLC 330.

[51] CA 1985, s.151(1).

[52] CA 1985, s.151(2).

[53] CA 1985, s.152(3).

[54] CA 1985, s.151(3).

[55] *Heald v. Connor* [1971] 1 W.L.R. 479, [1971] 2 All E.R. 1105, QBD.

[56] It is not unknown for plcs to become private again to take advantage of the whitewash rules.

if it is a private company and does not wish to go through the whitewash procedure, or if the assistance does not come within the list of exemptions mentioned above, how may assistance legitimately be provided? Is it impossible for a plc to provide financial assistance?

The answer is that section 153(1) states a company may give financial assistance for the purpose of buying shares in a company or its holding company if "(a) the company's principal purpose in giving that assistance is not to give it for the purpose of any such acquisition, or the giving of the assistance for that purpose is but an incidental part of some larger purpose of the company, and (b) the assistance is given in good faith". A similar provision applies in section 153(2) applicable to the provision of assistance by way of reducing or discharging any liability incurred by the purchaser for the purpose of the acquisition.

The words "principal purpose" and "incidental part of some larger   **6.18** purpose" have, however, given rise to much doubt.[57] They were considered in the case of *Brady v. Brady*[58] where two brothers whose group of companies were involved in the drinks and haulage trade engineered a complex reorganisation of their own and their companies' debts and shareholdings. The reason they engineered the reorganisation was to prevent the companies collapsing into deadlock while the brothers bickered. The reorganisation proceeded relatively smoothly until one brother decided that the terms were unsatisfactory for him and sought an excuse for withdrawing from the deal. The prohibition against financial assistance provided that excuse, but the other brother insisted on specific performance and the case eventually went to the House of Lords. The House of Lords specifically addressed the issue of "principle purpose". In order to give meaning to the opaque legislation, Lord Oliver drew a distinction between the "purpose" of the financial assistance, which was to reduce a liability incurred by the purchaser of shares, and the "reason" why a purpose is formed. He stated that the saving of the company from collapse was a by-product of the financial assistance, but would not accept that the avoidance of the collapse of the company was a principal or larger purpose of which the financial assistance was but an incidental part. It is evident that Lord Oliver found the wording of section 153 very difficult, and had trouble making sense of it; but if it comes to that, many people have found trouble making commercial sense of Lord Oliver's decision.[59] His restrictive interpretation of the wording was also not what had been intended by the rewording of the

---

[57] These words, and the good faith requirement, were introduced into the CA 1985 as they were omitted in the Companies Act 1958 which forbad any form of financial assistance. *Belmont Finance Corporation v. Williams Furniture Ltd (No. 2)* [1980] 1 All E.R. 393; and *Armour Hick Northern Ltd v. Whitehouse* [1980] 3 All E.R. 833 both raised issues as to the purpose of the assistance and the good faith of those involved and it was deemed necessary therefore to insert the principal purpose and the good faith rule into the CA 1985.

[58] [1989] A.C. 755, HL; [1988] BCLC 20, CA.

[59] This has not prevented it being followed: *Plaut v. Steiner* (1989) 5 B.C.C. 352.

sections in the CA 1985. What had been intended, it would appear, was that where the financial assistance was a small part of some much more complicated transaction, the financial assistance should be permitted. That this did not happen is not necessarily the fault of the Parliamentary draftsman: the deeper issue is more likely to be that Parliament did not truly understand the significance of the proposed wording, and let it through without proper consideration of its ramifications. To improve matters, the DTI Review[60] states that the *Brady* decision should be reversed and a clearer set of rules inserted instead, because Lord Oliver's decision has done nothing to enable plcs to know whether or not, or to what extent, financial assistance is acceptable.

An ironic feature of the *Brady* case was that Lord Oliver finally granted an order for specific performance on the grounds that as the company involved was a private company, it could have used the whitewash procedure anyway—and indeed was directed to do so.

6.19   So when may financial assistance be lawful? According to the *Brady* case, it would appear that any form of benefiting the shareholder will be unlawful, irrespective of the extent to which that benefit is an incidental part of some larger purpose,[61] unless it comes within one of the recognised exceptions. However where the assistance benefits the company, as opposed to preventing disputes between the members as happened in *Brady*, the financial assistance may be acceptable.[62]

It is to be hoped that any reform of the law will improve matters in this area significantly.[63] Because of the uncertainty arising from the *Brady* case, it is still not known whether certain forms of activity are potentially criminal—these including the payment of a venture capitalist's legal fees by a company in which he has just invested; the payment by a company to a stockbroker or other agent who has found an new investor for the company; the granting of floating charges by newly acquired subsidiaries as part of a continuing obligation under a loan whereby a company undertakes to grant floating charges over itself and all its present and future subsidiaries, irrespective of whether or not the

---

[60] *Modern Company Law for a competitive economy: Completing the Structure*, Chap. 7 and the DTI consultation document: *Company Law Reform: Financial Assistance by a Company for the Acquisition of Shares*.

[61] A management buy-out would normally be considered a "larger purpose" and it might therefore be legitimately possible for, say, company X to grant a security over its own assets to enable a bank to provide funds to enable a management buy-out team (and who used to work for X) to buy X's shares from X's shareholders. The bank would be repaid out of X's profits or the management buy-out team's earnings. But a more prudent course of action would be to ensure that X was a private company and to use the whitewash procedure rather than relying on the uncertain meaning of "larger purpose".

[62] It is no easy matter to think of such circumstances, since the members would indirectly benefit from the successful carrying out of a company's larger purpose.

[63] In many other countries, the USA for example, financial assistance is not seen as criminal or untoward, provided that its operation is transparent and disclosed to investors and creditors alike.

subsidiary was acquired using the lender's funds; and "piggybacking", whereby where illegal financial assistance is taking place, causing market manipulation, but astute investors follow the market any-way—are their trades all illegal too?

The whitewash procedure

A private company may provide financial assistance for the acquisi-tion of shares in itself, or its holding company (assuming that company is private too).[64] If a subsidiary wishes to provide financial assistance to a company to a holding company, and the subsidiary is a subsidiary of a plc, and the plc is itself a subsidiary of its holding company, such assistance is forbidden.[65] The financial assistance must be provided from distributable profits.[66] **6.20**

In order to provide the financial assistance, the members must pass a special resolution[67] to approve the financial assistance, and the direc-tors[68] must furnish the Registrar of Companies with a statutory declara-tion[69] relating to the continued solvency of the company. The resolution must take place within a week of the statutory declaration.[70] The statutory declaration is on a special form containing information about the company, the directors, the person to whom the financial assistance is being made available, together with the principal terms, form and date of the financial assistance. The directors also have to state that they believe that there will be no ground on which the company will be unable to pay its debts immediately after the provision of the financial assistance, that if the company is wound up within 12 months of the date of the financial assistance the company will be able to pay all its debts in full and that it can pay its debts as they fall due throughout the year following the date of the provision of the financial assistance.[71] In order to make their assessment of the company's continuing solvency, the directors should consider the same liabilities as would be relevant under compulsory winding up in terms of IA 1986, section 122.

Since there might be doubt as to the judgement of the directors, an auditors' report is required to indicate that having enquired into the state of the company the auditors are not aware of anything to indicate that **6.21**

---

[64] CA 1985, s.155(1).

[65] CA 1985, s.155(3). It is hard to know if this particular interpretation was what the draftsman intended, or whether what was intended was that there should be no assistance where there was a group involving a plc.

[66] CA 1985, s.155(2).

[67] CA 1985, s.155(4). Wholly owned subsidiaries do not need to do this, but any holding company in which shares are to be acquired following assistance from a subsidiary must also pass a special resolution: s.155(5).

[68] That is, the directors of the company providing the assistance and of the holding company too if applicable.

[69] CA 1985, s.155(6). It may be provided in an electronic form as well: s.155(6A).

[70] CA 1985, s.157.

[71] CA 1985, s.156.

the directors' opinion is unreasonable.[72] If it turns out that the directors' optimism was misplaced, the directors may suffer criminal sanctions.[73]

The directors' declaration, the auditors' report and the special resolution must be sent to the Registrar of Companies within 15 days.

In order to protect members of the company who are unhappy with the financial assistance, holders of 10 per cent or more of the company's issued share capital or any class thereof may apply to the court for the cancellation of the special resolution—but no member who previously voted in favour of the resolution may change his mind and apply to court.[74]

6.22 The assistance must not be provided for a period of four weeks from the resolution (unless the resolution was unanimous)[75] in order to allow time for applications to court. If there is an application the financial assistance will not take place until the application is determined. If there is no application the financial assistance may be provided within eight weeks of the statutory declaration unless the court provides otherwise.[76]

The whitewash procedure is very convenient where it applies, but there are still occasions where a private company for some reason does not go through the procedure, or sometimes tries to wriggle out of an obligation it had entered into previously by saying that the obligation involved financial assistance which was illegal—so the company not need abide by it. However it would appear that receiving a salary, a pension and a bonus from a company for which a shareholder worked in consideration of the transfer of shares from the shareholder to himself and his sons jointly, together with the provision of his services to his company, did not amount to financial assistance.[77]

PURCHASE AND REDEMPTION OF SHARES

6.23 Historically companies could not buy back their own shares. This was to prevent a simple fraud whereby the directors used the company's money to buy shares in the market, thus driving up the price. When the price was high enough, the directors sold their own shares and disappeared, and the remaining company members would then find the company had plenty of its own shares but no funds. Such a fraud was easier where the stock exchange could not monitor transactions as

[72] CA 1985, s.156(4).
[73] CA 1985, s.156(7).
[74] CA 1985, s.157(2).
[75] CA 1985, s.158(2).
[76] CA 1985, s.158(4).
[77] *Parlett v. Guppys (Bridport) Ltd* [1996] 2 BCLC 34.

effectively as can be done nowadays, and where the accounting rules were less closely followed than they are now.

The rules have now been changed, as will be seen shortly. Although a company may not own its own shares,[78] and nor may a subsidiary own its holding company's shares (except as nominee for some other interest[79]), a company may now acquire its own shares,[80] create redemption shares intended to be repurchased by the company, receive a gift of its own shares,[81] accept surrendered and forfeited shares[82] or be required by the court to acquire its members' shares under CA 1985, section 5, section 54 or section 459.

If a plc acquires shares in which it has a beneficial interest, or a **6.24** member's shares are surrendered or forfeited to the company, those shares must be cancelled within three years[83] unless the company provided financial assistance to a person to enable him to buy shares in the company and the company has a beneficial interest in the shares. In that case the time limit is 12 months.[84] If in the process the cancellation of the shares causes the company's issued share capital to fall below £50,000, the company must re-register as a private company.[85] While the company is holding the shares in the period up to their cancellation, no voting rights may be exercised in respect of the held shares.[86] These rules are also extended to shares in a private company which re-registers as a plc.[87]

Reasons for purchase of shares

A company may wish or agree to purchase its shares for the following **6.25** reasons:

- A member may be unable to find any other purchaser for his shares;
- The remaining members may be glad to "pay off" an unwelcome member but lack the funds to do so; instead the company may do so;
- Purchasing shares drives up the share price, thus possibly deterring takeover bidders (though it may also signal that the company has cash to spare and that the shares are undervalued);

---

[78] CA 1985, s.143(1).
[79] CA 1985, s.144. See also *Acatos and Hutcheson plc v. Watson* [1995] 1 BCLC 218.
[80] See CA 1985, ss.159–181.
[81] CA 1985, s.143(3).
[82] CA 1985, s.143(3)(d).
[83] CA 1985, s.146(3(a). There are suggestions that one possible reform to this rule should be that the company may keep such shares in "treasury", ready for re-issue at a later date.
[84] CA 1985, s.146(3)(b).
[85] CA 1985, s.146(2)(b).
[86] CA 1985, s.146(4).
[87] CA 1985, s.148.

- Buying back the shares will normally increase the net asset value per share for the remaining shares even taking account of the cost of re-purchase;
- Buying back the shares will increase the earnings per share for the remaining shares if the company continues to make the same level of profit notwithstanding the loss of capital;
- Employees' shares may be purchased by the company;
- It may be cheaper for the company to operate through borrowed funds (especially if interest rates are low) than to pay high dividends to preference shareholders.

Redemption of shares

6.26   A company, as stated in Chapter 5,[88] may issue shares in the knowledge that those shares will be bought back by the company at a predetermined price and a predetermined time, as determined in the articles. The rules that relate to the funding of the redemption of shares are exactly the same as the rules that relate to the funding of the purchase of shares. Redeemable shares must be fully paid up on redemption.[89] Once both redeemable shares and purchased shares have been redeemed or purchased, the shares must be cancelled[90] though this does not mean that the authorised share capital is reduced.[91]

The process of purchasing shares

6.27   If a company wishes to purchase its shares, there must first be the requisite power under the articles (as there usually will be[92]). If there is no such power, the company will need to pass a special resolution to alter the articles to permit it. If as a result of the repurchase there would be no other shares other than redeemable shares in existence, the purchase may not take place.[93]

There are two methods of purchasing shares: the off-market purchase and the market purchase.

Off-market purchase

6.28   This is designed for shares either in a private company, in a non-quoted plc or occasionally in a quoted plc where the company has been allowed to have private dealings with permission from the relevant investment exchange[94] where the company's securities are normally

---

[88] See para. 5.06.
[89] CA 1985, s.159(3).
[90] CA 1985, s.160(4).
[91] CA 1985, s.160(4).
[92] See Table A, reg. 35.
[93] CA 1985, s.162(3).
[94] Such as the London Stock Exchange or one of the other few recognised investment exchanges that exist.

traded.[95] The last of these is rare, since investment exchanges are not in general keen on private arrangements which may distort the market. An off-market purchase is basically a private transaction between the shareholder who wishes to sell his shares and the company in question.

In order for the off-market purchase to take place, there must first be a contract[96] drawn up between the company and the shareholder,[97] whose terms must be approved by a special resolution of the members,[98] thus giving authority to the directors to make the company enter into the contract; which authority in the case of a plc may not endure more than 18 months from the date of the resolution.[99] The contract must be available for inspection by the members for a period of 15 days before the meeting for the passing of the resolution.[1] In voting on the resolution, the member whose shares are to be repurchased is entitled to vote, but if the votes attaching to those shares that are to be purchased are the ones that cause the vote to reach the required approval level of 75 per cent, those particular votes are to be ignored and the vote should be taken again without voting by the member in respect of the votes attaching to the shares that are about to be purchased.[2] The member is however perfectly at liberty to vote in respect of those of his shares that are not to be purchased.

Market purchase

This takes place where the company's shares are traded on a recog- **6.29**
nised investment exchange, such as the London Stock Exchange, and approval for the purchase only requires an ordinary resolution.[3] The authority for the purchase endures for 18 months, and may be revoked, varied or renewed within that period by ordinary resolution.[4] The authority for which approval is given must specify the maximum number of shares to be acquired and the maximum and minimum prices which may be paid for the shares, together with the date of expiry of the

---

[95] CA 1985, s.163(1), (2).

[96] It is possible to have a memorandum instead if for some reason the parties wish to preserve some degree of confidentiality.

[97] CA 1985, s.164(1).

[98] CA 1985, s.164(2). It is also possible to vary, revoke or renew the terms of the authority given to the directors to make the company enter into the contract: CA 1985, s.164(3).

[99] CA 1985, s.164(4).

[1] CA 1985, s.164(6). It is also possible to have a "contingent purchase contract" which only comes into place on the fulfilment of certain conditions: CA 1985, s.165.

[2] CA 1985, s.164(5).

[3] CA 1985, s.166(2). There is no need for a contract, since shares are being bought in the market-place and it would be impossible to make separate contracts with everyone selling their shares to the company.

[4] CA 1985, s.166(4).

authority.[5] It is also possible to specify the maximum sum that the directors may spend in acquiring the shares, or to draw up an arithmetical formula for calculating how much may be spent acquiring the shares.[6] Where the company in question is listed, the London Stock Exchange must be informed of the transaction.[7]

Assignment of the right to purchase

6.30 Only the company has the right to purchase the shares, and that right may not be assigned.[8]

Contingent purchases

6.31 A company may enter into an option to purchase its own shares. This requires a special resolution and is only available under the off-market procedure.[9]

Disclosure

6.32 If the purchase takes place, within 28 days a Form 169 must be returned to the Registrar of Companies indicating the repurchase of the shares[10] and certain other items of information. A copy of the contract is required to be kept at the company's registered office, no doubt getting in the way and covered in dust, for 10 years.[11] The purchased shares must be cancelled.

Payment for the purchase or redemption

6.33 The method of payment for the purchase or the redemption is the same. The funds for the purchase of the shares, or redemption of redeemable shares, should be provided either out of distributable profits or out of the proceeds of a fresh issue of shares made for the purposes of the redemption. It may also be provided out of a combination of those two methods. As will be seen shortly, it is also possible in a private company to pay for the redemption or the purchase out of capital.[12]

If the purchased or redeemed shares are to be purchased or redeemed at a premium[13] that premium will normally be paid out of the company's distributable profits. However, if the company issued the original

---

[5] CA 1985, s.166(3). There is no virtue in specifying one price for the shares, since the company's purchase of the shares in the market will probably cause the price to fluctuate anyway.

[6] CA 1985, s.166(6).

[7] See the London Stock Exchange Listing Rules, Chap. 15.

[8] CA 1985, s.167.

[9] CA 1985, s.165. Without this prohibition, listed companies could purchase traded options and speculate against the value of their own share price movements.

[10] CA 1985, s.169(1).

[11] CA 1985, s.169(4).

[12] CA 1985, s.171.

[13] *i.e.* the company pays back not only the nominal value of the share but an extra portion as agreed in the original documentation.

shares (which were later purchased or redeemed) at a premium, it is also permissible for the company to pay for the premium on purchase or redemption out of the proceeds of a fresh issue of shares made for the purposes of the purchase or redemption.[14] However, this right is tempered by the requirement that the premium payable on purchase or redemption may only be paid out of the funds arising out of the proceeds of a fresh issue of shares up to an amount equal to whichever is the lesser of

(a) the total premiums received on the original issue of the shares about to be purchased or redeemed, or
(b) whatever happens to be in the share premium account at the time of the purchase or redemption, which amount includes any premiums paid on the issue of the new shares issued for the purpose of paying for the purchase or redemption.[15]

For example, if on the original issue five years ago of 10,000 ordinary **6.34** shares of £1.00 nominal value shares the total premium paid for the shares was, say, £2000, (a) would amount to £2000.

But if since the £2000 was paid into the share premium account, £1000 worth of that share premium account had been used to fund the creation of 1000 bonus shares, and £400 had been used to pay for some expenses arising on the allotment of some other shares, (b) would only amount to £600. The amount that could be taken out of the proceeds of the fresh issues of shares in order to pay for the premium on redemption will be the lesser of (a) or (b), in this case (b). Since that could potentially lead to a diminution of the share capital, the share premium account is reduced by the amount that it is taken out of the proceeds of the fresh issue of shares[16] so that although the share premium account goes down the share capital still reflects the true number of shares in issue.

The point of this provision, which is really an accounting exercise designed to maintain a company's share capital, is that it is possible to evacuate the share premium account if there is not much in it, but it is not possible to have a negative share premium account.

The capital redemption reserve

When a company purchases or redeems its own shares out of distrib- **6.35** utable profits, the company is treated as having cancelled the shares[17] and thereby the company's issued share capital is reduced. As this means a reduction of the creditors' buffer, it is necessary to create a new

---

[14] CA 1985, s.160(1)(a). In paying for the premium, a company might choose to use a combination of distributable profits and the proceeds of a fresh issue of shares.
[15] CA 1985, s.160(2).
[16] CA 1985, s.160(2).
[17] CA 1985, s.160(4).

capital fund, equal in value to the nominal value of the purchased or redeemed shares.[18] This is called the capital redemption reserve.[19] The value of the capital redemption reserve, when added to the reduced share capital, will be equal in value to the company's issued share capital position before the purchase or redemption. By this means the capital maintenance rule is not offended.

If the company already has a capital redemption reserve, each time the company purchases or redeems its own shares out of distributable profits, the company should transfer to the capital redemption reserve a sum equal in value to the nominal value of the purchased or redeemed shares.

6.36   Where the purchase or redemption is funded wholly or partly out of the proceeds of a fresh issue of shares, and those proceeds are less than the nominal value of the purchased or redeemed shares, the balance of the funding will have to be out of distributable profits[20] in which case the difference between the proceeds of the fresh issue and the nominal value of the purchased or redeemed shares is transferred to the capital redemption reserve.[21] There is no requirement to transfer sums to a capital redemption reserve where the funding of the purchase is wholly through the proceeds of a new issue of shares.

The capital redemption reserve may be used for the creation of bonus shares, and the rules relating to reduction of capital, as explained above, apply to this reserve.[22] One effect of the capital redemption reserve is that where a company pays for the purchase or redemption out of distributable profits, not only does the company have to hand over some of its distributable profits to its former shareholder, but it needs to set aside funds which might otherwise be available for distribution (such as retained profits) to be transferred into the capital redemption reserve. There is therefore less available for distribution to shareholders by way of dividend.

Purchase or redemption of own shares out of capital in private companies

The funding arrangements

6.37   Private companies are permitted to pay for the purchase or redemption of their shares out of capital. This is a deviation of the normal capital maintenance rule, and is only permissible because of the strict rules attaching to the procedure—rules in most respects identical with the whitewash rules for financial assistance. The word "capital" in this

---

[18] CA 1985, s.170(1).
[19] Or occasionally known as the capital redemption fund.
[20] Unless it is a private company.
[21] CA 1985, s.170(2).
[22] CA 1985, s.170(4).

context is also not quite the same meaning as "capital" elsewhere,[23] and so includes such funds as a revaluation reserve.

The company must have authority to make such a payment in its articles.[24] The amount that may be taken from capital is known as the permissible capital payment[25] ("PCP") and may be stated as follows:

PCP = the repurchase or redemption price
less any "available profits" of the company (if any) and less the proceeds (if any) of a fresh issue of shares made for the purposes of the purchase or redemption.

For example:

PCP = £100 (the purchase or redemption price)
less available profits of £30 and
less the proceeds of a not very successful fresh issue of shares, £60
= £10.

The term "purchase or redemption price" means the total of the nominal value of the purchased or redeemed shares and any premium payable on purchase or redemption.

The point of the PCP is to ensure that the company uses up such **6.38** distributable profits as it has, followed by the proceeds of any new issue of shares, before it dips into capital. The available profits are the company's normal distributable profits as shown in the accounts in the period of up to three months before the directors' statutory declaration referred to later,[26] but excluding from those profits any sums used by way of financial assistance or the purchase or redemption of shares.[27]

If the PCP plus the proceeds of any fresh issue amount to *less* than the *nominal* value of the share purchased or redeemed, the difference is transferred to the capital redemption reserve.[28]

For example, ABC Ltd agrees to redeem 120 £1.00 nominal value ordinary shares at par, making a total price of £120. The company has available profits of £45. The company has a fresh issue of shares to pay for the redemption, which brings in only £60. The PCP is £120 − £45 − £60 = £15.

Following section 171(4),[29] as the PCP (£15) plus the proceeds of the fresh issue (£60), making £75, is less than the nominal value

---

[23] As for example, in reduction of capital.
[24] CA 1985, s.171(1).
[25] CA 1985, s.171(3).
[26] CA 1985, s.172(6).
[27] CA 1985, s.172(5).
[28] CA 1985, s.171(4).
[29] Taking account of s.171(6), whereby one adds back into the PCP the proceeds of a fresh issue of shares if there are any.

of the redeemed shares (£120), the difference of £45 is transferred to the company's capital redemption reserve.

6.39   However, if the PCP plus the proceeds of any fresh issue amount to *more* than the *nominal* value of the shares purchased or redeemed, it is permissible to reduce the share premium account, capital redemption reserve, fully paid share capital or revaluation reserve by the amount by which the PCP exceeds the nominal value of the shares.[30]

> For example, DEF Ltd agrees to redeem 100 £1.00 nominal value ordinary shares at a premium of 20 pence per share, making a total price of £120. There is no share premium account out of which to pay the premium on redemption. The company has available profits of £15. There was no fresh issue of shares.
> The PCP is £120 − £15 − £0 = £105.
> Following s.171(5),[31] as the PCP of £105 is greater than the nominal value of the redeemed shares (£100), the company's share capital account may be reduced by £5 in addition to the cancellation of the 100 shares, and there is no requirement to transfer any sums to the capital redemption reserve.

As will be seen, the effect of either of these methods ensures that the capital is reduced, in the first case the share capital being reduced by £75, albeit that a capital redemption reserve of £45 is created; and in the second the share capital is reduced by £105, with no requirement to transfer any funds to the capital redemption reserve. Since this makes a mockery of the capital maintenance rule, it is worth noting that apparently originally it was intended that the shortfall in capital in each case was supposed to be made good in subsequent years by the company, but the legislation to that effect was omitted and never seen as sufficiently important since to be worthy of amendment.

Conditions for payment out of capital

6.40   There must be a special resolution of the company[32] which must be passed within one week[33] of the day the directors make a statutory declaration confirming that they have made full enquiry of the affairs and prospects of the company and believe that the company can pay its

---

[30] CA 1985, s.171(5).
[31] Taking account of s.171(6), whereby one adds back into the PCP the proceeds of a fresh issue of shares if there are any.
[32] CA 1985, s.173(1). As with the special resolution for approving the purchase of shares by the company under s.164(5), the votes attaching to the shares that are to be purchased must not be what causes the resolution to be passed. At the meeting the members must be allowed to inspect the directors' declaration and the auditors' report: s.174(4).
[33] CA 1985, s.174(1).

debts on the proposed day of the payment,[34] and that it will continue as a going concern, and able to pay its debts as they fall due,[35] for a further 12 months.[36] In case the directors' opinion is misjudged, the company's auditors are required to produce a report confirming that they too have inquired into the company's state of affairs, that the PCP is properly calculated, and that they are not aware of anything to indicate that the directors' statutory declaration is unreasonable under the circumstances.[37] Should the directors' declaration be found unreasonable at a later date, there are criminal sanctions against them, and under IA 1986, section 76(1)(a) the directors will be required to make good to the company any loss occasioned to their company by their misplaced views.[38]

Within a week of the resolution, the company must publish a note in the *Edinburgh Gazette* and an appropriate national newspaper stating that the company will be using capital to pay for the purchase or redemption of its shares, specifying the amount of the PCP and the date of the resolution, indicating the continuing availability of the directors' declaration and auditors' report[39] for inspection and intimating that any creditor may within five weeks of the resolution apply to the court for an order prohibiting the payment.[40]

6.41 If there is an objection by either a member or a creditor to the proposed payment out of capital, the court must consider the objection but is free to make such order as it sees fit in order to protect the dissentient members or dissentient creditors.[41] But if there is no such objection, the payment may take place within seven weeks of the original special resolution.[42]

Failure to purchase or redeem

6.42 If a company does not purchase or redeem its shares when it said it would, the company will not be liable in damages for its failure to purchase or redeem its shares,[43] and the court will not grant an order for specific implement if the company does not have the distributable profits with which to meet its obligation.[44] If the company is wound up and the purchase or redemption is incomplete by the time of the

---

[34] CA 1985, s.173(3)(a).

[35] In terms of IA 1986, s.122.

[36] CA 1985, s.173(3)(b).

[37] CA 1985, s.173.

[38] It is surprising that this provision applies to the purchase or redemption of shares out of capital, but despite the otherwise similar wording does not apply to financial assistance.

[39] These must also be sent to the Registrar of Companies: s.175(4).

[40] CA 1985, s.175.

[41] CA 1985, s.177.

[42] CA 1985, s.174(1).

[43] CA 1985, s.178(2).

[44] CA 1985, s.178(3).

commencement of the winding up, the members' rights in respect of the purchase or redemption will be postponed to all other debts of the company but is higher than the right to repayment of shareholders' capital, subject to any overriding terms in the articles relating to other shares' rights.[45]

SERIOUS LOSS OF CAPITAL

6.43 If the net asset value of a plc drops to below half or less than the company's issued share capital, the directors must within 28 days of their first awareness of the loss of capital convene an extraordinary general meeting (EGM) of the company to take place within 56 days of that first awareness.[46] Somewhat unhelpfully the legislation does not state what the company is supposed to do at the meeting. One option might be to put the company into voluntary liquidation before things get any worse.

SHARE PREMIUM ACCOUNT

6.44 A share premium account is the account where the premiums paid by subscribers for their newly issued shares are kept. The premium on a share (the difference between its nominal value and the market price paid to acquire it from the company) reflects the desirability of the share to the subscriber. The share premium account may be used to create bonus shares, pay for the company's incorporation expenses, pay the cost of any expenses (including commission) arising from the issue of shares or debentures and paying for the any premium arising on the redemption of debentures.[47] In addition, as already indicated sums in the share premium account may be used under limited circumstances to pay the premium on the re-purchase or redemption of shares.[48] There is no obligation on a company to seek the maximum premium.[49]

Special merger relief rules apply to share premium accounts. Where company A acquires company B, and B's shareholders are offered shares in A as consideration for selling A their shares, and where the total assets in B turn out to be greater in value overall than the value of the A shares offered to the B shareholders in exchange for selling A their shares, that difference in value would in theory normally be credited to the share premium account and would then be undistributable. Since this would then deny A any use of B's excess assets there

---

[45] CA 1985, s.178(5), (6).
[46] CA 1985, s.142.
[47] CA 1985, s.130(2).
[48] CA 1985, s.160(2).
[49] *Cameron v. Glenmorangie Distillery Co. Ltd* (1896) 23 R. 1092.

would be little incentive to carry out takeovers. Accordingly merger relief under CA 1985, sections 131–134 is permitted, whereby if A acquires 90 per cent[50] or more of B's shares and allots B's shareholders shares in A as consideration, the difference between the nominal value of newly allotted A shares (after the takeover) and the actual value of the B shares need not be credited to the share premium account.[51] The same relief applies where the consideration provided by A is a cancellation of any shares in B not already held by A. This means that the funds not credited to the share premium account could be used to pay dividends.

Group reconstruction relief applies where a wholly owned subsidiary **6.45** ("C") allots its holding company or another subsidiary shares in C in exchange for non-cash assets (including shares) from any company ("D") within a group comprising the holding company and C; and where those new C shares are issued at a premium, that premium in excess of the lower of cost or book value of the shares in D need not be credited to the share premium account.[52]

Further Reading

Cabrelli "In dire need of assistance? Sections 151–158 of the Companies Act 1985 revisited" (2002) J.B.L. 272–291

DTI Consultation Document October 1999, *Company Formation and Capital Maintenance*

DTI Consultation Document June 2000, *Capital Maintenance: Other Issues*

Davies *Gower's Principle of Modern Company Law* (6th ed., Sweet and Maxwell, 1997), Chap. 11

---

[50] This applies whether company A is acquiring all 90 per cent at once or if it is merely acquiring, say, 40 per cent of B's shares, having purchased 50 per cent of the shares on some previous occasion.
[51] CA 1985, s.131.
[52] CA 1985, s.132.

CHAPTER 7

DIVIDENDS AND ACCOUNTS

7.01   In the previous chapter we discussed the important principle of maintenance of capital. Part of this principle is that dividends may only be paid out of distributable profits and not out of capital. It is therefore necessary to define what is meant by "distributable profits". Distributable profits as a term is defined in the Companies Act 1985 ("CA 1985") primarily[1] at CA 1985, section 263(3):

> "For the purposes of this Part [of CA 1985], a company's profits available for **distribution** are its **accumulated**, **realised profits**, so far as not previously utilised by distribution or **capitalisation**, less its accumulated, **realised losses**, so far as not previously written off in a **reduction** or **reorganisation** of capital duly made."

These terms may be taken in order.

Distribution

7.02   Under the CA 1985, section 263, distribution means any method of handing back the company's assets to the members, whether in cash or in the form of any other assets of the company, with the exception of the following:

- an issue of partly or fully paid bonus shares[2];
- the redemption or purchase of any of the company's own shares out of capital (including the proceeds of any new issue of shares) or out of unrealised profits[3];
- the reduction of share capital in terms of the CA 1985, section 135(2)(a) or (c) (extinction or reduction of shareholders' liability

---

[1] There is an alternative definition of "distributable profit" at CA 1985, s.152(2) in the context of financial assistance.
[2] CA 1985, s.263(2)(a). See also Chap. 5.
[3] CA 1985, s.263(2)(b).

in respect of share capital not fully paid up, or the repayment to shareholders of paid-up share capital)[4];
- a distribution of assets on winding up.[5]

Accumulated

"Accumulated" means that previous year's profits, if they have not **7.03** been used for any other purpose, are amalgamated with the current year's profits and create an overall figure, known as the accumulated profits. The same principle applies to losses. Although historically if a company had suffered losses for several years and then made a profit, it was allowed to distribute that profit in the form of dividend, this is not now possible because of the use of the word "accumulated" in section 263(3) in respect of both profits and losses. In other words, a company must make good its accumulated losses out of subsequent profits before it starts to pay dividends—unless it reduces its capital in terms of CA 1985, section 135.

Realised profits and realised losses

"Realised profits" and "realised losses" are defined in CA 1985, **7.04** section 262(3). They are such profits and losses as:

> "fall to be treated as realised in accordance with principles generally accepted, at the time when the accounts are prepared, with respect to the determination for accounting purposes of realised profits or losses.
> This is without prejudice to—
>
> > (a) the construction of any other expression (where appropriate) by reference to accepted accounting principles or practice, or
> > (b) any specific provision for the treatment of profits or losses of any description as realised."

Profits must actually have arisen by the balance sheet date.[6] When an asset is sold at a profit, the profit will be recorded as a profit on the day of sale. However, if the asset is sold on credit, the profit is not treated as realised until payment has been made. Even if an asset has been upwardly revalued, the increase in value is not treated as a realised profit until the day of sale. Any interim increase in value prior to sale may instead be credited to a revaluation reserve.[7]

---

[4] CA 1985, s.263(2)(c).
[5] CA 1985, s.263(2)(d).
[6] CA 1985, Sched. 4, para. 12(a).
[7] See CA 1985, Sched. 4, Pt II which sets out company accounting principles.

7.05   "Principles generally accepted" is a deliberately vague term which covers the idea that accounting principles change over time and that it would be an impossible task to state exactly what principles would currently be applying. Without such a term there would need to be endless updating of the legislation to take account of new accounting principles as they are gradually adopted. Generally the phrase "principles generally accepted" puts the onus on companies to explain why they are using principles other than those generally agreed to be best practice. By way of limited help, there are two main sets of guidelines, these being Statements of Standard Accounting Practice ("SSAPs"), issued by the Accounting Standards Committee, and Financial Reporting Standards ("FRSs"), issued by the Financial Reporting Council. The FRSs are gradually replacing the SSAPs. When directors are preparing their companies' accounts, they have to state that the accounts have been prepared in accordance with applicable accounting standards (*i.e.* SSAPs and FRSs) and any material departures from those standards must be explained.[8] In *Lloyd Cheytham & Co. Ltd v. Littlejohn & Co.*[9] the judge stated that SSAPs are "very strong evidence as to what is the proper standard to which should be adopted and unless there is some justification, a departure from this will be regarded as constituting a breach of duty."[10]

Although a realised profit must genuinely have arisen, unrealised losses do not always have to have arisen at the time of the preparation of the accounts but as a matter of prudent accounting practice it is required that the accounts take the potential losses into consideration even if the actual losses do not take place for some time, if at all. Or to put it another way, although unrealised profits are not treated as realised profits, unrealised losses will sometimes be treated as realised losses. For example, under CA 1985, section 275(1) a provision,[11] such as a claim for damages following a negligence claim against the company, is treated as a realised loss. Although the company might ultimately win the case, the company's accounts should in the meantime be drawn up on the assumption that the claim against the company will be successful.

7.06   There is a proviso to the above rule concerning the unrealised losses provisions in CA 1985, section 275(1), namely, that if:

(a)   there is a revaluation of all the fixed assets of the company, or all the fixed assets save goodwill, and

---

[8] CA 1985, Sched. 4, para. 36A.

[9] [1987] BCLC 303.

[10] This case actually dealt with the liability of auditors, but it nonetheless established the principle of judicial approval of SSAPs.

[11] A future liability uncertain as to the amount or the date on which it may be due: CA 1985, Sched. 4, para. 89.

(b) the revaluation indicates that an unrealised profit overall in respect of all the revalued fixed assets (with or without goodwill) has been made,

(c) any one fixed asset which—

    (i) has in fact diminished in value, and

    (ii) whose diminution in value would normally be treated therefore as a provision,

need not have its diminution in value treated as a provision or as a realised loss.

It can therefore be set against the unrealised profits of the rest of the revalued assets.[12] This takes account of the realistic view that if all but one of a company's assets have gone up in value it is not unreasonable to set off the diminished value of the one fixed asset against the general upwards revaluation.

Unless the fixed asset or assets have actually been properly revalued **7.07** by an independent valuer, as opposed to merely being considered, the directors must have satisfied themselves (generally as evidenced by a board minute) that the overall current value of the assets is greater than the value that is stated for the assets in the company's account.[13] If the directors are satisfied that the revaluation figure for all the fixed assets is greater than the original historic-cost figures stated in the accounts, they must say so in a note to the accounts.[14] They must also state that they did genuinely consider the value of the assets in question and that their consideration is treated as a revaluation.[15] As the directors' consideration of their company's assets will no doubt be viewed with a certain scepticism, in practice it is wise to have the company's assets independently valued.

As a further part of the rules on revaluation, CA 1985, section 275(2) states that if:

    (iii) any fixed asset is revalued, and

    (iv) thereby makes an unrealised profit, and

    (v) on or after the revaluation a sum ("A") is taken off the value of the asset in respect of depreciation for each year (or such other period), and

    (vi) prior to the revaluation a sum ("B") used to be taken off the value of the asset in respect of depreciation,

the difference between A and B is treated as a realised profit.

---

[12] CA 1985, s.275(1).
[13] CA 1985, s.275(5).
[14] CA 1985, s.275(6).
[15] CA 1985, s.275(6)(a).

7.08   The reason for this is that if the depreciation is done on a percentage basis, an asset that was worth, say, £50,000 and was depreciated at the rate of 10 per cent a year would suffer a realised loss of £5,000 each year until such time as it written off. The figure of £5,000 represents B. If that property was revalued and now found to be worth £200,000, the annual depreciation charge would be £20,000. The figure of £20,000 would represent A in the above paragraph. The company might have been able to bear £5,000 a year as part of its losses, but £20,000 might impose an intolerable strain on its profits, and its profits might all be eaten up by the depreciation charge. What the CA 1985, section 275(2) allows the company to do is to treat £20,000 − £5,000 (*i.e.* A − B) = £15,000 as realised profit. Effectively the company may, if it wishes, continue to use the pre-revaluation depreciation charge.

Following this procedure may in practice suggest an unrealistic view of the company's accounts. Therefore, although the directors are permitted to treat the depreciation charge in this way, there must be a note in the accounts stating why the more usual statutory depreciation method has not been followed.[16]

If for some reason the original value of a fixed asset is not known, the earliest available recorded figure after the asset's acquisition will be deemed to be its acquisition value.[17]

Capitalisation

7.09   This means the conversion of retained and current net profits into bonus shares.

Written off

7.10   This means treated as no longer present in the accounts either as an asset or a liability.

Reduction

7.11   This means reduction in terms of the CA 1985, section 135 or any other permitted reduction such as the redemption or repurchase of a private company's own shares out of capital.

Reorganisation

7.12   Reorganisation means any valid form of rearrangement of capital such as a scheme of arrangement under the CA 1985, section 425 (see Chapter 19), or a reorganisation following, for example, a successful minority petition under the CA 1985, section 459.

---

[16] CA 1985, Sched. 4, para. 36A.
[17] CA 1985, s.275(3).

DISTRIBUTABLE PROFITS

Distributable profits are the net profits (*i.e.* profits after deduction of all **7.13** overheads) available for the payment of dividends to the members, either in cash or assets of the company (known as "specie"). The dividend is the amount of profit per share that the directors consider appropriate or is required (depending on the articles) to pay out of the company's distributable profits to the shareholders. Not all the profits of a company are usually paid out in dividends: what is not paid out is known as "retained profit" or "undistributed reserves". A prudent company always keeps enough retained profit to meet any unexpected liabilities, but not so much that the members claim that there is a poor income arising from their investment.

Furthermore, no distribution may be made except out of profits available for the purpose.[18] A company may not use the proceeds of an issue of new shares[19] nor use its existing capital to pay dividends, as that offends the principle of capital maintenance. The capital exists for the benefit of those who trade with the company. Directors who knowingly permit the payment of capital as dividend will be personally liable for the loss to the company and potentially to the company's creditors.

Non-cash dividends and revaluations

If any company is making a distribution of a non-cash asset, and that **7.14** non-cash asset has been revalued so that its book value (and therefore the value being placed on it for the purposes of the distribution) contains an element of unrealised profit (being the difference between its original value and its revalued value), that element of unrealised profit is deemed to be a realised profit[20] and the distribution itself is deemed to be legal—which it might not otherwise be, since normally one cannot distribute any part of an unrealised profit.

Treatment of development expenditure

Research and development expenditure can be dealt with by three **7.15** methods:

    (1) The costs can be paid for as they are incurred.
    (2) The company may choose to carry forward all the development costs together, and charge them all against the first year of sales. This would mean that:

---

[18] CA 1985, s.263(1).

[19] Paying dividends out of capital contributed by new shares is known as a "Ponzi" fraud, after an infamous American fraudster of that name who carried out this simple and much replicated fraud.

[20] CA 1985, s.276.

(a) the profits for the years while development was taking place would not show the extent of the development costs,

(b) the first year of production would be unlikely to show much profit for the new product, but (assuming it was successful)

(c) subsequent years might show very good profits.

(3) The company may save up all the costs until such time as the product is ready, and then set the costs off over a period of years during the time that the product is selling (also known as "amortisation").

Method (1)

7.16   Method (1) would require the development costs to be treated as a realised loss as they arose.[21]

Method (2)

7.17   Under method (2) the development costs are still treated as a realised loss, except where there is an unrealised profit arising out of any revaluation of those costs. The unrealised profit can be set against the realised loss of all the other development costs.[22]

Method (3)

7.18   Method (3) is also possible, but there must be special circumstances which justify the directors using this method.[23] Those circumstances must be explained in the notes to the accounts.[24]

Relevant accounts

7.19   Dividends can only be paid out of distributable profits, and distributable profits can only be calculated by reference to the company's accounts as prepared by the directors. Schedule 4 to the CA 1985 sets out extensive rules for the layout of accounts, the notes to the accounts and many other details. In order to calculate the distributable profits, one must refer to the last annual accounts made up to the most recent accounting reference date in respect of which the accounts were prepared[25] and tabled at a general meeting,[26] or, in the case of private companies which have been exempted from tabling their accounts at a general meeting following an elective resolution to that effect, sent to

[21] CA 1985, s.269(1).
[22] CA 1985, s.269(2).
[23] CA 1985, s.269(2)(a).
[24] CA 1985, s.269(2)(b).
[25] CA 1985, s.270(3).
[26] CA 1985, s.241.

the members.[27] Except where the company is exempt from the auditing requirements because of its small size[28] the accounts must be audited, and the auditors must indicate that the accounts give a true and fair view of the balance sheet and the profit and loss account.

The auditors must also state in their report on the accounts whether any qualification they are making to the report is material (*i.e.* significant and worth being concerned about) for determining whether the company would contravene CA 1985, sections 263–265 by making its proposed distribution. If it is a material qualification, the company should not make the distribution at all, or if it has already been made, it should not have been and may be required to be reimbursed so far as that is feasible. Such a distribution is classed as "unlawful" in terms of CA 1985, section 277, discussed later in this chapter.

Initial accounts

If the directors wish to declare a final dividend before the end of the company's first accounting reference period, they may refer to its initial accounts,[29] prepared in the same manner as ordinary accounts.[30] No auditor's certificate for initial accounts is required if the company is a private company, but if it is a public company, an auditors' report is required.[31] This must state any material qualification which affects the company's ability to make a distribution and which would make the distribution unlawful as above.[32] **7.20**

Interim accounts

A company may pay a dividend on the basis of interim accounts.[33] These do not need to be audited even in the case of public companies as there is no subsection specifically stating the need for auditing. Initial and interim accounts for public companies must be filed with the Registrar of Companies[34] (CA 1985, sections 273(6) and 272(4)). **7.21**

DISTRIBUTION RULES FOR PUBLIC LIMITED COMPANIES

Although a private company may not pay a dividend unless its accumulated realised profits are greater than its accumulated realised losses, **7.22**

---

[27] CA 1985, s.252(3).
[28] CA 1985, s.249A.
[29] CA 1985, s.270(4)(b).
[30] CA 1985, s.273(3).
[31] CA 1985, s.273(4).
[32] CA 1985, s.273(5).
[33] CA 1985, s.270(4)(a).
[34] CA 1985, ss.273(6) and 272(4).

there is a further rule for the payment of dividends that applies to public limited companies, known as the "net assets rule"[35]:

A public company may only make a distribution at any time—

(a) if at that time the amount of its net assets is not less than the aggregate of its called up share capital and undistributable reserves, and

(b) if, and to the extent that, the distribution does not reduce the amount of those assets to less than that aggregate.[36]

What this means in practice is that before any distribution is made,

(a) the net assets must be greater than the total of the called-up share capital and the undistributable reserves, and

(b) the payment of the proposed distribution must not cause the net assets to amount to less than that total of the called-up share capital and the undistributable reserves.

So, for example, if a company has net assets of £100,000, share capital of £50,000 and a share premium account of £10,000, the maximum distributable profits that could be distributed by way of dividend is £100,000—50,000—10,000 = £40,000. Any payment in excess of £40,000 would cause the net asset to fall below the required aggregate figure.

7.23   The term "undistributable reserves" is defined in CA 1985, section 264(3) as any of the following:

- share premium account;
- capital redemption reserve;
- the amount by which the company's accumulated unrealised profits, less any unrealised profits capitalised into bonus shares, exceed its accumulated unrealised losses, in so far as these have not been written off in a reduction of capital (*i.e.* its revaluation reserve);
- any other reserve which the company is prohibited from distributing either under statute or under the terms of the company's memorandum or articles.

A public limited company may not treat any uncalled share capital as an asset in terms of the net asset rule.[37]

There are special distribution rules for investment companies.[38]

---

[35] It is also sometimes known as the "full net worth" rule.
[36] CA 1985, s.264(1).
[37] CA 1985, s.264(4).
[38] CA 1985, ss.265, 266 (1)(a) and (b).

Payment of dividends

It is common for companies to pay final dividends and interim **7.24**
dividends, interim usually being half-yearly. A few companies pay
dividends quarterly. How dividends are to be paid is normally stated in
the articles, but commonly:

- a full dividend is only payable on a fully paid-up share, partly
  paid shares attracting only a proportion of the dividend;
- unless the articles say otherwise, there is no automatic right of
  the members to a dividend. The directors recommend the
  amount of the dividend to the members at a general meeting. The
  members then pass an ordinary resolution to approve the level of
  dividend or reduce it, but not increase it[39];
- dividends are payable in cash or in assets of the company[40];
- a dividend is a debt due to the members only once it has been
  declared. It is a deferred debt in a liquidation, and shareholders
  will only get their outstanding dividends once preferential and
  ordinary creditors have been paid[41];
- dividends can be paid in the form of further shares of the
  company provided there is sufficient authorised capital and unissued share capital to do so, and provided the company's articles
  permit it;
- dividends suffer tax before payment, so that the investor receives
  his dividend less the tax paid on it, on the investor's behalf, by
  the company. If the investor has a low income he may be able to
  reclaim the tax already paid; if he has a high income he may
  have to pay additional tax later;
- interim dividends do not need the approval of the members in
  general meeting;
- dividends are normally paid by cheque or paid straight into the
  shareholder's bank account. In the case of joint ownership of a
  share, the dividend is normally paid to the first-named holder
  unless there is written notice otherwise;
- unclaimed dividends are normally forfeited after a period of time
  specified in the articles. Table A provides for 12 years before
  forfeiture;
- in order to pay the dividends, companies may close their shareholders' registers for a period of time prior to the payment in
  order to send out the dividend cheques. Alternatively, dividends
  will be payable to all those registered as members on the date
  selected by the directors as the date of payment. The purchase

---

[39] Table A, reg. 102.
[40] Table A, reg. 105.
[41] IA 1986, s.74(2)(f).

price of the share will reflect whether the share is sold with a due dividend (known as cum) or if it is sold without (ex);
- an investor has a period of up to five years[42] in which to sue for non-payment of a declared dividend.[43]

Members' liability for an improper distribution

7.25   Under the CA 1985, section 277(1), any member of a company who receives a distribution knowing that the payment of the distribution was in contravention of the CA 1985, sections 263–265 is liable to repay it. This does not preclude any other liability to repay the distribution which might arise, say, through being a company officer.[44]

A member who receives an improper dividend, even if he does not know or has no reason to believe that the dividend is improper, may still be liable if there is a clause in the articles specifying this, or he has otherwise accepted liability. CA 1985, sections 277 and 281 also catch members who knowingly receive distributions (or other payments that were in essence distributions even if disguised as something else) that are illegal.[45] A purported ratifying resolution in general meeting by the recipients of the dividend cannot validate a payment that is illegal.[46]

Directors' liability for an improper dividend

7.26   Directors who negligently authorise a payment of a dividend which is improper are under common law jointly and severally liable for the sums paid on the grounds of the breach of their fiduciary duty[47] unless they can convince the court under the CA 1985, section 727 that they acted reasonably and honestly with regard to all the circumstances.[48] If the directors relied on accounts that were carelessly drawn up by accountants, or negligently audited, any liability suffered by the directors might then be passed on by them to the accountants or auditors. This, however, would not be a matter of concern to the members of the company or the company itself. This is because it is the directors' duty to ensure that the accounts present a true and fair view of the company's financial state. Directors who cause the company to be wound up because of unjustified distributions might also find that the liquidator

---

[42] Prescription and Limitation (Scotland) Act 1973, s.6.

[43] In England the position is five years: Limitation Act 1980, s.5.

[44] CA 1985, s.277(2).

[45] *Aveling Barford Ltd v. Perion Ltd* [1989] BCLC 626. In this case a subsidiary arranged for one of its assets to be sold at a considerable undervalue to its holding company, thus effectively making an illegal return of capital.

[46] *Precisions Dippings Ltd v. Precisions Dippings (Marketing) Ltd* [1986] Ch. 447.

[47] *Re Exchange Banking Co. (Flitcroft's Case)* (1882) 21 Ch. D. 519, CA; *Bairstow v. Queens Moat Houses plc* [2000] I BCLC 549; *Allied Carpets Group plc v. Nethercott* [2001] B.C.C. 81.

[48] *Re D'Jan of London Ltd* [1994] BCLC 561: this case concerns relief under s.727, though it is not a case dealing with the wrongful payment of dividends.

could ask the court under the IA 1986, section 218 to refer the matter to the prosecuting authorities. The directors might also be disqualified under the Company Directors Disqualification Act 1986.

Reform

The White Paper is proposing to revisit the rules relating to distribu- **7.27** tions and to codify them in a coherent manner in conjunction with advice from the Accounting Standards Board.

ACCOUNTING RECORDS

Under CA 1985, section 221(1) every company must keep accounting **7.28** records which are sufficient to show and explain the company's transactions, which disclose with reasonable accuracy, at any time, the financial position of the company at that time, and enable the directors to ensure that any balance sheet and profit and loss account complies with the requirements of CA 1985.

The accounts should record all receipts and expenditure and contain a record of the company's assets and liabilities.[49] Failure by the directors, without good excuse, to keep such records may well interest the Inland Revenue or Customs and Excise, be potential grounds for disqualification as a company director[50] or be grounds for prosecution.[51] Accounting records must be kept for three years for private companies and for six years for plcs.[52] The records will normally be kept at the company's registered office and are open to inspection by the company's officers at any time.[53] For reasons of commercial confidentiality members normally do not have access to the accounting records unless the company's articles permit it.[54]

Preparation and publication of accounts, directors' reports and auditors' reports

The accounts will normally[55] include a balance sheet, made up to the **7.29** end of the company's financial year, and a profit and loss account for the same period.[56] These accounts must give a true and fair view of the

---

[49] CA 1985, s 221(2).
[50] Company Directors Disqualification Act 1986, Sched. 1.
[51] CA 1985, s.221(5).
[52] CA 1985, s.222(5).
[53] CA 1985, s.221(1).
[54] Table A, reg. 109, permits access under statute or where authorised by the directors or members following an ordinary resolution.
[55] Listed companies are expected to include more information by way of accounts than non-listed companies.
[56] CA 1985, s.226(1).

company's financial position[57] and the form and content must comply
with the provisions of the CA 1985, Schedule 4. There are many notes
to the accounts may be used to explain any deviations from standard
accounting practice. Listed companies are expected to provide a great
deal more by way of explanatory notes than non-listed companies; and
listed companies also need to provide cash-flow statements.

The true and fair view

7.30   Under the EC Fourth Directive[58] annual accounts are required to give
a "true and fair view" of the company's assets, liabilities, financial
position and profit or loss.[59] Although there is no satisfactory definition
of "true and fair view", the consensus seems to be that a true and fair
view is that which accountants versed in company accounts consider in
the context of company law to be a true and fair view: some might call
this a circular definition. SSAPs[60] and FRSs[61] promulgated by the
Accounting Standards Board and its successor the Financial Reporting
Council try to maintain common standards in accounting so that
accounts should present true and fair views of companies' financial
positions.[62]

Accounting reference date

7.31   The accounts are made up to the end of the company's financial year.
A company's first financial year is from the date of its incorporation
until its accounting reference date—or up to seven days before or after,
at the directors' discretion,[63] provided that the period between those two
dates may not be less than six months nor greater than 18 months.[64]
Although a company may change its accounting reference date, in the
absence of any change, a company will have an accounting reference
date which ends on the last day of the month in which the anniversary
of its incorporation falls.[65] If this date is unsuitable, the company may,
within nine months of its incorporation, alter its accounting reference
date by sending the Registrar of Companies a Form 224 altering the
date[66] (CA 1985, section 224(2)). One reason for altering the date is to

---

[57] CA 1985, s.226(2).
[58] Directive 78/855.
[59] CA 1985, s.226(2).
[60] Statements of Standard Accounting Practice.
[61] Financial Reporting Standards.
[62] Since the Enron scandal in the USA, attention has been much focused on the intelligibil-
    ity and probity of accounts. Companies and their auditors have had to pay more
    attention than hitherto to the reality of the financial position and the need for accounts
    to be as truthful as possible.
[63] CA 1985, s.223(2).
[64] CA 1985, s.224(4).
[65] CA 1985, s.224(3) and 3A.
[66] CA 1985, s.224(2).

make a newly created subsidiary company have the same accounting reference date as its parent company.

A company's subsequent financial years

A company's subsequent financial year begins with the day that **7.32** immediately follows the company's last financial year and ends with the last day of its next accounting period (or up to seven days before or after, at the directors' discretion).[67] Normally an accounting reference period will be 12 months after the end of the previous one, unless altered by using the requisite form though it may be lessened or increased according to circumstances.[68] No change in the accounting reference date is possible if it means that an accounting reference period will be longer than 18 months[69] or if the company has already extended the accounting reference period within the previous five years (unless the Secretary of State grants a special exemption).[70] This five-year rule will not, however, apply if the purpose of the extension is to make the accounting reference dates of parents and subsidiary companies or undertakings coincide[71] or if an administration order under Part II of the IA 1986 is in force.[72]

Auditors

Auditors are required to check that the directors' assessment of the **7.33** accounts is correct. This topic is dealt with in Chapter 10.

The auditors' report must state whether, in the auditors' opinion, the accounts have been properly prepared in accordance with the Companies Acts, and whether a true and fair view has been given of the balance sheet, profit and loss account and of the consolidated accounts in the case of a group.[73] The auditors' report must be signed by the auditors[74] and a copy (usually the one signed by the directors) must be lodged with the Registrar of Companies.[75] When the auditors are preparing their report, they are required to investigate:

- whether proper accounting records have been kept[76];
- whether proper returns for the purposes of the audit have been sent from branches of the company which the auditors have not been able to visit[77];

---

[67] CA 1985, s.223(3).
[68] CA 1985, s.225.
[69] CA 1985, s.225(6).
[70] CA 1985, s.225(4).
[71] CA 1985, s.224(a).
[72] CA 1985, s.225(4)(b).
[73] CA 1985, s.235(2).
[74] CA 1985, s.236(1).
[75] CA 1985, s.236(3).
[76] CA 1985, s.237(1)(a).
[77] CA 1985, s.237(1)(a).

- whether the company's individual accounts are in agreement with the accounting records and returns[78].

7.34   If the auditors form the view that proper accounts and returns have not been kept or made, or if the auditors fail to obtain the information and explanations necessary for the preparation of the audit, they must say so in their report on the accounts.[79] They should also disclose in their report any information about directors' earnings, pensions, compensation or loans which might not otherwise be shown in the accounts.[80] Auditors are also required to qualify[81] their report if there are matters which might materially affect the ability of the company to make distributions.[82] These matters are stated in the CA 1985, section 270(2), being:

- profits,
- losses,
- assets and liabilities,
- provisions (*i.e.* depreciation, diminution in value of assets, retentions for liabilities),
- share capital, and
- reserves.[83]

Since August 11, 1994 certain small companies may be exempt from supplying audited accounts. Under such circumstances there is no need for an auditors' report. This will be discussed in the context of small companies later in this chapter.

Charities

7.35   In order to ensure that charities' money is properly accounted for, there are special rules relating to the accounts and audit of charities.[84]

Directors' report

7.36   The directors' report[85] states who the directors are and have been during the financial year, the principal activities of the company and its subsidiaries, and any significant changes from previous years. There is normally a review of the business of the company over the financial

---

[78] CA 1985, s.237(1)(b).
[79] CA 1985, s.237(2), (3).
[80] CA 1985, s.237(4).
[81] "Qualify" in this context means indicate by means of clause or statement in the report that the accounts are unsatisfactory or inadequate for some specified reason. It is obviously a matter of some concern to a company if its auditors' report is qualified.
[82] CA 1985, s.271(4).
[83] CA 1985, s.270(2).
[84] CA 1985, s.249A2, A(3), A(3A), A4, and s.249C.
[85] CA 1985, s.234.

year, a statement as to the forthcoming prospects for the company and the recommendation of the directors as to the level of dividend. Schedule 7 of CA 1985 requires the directors' report to state or provide:

- any changes in the value of the company's assets, directors' shareholdings, political and charitable contributions;
- information concerning the company's acquisition of its own shares or any charges on the company's shares;
- information about the training, employment and advancement of disabled people;
- information about the health, safety and welfare at work of the employees;
- information about the involvement of employees in the "affairs, policy and performance" of the company.

The directors' report is approved by the board of directors and signed on its behalf by a director or the company secretary.[86] The accounts are first approved at a board meeting[87] and then signed.[88] The directors' report, the accounts and the auditors' report are sent to all the members, debenture-holders and anyone else entitled to see a copy of the accounts[89] and a signed copy of each document, signed by a director or secretary as far as the directors' report and accounts are concerned and by the auditors for their report, must be sent to the Registrar of Companies.[90] It is common for the directors' report, the accounts and the auditors' report to be considered at a forthcoming annual general meeting, but in fact they may be tabled and approved at any general meeting, and in the case of a private company which has made an election in terms of CA 1985, section 252 to dispense with laying of accounts and reports at general meeting, there is no need to lay the accounts before a general meeting at all.[91]

---

[86] CA 1985, s.234A(1). Some directors resent the amount of effort that is required in the production of the report and the notes to the accounts. Sir Ron Brierley, chairman of Guinness Peat plc, memorably described his company's annual report in 2002 as "a product of the unceasing demands of a proliferating range of "corporate governance" academics and "do gooders", which results in pages and pages of superfluous dross, which is utterly meaningless but nevertheless expensive to compile" (*The Independent*, June 5, 2002).

[87] CA 1985, s.233(1).

[88] CA 1985, s.233(2).

[89] CA 1985, s.238.

[90] CA 1985, ss.234A(3), 233(4) and 236(3).

[91] It is however possible to revoke the elective resolution for dispensing with the requirement to lay the accounts before general meeting: such a revocation only requires an ordinary resolution and there are mechanisms to enable a shareholder to require the laying of accounts (CA 1985, s.253).

Time for lodging of accounts and reports

7.37   As indicated above, all companies are required to lay the accounts
and reports before a general meeting (except those which have elected
not to or dormant companies).[92] All companies must deliver a signed
copy of their accounts and reports to the Registrar of Companies.[93] The
time-limits for laying and delivering are as follows:

(a) for a private company, 10 months after the end of its accounting reference period[94];

(b) for a public company, seven months after the end of its
accounting reference period.[95]

If a company's first accounting reference period is greater than 12
months, the maximum period before laying and delivery is 10 (for a
private company) or seven (for a public) months from the first anniversary of the incorporation of the company[96]; or three months from the
end of the accounting reference period,[97] whichever is the later.

7.38   This means that a private company could have up to 22 months before
its first accounts had to be laid and delivered, and a public company
could have up to 19 months. Listed companies require the accounts and
reports to be laid and delivered within six months of the end of the
company's financial year.[98] Failure to lay and deliver the accounts is
treated very seriously by the Registrar of Companies and incurs substantial penalties.[98a] The directors can also be personally prosecuted for
failure to lodge the accounts in time.[98b]

The report and accounts may be sent by electronic means to the
Registrar of Companies and there are provisions for treating the publication of reports and accounts on the world wide web as equivalent to
delivery to those entitled to see them.[99]

Unlimited companies

7.39   In general, unlimited companies do not need to deliver accounts to the
Registrar of Companies[1] though the accounts still need to be laid before
the members in general meeting unless there has been an elective

[92] CA 1985, s.241.
[93] CA 1985, s.242.
[94] CA 1985, s.2441(a). There are moves to shorten this period.
[95] CA 1985, s.244(1)(b).
[96] CA 1985, s.244(2)(a).
[97] CA 1985, s.244(2)(b).
[98] Admission of Securities to Listing, Chap. 12, s.42(e).
[98a] CA 1985, s. 242A.
[98b] CA 1985, s. 242(2).
[99] CA 185, s.238(4A)–(4E).
[1] CA 1985, s.254(1).

resolution to the contrary. However, if an unlimited company at any stage during its accounting reference period was:

- to its knowledge, a subsidiary of an undertaking which was at the time limited; or
- to its knowledge, subject to the potential or actual exercise of rights held by two or more limited undertakings, which if or when exercised would have made the unlimited company a subsidiary of one of those undertakings; or
- a parent company of a company which was at the time limited; or
- a banking company or the parent company of a banking group; or
- a "qualifying company" in terms of the Partnerships and Unlimited Companies Accounts (Regulations) 1993[2]; or
- a company which was a promoter of a trading stamp schemes such as the Green Stamp scheme and Red Stamp schemes (popular in the late 1960s),

its accounts must be delivered.[3] This is to prevent the potential fraud of liabilities being hidden in unlimited companies which are subsidiaries of larger companies, thus disguising the true extent of the group's liabilities or solvency.

Summary accounts

A listed public company may send a summary of its accounts to those members who wish to receive a summary financial statement as opposed to the full accounts and reports.[4] Full accounts are still available to those who wish to have them. **7.40**

Small and medium-sized private companies

Private companies that fall into the above two categories must present their members with their full accounts in the normal way. However, if they are small or medium-sized they do not need to publish at the Registrar of Companies all their accounts: they need only present their accounts in terms of the formats outlined in CA 1985, Schedules 8 and 8A. **7.41**

A small company is one that under the CA 1985, section 247(3) in relation to a financial year comes within two or more of the following specifications:

---

[2] S.I. 1993 No. 1820, which deals with partnerships whose members are limited companies.
[3] CA 1985, s.254(2), (3).
[4] CA 1985, s.251(1). This takes account of the considerable expense of sending out full accounts to members, many of whom neither understand nor read the reports and accounts anyway.

- Turnover: not more than £2,800,000;
- Balance sheet total: not more than £1,400,000;
- Average number of employees per week: not more than 50.

A small company may publish accounts without any:

- profit and loss account[5];
- directors' report[6];
- information about the directors' remuneration[7];

7.42 The point of these provisions is to enable companies to retain some degree of commercial confidentiality. The White Paper is proposing to increase the above figures to £4,800,000 and £2,400,000 though keeping the number of employees the same, and similar figures will be promulgated in due course for small groups.

A medium-sized company is one that under the CA 1985, section 247(3) in relation to a financial year comes within two or more of the following specifications:

- Turnover: not more than £11,200,000;
- Balance sheet total: not more than £5,600,000;
- Number of employees: not more than 250.

A medium-sized company is similar to a small company, save that it does have to produce a profit and loss account, although within that account the details of the turnover, cost of sales and other operating income need not be specified, all being lumped together in one figure known as "gross profit or loss".[8] However, in all other respects a medium-sized company must provide full company accounts, notes and reports.

7.43 The small or medium-sized company exemption from preparing full accounts is not available to the following if at any stage the company is or was during the financial year to which the accounts relate:

- a public company;
- a banking or insurance company;
- an "authorised person" under the Financial Services Act 1986 (*i.e.* someone professionally involved in the provision of investment, insurance or other finance-related advice or services);
- a member of an ineligible group.[9]

---

[5] CA 1985, Sched. 8, para. 2.
[6] CA 1985, Sched. 8, para. 4.
[7] CA 1985, Sched. 8, para. 3.
[8] CA 1985, Sched. 8, para. 5.
[9] CA 1985, s.247A.

An ineligible group is a group of companies with at least one of its members a member of the above list.

Although many companies do take advantage of the opportunity to produce abbreviated accounts, the Inland Revenue, Customs and Excise and any prospective lender or investor may still wish to see full accounts. However, abbreviated accounts do provide some degree of commercial secrecy which some companies may find advantageous.

Small companies exemption from audit

In addition to the above dispensation for providing full accounts, **7.44** certain small companies (as defined earlier in this chapter) may be exempted from having their accounts audited, although under CA 1985, section 249B(1) the exemption does not apply to the following types of company:

- public companies;
- banks, insurance companies and insurance brokers;
- authorised persons and representatives under the Financial Services Act 1986;
- special register bodies and employers' associations under the Trade Union and Labour Relations (Consolidation) Act 1992;
- parent companies or subsidiary undertakings, unless part of a small group and within the terms of the CA 1985, section 249B(1B) and (1C).

The exemption is also not available to:

- charities with an income of more than £90,000[10];
- companies whose article require or whose members demand an audit.[11]

For a small company[12] (excluding charities) to be exempt from **7.45** audit:

- its turnover must be less than £1 million[13];
- its balance sheet total must be more than £1.4 million[14];
- there must be a statement by the directors on the company's balance sheet indicating that the company is exempt from audit under the CA 1985, section 249A(1)[15];

---

[10] CA 1985, s.249A(3A) and (4).
[11] CA 1985, s.249B(2).
[12] In terms of s.246.
[13] CA 1985, s.249A3(a).
[14] CA 1985, s.249A(3)(b).
[15] CA 1985, s.249B(4)(a).

- there must be a statement by the directors on the company's balance sheet confirming that the members have not lodged a notice demanding an audit in terms of the CA 1985, section 249B(2). This subsection states that holders of 10 per cent of the company's issued share capital, or 10 per cent of any class of shares, or in a guarantee company, 10 per cent of the members, may require the company to have the accounts audited. If the members wish to demand an audit, they must give written notice to the company at its registered office at least one month before the end of the company's current financial year[16];
- there must be a statement by the directors acknowledging that they are responsible for:

   (a) ensuring that the company keeps proper accounting records under the CA 1985, section 221;
   (b) preparing accounts which give a true and fair view of the company's financial affairs in accordance with the requirements of the CA 1985, section 226; and
   (c) otherwise complying with any other relevant requirements of the Companies Acts relating to accounts.[17]

The purpose of audit exemption is to save cost and inconvenience. However, lenders and investors may still require audited accounts before lending or investing, and investors and creditors in general may be somewhat sceptical of the value of unaudited accounts.

Group companies, and small and medium-sized groups

7.46   For the distinction between and significance of group companies and subsidiaries see Chapter 3. The directors of a parent company are obliged to prepare group accounts.[18] Group accounts combine the accounts of a parent company with its subsidiary undertakings' accounts and are known as consolidated accounts. These effectively ignore inter-company transfers which might be used to disguise the unsatisfactory financial position of some of the companies or undertakings within the group. Under the CA 1985, section 228 a parent company is exempt from preparing consolidated accounts in the United Kingdom if the parent company itself is part of a group elsewhere in the European Community and that group's consolidated accounts are drawn up and audited in terms of the provisions of the EC Seventh Directive (Directive 83/349).[19] This does not apply, however, if the parent company is listed on a stock exchange anywhere in the European Community[20] (CA

---

[16] CA 1985, s.249B(4)(b).
[17] CA 1985, s.249B(4)(c).
[18] CA 1985, s.227.
[19] CA 1985, s.228.
[20] CA 1985, s.228(3).

1985, section 228(3)). Each subsidiary undertaking's accounts must be included within the consolidated accounts unless the subsidiary undertaking comes within the terms of the exemptions specified in the CA 1985, section 229:

- the inclusion of the subsidiary undertaking's accounts would not be material for the purpose of giving a true and fair view of the consolidated accounts[21];
- the parent company is severely restricted from exercising any rights to the assets or management of the subsidiary undertaking, perhaps because of the terms of a shareholders' agreement[22];
- the information necessary for the preparation of the group accounts could not be obtained from the subsidiary undertaking without excessive time, trouble and expense[23];
- the parent company's interest in the subsidiary undertaking is restricted purely to a subsequent resale and at no previous stage have the subsidiary undertaking's accounts been included within the group accounts[24];
- the activities of a subsidiary undertaking are so very different from all the other undertakings within the group that the inclusion of the subsidiary undertaking's accounts would be incompatible with the need for the accounts to present a true and fair view of the group's financial standing.[25]

Just as companies can claim exemptions from some of the normal accounts rules requirements if they are small or medium-sized, so small groups and medium-sized groups can do this as well.

A small group is one that under the CA 1985, section 249(3) in **7.47** relation to a financial year comes within the following specifications:

- Aggregate turnover: not more than £2.8 million net or £3.36 million gross;
- Aggregate balance sheet total: not more than £1.4 million net or £1.68 million gross;
- Aggregate number of employees: not more than 50.

A medium-sized group is one that under the CA 1985 s 249(3) in relation to a financial year comes within the following specifications:

- Aggregate turnover: not more than £11.2 million net or £13.4 million gross;

---

[21] CA 1985, s.229(2).
[22] CA 1985, s.229(3)(a).
[23] CA 1985, s.229(3)(b).
[24] CA 1985, s.229(3)(c).
[25] CA 1985, s.229(4).

- Aggregate balance sheet total: not more than £5.6 million net or £6.72 million gross;
- Aggregate number of employees: not more than 250.

7.48   Under the CA 1985, section 264(4) a group is ineligible for the above exemptions available to small and medium-sized companies if any of its members are:

- a public company;
- a banking or insurance company;
- an authorised person under the Financial Services Act 1986.

The CA 1985, Schedule 4A applies to the preparation of group accounts and is broadly in line with Schedule 4 and with the exemptions for small and medium-sized companies save that inter-group transfers are ignored.

A small group may be audit-exempt in the same manner as a small company, but the group's turnover must not be greater than £1 million gross and the aggregate balance sheet must not be greater than £1.4 million net.[26]

Dormant companies

7.49   Dormant companies are also referred to in Chapter 3. Providing there has been no accounting transaction in the company records a company may be treated as dormant and is not required to have an audit.[27] For each year that the company is dormant the directors will prepare their own accounts showing the company's assets (commonly the capital value of just one or two shares) and stating that there has been no change in the company's financial position. The dormant state of the company stops the moment there is an significant accounting transaction,[28] and thereafter accounts will need to be prepared in the normal manner.

Revision of defective accounts or reports

7.50   If the directors consider that the published accounts or reports are defective, they may voluntarily prepare revised ones, as permitted by the CA 1985, section 245. If, however, the accounts come to the notice of the Secretary of State as to whether the accounts have been properly prepared within the terms of the Companies Acts, he may ask the

---

[26] CA 1985, s.249B(1B), (1C). There are separate rules for charities.
[27] CA 1985, s.249AA.
[28] Accounting transactions that are not significant are such matters as payment of the annual registration fee to the Registrar of Companies, etc. See CA 1985, s.249AA(5)–(7).

directors to explain any non-compliance with the terms of the Companies Acts[29] and if necessary apply to court to insist that the accounts be revised[30] (CA 1985, section 245B). At present the Secretary of State delegates his authority in this matter to the Financial Reporting Review Panel Limited, part of the Review Panel, which, in turn, is part of the Financial Reporting Council which advises on Financial Reporting Standards (FRSs). Understandably companies are sometimes reluctant to revise their accounts, but refusal to do so when asked may invite more attention from the financial press than compliance.

Proposals for reform

It is anticipated that the figures for small and medium sized companies and groups will shortly be revised upwards in order to remove more companies from the auditing requirements. There are expected to be other deregulatory moves in order to make life easier for such companies. **7.51**

Further Reading

Davies, *Gower's Principles of Modern Company Law* (6th ed., Sweet and Maxwell, 1997), Chap. 12

---

[29] CA 1985, s.245A.
[30] CA 1985, s.245B.

CHAPTER 8

DIRECTORS I: APPOINTMENT, DISMISSAL AND DISQUALIFICATION

THE DEFINITION OF A DIRECTOR

8.01 What is a director? A director is a person, either authorised under the company's constitution and appointed by one of the methods of appointment outlined under the company's constitution or other legal method, to whom the members have delegated the task of managing the company, usually in terms of Table A, regulation 70 (or variants thereof) but subject to any special resolutions passed by the members; or a person who is deemed in law to be a director, either because the company has willingly held him out to be a director and/or he is treated as a director by the company (known as a *de facto* director) or a shadow director, who causes the company to act according to his instructions, but who does not generally wish to be seen to be managing the company, both of which latter types of director are treated in law as directors, irrespective of their wishes in the matter.[1] A director does not need to be human, but must have a legal persona: consequently any registered company could be a director,[2] a Scottish partnership could be a director and a limited liability partnership could be a director. A director need not have any educational or other qualifications. There is no lower age limit on being a director, and as regards an upper limit, plcs may not, without the approval of their members, or as permitted by the articles, have directors over the age of 70.[3] Directors may simultaneously be shareholders and may also be company secretaries. As indicated later, certain persons are forbidden to be directors either under the terms of the company's own articles or because they are banned under the Company Directors Disqualification Act 1986 ("CDDA 1986").

---

[1] See also CA 1985, s.741(1): "In this Act, 'director' includes any person occupying the position of a director, by whatever name called."

[2] The White Paper proposes that this practice should cease, and that corporate directors should no longer exist, as is the case in many other jurisdictions.

[3] CA 1985, s.293.

The director's primary task is to manage the company, but a director does not generally have a completely free hand.[4] The members own the company and so retain residual rights in the management: for example, although directors may wish to change the company's name, change of name is a matter reserved to members alone,[5] and while the directors may recommend the change, ultimately the decision belongs to the members, though those directors who are members are entitled to vote for their own proposals at general meetings. Generally speaking, the directors deal with the commercial and administrative matters of the company, and the members are content to let them do so, on the grounds of the directors' probable greater expertise and because members may not themselves wish to bother with the management of the company as long as they receive a reasonable return on their investment. The directors carry out the management usually through meetings of the board of directors, and a well-run company will have monthly board meetings and keep accurate records of all its decisions. A disorganised, commonly private, company will rarely hold meetings[6] and even more rarely have minutes of those meetings, but it would nonetheless be wise to have them: board minutes may be examined by the auditors or the courts and in the event of impropriety by the directors, minutes indicating who approved which decisions may prove decisive in apportioning liability for problems attaching to the company. The minutes are also *prima facie* evidence of what was decided at the meetings.[7] The absence of minutes may also impugn the credibility of directors' statements of what they assert the board decided.[8] The company's own articles will generally indicate the extent of any delegation of authority extended to directors (subject to any over-riding statutory requirements) and where the directors transgress that authority, the directors will be liable.[9]

Guinness plc v. Ward and Saunders [1990] All E.R. 652
    Three Guinness directors, to whom had been delegated the business of the takeover of Distillers plc, secretly agreed between themselves that in the event of the successful takeover of Distillers plc, one of them, Ward, should receive a success fee of 0.2 per cent

---

[4] Even in a single member private limited company, where the director has in his capacity as shareholder all the shares, the artificial division between director and shareholder must be maintained and reflected in the company's minutes. Some decisions may still only be taken by that person in his capacity as shareholder and not in his capacity as director—for example, changing the company's articles of association.

[5] CA 1985, s.28.

[6] Board meetings require reasonable notice: a chance encounter at Paddington station does not constitute a proper board meeting: *Barron v. Potter* [1914] 1 Ch. 895, 83 L.J. Ch. 646.

[7] CA 1985, s.382.

[8] This is particularly true of single member private limited companies: *Re Neptune (Vehicle Washing Equipment) Ltd* [1995] 3 W.L.R. 108, [1995] 3 All E.R. 811.

[9] See also *Mitchell and Hobbs (UK) Ltd v. Mill* [1996] 2 BCLC 102, where a director raised an action without seeking the approval of the board first.

of the purchase price of Distillers plc, being £5.2 million. Although this matter should have been referred back for approval to the main board of directors of Guinness, as indicated in Guinness's articles, no such reference was made, and when the takeover duly took place, Ward received his funds. He was held liable as constructive trustee for the money purloined from the company.[10]

8.02   As far as outsiders are concerned, where the directors carry out the management of the company, it is on the whole expected that directors will have the authority to carry out the acts that they are doing. Even if that is not the case, under CA 1985, sections 35, 35A and 35B it is probably safe to assume that even if directors do not have the requisite authority to carry out certain acts, outsiders can still expect that the company will have to accept responsibility for the directors' actions, even if those actions are technically *ultra vires* the directors' powers under the company's constitution.[11]

Directors of listed companies are expected to follow the Combined Code, which is to be found at the back of the Admissions of Securities to Listing (also known as the Purple Book). The Combined Code is the agreed best practice for directors as recommended in the Cadbury, Greenbury and Hampel Reports. There is no statutory obligation to follow the Combined Code and no penalties—apart from obloquy—for transgression.

8.03   Apart from attending board meetings and managing the company, directors have various other tasks. They are required to sign the directors' report and accounts,[12] sign various statutory declarations from time to time,[13] consider the interests of the company's employees,[14] return various forms to the Registrar of Companies,[15] convene meetings when required to do so following a requisition by the members to do so[16] or following a serious loss of capital in a plc,[17] produce proposals for approval of creditors in a company voluntary winding up,[18] and many

---

[10] Saunders arranged for the conduit of Ward's payment through Switzerland to the USA. As a result of the Guinness scandal, Ernest Saunders, the former managing director of Guinness, was imprisoned in Ford open prison in Sussex. Once there, he persuaded the Court of Appeal that he was suffering from pre-senile dementia and should be released on compassionate grounds. Since then he has enjoyed excellent health and made the only known recorded recovery from this sad ailment.

[11] See Chap. 4.

[12] CA 1985, s.242.

[13] Such as, for example, purchasing a company's own shares out of capital (CA 1985, s.173(3)) or indicating the likely continued solvency of a company in a members' voluntary winding-up (IA 1986, s.89).

[14] CA 1985, s.309. This is discussed further in the next chapter.

[15] Such as the annual return under s.363; though in practice this is often a task carried out by company secretaries.

[16] CA 1985, s.368.

[17] CA 1985, s.142.

[18] IA 1986, s.1.

other duties under Health and Safety legislation, tax and Customs and Excise legislation, etc. They have certain statutory and common law duties to follow which will be examined in detail in the next chapter.

The significance of being a director

While on the one hand it is normally quite an achievement to be a **8.04** director of a major listed company, on the other it is easy to set up a company and appoint oneself a director. However, in either situation, a director, once appointed, or, as the case may be, deemed in law to be a director, is potentially liable to the company for any breach of any statutory or common law duty (as discussed in the next chapter). In addition, in the event of the company's insolvency, a liquidator or administrator may apply to the court to make a director compensate the company for any loss occasioned to the company (and thereby its creditors) for misfeasance,[19] fraudulent trading,[20] wrongful trading[21] or phoenix trading.[22] There are also numerous criminal penalties[23] under company law, revenue law, health and safety law, etc., for directors who fail to carry out prescribed tasks. There are extensive disclosure requirements for directors and various prohibitions on loans to directors[24] from the company. For plcs and listed companies there are extra requirements of disclosure, not all of which are welcome to directors. As indicated above, directors of listed companies are expected to follow the Combined Code, or explain why they are not doing so (known as "comply or explain"). There have been moves afoot in the recent past to introduce a crime of corporate homicide in England and it is not impossible that a similar bill will be introduced one day in Scotland; these too may have personal consequences for directors. Most trying of all for directors, or putative directors, is that they may be disqualified from acting as a director for up to 15 years if they fall foul of the CDDA 1986.

These collective inconveniences are often palliated by the fact that directors of successful companies are on the whole well rewarded for their activities.

Types of Directors

There are various different types of director. These are definitions by **8.05** convention, as opposed to definitions with legal status. They are as follows:

---

[19] Misfeasance is a general term for any breach of duty to the company: IA 1986, s.212.
[20] IA 1986, s.213.
[21] IA 1986, s.214.
[22] IA 1986, s.216.
[23] On the whole very rarely used.
[24] CA 1985, s.330.

- Managing director
- Executive director
- Non-executive director
- Chairman of the Board of Directors
- Nominee directors
- Alternate directors
- *De facto* directors
- Shadow directors
- "Directors" by title but not directors recognised as such in terms of company law

Managing director

8.06 The managing director is sometime known as the CEO (Chief Executive Officer). His task is to implement the policies of the company. It is not obligatory to have a managing director, but Table A, regulation 27 provides for a company to have one or more if it wishes and if so a managing director will not be subject to retirement by rotation.[25] Under the Combined Code it is considered bad practice for the managing director also to be the chairman. A managing director will normally be an employee of the company. If a company does not have a managing director, but the company holds out a person to be its managing director, even if that person was not actually appointed as such, that person will be nevertheless be deemed to be its managing director.[26] A managing director has no specific role in law: in each case it is a question of what powers the company chooses to grant him.[27]

Executive director

8.07 An executive director is generally a director who is an employee of the company, or even if not actually an employee, fulfils an executive role within the company.

Non-executive director

8.08 A non-executive director is generally a director who is not an employee of the company, but who is appointed for other skills or connections that he may have. Sometimes a non-executive director is a substantial shareholder whose interests in the company the other directors would be wise to consider. The idea behind non-executives is that at least some of them (and the majority in listed companies[28]) should bring to the director's role an independence of mind that allows them to

---

[25] reg. 84.
[26] *Freeman & Lockyer v. Buckhurst Park Properties (Mangal) Ltd* [1964] 2 Q.B. 480, [1964] 2 W.L.R. 618.
[27] *Harold Holdsworth & Co. (Wakefield) Ltd v. Caddies* [1955] 1 W.L.R. 352, [1955] 1 All E.R. 725; *Mitchell & Hobbs (UK) Ltd v. Mill* [1996] 2 BCLC 102.
[28] Combined Code, A.3.2.

ask questions about the company that otherwise might not be asked. Although good non-executives are a considerable asset to a company, sadly it is not unknown for non-executives merely to be the managing directors' placemen, content to pick up directors' fees[29] for rubber-stamping the managing director's opinion or for contributing little to the efficacy of the company.[30]

In a listed company the non-executives should comprise at least one third of the board.[31] Non-executives alone should sit on the remuneration committees.[32]

Chairman of the Board

Not all companies need a chairman, in smaller companies the more **8.09** usual practice being for the managing director to take the chair at any meeting. But in larger companies it is common for there to be a chairman, ideally an independent and respected person, who commands the authority of the members and the other directors, who is able to provide an overview of the company's progress and who ideally is able to stand up to the managing director if necessary. His task is to chair meetings, to ensure that meetings are properly run and that decisions are validly reached.

Under the Combined Code it is recommended that the chairman and managing director should not be the same person. Where they are the same person there will be no-one to call the managing director to account apart from a few intrepid shareholders, and this is not necessarily good for a company. The City has noticed over many years that, with a few notable exceptions, companies tend not to prosper in the long run where too much power is concentrated in the hands of one person.

Nominee director

A nominee director is a director who represents a vested interest in **8.10** the company, such as bank, a class of shareholders, a trades union representative or some other stakeholder in the company. The difficulty for a nominee director is that strictly speaking he should always consider the interests of the company as a whole as opposed to the interests of the body he represents; and if he strongly dissents with what the company is doing, he may have to resign, thereby further limiting his opportunity for bringing his guidance to the company. Furthermore,

---

[29] At the time of writing, the average fee for a non-executive's services for a listed company are between £25,000–£30,000 a year (*Independent*, April 30, 2002).
[30] The corporate buccaneer Tiny Rowland, who formerly controlled Lonrho, memorably described non-executives as "decorations on the Christmas tree".
[31] Combined Code, A.3.1. In a listed company there is no sanction for failure to adhere to this practice. Some very successful companies make no secret of their contempt for non-executives and see no reason to obtain any.
[32] Combined Code, B.2.2.

being a director, if he is not careful he may be liable for some of the penalties attaching to being a director.

Sometimes a nominee director exists purely for the purpose of establishing residency or as a front for other interests. This will not necessarily protect the nominee director from disqualification proceedings.[33]

Alternate director

8.11   Under Table A, regulations 65–69 where a director is away or ill he may appoint an alternate who will stand in as his proxy at meetings—particularly useful where there is a quorum required for board meetings. An alternate director may be an existing director, who may thus be entitled to vote both in his own right and as an alternate.

De facto director

8.12   A *de facto* director is a person who is treated as a director even though he has not been formally appointed as a director, and his name is not on the company's documentation as being a director. Generally speaking, a *de facto* director is someone whom the law treats as being a director,[34] because of the way he is treated by the company and by the fact that the company does not do anything to counter the impression that he is authorised to act as a director[35] even if he holds some other title. A dutiful spouse, who carried out a secretarial role within a company, who had not been appointed a director but merely tried to help her director husband, was not held to be a *de facto* director,[36] but an investor who did take an active role in a company but without being appointed as a director was held to be a *de facto* director.[37]

Shadow director

8.13   By contrast a shadow director is one "in accordance with whose directions or instructions the directors of the company are accustomed to act"[38] but who generally does not wish to be seen as a director. The familiar example of this is the person who for nefarious purposes does not wish to be seen to be associated with the company[39] but whose orders the other directors follow. A matter of some concern for banks[40]

---

[33] *Secretary of State for Trade and Industry v. Croshaw*, unreported, 1999.

[34] CA 1985, s.741(1).

[35] In this respect there is an element of holding out under agency law or personal bar under contract.

[36] *Re Red Label Fashions Ltd* [1999] BCLC 308.

[37] *Secretary of State for Trade and Industry v. Jones* [1999] B.C.C. 336.

[38] CA 1985, s.741(2).

[39] Perhaps because he is disqualified or because his professional reputation leaves something to be desired.

[40] For the potential position of banks, see *Re a company (No. 005009 of 1987) ex p. Copp* [1989] BCLC 13.

and "company doctors" who are sent in by banks to sort out companies in difficulties is the extent to which the banks or company doctors could be held to be shadow directors and thus liable for the penalties attaching to directors of companies in liquidation. A prudent bank, or important creditor, however tempted, should present options to a company that is one of its customers without insisting that the company follow its demands: any decisions should be taken by the company's directors and not by the bank or creditor.[41] In the important case of *Re Hydroban (Corby) Ltd*[42] the court stated that for a person to be a shadow director that person should have directed the existing directors of the company, that the directors followed that person's directions, and that they were used to following that person's directions. This case also established that the directors of a parent company were not themselves shadow directors, merely the agents of the parent company. Having the right to appoint some directors does not necessarily make a person a shadow director.[43] Shadow directors are also referred to in CDDA 1986, s.22(5).

The provision of professional advice by, say, an accountant advising the company, will not normally make the accountant a shadow director; but equally advice not given by a professional could still make that person a shadow director.[44]

"Directors" by title but not recognised as such under company law

Sometimes companies will give their senior executives important **8.14** titles, such as "marketing director" or "sales division director" without actually having such executives on the board of directors. In this case the titles carry no significance in terms of company law, and the executives will not be treated a directors in law unless they happen to be *de facto* or shadow directors as above.

Persons who may not be directors

The following persons may not be directors: **8.15**

- those who have been sequestrated; where a debtor in sequestration is involved in the management of a company without the permission of the court,[45] and where the debtor was compulsorily sequestrated the permission of the court that sequestrated him, he may be fined or imprisoned, and he will be jointly and

[41] See *Re a Company* (1988) 4 B.C.C. 424; *Re Tasbian (No. 3) Ltd* [1992] BCLC 358, CA.
[42] [1994] 2 BCLC 180.
[43] *Kuwait Asia Bank E.C. v. National Mutual Life Nominees Ltd* [1990] BCLC 868.
[44] *Secretary of State for Trade and Industry v. Deverell* [2000] Ch. 340, [2000] 2 All E.R. 365, [2000] 2 W.L.R. 907.
[45] CDDA, s.11.

severally personally liable (for what it is worth) along with the
company and with anyone who acted on his instructions while
knowing of his sequestration for the debts of the company with
which he was involved while sequestrated[46];

- those who have been disqualified under the CDDA 1986;
- a person aged over 70 in a plc (or a private subsidiary of a plc)
  unless the company's articles permit it or the members, having
  been given special notice beforehand, have approved the director's appointment[47];
- directors who have failed to obtain their qualification shares
  within the required two months (or lesser) period.[48] Not every
  company has a share qualification for its directors, but those that
  do usually require that the director obtain the shares within the
  time required, and if he does not, he ceases to be a director.[49]
  Despite this, if a director acts despite not having the requisite
  share qualification, his acts will still be valid[50];
- those not permitted to be directors under the terms of the company's articles (for example, Table A states that directors suffering from a certified mental disorder or absent without leave for
  more than six months will cease to be directors[51]);
- in a company with only one director, which is a company in its
  own right, where that second company's sole director is the
  company secretary of the first company[52];
- the company's auditor.

Formal appointment as a director

8.16   All but the last three types above will generally be formally
appointed, but even in the absence of formal appointment, the law
recognises that anyone who occupies the position of director, irrespective of his actual label, is a director.[53] Formal appointment as a director
is generally publicised by means of signing the Form 10, if one of the
original directors, or a Form 288a, if a subsequent director, and insertion
in the register of directors.[54] It is common for directors to sign service

---

[46] CDDA, s.15(2).
[47] CA 1985, s.293.
[48] CA 1985, s.291(1).
[49] CA 1985, s.291(3). Bizarrely, the director will also be liable to a fine.
[50] Table A, reg. 92.
[51] Table A, reg. 81.
[52] CA 1985, s.283(4)(b).
[53] CA 1985, s.741(1).
[54] However, having one's name registered as a director does not necessarily mean that one
is director: *Pow Services Ltd v. Clare* [1995] 2 BCLC 435. A degree of intention to be
a director is required, even if (as will be seen later) no great commitment to the post
once appointed is necessary.

contracts, but not obligatory to do so. The actual method of appoint-ment, will vary from company to company, depending on the com-pany's articles, and may even be by being named as a director in the company's articles. It is however common that new directors are appointed at AGMs, or appointed by existing directors but ratified by the members at the next available AGM. Some companies' articles require that directors be re-appointed every three years (as under Table A) or such lesser period. Table A contains complicated provisions for rotation of directors, the complexity of which ensures that they are frequently ignored by the companies that have adopted them. Nonethe-less, strictly speaking such provisions should be followed unless the members choose to re-write them—as many do. Some companies will specify a minimum or maximum number of directors. In a plc, directors must be voted for separately unless there has been an unanimous resolution to the contrary passed beforehand.[55]

The remuneration of directors

Directors are entitled to be remunerated[56] and to be reimbursed their **8.17** expenses.[57] Although the normal method of remuneration will be through a salary, salaries attract income tax and national insurance, and sometimes it is therefore more tax-efficient for a director to receive less by way of salary and more by way of dividend on his shares (partic-ularly if he has most of the shares in his company) since he does not have to pay national insurance on dividends. Other methods of reward-ing directors are by means of share option schemes[58] the exercise price of which is sometimes geared to the profitability of the company. Further methods of rewarding directors include the use of employee shares and by issuing redeemable shares which will be purchased by the company on the fulfilment of certain criteria. Whatever methods are involved, they must be displayed in the director's service contract which is available for the members' inspection[59] and which, if in excess of five years in duration without being easily terminable by the company, will need to be voted upon before the company enters into the service contract.[60] Likewise any payments in consideration of loss of office must be disclosed to and voted upon by the members.[61] Information about the directors' remuneration must be disclosed in the company's

---

[55] CA 1985, s.292. This is to prevent "packages" of directors where the price of some good directors is the simultaneous appointment of some lesser directors.
[56] Table A, reg. 82.
[57] Table A, reg. 83.
[58] Not to be confused with traded options, which involve the purchase of shares already in the market: share options are the entitlement to acquire newly issued shares from the company at a predetermined price. Directors and their families are forbidden from dealing in traded options in their own companies: CA 1985, ss.323 and 327.
[59] CA 1985, s.318.
[60] CA 1985, s.319.
[61] CA 1985, s.312.

accounts.[62] In the last few years there has been much criticism of directors for receiving very high salaries at a time when workers are either being laid off or having wage freezes, or for receiving substantial pay-offs even when they are being "retired", thus apparently rewarding failure. From a legal point of view, provided the terms of the directors' remuneration and any perquisites have been properly disclosed to and approved by the directors (if the contract is less than five years and there are no terms to the contrary in the articles) it is generally difficult for members or employees to do anything other than cause the well-rewarded director embarrassment at such largesse. In any case, the few executives who are capable of holding the post of managing director of a listed plc are generally in a strong position to command whatever salary the market can stand, and on whatever terms they see fit.

Disclosure of information by directors

Disclosure to the Registrar of Companies

8.18   Each company must keep at its registered office a register of directors and secretaries[63] and as far as directors are concerned, the register will contain details of each director's full name, address,[63a] business occupation, nationality, other relevant directorships within the last five years and date of birth. Any changes must be notified to the Registrar of Companies within 14 days.[63b]

Disclosure to the company of any interest in securities

8.19   A director who has securities in a company must within five days of his directorship, or within five days of his awareness of the following obligation, disclose to the company any interest he may have in securities in his company or companies with which his company is associated.[64] This information is inserted in a special register.[65] This rule applies to shadow directors as well, and applies not only where the director acquires securities but also where he disposes of them. In addition, this rule applies to the director's spouse and children, including adopted and step-children,[66] and to any companies in which he has one-third of the voting control or the board of directors acts according to his wishes,[67] or a trust of which he is the beneficiary.[68] If the company's securities are traded on a recognised investment exchange,

---

[62] CA 1985, s.232 and Sched. 6, Pt I.
[63] CA 1985, s.288(1).
[63a] Confidentiality Orders may be obtained from the Secretary of State: See para. 3.01.
[63b] CA 1985, s.288(2).
[64] CA 1985, s.324, and Sched.13.
[65] CA 1985, s.325.
[66] CA 1985, ss.327 and 328.
[67] CA 1985, Sched. 13, Pt I, para. 4(a), (b).
[68] CA 1985, Sched. 13, Pt I, para. 2.

and the director or his family buy or sell securities in his company, this fact must be communicated to the recognised investment exchange before the end of the following business day.[69]

Disclosure of interest in any contracts entered into by the company

Although this matter is dealt with in greater detail in the next chapter, **8.20** under CA 1985, section 317 a director is supposed to declare his interest in any contract with the company at the next available meeting of the board of directors. On that occasion, and if the company adheres to Table A, regulation 94, the director should not vote at that board meeting in respect of the contract in which he has an interest if his interest is "material"—"material" being defined by the other directors.[70] Although this may appear to be a licence to directors to have self-interested transactions, this rule is eminently pragmatic. It would be awkward and slow to refer every decision involving a director's interests back to the members, however trivial, and so the members, by accepting the terms of regulation 94, in effect delegate their power to query self-dealing transactions to the directors. On the other hand, since this is clearly open to abuse by directors mutually agreeing on flexible definitions of the word "material", listed companies insist on proper disclosure to shareholders instead.[71]

In companies with Table A the members retain an over-riding power to relax the rules in regulation 94, thereby permitting the director to vote on a matter in which he has an interest, material or otherwise.

Termination of directorship

The unsatisfactory director

What may the members do if one or more of their directors is **8.21** unsatisfactory? If a director loses the confidence of the members, the members have a number of options:

- They may dismiss him under CA 1985, section 303;
- They may rewrite the company's articles or pass a special resolution to impose controls on that director (assuming the disgruntled members have the votes to command a special resolution)—though this does not of itself terminate his directorship;
- They could refuse to re-elect the director when he stands for re-election as a director if the company has (as does Table A) triennial re-election by rotation of directors;

---

[69] CA 1985, s.329.
[70] It is nonetheless open to companies, if they wish to do so, to have articles that permit the directors to vote at board meetings on matters in which they have an interest.
[71] See Listing Rules, Chap. 11.

- As a last resort the company could be wound up on the just and equitable grounds of Insolvency Act 1986 ("IA 1986"), section 122(1)(g)—though the company would have to be solvent and no better remedy should be available.[72]

Other methods of termination of directorship

8.22   These include the following:

- death;
- dissolution and striking from the register (if the director is a limited company or a limited liability partnership);
- sequestration (if the director is a Scottish partnership);
- sequestration (if the director is a person);
- expiry of his service contract;
- breach of his service contract by the director himself;
- failure to obtain qualification shares[73];
- insanity[74];
- absence for more than six months without reasonable excuse[75];
- retirement[76];
- attainment of the age of 70 in plcs unless the members have voted, following special notice, to retain the director[77];
- disqualification under CDDA 1986.

The company is required to intimate to the Registrar of Companies the termination of the directorship.[78] Any director forced to leave office before he was contractually due to do so may be entitled to damages for breach of contract by the company—usually amounting to the value of the unexpired portion of his contract. Astute directors will normally negotiate a clause in their contracts entitling them to substantial awards if the event of early termination of their contracts. Alternatively they may be able to negotiate a substantial sum if they "promise to go quietly" without speaking to the financial press about the circumstances of their termination.

Dismissal of a director under Companies Act 1985, section 303

8.23   Under CA 1985, section 303 a director may be dismissed by means of an ordinary resolution provided special notice of 28 days has been

---

[72] IA 1986, s.125(2).
[73] CA 1985, s.291(3).
[74] Table A, reg. 81.
[75] Table A, reg. 81 (though not all companies will choose to adopt this regulation).
[76] Table A, reg. 81.
[77] CA 1985, s.293.
[78] CA 1985, s.288(2). Companies should also tell the Registrar of any changes to the particulars relating to their directors.

given to the company of the intention that the resolution be moved at the forthcoming meeting where the resolution will be moved. The idea behind the 28 days is to allow the insertion into the notice of the next general meeting of the words "special notice"[79] in front of the wording of the resolution for dismissal. The words "special notice" are supposed to draw members' attention to the significance of the matter.[80] The 28 days notice also allows the director in question time to prepare a statement concerning his dismissal. This statement must be of reasonable length and the director may insist that it be circulated to the members before the meeting[81] (unless it is received too late to be so) and if it is not sent out as it should be, it may be read out at the meeting itself.[82] The director may in any event insist on speaking at the meeting.[83] The statement itself need not be read out if the company, or any person referred to in the statement, persuades the court that the statement should not be read out because the statement is being used to obtain "needless publicity for defamatory matter".[84] The intention behind the legislation is to allow directors to bring to members' attention any matters which the director feels they ought to know and for which he may be being dismissed. It is arguable how beneficial a solution it is to have this protection, since if the members are determined to remove the director, his protests may carry little weight. It is not permissible to dismiss a director by means of a written resolution because of the director's right of protest.[85]

DISQUALIFICATION OF DIRECTORS UNDER THE COMPANY DIRECTORS DISQUALIFICATION ACT 1986

In a book of this length there is insufficient space to give anything other **8.24** than the broad outlines of this particular issue. The law relating to disqualification of directors was consolidated in 1986 as part of the various reforms to company law which were designed to encourage more responsible behaviour by directors. Not only could directors be found liable to their insolvent companies in terms of IA 1986, sections 212–216, but they could also be banned from being directors for up to 15 years. The purpose of this was primarily to protect the public as opposed to punishing the directors, although it undoubtedly has that

---

[79] Alternatively, the notice of the general meeting may say "Special notice has been received by the company of the following resolution" following by the wording of the s.303 resolution.

[80] Given that most private shareholders rarely even read their company reports and even more rarely vote, it is debatable how useful this provision is.

[81] CA 1985, s.304(2).

[82] CA 1985, s.304(3).

[83] CA 1985, s.304(1).

[84] CA 1985, s.304(4).

[85] CA 1985, Sched. 15A1(a).

effect as well. The Registrar of Companies now has a register of disqualified directors and even a "Defiant Directors' Hotline" for those who wish to phone in to complain that a disqualified director is still, in practice, conducting business through a company.

Disqualifying directors has thrown up some difficulties: the disqualification of a director who controls many businesses, and who was the victim of unfortunate circumstances rather than any particular vice, may result in substantial job losses for his employees as his businesses collapse without him to manage them. Unscrupulous directors who have been disqualified merely get their spouses to run their businesses for them, and if ultimately found to be shadow directors commonly ensure that they are bankrupt anyway, so that the law holds few terrors for them. Directors, who were directors in name only, who took no part in management and received no remuneration for their directorships, have sometimes been disqualified, on the grounds that by accepting the position of director, they have to accept the responsibilities that come with directorship, even if they have not exercised any directorial role and never sought to do so.[86]

Disqualification orders in general

8.25   There is a common misconception that members of a company may disqualify directors: this is not the case. Only the courts may disqualify directors, and they will do this on a discretionary basis unless they are obliged to do this in terms of section 6 (unfitness of directors of insolvent companies). Furthermore, just because a director of a solvent company breaches some duty or acts negligently does not mean that he will be disqualified. In order to give some degree of protection to directors, and not to have the converse effect of driving entrepreneurs from the United Kingdom, directors will only be disqualified by the courts under the restricted circumstances indicated in the Company Directors Disqualification Act ("CDDA").

The legislation applies both to company directors and to insolvency practitioners, (for the purposes of the rest of this chapter known collectively as "directors") and prohibits such persons from being involved in any company in any way as directors, promoters, managers or founders of a company except with leave of the court.[87] The maximum period of disqualification is 15 years, but if a director is disqualified in respect of more than one company, the period of disqualification is concurrent. It is now permissible for a director to give an undertaking to the Secretary of State, known as a disqualification undertaking, whereby

[86] *Re Park House Properties Ltd* [1997] 2 BCLC 530.
[87] CDDA 1986, s.1. Directors includes bodies corporate (CDDA 1986, s.14, and see *Official Receiver v. Brady* [1999] B.C.C. 258) and includes *de facto* directors and shadow directors. For shadow directors, see *Secretary of State v. Deverell* [2001] Ch. 340, [2000] 2 All E.R. 365, [2000] 2 W.L.R. 907, [2000] 2 BCLC 133, [2000] B.C.C. 1057.

as a form of fast-track procedure a director undertakes to accept his disqualification on agreed terms. This saves unnecessary dispute and expense in the courts, may cause the period of disqualification to be lessened, and lets it both start and finish earlier.[88] The court has power to vary the disqualification undertaking if necessary.[89]

The grounds for a disqualification order

Under CDDA 1986, section 2 a disqualification order may (as opposed to "shall") be made where the director has been convicted of an indictable offence in connection with the promotion, formation, management, liquidation, striking off or receivership[90] of a company. This section has been used for such matters as insider dealing[91] or carrying on a business for which the director lacked the appropriate authority.[92] **8.26**

Under section 3 a director may be disqualified for persistent breaches of companies legislation with regard to the delivery of documents or accounts to the Registrar of Companies, such as repeated failure to send in proper returns.[93] "Persistent" here means at least three defaults in the previous five years.[94]

Under section 4 a director may be disqualified for fraud in winding up[95] or of a breach of duty to a company in liquidation or receivership.[96]

Under section 5 a director may be disqualified on summary conviction for any failure to make proper returns, such failure being established by at least three defaults in the previous five years.[97] The difference between section 3 and section 5 is that under section 5 the judge may impose a disqualification order at the same time as convicting the director for his failure whereas under section 3 a judge can impose a disqualification order without an accompanying conviction. **8.27**

---

[88] CDDA 1986, s.1A. This was introduced by the Insolvency Act 2000 and replaces the uncertainty in the law as to whether or not undertakings were acceptable. There was also a form of summary disqualification, known as the Carecraft procedure, the need for which is diminished by the acceptability of disqualification undertakings.

[89] CDDA 1986, s.8A.

[90] And in England and Wales, administrative receivership.

[91] *R. v. Goodman* [1994] 1 BCLC 349.

[92] *R. v. Georgiou* (1988) 4 B.C.C. 322. Georgiou carried out an insurance business through a company without having complied with the requirements of the Insurance Companies Act 1982.

[93] *Re Arctic Engineering Ltd* [1986] 1 W.L.R. 686, [1986] 2 All E.R. 346, [1986] BCLC 253.

[94] CDDA 1986, s.3(2). The defaults in question relate to default orders under CA 1985, ss.244 and 713, and IA 1986, ss.41 and 170.

[95] Following his guilt if involved in the crime of fraudulent trading under CA 1985, s.458 (and applies even if he is not convicted).

[96] CDDA 1986, s.4(1)(b).

[97] CDDA 1986, s.5.

The maximum duration of the disqualification under both sections is five years.[98]

Under section 10 where a director has been found liable by the court to make a contribution to his insolvent company's assets in terms of IA 1986, section 213 (fraudulent trading) or section 214 (wrongful trading), the court may, at the same time, disqualify the director.

Bankrupts are not permitted to be directors, or directly or indirectly involved in the promotion, formation or management of a company except with leave of the court.[99] If they do so, they are liable to prosecution,[1] and indeed to further disqualification.

The unfit director of an insolvent company

8.28   Section 6 obliges the court to disqualify a director for "unfitness" of a company which has become insolvent.[2] This is possibly the most problematic of the disqualification criteria and has led to a great deal of caselaw. The word "insolvent" in this context means not only insolvent liquidation and administration, as might be expected, but also receivership.[3] In order to catch shadow directors the legislation specifically applies to them as well.[4] The minimum period of disqualification is two years and the maximum 15.[5]

Who may apply for a disqualification order for an unfit director?

8.29   The Secretary of State may apply for a disqualification order for an unfit director of an insolvent company if it appears to him, on the basis of information received by him from the company's liquidator, administrator, receiver or in England the Official Receiver,[6] to be "expedient in the public interest"[7] to do so. This must be done within two years of the date of the director's company's insolvency[8] unless leave has been granted by the court otherwise. Leave is less likely to be granted where the delay is not the fault of the director or where there is a risk of prejudice to the director, although in each case the public interest will still have to be taken into account.[9] Even if the action for disqualification has been raised timeously, the Secretary of State must still be seen

---

[98] CDDA 1986, ss.3(5), 5(5).

[99] CDDA 1986, s.11.

[1] CDDA 1986, s.12. *R. v. Brockley* [1994] 1 BCLC 606.

[2] The previous sections apply to both solvent and insolvent companies.

[3] CDDA 1986, s.6(2).

[4] CDDA 1986, s.6(3C).

[5] CDDA 1986, s.6(4).

[6] CDDA 1986, s.7(3).

[7] CDDA 1986, s.7(1).

[8] CDDA 1986, s.7(2).

[9] *Re New Technology Systems Ltd* [1997] B.C.C. 810; *Re Polly Peck International plc (No. 2)* [1994] 1 BCLC 574, [1993] B.C.C. 890.

to prosecute the case with some degree of urgency, since in the intervening period until the decision on disqualification the director cannot practise as a director. A total delay of four and a half years was held to be unacceptable under Human Rights legislation.[10]

The Secretary of State may accept an undertaking by the director to be disqualified if the Secretary of State believes this to be in the public interest.[11]

The Secretary of State may also apply for a disqualification order on the strength of the report or other documentation following a DTI inspection.[12] The two year rule does not apply in this case, generally because DTI reports take so long to prepare. The Secretary of State may also accept a disqualification undertaking by a director who is featured in the report or other documentation.[13]

How unfit is "unfit"?

As a guide to the degree of unfitness required for disqualification, **8.30** section 9 refers to Schedule 1 for general unfitness as regards the directorship of any company and Schedule 2 for unfitness as a director of an insolvent company. The reason for the two matters is that while unfitness primarily refers to the directorship of insolvent companies, a director might simultaneously be a director of an insolvent company and of a solvent company and might need to be disqualified from the solvent companies too. Schedule 1 refers primarily to breaches of duty to the company, failure to keep proper records and the failure to send in returns to the Registrar of Companies. Schedule 2, which is inherently vaguer, refers to the extent of the director's responsibility for the company's insolvency, his responsibility for his company's failure to provide services or goods which have been paid for, his responsibility for any unfair preferences or gratuitous alienations made by the company, his failure to call creditors' meetings in a creditors' voluntary winding up and various failures to co-operate or provide information to liquidators, administrators, receivers, etc.

As all this gives wide scope for argument, the courts have tried to lay down guidelines as to the degree of unfitness which qualifies as worthy of disqualification. In principle, unfitness contains some degree of lack of probity or negligence. The courts appear unwilling to condemn mere commercial misjudgement or minor incompetence,[14] but a breach of commercial morality or gross incompetence, such that the director

---

[10] *EDC v. U.K.* [1998] B.C.C. 370, ECHR.
[11] CDDA 1986, s.7(2A).
[12] CDDA 1986, s.8(1).
[13] CDDA 1986, s.8(2A).
[14] Browne-Wilkinson VC in *Re Lo-Line Electric Motors Ltd* [1988] Ch. 477 at 479.

would be a danger to the public, would be unacceptable.[15] In *Secretary of State for Trade and Industry v. Griffiths*[16] the Court of Appeal recommended the use of common sense combined with a practical and flexible approach to case management in ascertaining the degree of unfitness. Matters that the court should take into consideration are the fact that the purpose of disqualification is to protect the public, to serve as a deterrent to other directors and to ensure that directors generally recognise that being a director brings inescapable personal responsibilities.

8.31   Examples where disqualification orders have been granted (and there are many) include the following:

- causing the company to trade while insolvent, and in particular, not paying some creditors (such as the Inland Revenue) and using the money for those creditors to pay other less pressing creditors[17];
- drawing excessive salaries at a time when the company could not afford it[18];
- failure on the part of a director of a major company to monitor his undermanagers.[19]

For how long should the director be disqualified?

8.32   Broadly speaking the courts have adopted the guidelines set out in *Re Sevenoaks Stationers (Retail) Ltd*[20] whereby an order of two to five years is appropriate for first cases involving negligence and incompetence, six to 10 years is for cases involving misappropriating assets and prejudicing creditors, and 11 to 15 years is for very serious cases and repeat offences.

Application for leave

8.33   It is possible for the courts to exercise their discretion under CDDA, section 17 to lift the disqualification order or disqualification undertaking in respect of one or more particular companies, usually because the company might collapse without the director present[21] or because there is no danger to the public. The courts may impose a condition: for

---

[15] Hoffman J. (as he then was) in *Re Dawson Print Group Ltd* (1987) 3 B.C.C. 322 at 324; *Re Barings plc (Secretary of State v. Baker (No. 5))* 1 BCLC 433, aff'd [2000] 1 BCLC 523, CA.
[16] [1998] 2 BCLC 646, CA.
[17] *Secretary of State v. Laing* [1996] 2 BCLC 324.
[18] *Secretary of State v. Lubrani* [1997] 2 BCLC 115.
[19] *Secretary of State v. Baker (No. 5)* 1 BCLC 433.
[20] [1991] BCLC 325, CA.
[21] *Re Chartmore Ltd* [1990] BCLC 673; *Re Cargo Agency Ltd* [1992] BCLC 686; *Re Gibson Davies Ltd* [1995] 11.

example in *Secretary of State v. Rosenfield*[22] the courts permitted Rosenfield to act as a director provided the company produced quarterly accounts and that someone with financial expertise was appointed to the board of directors.

Consequences of breach of disqualification order

If a disqualified director continues to act as a director, or as a *de facto* **8.34** or shadow director, in addition to any criminal consequences under CDDA 1986, section 13 he may be held jointly and severally personally liable, along with the company and with anyone who is involved with him in the company while knowing that the disqualified director is disqualified.[23] Any person acting on the disqualified director's instructions is presumed to have been aware that he knew that the director was disqualified. This provision is designed to catch, in particular, spouses or other business partners who act at the disqualified director's bidding.

It would be pleasant to think that disqualification acts a deterrent. Sadly the incidence of cases such as *Re Moorgate Metals Ltd*[24] suggests that it does not. In this case, a former bankrupt teamed up with a thrice bankrupted and undischarged scrap metal merchant to run a scrap metal business. The second bankrupt persuaded his wife to act as a director but to his order, and they ran a completely hopeless business with bogus accounts. What little money the business made in its short existence was spent on large salaries, bigger cars and expensive holidays in France. Both directors were disqualified for further periods.

If an honest director realises that the company with which he is **8.35** involved may collapse and that he may be disqualified, he should resign where possible, and he should also ensure that his opposition to any improper or foolish decisions is noted in the board minutes. By such means in *Re CS Holidays Ltd*[25] a prudent director was able to protect himself while his fellow directors were all disqualified.

The Human Rights Act 1998 and directors

A director, and indeed any person, is entitled to a fair trial under **8.36** Article 6 of the European Convention on Human Rights ("ECHR"). This issue particularly arose in the case of *Saunders v. United Kingdom*[26] where Saunders argued that information that he had been compelled to give DTI inspectors should not be used against him in criminal proceedings. As a result of this the parts of the CA 1985 that refer to

---

[22] [1999] B.C.C. 413.
[23] CDDA 1986, s.15.
[24] [1995] BCLC 503, [1995] B.C.C. 143.
[25] Also known as *Re a company (No. 004803 of 1996)* [1997] 1 W.L.R. 407.
[26] (1997) E.H.R.R. 313.

DTI inspections have been amended to prevent a director being penalised through self-incrimination as a result of responding to questions as part of a DTI inspection.[27]

On a separate issue, a five year delay in bringing disqualification proceedings against a director in *EDC v. United Kingdom*[28] was held to be unacceptable in terms of Article 6 of the ECHR.

Further Reading

Griffin, *Personal Liability and the Disqualification of Company Directors* (Hart Publishing, 1999)

---

[27] For example, see CA 1985, s.434(5A) and 5(B).
[28] [1998] B.C.C. 370.

CHAPTER 9

DIRECTORS II: RIGHTS, DUTIES, LIABILITIES AND OTHER OBLIGATIONS

DIRECTORS' RIGHTS

Most companies adopt a form of Table A, regulation 70 which states: **9.01**

> "Subject to the provisions of the Act, the memorandum and articles and to any directions given by special resolution, the company shall be managed by the directors who may exercise all the powers of the company."

Within these parameters, directors have a relatively free hand as regards their rights. This is convenient for the members, who are not interested in managing the company and merely seek a return on their investment, and convenient for the directors, who will not wish to seek members' approval for everything of a commercial or administrative nature that the directors wish to do. Some companies' articles are more restrictive than Table A, regulation 70. For example, many companies will have a regulation in their articles stating that before the directors make the company borrow more than a certain pre-determined amount the directors must seek the members' approval. Furthermore, as indicated in the previous chapter, directors cannot alter the articles or the company's name or capital, these being matters reserved under statute to the members.

Directors may have rights under their service contracts (for which see later) if they have them.

But with rights come duties, and the failure to carry out those duties **9.02** properly brings sanctions.

DIRECTORS' DUTIES

There are three main types of duty that a director owes to his com- **9.03** pany:

- The fiduciary duty

- The duty of skill and care
- Statutory duties.

There are other duties that arise under certain circumstances:

- Duty to creditors
- Duty to employees
- Duty to members

9.04 Certain other duties have already been discussed in the previous chapter:

- Duty of disclosure of directors' interests in the company's securities.

Certain other duties arise on insolvency:

- Duty to co-operate with insolvency practitioners
- Duty to contribute to the company's assets on insolvency under certain circumstances (this is dealt with under "directors' liabilities" later).

The fiduciary duty

9.05 The fiduciary duty is the duty to act in good faith in the best interests of the company as a whole with a proper purpose in mind. It is the same duty that an agent owes to a principal, a partner to his partnership and co-partners, and a solicitor to his client. There should be no conflict of interest between the director and his company. With such a duty, if the director wishes to take any advantage whatsoever from his position, or to benefit any other person, or to do anything other than what he is supposed to do, he may only do so provided he has received authority from the company to do so, either in advance, or later when the company ratifies it, and provided the proposed action is within the proper exercise of his powers. If he receives any benefit from his position, he may only keep that benefit if he discloses it and seeks authority to keep it. The key words are "disclosure" and "approval by the members".

In its purest form this is a very strict duty. In *Aberdeen Railway Co. v. Blaikie Bros*[1] the chairman of a railway company also was a partner in a firm of outfitters which was furnishing the railway carriages. There was no suggestion that the chairman had actually behaved improperly, but nonetheless he had neither disclosed his interest in the outfitting firm nor sought approval from the members for him to receive a benefit from the work being placed with his firm. Consequently he had breached his

[1] (1854) 1 MacQ. 416 (HL).

fiduciary duty and was held liable to repay to the railway company the unauthorised benefit that he had received.

Since the *Aberdeen Railway* case, the principle has remained the **9.06** same, but has been adapted to take account of the practicalities of the situation: to save the members having to approve every single transaction in which directors have the slightest personal interest, the directors are usually (depending on the articles) permitted to carry out any required approval on the members' behalf instead.

Directors' personal interests and conflicts of interest

The combination of the Companies Act 1987 ("CA 1987"), section **9.07** 317 and Table A, regulation 94 (if adopted by the company) allows directors to have personal interests in matters involving their companies. Directors must declare their personal interests in any matter involving the company to their fellow directors, and where the interest is "material" the director must not vote on the matter at the board meeting where the matter is discussed, but otherwise may be involved. By virtue of regulation 94 the members delegate to the directors the business of checking that a fellow director who has a personal interest is not taking unauthorised advantage of his position. At the heart of regulation 94 is an inherent paradox: are directors really the best persons to judge whether one of their own is taking unauthorised advantage of his position? The answer is, possibly not, but short of remitting every matter back to the members, there is unlikely to be any other satisfactory alternative.

Where this procedure is not followed when it should be, there may be a breach of fiduciary duty. With such a breach, the director will usually be required either to hand over the profit he had improperly made or otherwise return to the company what he had improperly gained or obtained from the company. In *Boston Deep Sea Fishing Co. Ltd v. Ansell*[2] the defendant, the managing director of the plaintiffs, was given a commission for placing an order for a new trawler with a firm of shipwrights, and secretly kept the commission instead of declaring it to his company and seeking permission to keep it. Had he received permission he might have been allowed to retain it: as it was, his company, whose interests he as managing director was supposed to uphold, had effectively overpaid the cost of the trawler to the extent of the commission and he had to repay it. In *Regal Cinemas (Hastings) Ltd v. Gulliver*[3] the directors of a cinema company had the opportunity (which came to them in their position as directors) of buying further cinemas in Hastings. They formed a company to acquire the cinemas and then sold the

---

[2] (1888) 39 Ch. D. 339.
[3] [1967] 2 A.C. 134, [1942] 1 All E.R. 378.

company to the plaintiff company of which they were directors, thereby making a profit. Had they sought approval from the members of the plaintiff company—which would have been easily achieved, since the directors collectively owned most of the shares—they could perfectly well have kept the profit; but they failed to obtain such approval. When in due course they sold the company, the new owner of the company's shares realised what the by now former directors had done and was able to recover the profit from those directors.

9.08   In *Gencor ACP Ltd v. Danby*[4] the managing director of a road-building company used to divert business opportunities that came to his company to another business in which he had an interest, and used the company's funds for the redecoration of his home and the payment of his credit card bills. He, too, unwisely sold his business without destroying the evidence of his past transactions, so that the incoming owner was able to see what had been purloined from the company by the former managing director.

The process can work retrospectively: in *Industrial Developments Consultants Ltd v. Cooley*,[5] Cooley, in his capacity as a director of the plaintiffs, had been approached by Gas Board officials to see if his company would carry out some work for them. The officials at the Gas Board then indicated that they were interested in his particular skills rather than the skills of his company, and that they were willing to give him, personally, the contract for the required work. Assenting to this arrangement, Cooley persuaded his company that he should take early retirement on health grounds. Once he had retired, he took up the contract from the Gas Board as arranged. When his former company heard what he had done, it successfully sued him to make him return to the company the contract (or the value thereof) that he had been able to obtain through his position as a director of the company.

9.09   In *Bishopsgate Investment Management Ltd (in liquidation) v. Ian Maxwell (No. 2)*[6] Maxwell had transferred, at his father's direction,[7] a substantial number of shares, being an investment by the Mirror Group pension fund of which he was a director, to other companies owned by the Maxwell family, which thereby benefited. Ian Maxwell was liable for the misapplication of funds: when signing the stock transfer forms he had not been acting in the best interest of the pension fund company[8] as he should have been.

---

[4] [2000] 2 BCLC 734.
[5] [1972] 1 All E.R. 443.
[6] [1994] 1 All E.R. 261, [1993] BCLC 1282.
[7] His father being the late Robert Maxwell, the alarming and ultimately fraudulent former proprietor of the *Mirror* newspaper.
[8] The case was of little consequence other than to make Ian Maxwell bankrupt, since he was quite unable to restore the missing securities to the pension fund.

Directors acting in good faith but not necessarily in the best interests of the company as a whole

Occasionally a director will claim that he was genuinely acting for the **9.10** good of the company and was acting in good faith—and that he was not therefore in breach of his fiduciary duty. In *Howard Smith Ltd v. Ampol Petroleum Ltd*[9] the directors genuinely believed that it was desirable for the company to be taken over by another company. Using authority to allot shares (which the members had given them earlier) the directors used that authority to allot shares to their preferred takeover bidder, so that the combination of the directors' shares and the bidder's shares outweighed the other shareholders who had hitherto been in a majority and who had opposed the proposed takeover by the bidder. The other shareholders objected to the directors' misuse of their undoubted authority to allot shares, and it was held that while the directors were entitled to use their authority to allot shares they were not entitled to use that authority for the purpose of wrecking an existing majority—and so they were not acting in the best interests of the company as a whole. A slightly similar issue arose in the case of *Hogg v. Cramphorn*[10] where directors allotted shares to the employees' pension scheme as part of a successful attempt to prevent a takeover bid. The directors genuinely believed that this was in the best interests of the company, but notwithstanding the directors' good faith in the matter, it was held that this was an improper use of their power. In order to resolve the matter, Buckley J. said that the members should be allowed, if they wished, to ratify what the directors had done, but those to whom the newly allotted shares had been issued should not be allowed to vote on the matter.[11]

Acting in the best interests of the company as a whole?

Sometimes the directors are put in a difficult position in that they may **9.11** have undertaken to commit themselves to a course of action which at the time was in their view in the best interests of the company. Does this decision fetter their future discretion? May they change their minds in the best interests of the company as a whole? It would appear that in principle they can,[12] provided there is no breach of any contract[13] —much therefore depending on the extent to which the directors have actually made their company form a contract with the other party, and if there has been any consideration.

---

[9] [1974] A.C. 821, [1974] 2 W.L.R. 689.
[10] [1967] Ch. 254, [1966] 3 W.L.R. 995.
[11] A similar approach was followed in the case of *Bamford v. Bamford* [1970] Ch. 212, [1969] 1 All E.R. 969, CA.
[12] *Dawson International plc v. Coats Paton plc* [1989] 5 B.C.C. 405.
[13] *Fulham Football Ltd v. Cabra Estates plc* [1994] 1 BCLC 363.

Remedies for breach of fiduciary duty

9.12   If a director breaches his fiduciary duty, the company may call upon
him to reimburse the company for any loss it has suffered, indemnify the
company for any expenses, hand over any profit which he has obtained
and which rightfully should be the company's, and to return to the
company any assets which he has misappropriated. If those assets are in
the hands of a third party who has acquired them in good faith for a fair
price from the director, it is unreasonable to expect the third party to
hand them back, but the director can still be required to account to the
company for the value of the assets themselves. The company may also
take out an interdict to prevent the repetition of the breach. If necessary,
the members could also vote to dismiss the director under Companies
Act 1985 ("CA 1985"), section 303.

Forgiveness for the breach

9.13   The members, however, may be content for their director to have
breached his duties—and indeed, despite the apparent conflict of interest, there is nothing usually to prevent a director voting in his own
interest to forgive his own breach[14] unless there is a question of a fraud
on the minority[15] or there is a contravention of some other rule of law
which is inherently unratifiable. An example of something that is unratifiable is illegal financial assistance or an improper return of capital.[16]
Forgiveness, or ratification of the breach, has to be done by the members
in general meeting by ordinary resolution, following full disclosure of
the entire matter.[17] If what the directors have done is contrary to the
memorandum or articles of association, then a special resolution is
required.[18] However, it is not possible to have a clause in the articles or
in any contract with the company pre-emptively absolving the directors
from any liability for any breach of their fiduciary (or indeed any other)
duty.[19] Despite this, the courts may forgive a breach where in their
opinion the director has acted honestly and reasonably.[20]

---

[14] *North-West Transportation Co. v. Beatty* (1887) 12 App.Cases. 589, PC.

[15] *Cook v. Deeks* [1916] 1 A.C. 554, PC.

[16] *Aveling Barford Ltd v. Perion Ltd* [1989] BCLC 626. In this case a holding company
engineered the disposal of a subsidiary's asset to the holding company for much less
than its true value. The subsidiary then went into insolvent liquidation. The holding
company claimed that as shareholders of the subsidiary it was entitled to ratify the
disposal, but the liquidator successfully argued that the disposal had been an improper
return of capital and that the company had failed to follow the proper procedures
required for a return of capital; a return of capital was inherently unratifiable and could
only be carried out by the required procedures.

[17] *Bamford v. Bamford* [1970] Ch. 212, CA.

[18] CA 1985, s.35(3).

[19] CA 1985, s.310.

[20] CA 1985, s.727, to be discussed later.

The duty of skill and care

Historically the standard of care that a director was expected to **9.14** exercise in the management of his company was, by modern standards, very low. It was even possible to provide in a company's articles that the directors would not be personally liable for any actions carried out by them in the course of their directorship of the company, and the courts' view, to justify this, was that no-one was obliged to be a member of a company, and anyone who did was bound to accept that the company's articles might allow directors such freedom.[21] The rationale behind this was that directors should not be trammelled by anything that would interfere with the free market.

Such licence is not available now, since the advent of CA 1985, section 310, which provided that the only protection the company may supply is insurance for its officers' liabilities in the event of actions being raised against them, though such insurance would only cover officers' expenses in successfully defending any actions against them.

Furthermore the climate of opinion has also changed in the light of **9.15** various scandals, such as BCCI, the Mirror Group Pension fund, and Barings Bank. No longer is it acceptable, on the grounds of letting the free market operate, for directors to walk away from the problems their negligence or deceit has engendered. The Company Directors Disqualification Act 1986 interacts with the Insolvency Act 1986 to provide for the disqualification of directors who have allowed their subsequently insolvent companies to trade fraudulently[22] or wrongfully[23]; and even if the company is solvent, as indicated in the previous chapter, a director may be disqualified. The rules on minority protection under CA 1985, section 459 have limited some of the worse excesses of directorial powers. The Combined Code for directors of listed companies requires high standards of disclosure and probity. Non-executive directors are expected to keep an eye on their fellow directors. The financial press has grown more sceptical of directors' behaviour in the light of the increase in directors' salaries irrespective of the success of their companies. Furthermore, it is increasingly becoming evident that unprofessional behaviour by directors leads to a lower share price[24]: it is thus in everyone's interests that directors behave properly.

---

[21] *Re City Equitable Fire Insurance Co. Ltd* [1925] Ch. 407. In this case the chairman himself was a "daring and unprincipled scoundrel" but as the articles provided that directors would not be liable even for their own "wilful neglect or default" the directors escaped scot-free. For a discussion on how this case was nevertheless an advance on previous cases, see Walters, "Directors' duties: the impact of CDDA 1986" (2000) *Company Lawyer* 110.

[22] IA 1986, s.213.

[23] IA 1986, s.214.

[24] The shares in Robert Maxwell's Mirror Group, while he was at the helm, consistently traded at a discount to the underlying value of the business, because of the "Max" factor which reflected his general unreliability and questionable integrity.

From a legal, as opposed to a commercial, point of view, the standard
of care that is now expected of a director is both objective—that of a
person in a similar position to the director—and subjective, in that if a
director has a qualification, such as accountant or lawyer or other
professional position, more is expected of him.[25] Lord Hoffman stated
in *Re D'Jan of London Ltd* that the duty of care to be exercised by a
director was as indicated in IA 1986, section 214(4), being that of

"a reasonable diligent person having both—

(a) the general knowledge, skill and experience that may
reasonably be expected of a person carrying out the same
functions as are carried out by that director in relation to
the company, and
(b) the general knowledge, skill and experience that that
director has."

9.16   Lord Hoffman's view has the happy merit of matching the standard
expected of a competent director of a company with the standard
expected of a director trying to avoid being found liable for wrongful
trading where a company has gone into insolvent liquidation.

It is true that if a director has failed to exercise a duty of care towards
his company, it is open to the members to forgive him, as indicated
above, and ratify his breach of duty of care. This means that a director
with a majority shareholding could use his votes in general meeting to
absolve himself of any breach unless he was using his votes in such a
way as to prejudice the minority shareholders, or, at worst, perpetrate a
fraud on the company. But, as Lord Hoffman pointed out in *Re D'Jan
of London Ltd*, if a director wishes to be absolved by voting in his own
interest, as Mr D'Jan could possibly have done, he needs to do so
swiftly before the company goes into liquidation—as did not happen in
that case.

9.17   If the members do not forgive the director, the courts may possibly do
so, under CA 1985, section 727. This section acts as complete or partial
relief (at the court's discretion) for directors who have acted honestly
and reasonably under the circumstances. Mr D'Jan, who failed to check
his insurance documentation for his company property, was held to be
only partly liable for the loss to the company occasioned by his care-
lessness in failing to check the paperwork; but Mr Selby, in *Cohen v.
Selby*,[26] who, in his capacity as a shadow director of his jewellery
company, took uninsured jewels (paid for by post-dated cheques, but
owned by his company) from the south of England in a canvas hold-all
on a cross-channel ferry, apparently lost them on the ferry, thereby
failed to sell them at Antwerp, consequently failed to provide funds to

[25] *Dorchester Finance Co. Ltd v. Stebbing* [1989] BCLC 498.
[26] [2001] BCLC 176, CA (and confirmed on appeal).

enable the cheques to be honoured, and who also tried to avail himself
of the benefits of section 727, was unable to persuade the courts that his
actions were "honest and reasonable".[27]

It is probably the case that the standard of care required of directors
has never been higher. In the USA the test that is applied to directors as
to the competence of their decisions is the "business judgement rule",
which, broadly speaking, states that provided a director has applied his
mind to the matter in hand, exercised a degree of prudent judgement and
acted honestly and sensibly, on the whole he will not be liable for his
mistakes. It is submitted that increasingly a similar test is being or will
be applied in the United Kingdom.[28]

Statutory duties

It is arguable that there is no need for any statutory duties at all, since **9.18**
the wide terms of the fiduciary duty cover a multitude of obligations,
and the wide terms of the duty of care cover most of the remaining ones.
Nevertheless, a number of statutory duties were introduced mainly as a
result of various corporate scandals in the 1960s and 1970s. The duties
were enacted, sometimes in haste, and sometimes not with the consideration that might have been expected. It is well recognised now that
having statutory duties, though not always without its benefits, has
difficulties, these being the difficulty of changing the statutes, and more
significantly, having duties on a statutory basis encourages a mind-set of
directors which tries to find loopholes in the legislation. At the time of
writing, and following the Company Law Review, it is anticipated that
a new code for directors, similar to that which is used elsewhere in
Europe, will be promulgated and put out for discussion, in the hope that
a code will have the flexibility and alertness to circumstances and
change that legislation clearly lacks.

Tax-free payments to directors—Companies Act 1985 section 311

This was introduced because some directors had been able to per- **9.19**
suade their companies to pay them remuneration free of income tax; but
any attempt to be paid free of tax would nowadays be caught much more
effectively by the Inland Revenue. This section is generally agreed to be
completely pointless.

Payments to directors for loss of office—Companies Act 1985 section 312

Should a director receive a payment for loss of office or retirement, **9.20**
on takeover or on any other occasion, that payment should be disclosed

---

[27] The unkind might suggest that the uninsured jewels never actually left England.
[28] On the subject of directors' duty of care generally, see also Lord Hoffman's Leonard
Sanger Lecture, published in *The Company Lawyer*, July 1997, p. 1994.

to and approved by the members first, without which the company may demand it back from the director.[29] This requirement is easily evaded by providing for payment for early termination or other termination of office in the director's service contract which, if for less than five years and approved by the other directors, need not be approved by the members.

Company approval for property transfer or share transfers— Companies Act 1985 sections 313, 314

9.21   If a director receives payment for loss of office on the occasion of the transfer of some or all of the company's property or undertaking, that payment should be declared and approved; and if the director receives such payment without approval he is to hold it in trust for the company. The rationale of this is if the director is in effect receiving an inducement to sell some or part of the company's property, he is personally benefiting from a payment that really ought to be shared out amongst all the shareholders. A similar provision applies under section 314 where the director receives payment for loss of office following the sale of all or part of the company's shares. This section attracts criminal consequences and any unauthorised benefit must be returned to the members. This again is designed to prevent directors receiving bribes to persuade the shareholders to sell their shares to a bidder. How such bribes could in practice be detected is not explained.

Directors to declare their interest in contracts—Companies Act 1985 section 317

9.22   See *Directors' personal interests and conflicts of interest* above.

Directors' service contracts

9.23   Directors obtain rights from their service contracts. If a director has a service contract, the contract will first need to be approved by the other directors in terms of CA 1985, section 317.[30] Directors' service contracts are available for inspection at the company's registered office.[31]

Companies Act 1985, section 319 states that any term of a director's contract which provides that the contract is to continue for a period in excess of five years and which may be terminated at the director's instance, but not the company's, or may only be terminated by the company only under specified circumstances, will only be valid if the

---

[29] *Lander v. Premier Pict Petroleum Ltd*, 1997 S.L.T. 1361. This case concerned the viability of a "golden handshake" on a director's departure.
[30] *Neptune (Vehicle Washing Equipment) Ltd v. Fitzgerald* [1995] 3 All E.R. 811, [1995] BCLC 352.
[31] CA 1985, s.318.

contract with the offending term has been approved by the members first.[32] Any term contravening this will be void and the company will then be able to terminate the contract by giving reasonable notice.[33]

There are further rules to prevent the overlapping of directors' service **9.24** contracts in an attempt to avoid the rules stated above.[34] Ingenious directors apparently instead avoid the rules by having lengthy notice periods.

Substantial property transactions

In order to prevent directors selling assets to their companies for an **9.25** excessive value, or buying assets from their companies for less than proper value, section 320 requires that members give approval to the directors before the directors either sell an asset to their company, or buy an asset from their company, if that asset is either worth more than £100,000 or 10 per cent of the company's net asset value, subject to a *de minimis* exception where the asset is less than £2,000 in value. Where the directors fail to obtain such approval, the transaction is voidable at the instance of the company,[35] the asset (where possible and if not in the hands of a third party who has acquired it in good faith and for value) or its value returned to the company unless the members have ratified the transaction within a reasonable period of time.[36] It is acceptable to take a subjective valuation of the asset since Parliament did not state that the value should be market value.[37]

Directors and ultra vires *contracts*

Directors, of all people, ought to know which contracts the company **9.26** enters into are *ultra vires*, and in particular, if a company enters into a contract with a director (or someone connected with the director), in his personal capacity, or the board of directors exceeds its powers under the company's constitution, that contract, or any transaction exceeding those powers, may be rendered voidable at the instance of the company.[38] The company's normal remedies against directors would then be

---

[32] In *Wright v. Atlas Wright (Europe) Ltd, The Times*, February 3, 1999, the courts permitted a single member company to approve an indefinite directorship for its sole director (and indeed shareholder).
[33] CA 1985, s.319(6).
[34] CA 1985, s.319(2).
[35] CA 1985, s.322(2). See also *Re Duckwari plc (No. 1)* [1997] 2 BCLC 713.
[36] CA 1985, s.322(2)(c). See also *sub nom Re Duckwari plc (No. 2)*, *The Times*, May 18, 1998.
[37] *Micro Leisure Ltd v. County Properties and Developments Ltd, The Times*, January 12, 2000, (OH).
[38] CA 1985, s.322A.

available as above unless the members ratify the contract or the transaction, or the courts exonerate them.[39]

Contracts with sole members/directors

9.27   Where a company is a single member private limited company, any contracts between the company and its single member who is also a director of the company must either be in writing, set out in a memorandum or recorded in the minutes of the first meeting of the company after making the contract.[40]

No dealing in traded options

9.28   Directors of listed companies may not deal in traded options to buy or sell their own company's securities,[41] since this could lead to manipulation of the share price. There are criminal penalties for transgression though no civil sanctions are indicated in statute.[42] It is however permissible for the director to have share options.[43]

Restrictions on loans to directors

9.29   Technically it is not a duty of a director not to borrow money from his company or a company's holding company or subsidiary; rather there is a prohibition on a company lending money to a director, subject to certain exemptions. But for convenience sake the topic is being dealt with here. Companies may not lend money, or provide security for a loan or undertake to indemnify a loan to a director,[44] unless the sum in question is less than £5,000.[45] The reason for this prohibition is that if a director is reduced to borrowing money from his own company it suggests his credit is poor elsewhere and he is therefore a potentially risky borrower from the company, and because it is not a proper use of shareholders' funds. Lending to a director is a criminal matter for the director who received the loan if the company in question is a "relevant company",[46] for the relevant company that gave the loan and for anyone

---

[39] *Re Torvale Group Ltd* [1999] 2 BCLC 605.
[40] CA 1985, s.322B(1). See also *Re Neptune (Vehicle Washing Equipment) Ltd (No. 2)* [1995] B.C.C. 1000.
[41] CA 1985, s.323.
[42] If market manipulation did take place it could lead the director open to sanctions under the Financial Services and Markets Act 2000, Pt VIII.
[43] A traded option entitles the person exercising the option to acquire a share already in the market at a designated price; a share option (in the USA known as a stock option) is the entitlement to buy a newly created share from the company. There is much controversy about the method of accounting for share options.
[44] CA 1985, s.330(1).
[45] CA 1985, s.334.
[46] A "relevant company" is a plc, a subsidiary of a plc, a subsidiary of a company which has another subsidiary which is a plc or has a subsidiary which is a plc (CA 1985, s.331(6)).

who procures that the relevant company gives the loan while knowing that the relevant company should not be giving the loan. In addition the loan is voidable at the instance of the company[47] subject to the usual caveats[48] and the director is liable to make good the loss to the company or account to the company for any gain he may have made.[49]

Relevant companies have further restrictions. If a relevant company grants a "quasi-loan" to a director, that too is forbidden[50] and voidable at the instance of the company.[51] A quasi-loan is a loan arrangement whereby the company lends money to the director, but the director undertakes to reimburse the company at a later stage—the standard example being using the company credit card to buy personal goods.[52] However a quasi-loan is permitted if the reimbursement must take place within two months and if the quasi-loan is not in excess of £5,000.[53]

In addition a relevant company may not make a "credit transaction" **9.30** which enables the director to defer payment for goods or land because the company, on a hire purchase agreement or a conditional sale agreement, acquires the goods on the understanding that the director will ultimately repay the company.[54] However it is permissible for a company to enter into a credit transactions if the sum involved is less than £10,000[55] and if the credit transaction is in the ordinary course of business and the terms of the credit transaction are no different from the terms that would be offered to anyone who was not involved in the company.[56]

Notwithstanding the general restriction on loans, quasi-loans and credit transactions, there are still further exemptions from the overall rule. Companies within a group may lend sums to each other by way of loans or quasi-loans.[57] A company may give a loan or a quasi-loan to its holding company[58] or enter into a credit transaction for its holding company.[59] Companies may lend money to their directors to enable them to meet expenditure on behalf of the company or to carry out their duties[60] provided the matter is approved by the members in advance,

---

[47] CA 1985, s.431(1). This applies to all companies, whether relevant companies or not.
[48] CA 1985, s.341(1)(a) and (b).
[49] CA 1985, s.341(2).
[50] CA 1985, s.330(3).
[51] CA 1985, s.341.
[52] CA 1985, s.331(3).
[53] CA 1985, s.332.
[54] CA 1985, s.331(7).
[55] CA 1985, s.335(1).
[56] CA 1985, s.335(2).
[57] CA 1985, s.333.
[58] CA 1985, s.336(a).
[59] CA 1985, s.336(b).
[60] CA 1985, s.337(1).

failing which the expenditure must be repaid within six months[61] and provided the expenditure is no greater than £20,000.[62]

9.31 Yet further exemptions apply in respect of money-lending companies.[63] This is because traditionally one of the perquisites of working for banks and similar institutions is a cheap mortgage and low rates of interest on loans. Accordingly a money-lending company may give a director a loan or a quasi-loan, or guarantee a loan or a quasi-loan, provided the loan or quasi-loan is in the ordinary course of business and is on the same terms as would be given to anyone not connected with the money-lending company provided the sum involved is not more than £100,000.[64] Specifically this does not prevent a money-lending company providing loans to its directors to enable them to buy their own homes[65] (even though such benefits might not be provided to others not connected with the company but with comparable financial standing).

All the above rules relating to loans, quasi-loans and credit transactions apply not only to directors but to those connected with them, these being directors' children, step-children, spouses, companies with which the directors are associated,[66] trustees of any trust for the benefit of the directors, their children, step-children and spouses, the trust itself, partners (in terms of partnership law) of the directors and those connected with the directors. Curiously the word "connected" does not include employees or in these liberal days, girlfriends, lovers, significant others or siblings.

9.32 The rules relating to loans are little understood and much ignored in practice, mainly because of their complexity and because of the failure, certainly in smaller companies, of the directors to see any significance in borrowing from what is effectively their own business anyway. The rules is still important, and a common feature of certain financial scandals in the USA in 2002 was directors' borrowings from their companies at below market rates.

Restriction on political donations

9.33 Companies are permitted to make donations to political parties of up to £5,000 a year without the need for prior authority from the members,[67] but for sums greater than this, the directors must seek the approval of the members by means of an ordinary resolution.[68] If this

[61] CA 1985, s.337(3).
[62] CA 1985, s.337(3).
[63] CA 1985, s.338.
[64] Unless the company is a bank (CA 1985, s.338(4)) in which case the financial limit of £100,000 is waived.
[65] CA 1985, s.338(6).
[66] This means that the director has at least a 20 per cent interest either in share capital or voting power (CA 1985, s.346(4)).
[67] CA 1985, s.347B(4).
[68] CA 1985, s.347C(1).

approval is not obtained, the directors will become jointly and severally personally liable for the donation and for any damages for loss suffered by the company arising out of the donation, together with interest.[69] It is therefore a duty of the directors to obtain prior approval before any political donation is given.

Directors' duties to creditors

In principle, directors have no duty of care to creditors,[70] at least **9.34** while the company is solvent. The whole point of the limited liability company is to insulate the directors and members from the claims of the company's creditors provided, that is, that the company is not being run as a sham or façade, or provided that some other occasion for the lifting of the corporate veil has not taken place.[71] Creditors are not obliged to deal with limited companies, and if a creditor chooses to deal with a limited company, he must take the risk that the company may be run badly or without any consideration for creditors' interests. If the creditor is anxious about the trustworthiness of directors of a company, he should take adequate precautions such as obtaining personal guarantees, inspecting the company's accounts in the Register of Companies, seeking performance bonds or some other method of safeguarding his position.

If the company is heading towards insolvency, the position may be different[72] though the Scottish case of *Nordic Oil Services Ltd v. Berman*[73] suggests that directors are not responsible for economic loss suffered by a creditor as a result of the directors' actions, and the case of *Williams v. Natural Life Health Foods Ltd*[74] bears this out—provided that on balance the director has been acting through the company and not taking personal responsibility for his company's actions. Furthermore, the directors will not in general be liable for something their company's employees have done, unless the directors procured that those acts be done by the employees.[75]

A particular issue in England is where a director has been the sole **9.35** member of a company, or is otherwise in a position to procure that a company acts to his instruction[76] in which case, if the company commits a tort on the instruction of the director, the director will be joint tortfeasor with the company—so that if the company is insolvent or not worth suing the director may be made liable himself. This very much

---

[69] CA 1985, s.347F(2) and (3).
[70] *Multinational Gas and Petrochemical Co. Ltd v. Multinational Gas and Petrochemical Services Ltd* [1983] Ch. 283, [1983] 2 All E.R. 563, *per* Dillon L.J.
[71] See Chap. 2.
[72] *Liquidator of West Mercia Safetywear Ltd v. Dodd* [1988] BCLC 250, CA.
[73] 1993 S.L.T. 1168 (OH).
[74] [1998] 1 W.L.R. 830.
[75] *C. Evans Ltd v. Spitebrand Ltd* [1985] 1 W.L.R. 317.
[76] *Trustor AB v. Smallbone* [2001] 1 W.L.R. 1177.

becomes an issue with a single member company, where if there is only one director, that director is in a position to procure that his company does whatever he wants; and he could then be liable, particularly if that director has deceived creditors.[77] But where there is more than one director, it becomes harder, in practice, to prove that the director himself procured the company to carry out the tort—there is always the possibility that some other director was at fault.[78]

There have not been at the time of writing any major cases in Scotland on this point, but it is submitted that the principle in Scotland would be the same as in England—and in the interests of commercial certainty it would be wise for it to be consistent—that a director is not in general personally liable for the delicts committed by his company, unless he has assumed personal responsibility, or unless it can be proved that he personally procured the delict through the company so that the company was a sham or façade concealing his true intentions.

Directors' duties to creditors, and the need for a code to outline what those duties are, are extensively discussed in the Company Law Review Final Report[79] without coming to a final view on whether or not, or to what extent, directors should be liable to the creditors as their company approaches insolvency.

Duty to employees

9.36   While companies may have obligations to employees under employment law, and directors are expected to carry out such duties as paying employees' wages and taxes under the PAYE system, in general there is no common law duty of care to employees as being different from any other creditors. However, under CA 1985, section 309 the directors are required to have regard to the interests of their companies' employees. The duty to "have regard" (whatever that may mean) is owed by the directors not to the employees directly, but to the company, and is enforceable in the same manner as any other fiduciary duty owed by the directors. This means that only if the members collectively decide that the employees' interests are not being regarded may they exert pressure

---

[77] *Daido Asia Japan Co. Ltd v. Rothen*, unreported, Chancery 1997, July 24, 2001.
[78] At the time of writing there is a case awaiting a hearing in the House of Lords, *Standard Chartered Bank v. Pakistan National Shipping Corporation (No. 2)* in which the claimants ended up with a bill of lading that had been deliberately falsely dated by the director of the fourth defendant, Mr Mehra, who was one of four directors of his company, Oakprime Ltd, as part of an ingenious and wholly successful fraud against the Vietnamese Government. The Court of Appeal held that the claimant had no claim against Mr Mehra, because the claimant at all time had dealt with Mr Mehra's company, Oakprime Ltd (subsequently in liquidation). Furthermore, although a claim could have been made out against Mr Mehra as a joint tortfeasor, such a claim should have been put in the pleadings earlier and it was unjust to insert it at such a late stage. It will be interesting to see if the House of Lords continue to maintain the corporate veil in the face of such deliberate deceit as arose in this case.
[79] At paras 3.12–3.20.

on the directors to have some regard for the employees. As in many cases, except perhaps companies where the employees have a large shareholding in the company, the members' interests will be antithetical to the employees' interests and this section is widely ignored.[80]

The directors also have extensive duties under Health and Safety legislation which may not be avoided by the exercise of the corporate veil.[81] This book does not address these large issues and reference should be made to other literature on the subject.

The duty to members

If the directors had to bear in mind the interests of every member individually, there would be no end to their responsibilities or to the possibilities for litigation. It would be unreasonable to expect directors to carry such a burden. Directors certainly have a responsibility to the members as a collective whole, but not necessarily to each member.   **9.37**

The case of *Percival v. Wright*[82] involved a member asking the company secretary to find a purchaser for his shares. The company secretary found that a director was willing to buy the member's shares, but the director did not disclose that the reason he wanted to do so was because there was talk of a takeover which meant that he could quickly have sold the former member's shares at a profit. It was held that the member had no claim against the director. On the one hand this case makes sense in that the member had been given what he wanted—a purchaser,[83] but on the other, the director appears to have been less than frank in his behaviour.

A more recent case casts doubt, not necessarily on the overall practical point of directors' not being liable to individual members, but on whether such lack of good faith is acceptable. In *Platt v. Platt*[84] one director, who was also a shareholder, deliberately lied to his fellow shareholders (indeed, his own brothers) about the value of their company's shares, and exhibited a lack of candour in his dealings with them. Under these circumstances it was held that he did have a fiduciary duty towards them. It would appear that while the overall principle of freedom from responsibility to individual members still applies, that principle may be disapplied under certain circumstances, and it remains to be seen how this particular area develops.   **9.38**

---

[80] The reason this section was inserted was that one of the terms of entry to the European Union was a greater regard for employees' interests; the wording was ingeniously drafted apparently to satisfy this requirement but without it actually being any use to employees.

[81] *R. Rollco Screw and Rivet Co. Ltd, The Times*, April 29, 1999.

[82] [1902] 2 Ch. 421.

[83] The plaintiff could, after all, have asked the company secretary to find someone who would buy his shares at the best price. It should also be noted that this case took place in 1902 when the courts were more much accepting of the idea of directors' freedom from accountability than we are today.

[84] [1999] 2 BCLC 745.

178 *Company Law*

Duty to co-operate with insolvency practitioners and others

9.39   When a company goes into administration, receivership or liquidation the directors and any other officers of the company are expected to supply such information as those persons may require. Failure to do so is a criminal offence.[85] Where a company is in liquidation and the directors have carried out a fraud or other deception, such as destruction of or failure to maintain the company's records, false representations to creditors and so on, further criminal sanctions will be applied.[86]

Where the company is undergoing a DTI inspection, there is a duty on the directors to co-operate to the fullest extent with the DTI inspectorate[87] at the risk of being liable for contempt of court.[88]

DIRECTORS' LIABILITY

9.40   When a company is solvent, a director will only be liable to his company where he has breached his fiduciary duty to the company, his duty of care to the company or his statutory duties, all to the extent indicated earlier in the chapter and subject to the rights of any third parties involved. He may, also as indicated earlier, be liable to the extent of the loss suffered by creditors and members under limited circumstances.

Directors' liability on insolvency

9.41   But when the company is wound up, the liquidator can use IA 1986, sections 212–217 to make the directors compensate the company for its losses. If a company is insolvent but is not wound up, mainly because there are no funds available to pay for a liquidator, the directors may, regrettably, be able to avoid such penalties.[89] If the directors have committed any criminal offences in the period leading up to winding up, such as fraud, concealment of assets, removing or destroying the company's assets, making or keeping false records, falsifying the company's books, defrauding creditors or failing to provide proper information to the liquidator, etc., the directors may be imprisoned or fined.[90] Again, if the company is not wound up, these sanctions may not be applied.

The civil sanctions outlined in IA 1986, sections 212–217 were introduced in order to concentrate directors' minds as a result of various

---

[85] IA 1986, ss.22, 66, 157 and 208.
[86] IA 1986, ss.206–211 and 218–219.
[87] CA 1985, s.434.
[88] CA 1985, s.436.
[89] In England and Wales, under such circumstances, the Official Receiver would be appointed as the liquidator. Apparently it was considered too much of a drain on the public purse to have Official Receivers in Scotland.
[90] IA 1986, ss.206–211.

scandals in the 1970s and 1980s. There was great alarm at their introduction on the grounds that the provisions were eroding the sanctity of limited liability, but the Government's view was that honest directors had nothing to fear and that there had been too many instances of directors abusing the privileges of limited liability. In practice, the various remedies are not greatly used, mainly because of the cost of having the liquidator apply to the court for compensation order (unless some of the creditors are willing to fund the action, liquidators in general being unwilling to fund the actions themselves), the uncertainty of obtaining the order, the fact that many directors are not in practice worth suing anyway once their companies are in liquidation, and the fact that any creditor who feels sufficiently strongly to persuade the liquidator to take action against the errant directors may well find that such sums as the directors provide by way of compensation are distributed amongst the creditors generally rather than to the aggrieved creditor himself.

Nonetheless the sanctions are some deterrent to misbehaving directors. There are also extensive criminal sanctions against fraudulent practices by directors and officers of insolvent companies.[91]   **9.42**

Breach of duty to the company under Insolvency Act 1986 section 212

Where an officer of the company,[92] or promoter, manager or someone   **9.43** otherwise involved in the formation of the company, has misapplied or retained the company's assets, or been guilty of misfeasance or breach of any fiduciary or statutory duty to his company, including being negligent, any creditor, the Official Receiver in England, the liquidator or a contributory,[93] but not an administrator, may apply to court in order to have the court examine the person alleged to be liable, and if necessary the court can compel that person to repay any sums or return any assets due to the company and to contribute to the company by way of compensation such sums as the court sees just. A significant advantage of section 212 is that the procedure is summary, so that the process may be carried out expeditiously, and receivers (and in England administrative receivers) may use it against directors and others.

In many respects it is a "catch-all" provision and whereas IA 1986, sections 213 and 214 have their difficulties, section 212 is relatively easy to operate. It is not unknown for an application to be made both

---

[91] IA 1986, ss.206–211.

[92] In the context of a company in liquidation, this means not only a director, the company secretary and the auditor, but also any receiver, administrator, administrative receiver (in England) or liquidator.

[93] A contributory is a person who has a partly paid share and is still due to repay the unpaid amount on his share. The rights and definition of contributory are more fully explained in Chap. 16.

under section 212 and section 214.[94] An example of the exercise of
section 212 is *Re D'Jan of London Ltd*,[95] referred to above, where the
director failed to complete an insurance proposal form properly, thus
invalidating a later claim for fire damage. The important issue concerning section 212 is that the liquidator or other applicant is claiming sums
back from the director as a result of the breach of the director's duties
to the company as a whole, as opposed to sections 213 and 214 which
involves claims by the liquidator arising out of the director's failure to
consider properly the interests of creditors. The relief afforded by CA
1985, section 727 therefore does apply to section 212 orders, but not to
section 213 or 214 orders.[96]

9.44   In the event of a company being put into liquidation and a successful
claim being made against the director under section 212, a receiver
operating under the terms of a crystallised floating charge would be able
to seize the recovered funds at the expense of the liquidator on the
grounds that what the director returned to the company was originally
funds of the company's and therefore covered by the terms of the
floating charge.[97]

Fraudulent trading under Insolvency Act 1986 section 213

9.45   Only a liquidator (and not a receiver or administrator) may apply to
court for an order that anyone[98] knowingly party to the carrying on of
a business through a company (whether solvent or not) with the intent
to defraud creditors of the company, creditors of any other person, or for
any fraudulent purpose will be liable to make such contributions to the
company's assets as the court thinks proper. The difficulty with fraudulent trading is having to prove the deliberate intent to defraud,[99] and
since the effort of doing so may not be worth the return, liquidators
rarely use this provision. But from time to time it is still used, generally
where the evidence of directors' *mens rea* is unequivocal.[1]

There is also a criminal offence of fraudulent trading which applies to
directors, irrespective of the company's solvency.[2]

Wrongful trading under Insolvency Act 1986 section 214

9.46   Wrongful trading is also problematic. A liquidator (but not a receiver
nor an administrator) may apply to the court for an order to make a

---

[94] *Re DKG Contractors Ltd* [1990] B.C.C. 903; *Re Brian D. Pierson (Contractors) Ltd*
[1999] B.C.C. 26.
[95] [1994] 1 BCLC 561.
[96] *Re Produce Marketing Consortium Ltd* [1989] BCLC 513.
[97] *Re Anglo-Austrian Printing and Publishing Union* [1895] 2 Ch. 981.
[98] The word "anyone" covers not only directors and officers of the company, but also
members who are aware of what is taking place. See *Morris v. Banque Arabe Internationale d'Investissement SA (No. 2)* [2001] BCLC 263.
[99] *Galoo Ltd v. Bright Grahame Murray* [1994] 1 W.L.R. 1360.
[1] *Morphites v. Bernasconi* [2001] 2 BCLC 1.
[2] CA 1985, s.458.

director, or past director, of a company that has gone into insolvent liquidation liable to make such contribution to the company's assets as the court thinks proper.[3] The director will be liable for this if:

- the company is in insolvent liquidation;
- at some time before the commencement of the winding up, that director knew or ought to have concluded that there was no reasonable prospect that the company would avoid going into insolvent liquidation, and
- that person was a director of the company at the time.[4]

The courts will not make such an order if they are satisfied that the director took

> "every step with a view to minimising the potential loss to the company's creditors as (assuming he knew there was no reasonable prospect that the company would avoid insolvent liquidation) he ought to have taken".[5]

As to the facts the director ought to have known or found out, the **9.47** conclusion he ought to have reached and the steps he ought to have taken, are those which should be known, found out, reached and taken by:

- a reasonably diligent person having
- the general knowledge, skill and experience as may be expected of a person carrying out the same functions as are carried out by that director in relation to the company, and
- the general knowledge, skill and experience that that director has.[6]

This test is a demanding one, and the point of the above wording is deliberately to encourage directors to seek professional advice before the company's financial position deteriorates any further, in order to protect the interests of creditors. There has been concern with the wording of this section in that it imposes a standard that is easy to deliver in hindsight, especially by a judge who himself has probably never entered the commercial arena, and concern that it may drive companies into administration or liquidation (erring on the side of prudence) when in fact the company could in fact continue perfectly viably. As indicated earlier, the standard that is expected of a director is the dual standard both of any director in the same position as the

---

[3] IA 1986, s.214(1).
[4] IA 1986, s.214(2).
[5] IA 1986, s.214(3).
[6] IA 1986, s.214(4).

director in question and, where applicable, an higher level if the director has extra skill or experience, such as a professional qualification or many years' practice.

9.48 As an example of the operation of section 214, in *Re Produce Marketing Consortium Ltd (No. 2)*[7] the directors deliberately ignored auditors' advice and overstated the value of stock in their refrigerated warehouse in order to present a more viable impression of the company's solvency. They did this, amongst other reasons, because they had given personal guarantees to a bank for their company's loans and wished to avoid having to honour the guarantees. Another case suggests that poor judgement by one director when he could have taken advice rendered him liable, while his wife, who although also a director, played no part in the management of the company nevertheless was also held liable on the grounds that ignorance is no excuse.[8]

If a director is found liable under section 214, the courts may in addition disqualify the director under the Company Directors Disqualification Act 1986.

"Phoenix trading"

9.49 Phoenix trading is the loose term[9] for the re-use of an insolvent company's name by the directors who were involved in the insolvent company. Sometimes companies collapse, leaving creditors empty-handed, whereupon the former directors quickly re-establish themselves as directors or promoters of a new enterprise with a similar name in the same line of business. Where the director, or person who had been a director in the last 12 months, of an insolvent company does this within five years of the insolvent company's liquidation, he commits a criminal offence by having the new enterprise's name identical or very similar to the insolvent company's name,[10] unless the courts have expressly permitted such a name.[11] Although the Registrar of Companies would probably detect the re-use of a name or the use of a similar name if a new company were formed, he would not be aware of a partnership with such a name—and the legislation specifically refers to that possibility.[12]

---

[7] [1989] BCLC 520.

[8] *Re Brian D.Pierson (Contractors) Ltd* [1999] B.C.C. 26.

[9] A phoenix is a mythical Arabian bird, the only one of its kind, which after many years makes itself a nest of spices, sings a melancholy song, and flaps its wings to set its nest on fire, in the process of which it is burnt to ashes and is born anew. In the same manner the phoenix company rises out of the ashes of its own immolation.

[10] *R. v. Cole* [1998] 2 BCLC 234.

[11] IA 1986, s.216(3). The courts permitted the re-use of a name in *Re Bonus Breaks Ltd* [1991] B.C.C. 491, subject to certain undertakings by the directors. In this case the creditors of the original insolvent company were willing to allow the new company to be set up. For the procedure on how a name may be re-used, see the Insolvency (Scotland) Rules 1986, rr. 4.78–82.

[12] IA 1986, s.216(3)(c).

In addition if the new enterprise becomes insolvent and is a company, the directors involved in the new company will be jointly and severally liable along with the company and anyone else who knew of the contravention and ignored it and who was involved with the management of the company.[13]

NON-STATUTORY DUTIES

There are some duties that perhaps do not count as "duties"—more as expectations. **9.50**

The directors of listed companies are expected to adhere to the Combined Code, which is a voluntary non-binding code being an amalgam of the recommendations of the Cadbury, Greenbury and Hampel reports in the interests of best corporate governance. Being only a code, there are no sanctions against failure to adhere to its requirements, other than public disapprobation and possible criticism at general meetings and in the financial press. If directors choose not to adhere to the provisions of the Combined Code, they are expected to explain why they are not doing so. The Combined Code promulgates the virtues of accountability, integrity and transparency in corporate transactions by the directors. On the whole, most listed companies comply with the Combined Code—some more grudgingly than others—but it is difficult for listed companies' directors to complain too vociferously about the Combined Code's requirements without the directors being asked what they have to hide. Only if a company is conspicuously successful can it afford to ignore the Combined Code's requirements.[14]

The duty to non-corporate interests

Although it is not strictly speaking part of company law, over the last 15 years or so, with the rise in corporate governance, questions are being asked about companies' and their directors' responsibility to wider groups other than shareholders but who will be affected by the directors' actions, such wider groups being known as stakeholders. Some years ago it was acceptable (and some would say, still should be) for directors to say that their primary concern was delivering shareholder value, irrespective of other stakeholders' considerations. However, with the rise in living standards for shareholders generally, some shareholders have begun to call into question the practices of some companies, particularly as regards exploiting employees, the environment, the public purse (by taking advantage of every loophole in the tax **9.51**

---

[13] IA 1986, s.217(2).
[14] For example, Morrisons, the English supermarket chain, ignores the requirements for non-executives on the grounds that the company is very well run already, profitable and successful—all of which was certainly true at the time of writing.

and VAT legislation), weak foreign governments, considering or carrying out unethical practices such as bribery, market manipulation, commercial blackmail and threatening to close businesses down in order to
take advantage of cheap and non-unionised labour abroad. At present
there are no legal duties compelling company directors to consider
stakeholders' interests although a Corporate Responsibility Bill was
promulgated in June 2001. There is considerable debate about the
wisdom of any such compulsion and the practicalities of enforcement.
At present the main lever that those who would favour the stakeholder
approach can use is the threat of bad publicity and, at worst, public
boycotts of the company's products.[15] This debate will no doubt continue.

Reform

9.52 The White Paper proposes a revamped, modern and coherent set of
statutory rules for directors and a new code of directors' conduct,
enumerating the duties and responsibilities of directors to their companies, to their companies' members, their companies' employees, their
companies' creditors and to a slender extent stakeholders. A draft code
is printed at the end of the Final Report of the Company Law Review.
The code will be non-statutory, but it will be for directors to explain why
they have not adhered to the code—a practice known as "comply or
explain". It remains to be seen whether this will indeed replace the
present mish-mash of common law and statute.

Further Reading

Worthington "Corporate Governance: Remedying and Ratifying Direc-
tors' Breaches" [2000] L.Q.R. 638
Worthington "Reforming Directors' Duties" [2001] M.L.R. 439
Watson and Willikes "Economic Loss and Directors' Negligence"
[2001] J.B.L. 217
The Law Commission and the Scottish Law Commission, *Company
Directors: Regulating Conflicts* (No. 261) and *Formulating a
Statement of Duties* (No. 173)

---

[15] As happened in Germany following the proposals to dump the Brent Spar oilrig in the
ocean.

CHAPTER 10

COMPANY SECRETARY AND AUDITOR

Both the company secretary and the auditor are treated as officers of the **10.01** company, which means that where statute specifically refers to "officers" as opposed to directors, the intention is that the legislation should catch these other officials in the company.[1-2]

At the time of writing, every company must have a company secretary but the White Paper on the reform of company law suggest that company secretaries be optional at least as regards private companies. This is in the interests of deregulation. Public companies will continue to need company secretaries. Small private companies already do not need an auditor, though they are needed for medium sized companies and for public companies. Again, this is in the interests of deregulation.

It is expected that many companies, whether or not they are obliged **10.02** to have either company secretaries or auditors, will continue to retain them, in the interests both of credibility and efficiency.

THE COMPANY SECRETARY

The company secretary was historically a person of little importance, **10.03** whose role was a mere minute-taker and organiser of meetings, but increasingly he is now seen as a useful and professional member of the senior management of the company. Company secretaries have their own professional body, the Institute of Chartered Secretaries and Administrators,[3] and most company secretaries have either a legal or an accounting qualification. Although it is possible simultaneously to be a director and secretary,[4] and in many small family companies the practice is that one spouse is the managing director while the other spouse is the other director and company secretary, it is also possible to have a

---

[1-2] For example, IA 1986, s.212.

[3] Based at 16 Park Crescent, London.

[4] Unless there is only one director—under which circumstances that one director may not be company secretary as well (CA 1985, s.283(2)).

professional company secretary[5] who or which carries out the necessary work. Sometimes a firm of solicitors, or a partner in a firm of solicitors or accountants, acts as a company secretary.[6]

In a plc, the company secretary must either be a chartered secretary, a lawyer, an accountant,[7] a person who has held the office of a company secretary of a plc within three of the previous five years, or someone who by virtue of his holding any office or position or being a member of some professional body appears to the directors to be capable of holding the office of company secretary of a plc.[8] A sole director (of any company) may not be company secretary.[9] It is also unacceptable for a company to have as its company secretary a company which in its own right has a sole director the same person as the sole director of the original company,[10] or have as sole director of the company a company which in its own right has a sole director who is the secretary of the original company.[11] The purpose of these perplexing rules is to ensure that two separate human beings are involved in every company.

10.04   A company secretary is an employee of the company and the company is vicariously liable for his acts in the course of his duty.[12] Unlike a director or auditor he has no right of protest on dismissal. There is usually a provision in a company's articles providing for the appointment of a company secretary and providing that he may have the authority to sign documents on behalf of the company—sometimes without the need for a director to sign as well. Normally most company documents will be signed by both a director and the secretary but it is open to a company to permit either one of these to execute documents in the presence of a witness. A company's articles may also authorise a deputy company secretary to sign documents in the absence of the company secretary. Even where there is no such specific authority to permit company secretaries to enter into contracts on behalf of the company, it is likely that Companies Act 1985 ("CA 1985"), section 35B would protect third parties dealing with the company secretary in good faith.

The first company secretary indicates his willingness to take up office on the Form 10 and thereafter new ones will sign a Form 288a. Company secretaries do not need to give information about themselves

---

[5] A professional company secretary can be a limited company or a Scottish partnership providing company secretarial facilities.

[6] This is increasingly less common, because of the potential risk of liability. Most large solicitors' practices have in-house limited companies to act as company secretaries if clients wish the firm to provide company secretarial facilities.

[7] Qualified under any of the various professional accountancy bodies such as ACCA, CIMA, ICAS, etc.

[8] CA 1985, s.286(1).

[9] CA 1985, s.283(2).

[10] CA 1985, s.283(4)(a).

[11] CA 1985, s.283(4)(b).

[12] *Panorama Developments Ltd v. Fidelis Furnishing Fabrics Ltd* [1971] 2 Q.B. 711, [1971] 3 W.L.R. 440.

other than their name and address. Company secretaries are under no obligation to disclose to the directors or members any personal contracts they may have with their companies, and while they may owe duties of allegiance and good faith to their employers, the fiduciary duty, so highly developed for directors, does not directly apply to company secretaries. However, certain statutory duties, such as the receiving by the company secretary of any loans, quasi-loans or credit transactions in excess of £2,500 need to be disclosed in the accounts.[13] A company secretary who took too great an involvement in a company's management could in theory be a shadow director, though there are no cases on this point.

The duties of a company secretary

There are very few duties laid down in statute concerning the duties **10.05** of a company secretary, and many of the tasks they traditionally fulfil may equally well be carried out by a director. However, by convention, the following tasks are commonly carried out by company secretaries:

- taking the minutes of general and board meetings;
- organising and preparing the paperwork for general and board meeting;
- signing of company documents and contracts;
- keeping the company's statutory registers, such as the register of shareholdings, etc.;
- sending registrable documents to the Registrar of Companies.

In addition, the following duties are often carried out by company secretaries:

- any legal work or work connected with such matters as employment, banking, tax, pensions, insurance and office administration;
- ensuring compliance with Health and Safety legislation;
- in finance companies, acting as compliance officer[14];
- any other reactive tasks the directors cannot face dealing with themselves.

The Institute of Chartered Secretaries and Administrators is trying to **10.06** raise the profile of company secretaries, and in this respect they were helped by the Combined Code which indicated that company secretaries of listed companies were to act as the conscience of the company, there

[13] CA 1985, Sched. 6, Pt III.
[14] A compliance officer has the unenviable task of monitoring his company's employees' personal shareholdings in order to deter insider dealing.

to provide best advice on how to comply with the requirements both of corporate law and also of current best practice in terms of corporate governance.

AUDITORS

10.07 As indicated in Chapter 7, all companies need auditors with the exception of dormant companies and certain small companies.[15] An auditor may be either an individual, a firm or a registered company[16] but under whatever form the auditor is operating, the auditor must be independent of the company,[17] and eligible in terms of his professional requirements by being a member of a recognised professional supervisory accountancy body.[18] Should the auditor turn out not to be eligible the Secretary of State may order a second audit.[19]

Appointment of auditors

10.08 A company's first auditors are appointed by the directors,[20] and they hold office until the first general meeting at which accounts are laid, whereupon they may be reappointed for the period up to the next general meeting at which accounts are laid.[21] Thereafter the auditors are usually re-appointed annually or until the next general meeting at which accounts are laid.[22]

Where there is a casual vacancy in the office of auditor, the directors or the company in general meeting may appoint another auditor to fill the post.[23] Special notice is needed where there is a resolution in general meeting either to fill a casual vacancy or to reappoint as auditor a retiring auditor who was appointed by the directors to fill a casual vacancy.[23a]

10.09 The Secretary of State has the power to appoint auditors if the company does not do so. The company is supposed to tell the Secretary of State within one week of the expiry of the time for appointing auditors[24] with criminal sanctions for failure to do so.

Accounts, as indicated in Chapter 7, do not need to be laid at annual general meetings, though it is conventional to do so. They may be laid

---

[15] CA 1985, s.388A(1).
[16] CA 1989, s.25(2) and 53(1).
[17] CA 1989, s.27.
[18] CA 1989, s.25. The main bodies are ICAS, ICAEW, ACCA and AAPA.
[19] CA 1989, s.29.
[20] CA 1985, s.385(3)—though if the directors do not get round to appointing them, the members may (CA 1985, s.385(4)).
[21] CA 1985, s.385(2).
[22] CA 1985, s.385(2).
[23] CA 1985, s.388(1).
[23a] CA 1985, s.388(3).
[24] CA 1985, s.387.

at any general meeting, but any reappointment of auditors starts from the meeting at which the accounts are laid.[24a]

Private companies

Private companies may pass an elective resolution[25] under CA 1985, **10.10** section 252 to dispense with the laying of accounts in general meeting. Where such a resolution has been passed, auditors will still need to be appointed in general meeting unless the members have passed a further elective resolution to dispense with the annual appointment of auditors under section 386. In the absence of that further elective resolution, the auditors must be appointed in general meeting before the end of the period of 28 days beginning with the day on which copies of the company's annual accounts for the previous year are sent to members in accordance with CA 1985, section 238. If notice has been given under section 253(2) that the accounts are to be tabled at general meeting,[26] the appointment must be from the conclusion of that meeting.

Most private companies will pass the further elective resolution to dispense with the annual appointment of auditors under section 386 if they have already passed the elective resolution to dispense with the laying of accounts in general meeting. Where the elective resolution to dispense with annual appointment of auditors has been passed, the auditors are deemed to be reappointed year after year unless the company becomes audit-exempt under CA 1985, sections 249A or 249AA or an ordinary resolution is passed revoking the elective resolution.[27]

The rights of auditors

In order to carry out their task of auditing a company's accounts, **10.11** auditors have the right of access to all the company's books and accounts, and are entitled to obtain such information and explanation from the company's officers as they need.[28] Misleading the auditors is a criminal offence.[29] Auditors of subsidiaries are required to give the auditors of holding companies all the information that the auditors of the holding company may reasonably require.[30]

Auditors have the right to receive notices of and attend all general meetings and to speak at such meetings. Auditors should also receive

---

[24a] CA 1985, s.385(2).

[25] For elective resolutions, see CA 1985, s.379A.

[26] This is where the elective resolution to dispense with the tabling of accounts is in operation, but a member or the auditor insists on a general meeting being held at which the accounts are to be tabled.

[27] CA 1985, 386(2).

[28] CA 1985, s.389A(1).

[29] CA 1985, s.389A(2).

[30] This is to prevent the old ruse whereby subsidiary companies had different auditors from the holding companies and information could artfully be mislaid between the two sets of auditors.

copies of resolutions which are proposed to be passed by means of written resolution (in the case of private companies) before the resolutions are passed. This is an attempt to prevent private companies passing either inappropriate resolutions or resolutions that require a particular procedure. For example, a private company could attempt to reduce its capital by written resolution, but as the procedure requires an application to court, the auditors should in practice (though there is no statutory duty to do so) warn the members that reduction of capital is more complicated than a mere resolution.

10.12   Auditors are entitled to be paid for their services but their fee must be indicated in the annual accounts.[31] Furthermore, auditors and their associates must also disclose what other benefits the firm of accountants carrying out the audit receives from the audited company.[32] This is because auditing is not particularly remunerative for accountants but serves as a loss-leader for more lucrative consultancy work, the preservation of which may, in some cases, cause auditors' independence to be compromised.

Removal and resignation of auditors

10.13   A company may at any time by ordinary resolution, of which special notice has been given, remove an auditor from office,[33] notwithstanding any contract between the company and the auditor.[34] If this takes place, the company must tell the Registrar of Companies of the removal within 14 days.[35] The removed auditor may still be notified of and attend any general meeting which had he not been removed he would still otherwise have been entitled to be notified of or attend had his term of office expired at it or at which the vacancy caused by his removal would have been filled.[36]

Because of the special notice provisions for the removal of an auditor before the expiry of his term of office, or appointing someone other than the retiring auditor as auditor,[37] the members should, at least in theory, be aware of the significance of the removal or the non-reappointment of the existing auditor. If the directors or a body of members wish to remove an auditor, or an existing auditor does not wish to be reappointed, there is inevitably a suspicion that the auditor may have uncovered something untoward that either the directors or some of the

---

[31] CA 1985, s.390A.

[32] CA 1985, s.390B. For the details of what must be disclosed see the Companies Act 1985 (Disclosure of Remuneration for Non-audit Work) Regulations (S.I. 1991 No. 2128).

[33] CA 1985, s.391(1).

[34] Removal before the expiry of his term of office may entitle the auditor to a compensation for breach of contract (CA 1985, s.391(3)).

[35] CA 1985, s.391(2).

[36] CA 1985, s.391(4).

[37] CA 1985, s.391A.

members may not wish revealed. Accordingly the special notice provisions require that the auditor in question be informed of the resolution, in which case he may make representations in writing of a reasonable length which should then be notified to the members of the company.[38] Unless the representations arrive too late to make it possible, the company must tell the members in the notice of the general meeting (at which the resolution is to be moved) of the receipt of the representations and send a copy of them to each member entitled to receive a notice of the meeting.[39] If the representations do arrive late, or the company fails to send them out, the auditor may require that the representations be read out at the meeting.[40] However, if the right to make representations is being abused in order to "secure needless publicity for defamatory matter" (as the statute pompously puts it) the court may rule that the representations should not be sent out or read out.[41]

The above rules relate to the removal or non-reappointment of an **10.14** existing auditor. If, however, an auditor resigns he may do so by leaving a notice to that effect at the company's office,[42] but such notice will not be effective unless it is accompanied by a section 394 statement. If the auditor is resigning because he feels that there are circumstances which he considers should be brought to the attention of the members, he may supply a statement of those circumstances[43] which must be circulated in the same manner as the representations above.[44]

There are special rules to deal with the situation where a private company has elected not to appoint auditors annually and any member wishes to terminate the auditors' appointment. In such a case, the member may by notice require the directors within 28 days of the notice to convene a general meeting at which the resolution to bring the auditors' appointment to an end may be moved. If the directors delay or refuse to do this, the member may convene the meeting himself and his expenses will be met by the company which in turn can recover them from the directors.[45]

The section 394 statement referred to above is a statement required to **10.15** be deposited at the company's registered office by the auditor if for any reason (including the above methods) that auditor ceases to hold office. The statement must disclose any circumstances in connection with the auditor's ceasing to hold office and which he considers should be brought to the attention of the members or creditors of the company.

---

[38] CA 1985, s.391A(3).
[39] CA 1985, s.391A(4).
[40] CA 1985, s.391A(5). This is in addition to his normal right to be heard at a general meeting anyway.
[41] CA 1985, s.391A(6).
[42] CA 1985, s.392.
[43] CA 1985, s.392A(1).
[44] CA 1985, s.392A(2)–(8).
[45] CA 1985, s.393(4), (5).

Equally, if there are no such circumstances, the auditor must say so.[46] This statement must be deposited within 14 days of the notice of resignation, within 14 days before the end of the time allowed for next appointing auditors or in any other case within 14 days of the date when the auditor ceases to hold office.[47]

The statement, if it does contain circumstances which the auditor considers should be brought to the attention of the members and creditors, must then be sent by the company to all those entitled to receive copies of the accounts[48] or, in the event of the statement containing needlessly defamatory matter (as above) there must be an application to the court to prevent the publication of the statement.[49] If, however there is no application to the court, or if there is an application to the court but it is rejected, the auditor must send in his statement to the Registrar of Companies within 28 days of the date of the original statement[50] or within seven days of receiving notification of the court's rejection of the application.[51] If the court upholds the application the statement need not be sent out, the auditor may have to pay the costs and all those entitled to receive the accounts will be informed of the court's decision.[52]

10.16 The purpose of this procedure, which is backed up by criminal sanctions for failing to comply with it,[53] is to prevent auditors from sitting on their hands if they discover something unpleasant in the accounts. In the past auditors who were scared by the directors of the company they were auditing, and who were worried by the prospect of being sued for not approving the accounts,[54] could resign in mid-office without having to give any reason for doing so.[55] Nowadays, auditors must either indicate what there is that causes them concern, or state unequivocally that there is nothing that does give them concern.

The role of the auditor

10.17 Auditors have various tasks, of which the primary one is the scrutiny of the company's accounts. Auditors normally draw up a contract with the company for which they are working, indicating the terms on which they will carry out the audit and what they expect the company and its officials to do. Notwithstanding the common misconception to the

---

[46] CA 1985, s.394(1).

[47] CA 1985, s.394(2).

[48] This does not just include members: it may include certain creditors such as debenture-holders.

[49] CA 1985, s.394(3).

[50] CA 1985, s.394(5).

[51] CA 1985, s.394(7).

[52] CA 1985, s.394(6).

[53] CA 1985, s.394A.

[54] Qualifying the accounts might call the directors' integrity in question, giving rise to the possibility of an action for defamation.

[55] As happened during the audit for the later Robert Maxwell's Mirror Group. The law was changed to ensure that resignation without explanation was no longer possible.

contrary, auditors have never held themselves out as checking that a company's accounts are all satisfactory. They could not possibly inspect every single entry in the company's books. They merely provide some degree of reassurance as to the accuracy of the company's finances, but are not there to track down every transgression. In the famous phrase of Lopes L.J. in *Re Kingston Cotton Mill (No. 2)*,[56] "the auditors are watchdogs not bloodhounds". It is the directors' duty to prepare the accounts, even if the directors have accountants to do the work for them, and it is the directors who are responsible for the accounts. Once the accounts have been prepared, the auditors add a report to the accounts confirming that the accounts, as stated above, present a true and fair view of the company's finances, but if there is something in the accounts with which the auditors are not satisfied, a "qualification" will be added to the report, which will indicate in what respects the accounts fall short of the requirements of normal accounting practice and the requirements of the Companies Acts. Having a qualification to the accounts is not in itself fatal for the company, for the members may be sufficiently close not to mind. However, creditors and potential investors will be concerned, and a company that has the report to its accounts qualified will have trouble maintaining its credibility.

Auditors are also required to certify certain matters under the requirements of CA 1985. For example, a private company converting itself into a plc will need the auditors to confirm the company's capital position, and a private company providing financial assistance to a shareholder will need confirmation by the auditors that the directors' own estimate of the continuing solvency of the company is not unjustified.[57]

The liability of auditors

Although there may be contractual arrangements to the contrary, the **10.18** primary duty of care that auditors owe is to the company that hires them to carry out the audit. This was established in the case of *Caparo Industries plc v. Dickman Touche Ross*[58] where the plaintiffs, who had been shareholders in a company they had taken over, sued the defendant auditors for their failure to carry out the audit of the target company properly, thus misleading the plaintiffs into believing that the target company was more viable than it was and therefore worth taking over. While the audit was undoubtedly inaccurate, the important issue in law was whether shareholders themselves had a right to sue the auditors. It was held that while the company had the right, not least because of the contractual arrangements between the company and the auditors to carry

---

[56] [1896] 2 Ch. 279.
[57] In *Coulthard v. Russell* [1998] 1 BCLC 143, a company carried out improper financial assistance. This should have been spotted by the auditors and stopped.
[58] [1990] 2 W.L.R. 358, [1990] 1 All E.R. 568.

out the audit, to sue the auditors, that right did not extend to individual members. Were individual members given that right, there might be no end of litigation, and the auditors could not possibly be expected to have such an indeterminate duty of care to such an indeterminate group of people. It would be impossible to insure against such risk, and carried to its logical extension accountants would then all pull out of auditing. The only way the auditors could have a responsibility to individual members or bodies other than the company which commissioned the audit was if they were put on notice that a particular member or body was relying on the audit,[59] or where it could be reasonably anticipated that a particular member[60] or body would be relying on the audit even if there were no contractual relationship.[61] Auditors of subsidiaries can reasonably expect that the holding company members will have an interest in their subsidiaries accounts and auditors may then be liable to the holding company.[62]

The *Caparo* decision, much welcomed by auditors, is still the current law, but increasingly the duty of care that is to be expected in each case will be specified in the terms under which the audit is carried out.

10.19   Auditors will not in general be liable if they had been misled by fraudulent directors[63] but if they uncover fraud they are expected to report it to the relevant authorities and will be liable for any loss to the company arising out of his failure to do so.[64] Auditors are allowed to obtain indemnities for their legal costs from the companies for which they work in the event of their successfully defending any action raised against them,[65] and in the event of a claim against them from the company which they are auditing, the auditors may be able to obtain the benefit of the court's protection if they have acted fairly and reasonably in terms of CA 1985, section 727.

Contemporary issues involving auditing

10.20   The recent scandals in the USA involving the destruction of Enron's financial records by Andersens, the firm of accountants that was supposed to be auditing Enron, has focussed minds on some of the intrinsic problems surrounding auditing, including an unhealthy lack of distance between auditor and auditee and a reluctance on the part of the auditor to queer the pitch of a high-paying client. As a result, auditing and accounting practice in the USA is likely to be brought more into line

---

[59] *ADT Ltd v. Binder Hamlyn* [1996] B.C.C. 808.
[60] *Electra Private Equity Partners v. KPMG Peat Marwick* [2000] B.C.C. 368.
[61] In *Andrew v. Kounnis Freeman* [1999] 2 BCLC 641, the Civil Aviation Authority was able to claim against negligent auditors since the auditors must have known that the CAA would be relying on their audit.
[62] *Barings plc v. Coopers and Lybrand* [1997] 1 BCLC 427, [1997] B.C.C. 498.
[63] *Galoo Ltd v. Bright Graham Murray* [1994] BCLC 319.
[64] *Sasea Finance Ltd v. KPMG* [2000] 1 BCLC 236, [2000] B.C.C. 989.
[65] CA 1985, s.310.

with the standards in the United Kingdom and Australia. There are
suggestions in the White Paper on Company Law reform to introduce
new rules into auditing, such as having new auditors every five years,
and it is likely that the role of the auditor will be increased to take
account of today's ever greater requirements for transparency and
accountability.

Further Reading

Company Secretaries

See the website for the Institute of Chartered Secretaries and Administrators www.icsa.co.uk

Auditors

Davies, *Gower's Principles of Modern Company Law* (6th ed., Sweet
and Maxwell, 1997), Chap. 20

CHAPTER 11

MINORITY PROTECTION AND DTI INVESTIGATIONS

MINORITY PROTECTION

11.01 Those who have the most shares in a company generally have the most to gain and most to lose from the company. It is therefore only fair that they should have the most say in the management of the company. Unfortunately, over the years it has sometimes been found true that those who have most shares in the company see the company's interests purely as an extension of their own interests, at the expense of the minority. If the minority shareholders dislike this, they may:

- sell their shares, if they are able to;
- accept the fact that they are outvoted;
- in limited circumstances raise an action to protect their own interests;
- under certain circumstances ask the DTI to investigate the company;
- petition to have the company wound up;
- (in Scotland only) have a judicial factor appointed to run the company.

This at least is the current position. But for many years, the courts found it very difficult to cope with the idea of a minority of shareholders having a justified grievance against a majority. There were various reasons for this:

(1) When you become a shareholder, under the Companies Act 1985 ("CA 1985"), section 14 you become a member on the terms and conditions of the memorandum and articles of association, one of which is that in general the majority rule prevails.

(2) It was not always clear whether a minority shareholder treated badly by the majority was seeking redress for himself,

or the company or for both. Whom should the minority
shareholder sue? Should he properly be suing the company,
the majority shareholders or the directors?

(3) If every disgruntled minority shareholder were entitled to
rush to the courts to complain every time the company made
a decision with which the minority disagreed, the courts
might be full of pointless and expensive actions.

(4) The courts are very reluctant to question commercial decisions. When is a resolution passed by the company a commercial decision which is entirely the company's business,
and when is it mistreating a minority?

At the same time, there are occasions when it is clear that a minority **11.02**
is being mistreated by the majority:

(1) Majority shareholders may use their strong voting position to
change the company's articles in such a way as to disadvantage a minority.

(2) If the majority shareholders are also directors, they might
award themselves high salaries and pension contributions as
directors while giving the minority shareholders little or nothing by way of dividends.

(3) Directors are not obliged to discuss all business and financial
matters with the shareholders. If the directors are also the
majority shareholders, they could deliberately keep the
minority in the dark to prevent the minority asking awkward
questions.

(4) If the directors are also the majority shareholders, it becomes
impossible for the minority shareholders to dismiss the directors under CA 1985, section 303, however badly the directors
might behave.

(5) The minority shareholders may find the cost of raising an
action against the majority expensive, and the majority may
take advantage of the minority's reluctance to incur costs.

(6) Although it is easy to say to a disgruntled minority shareholder that he should sell his shares, in practice in any but a
publicly quoted company (and sometimes not even then) it
may be difficult to find purchasers for the shares.

(7) If the directors are doing something which they should not be
doing, the company should raise an action against them. But
if those directors are also the majority shareholders, they are
not going to vote to make the company raise an action which
might ultimately be to their personal detriment.

(8) The majority shareholders in company A Ltd might be shareholders in company B Ltd, with which A Ltd is in dispute.
Even if A Ltd had a good claim against B Ltd, the majority

shareholders in A Ltd might be unwilling to raise an action against B Ltd because of their personal interest in B Ltd.

11.03   Historically the progress of legal protection for minority shareholders has proceeded as follows:

> (1) Following the rule in *Foss v. Harbottle*[1] (to be discussed below) minority shareholders could not obtain redress against a majority of shareholders unless the company in general meeting authorised action against the majority. Only the company had title to sue the majority shareholders—clearly on unlikely prospect.
>
> (2) It was soon realised that this was unduly oppressive to minority shareholders who had been treated unfairly. Under the common law four categories of unfairness were established, and these acted as permitted exceptions to the rule in *Foss v. Harbottle*.
>
> (3) Despite having admitted those categories, the courts were extremely reluctant to use them or to expand them, though the position of directors (who often were the same people as the majority shareholders) was increasingly brought under control by statute and the common law.
>
> (4) After an unsatisfactory statutory attempt in CA 1948, section 210 to protect minority shareholders, CA 1980, 1985 and 1989 all improved the position of the minority shareholder significantly. The CA 1985, section 459 (as amended by the CA 1989) contains the current statutory remedy for the minority shareholder. However, as the use of section 459 developed, it began to be recognised that the scales were increasingly tipping in favour of the minority shareholder. As most companies did not wish to be tied up in litigation, and because the courts appeared to be becoming ever more sympathetic to minority shareholders, it became easier to pay the aggrieved minority shareholders to go away even if their case was not very strong. However, the case of *O'Neill v. Phillips*,[2] and Lord Hoffman's pronouncements therein, have restored the scales to a more balanced position.

The *Foss v. Harbottle* rules and the exceptions thereto

11.04   The case of *Foss v. Harbottle* predates the first Companies Acts but deals with a fundamental problem in company law.

---

[1] (1843) 2 Hare 461.
[2] [1999] 1 W.L.R. 1092, also known as *Re a Company (No. 00709 of 1992)*.

Foss and Turton were minority shareholders in a company of which Harbottle and his associates were directors and majority shareholders. In their personal capacities Harbottle and his associates sold a plot of land to the company at an inflated price. At that time the present rules on fiduciary duties of directors were undeveloped and there was little judicial control over companies. Foss claimed that Harbottle and his associates had made the company pay too much for the land, thus unduly benefitting the majority shareholders. Harbottle replied that as directors they were entitled to decide what price the company should pay for its acquisitions. Foss and the other minority shareholders sued Harbottle and his associates. It was held that it was not for Foss and his fellow minority shareholders to raise an action against the directors for making the company lose money on expensive purchases. The proper plaintiff (*i.e.* the person or body who ought to be raising the action) was the company itself, as it was the company as a whole that was being defrauded or mismanaged. As the plaintiffs (Foss and Turton) were not the company (because of the separate legal personality rules —see Chapter 1), the issue of overpayment need not be decided upon.

This case is renowned both for its logic and its unfairness. The decision is logical because it is true that the company was the direct victim of the overpriced sale. The company had suffered: Foss personally had not suffered, except indirectly as his shares were now underrepresented by assets. If the company had suffered, it was for the company to raise an action. To do this would need the approval of the members, and Foss and Turton had not sought shareholders' approval for an action against the directors. Had a resolution to this effect been passed, the company could have raised the action against the directors.

The decision is unfair because of the requirement of shareholders' **11.05** approval for action against the directors. The decision in *Foss v. Harbottle* took no account of the fact that the majority shareholders, whose approval would have been needed for any action, were the perpetrators of the overpayment. They would have been most unlikely to vote for an action to be raised against themselves.

The exceptions to the rule in *Foss v. Harbottle*

Gradually the courts realised that the "proper plaintiff"[3] rule, **11.06** although not without its merits, did lead to injustice. Four exceptions have been permitted to the rules:

---

[3] A "plaintiff" would nowadays be called a "claimant" but the phrase is still extant and no doubt will continue to be for some time.

(1) *ultra vires* or illegal transactions;
(2) failure to follow proper procedure;
(3) infringement of the personal rights of the shareholders;
(4) fraud on the minority by the majority.

Although separating the exceptions gives the impression that they are all distinct, there is considerable overlap between them and the fiduciary duties applicable to directors, since majority shareholders commonly are directors.

Ultra vires *or illegal transactions*

11.07 If a company embarks upon an *ultra vires* transaction, technically the company should not be doing it (see Chapter 4). The company can be restrained from doing it by an interdict raised by any shareholder.

Although obtaining an injunction in this manner under this exception to the rule in *Foss v. Harbottle* would still potentially be valid, in practice any attempt to do this would be heavily qualified by the operation of the CA 1985, section 35(2)[4] which protects third parties[5] entering into transactions with a company without having any reason to believe that the company was not authorised to enter into the transaction and in any event provides statutory (though little used) remedies for members to insist on their companies adhering to their objects clauses. But nowadays most companies' objects clauses are so widely drawn there is little that is *ultra vires* most companies anyway.

As regards illegal transactions, any shareholder can stop any illegal transaction by means of an interdict.[5a]

Failure to follow proper procedure

11.08 If a company's articles state that a particular procedure must be followed for a particular matter, that procedure has to be followed. Although this might seem self-evident, in the case of *Quin and Axtens Ltd v. Salmon*,[6] the company failed to follow its own procedure. Its articles stated that certain transactions required the approval of both managing directors. One of the managing directors would not approve a particular transaction that required joint approval. The shareholders thought they would obviate his refusal by passing an ordinary resolution authorising the transaction anyway. This was held to be unacceptable. What the shareholders should have done was to pass a special resolution to rewrite the articles so that joint approval was no longer necessary.

---

[4] See Chap. 4, paras 4.04–4.07.
[5] Unless the third party is a director, in which case CA 1985, s.322A, would apply to protect the company.
[5a] CA 1985, s.35(2).
[6] [1909] A.C. 442.

If they were unable to pass the special resolution, then no authorisation could take place.

A similar case is *Edwards v. Halliwell*.[7] This case involves a trade **11.09** union, but is significant because the constitution of the trade union was similar to the articles of association of a company. The executive of the trade union decided that members' subscriptions should be increased, but did not first obtain the approval of a two-thirds majority of the members—as was needed under the trade union's constitution. A union member successfully challenged the executive's authority to increase the subscription without members' approval.

These two examples should not, in an ideal world, have arisen: a careful reading of the company's articles in the first case, and the trade union's constitution in the second, would have shown what the procedure was in each case.

Infringement of the personal rights of a shareholder

Whereas in the cases above the company in each case had failed to **11.10** follow procedures so that all the members are potentially affected, this exception arises when a particular minority is affected.

In *Pender v. Lushington*,[8] a company had unusual articles which stated that for every 10 shares a member had, he was entitled to one vote, but that no member could have more than 100 votes irrespective of the number of shares he held. In order to vote, the shares had to have been held for more than three months, and no shares could be held on trust for another member. A member, Pender, had a large number of shares but was only able to exercise his maximum of 100 votes. Pender also wished to ensure that certain general meeting decisions went his way. To get round the 100 vote rule he therefore transferred shares to friends who had been primed to vote in accordance with Pender's instructions and who, unlike Pender, were able to use the votes attaching to the shares he had transferred to them. On the occasion of a general meeting, held over three months later, Pender's friends wished to exercise their votes, but the chairman (Lushington) refused to count the votes, saying that Pender's transfers of shares were merely a ruse so that Pender could increase his influence. Had the votes been counted, the decision would have gone Pender's way. Pender then sued the chairman in a representative capacity on behalf of himself, the other shareholders and the company for the chairman's failure to count the votes. The courts had no difficulty agreeing with Pender, because there was nothing in the articles to prohibit the transfer of the shares; the motive for the transfer was irrelevant to the current proceedings, the friends were entitled to their votes and Pender was entitled to his.

---

[7] [1950] 2 All E.R. 1064.
[8] (1877) 6 Ch. D. 70.

Fraud on the minority by the majority

11.11   For the purposes of this exception it is important that there be a fraud,
carried out by the majority, (who are commonly also the directors), at
the expense of the company as a whole. Although the whole company
may suffer as a result of the fraud, in practice the majority shareholders
will not be distressed because they personally will have received the
benefit of the fraud. The minority shareholders will be distressed
because, for example, their shares may be worth less than if the fraud
had not taken place.

> *Cook v. Deeks*[9]
> Cook, a director and shareholder of the Toronto Construction
> Company, raised an action against Deeks and two other directors of
> the same company on the grounds that Deeks and the others had
> misappropriated a contract that in equity belonged to the company.
> Deeks and his fellow directors were majority shareholders in the
> company. The company had obtained a lucrative construction con-
> tract. Deeks and his friends decided that it would be better if they
> took the contract themselves personally rather than divide the
> profits amongst all the shareholders. As Deeks and his fellow
> directors commanded a majority of the votes, they passed a resolu-
> tion making the company renounce its interest in the contract.
> Deeks and his friends then took the contract for themselves. It was
> held that this was not only a breach of the directors' fiduciary duty
> but was also an abuse of the majority voting power. The contract
> had to be handed back to the company.

The issue here is that what Deeks did was unacceptable because it
was plainly fraudulent. Deeks had deliberately intended to deprive the
company and the other shareholders of something that rightfully
belonged to the company. By contrast, it is possible in general for a
majority legitimately to approve or ratify actions, even if the minority
are unhappy, provided those actions in themselves do not involve fraud,
show evidence of bad faith, or involve directors appropriating assets
which belong to the company. This was explored in the case of *Pavlides
v. Jensen*,[9a] where a mine was sold to an outsider at a very low value,
owing to the incompetence of the directors. The decision to sell was
ratified in general meeting, but the minority shareholders objected. It
was held that the directors'/majority shareholders' actions may have
been negligent but were not fraudulent, and therefore the ratification
was acceptable. By contrast, in *Daniels v. Daniels*[10] the directors sold an
asset at an undervalue to one of the directors. This was held not to be

---

[9] [1916] 1 A.C. 554, PC.
[9a] [1956] Ch. 565.
[10] [1978] Ch. 406.

ratifiable because it was a misappropriation by a director (who ought to have known better) of company assets.

Interestingly, no one is sure what the position would be in the United **11.12** Kingdom if a company in general meeting renounced a contract without any suggestion of fraud, and if a director or majority shareholder in his personal capacity then approached the other party to the contract to ask if he could take over the contract instead. Presumably provided he declared his interest to the other directors and members there would be no reason in principle why he could not then take the contract. His position would be strengthened if, in any vote on whether or not the company should renounce the contract so that he could get it instead, he abstained from voting. There would then be no question of a conflict of interest affecting his voting. Well-drafted articles might well permit this.

Difficulties with the common law remedies

The exceptions to the rule in *Foss v. Harbottle* have over the years **11.13** come to be seen as restrictive, confusing, and, particularly in England, tangled up with procedural matters.[11] There is also a difficult issue regarding the distinction between personal rights (the right to assert some provision of the memorandum or articles which is of particular significance to the member in question) and corporate rights (the right to seek a remedy for the company as a whole which the majority shareholders are unwilling to assert), the former of which may be asserted by a personal or representative action, and the latter by a derivative, the distinction between the two not always being as clear cut as might be hoped. The Law Commission Consultation Paper No. 142 followed by its Report[12] both recommend a new revised form of derivative action, to some extent modelled on CA 1985, section 459, which would be a great deal more "user-friendly". In any case derivative actions are a feature of the English law of equity and of English procedural laws and accordingly of less significance in Scotland. In Scotland the same result, it was argued in *Anderson v. Hogg*,[13] could be obtained by the use of the *nobile officium*.

Common law actions are not entirely obsolete, but the main reason for avoiding them is that the exceptions are narrow and unless the facts fit easily within the one of the exceptions an action may not be possible. By contrast section 459 is fairly broadly drafted to cover a wide range of prejudice to the minority and section 461 (which permits the court to give such remedy as it sees fit in response to a section 459 petition)

---

[11] A major issue is whether the action is derivative, thereby intended to benefit the company overall, or representative, meaning that the litigant is suing on behalf of himself and other shareholders (excluding those whom the claimant is suing) but not necessarily benefiting the company overall.

[12] Cm 3769.

[13] At the Outer House hearing, 1999 S.L.T. 634.

offers a breadth of remedies for the minority shareholder. Even where the facts might have warranted a derivative action (under the common law), said Lord Coulsfield in *Anderson v. Hogg*,[14] a petition under section 459 is not barred,[15] while in the English case of *Barret v. Duckett*[16] the Court of Appeal made it very clear that the plaintiff should have been seeking a buy-out remedy following a section 459 petition rather than trying to raise a derivative action. Nonetheless the fact remains that there are occasions when the common law is appropriate, and where the facts of the situation do not fall within the parameters of "unfairly prejudicial conduct" as required under section 459. Although in practice section 459 is by far the easiest method of dealing with minority protection, the common law is not dead[17] though it is perhaps worth noting that of the few recent derivative actions in England[18] most involve directors in their capacity as majority shareholders failing to act in good faith and perpetrating frauds on their companies—which in its own right would be a breach of fiduciary duty.

11.14 It might indeed be arguable that were the facts of *Foss v. Harbottle* to be replicated today and in a listed company, the current requirements under the City Code for directors to act in accordance with best professional practice would make it difficult for the directors' behaviour, even as majority shareholders, to be acceptable. In some ways it seems absurd that merely because the directors could use their majority shareholding in 1843 in *Foss v. Harbottle* to legitimise their overpayment, directors should still be able to hide behind the shield of their majority shareholding to avoid having to accept responsibility for their own failure to act in good faith with a proper regard for the company as a whole. If proper valuation requirements were introduced for directors and majority shareholders alike, minority shareholders would have no grounds for complaint, and majority shareholders and directors would have no opportunity for self-dealing or conflicts of interest.

---

[14] 2002 S.L.T. 354.

[15] As evidence he refers to *Gore-Brown on Companies* at s.28.13.7 and *Lowe v. Fahey* [1996] 1 BCLC 262. In any event, if the use of s.459 were barred wherever a derivative action could be used instead, it would negate the point of s.459 which was expressly to provide a remedy where the exceptions to the rules in *Foss v. Harbottle* were insufficient.

[16] [1995] 1 BCLC 73, [1993] B.C.C. 778, revs'd [1995] 1 BCLC 243, [1995] B.C.C. 362, CA.

[17] See Parker Hood "Section s.459 of the Companies Act—A new dawn or false sunrise?" 2000 *Juridical Review* 357. The author has also had the benefit of reading an article about to be published in Autumn 2002 in the *Edinburgh Law Review* by Robert Goddard: "Shareholder remedies in Scotland: *Anderson v. Hogg*", both of which illuminate the position of the s.459 remedy and the derivative action in Scotland.

[18] For example, *Konamaneni v. Rolls Royce Industrial Power (India) Ltd* [2002] 1 W.L.R. 1269, [2002] 1 All E.R. 979, [2002] 1 All E.R. (Comm.) 532, [2002] 1BCLC 336; and *Knight v. Frost* [1999] B.C.C. 819, [1999] 1 BCLC 364.

STATUTORY PROTECTION UNDER THE COMPANIES ACT 1985
SECTION 459

The Companies Act 1985, section 459 reads as follows: **11.15**

> "A member of a company may apply to the court by petition for an
> order under this Part on the ground that the company's affairs are
> being or have been conducted in a manner which is unfairly
> prejudicial to the interests of its members generally or of some part
> of its members or that any actual or proposed act or omission of the
> company (including an act or omission on its behalf) is or would be
> so prejudicial."

There is a number of points to note from this.

A member

Any member, however small his interest, may apply, provided he sues **11.16**
in his capacity as a member, and not as an employee or a director.
"Member" is also deemed to mean those who have shares transferred or
transmitted to them by operation of law, such as trustees in bankruptcy
or executors under a will.[19] A former member may not apply even
though the prejudicial conduct occurred while he was still a member.[20]

Order

Under CA 1985, section 461 the courts have wide discretion as to the **11.17**
type of order that they may grant in response to the petition, and may
impose any order that they see fit. The commonest order is that the
company or the majority shareholders buy out the petitioner's shares at
a fair price reflecting the value of his shares prior to the behaviour to
which the petitioner is objecting took place.

Are being or have been conducted

The use of the present and past tense enables the petitioner to petition **11.18**
in respect of current mistreatment or of past mistreatment, providing, it
would seem, that he was a member at the time of the past mistreatment.
However, once the member has left the company he forfeits his rights to
petition for past mistreatment.

---

[19] CA 1985, s.459(2).
[20] *Re a Company* [1986] 2 All E.R. 253.

A manner that is unfairly prejudicial

11.19   This phrase is interpreted to mean what it says: there is a requirement both of unfairness and of prejudice. For example, in the case of *R. A. Noble (Clothing) Ltd*[21] (to be discussed later) the petitioner had indeed suffered some prejudice, in the sense that he had suffered loss, but in view of his own behaviour it could not be said that he was treated unfairly.

To the interests of the members generally or of some part of the members

11.20   Companies Act 1989, Schedule 19, introduced the word "generally" into section 459, thus allowing a claim to be made even if the entire body of shareholders was unfairly prejudiced. It should be noted that the word "interests" is used, rather than "rights", specifically to widen the range of matters which might be the subject of unfairly prejudicial conduct.

Actual or proposed

11.21   The conduct being complained of need not already have taken place; it is sufficient if the majority are going to do it as evidenced by past conduct or by proposed conduct of a similar nature.

Statutory protection under the Companies Act 1985 section 460

11.22   The Secretary of State is empowered under the CA 1985 to investigate companies for various reasons such as fraud or unfairly prejudicial conduct.[22] If he has received a report from inspectors confirming the existence of such conduct, he can petition the courts in the same manner as described above. This does not preclude the Secretary of State having the company wound up.[23]

The court's remedies

11.23   The CA 1985, section 461 states that "[i]f the court is satisfied that a petition under this Part is well founded, it may make such order as it thinks fit for giving relief in respect of the matters complained of". This gives the court wide discretion, provided that the court agrees that the complaint is justified. The rest of section 461 gives various specific

---

[21] [1983] BCLC 273.
[22] CA 1985, s.423(2).
[23] CA 1985, s.460.

examples of remedies that the court could grant if it saw fit. In essence they are:

- Ordering the company or the majority shareholders to buy the minority out at a fair price, taking account of the value of the minority shareholding prior to the prejudicial conduct.[24]
- Preventing the company doing something the majority wished it to do, or making the company do something the majority did not wish it to do, or convening an extraordinary general meeting.
- Altering the memorandum or articles to a particular effect, or insisting that the existing memorandum or articles be not altered, or permitting any subsequent alteration only with leave of the court.

Where the court orders shares to be bought back by the company, it **11.24** may be necessary for the company's capital to be reduced as well. This is usually taken account of in the court's interlocutor. The price that at which the shares are bought back is generally speaking the price most favourable to the petitioner with regard to all the circumstances. This might be the value at the date of the petition, the value at the date of the court's decision or the value at the date when the prejudicial conduct took place, depending on what would be fairest.

These sections have been productive of much caselaw, much of it illustrating the remarkable high-handedness of majority shareholders. Below are examples of various remedies or decisions that have been given over the years.

Purchase of the minority shareholding by the majority at a fair value

Re Bird Precision Bellows Ltd[24a] **11.25**

The petitioner was unhappy with the way the majority shareholder was running the company. The petitioner believed that the majority shareholder in his position as managing director was paying bribes to obtain business opportunities. The minority shareholder asked the DTI to investigate. The DTI declined to do so. By way of retaliation the majority shareholder convened a general meeting at which he was able to use his majority shareholding to dismiss the petitioner from the directorship. The judge held that the petitioner should have his shares bought by the majority shareholder at a price that ignored the discount in value normally

---

[24] There are cases where the minority has been allowed to buy the majority instead—see *Re a Company ex p. Shooter* [1990] BCLC 384 and *Re Brenfield Squash Racquets Club Ltd* [1996] 2 BCLC 384.
[24a] [1986] 2 W.L.R. 158.

attributable to a minority shareholding because of a minority's minimal voting power.

The minority shareholder need not come to the court with clean hands

11.26 *Re London School of Electronics Ltd*[24b]

"Coming to the court with clean hands" is a term in English law, meaning that if the claimant seeks an equitable remedy against someone, the claimant must not have himself behaved dishonourably. In this case, neither party had behaved particularly honourably. The petitioner, Lytton, was a teacher at the London School of Electronics ("the School"), and was a director and shareholder in the company that ran the School. The majority shareholder was a company run by two Greek brothers, who were also directors of the School. The Greek brothers considered Lytton's work unsatisfactory and diverted some students to another school they had set up, thus depriving Lytton of his work. Lytton then set up a school himself and diverted some other of the School's students to it. The Greek brothers then convened a meeting at which they dismissed Lytton from his directorship. When the matter came to court the respondents argued that Lytton was no better than they were and that he had not come to the court with clean hands. However, Nourse J. held that having "dirty hands" was not of itself a barrier to seeking redress under section 459 though it might affect the extent and type of the remedy granted. Lytton was duly entitled to his redress.

The petitioner must however look after his own interests, and must not act unreasonably

11.27 *R. A. Noble (Clothing) Ltd*[24c]

The petitioner was a director of the above company, but had taken little interest in its affairs. He later complained that he had been excluded from management of the company. It was held that if he had taken the trouble to attend board meetings he would have been able to remedy the situation without recourse to court. He was not therefore able to seek redress under section 459. Where a shareholder could have used his own votes at general meetings to remedy his situation, his failure to do so prevented him obtaining his desired remedy.[25]

[24b] [1986] Ch. 211.
[24c] [1983] BCLC 273.
[25] *Re Baltic Real Estate Ltd (No. 2)* [1993] BCLC 503; *Re Legal Costs Negotiators Ltd* [1999] 2 BCLC 171.

Even if the majority shareholder disposes of his shares, he may still have a complaint raised against him

Re a Company (No. 005287 of 1985)[25a] **11.28**

The majority shareholder took all the profits out of the company in the form of management fees and then transferred all his shares to a Gibraltar registered company. He was made to account for the abstracted money even though he was no longer a shareholder.

The court may give a remedy appropriate to the facts of the case

Re H. R. Harmer Ltd[25b] **11.29**

This case was decided under previous legislation but is still a good example. At the age of 82 H. R. Harmer set up a company to acquire and manage his stamp-selling business. He and his wife were the majority shareholders with 78.6 per cent of the votes, but had contributed only about 10 per cent of the capital, the rest being contributed by Harmer's sons. Harmer and his wife were thus able to direct the management of the company as they pleased, notwithstanding that he and his two sons were stated in the articles to be directors for life. He also had a casting vote as chairman of the board of directors. Harmer did not trouble himself with other people's views and ran the company as if it were his own private fiefdom. In the process he made several unwise investment and personnel decisions. He even hired a private detective agency to spy on the staff. His sons became so vexed by the father's conduct that they petitioned for relief. By the time of the court case Harmer was deaf, confused and had trouble understanding what the case was about. The judge ordered that Harmer be made a consultant to the company, that the articles be amended so that he could no longer be a director for life with a casting vote, that he was not to interfere in the management of the company and that he was to be appointed president of the company but without any duties or rights whatsoever.

The majority may not use its controlling position to further weaken the position of the minority

Re Cumana Ltd [1986] BCLC 430 **11.30**

The majority and minority shareholder agreed that the company's profits should be divided in three, with the majority shareholder receiving two-thirds. The majority shareholder then diverted some of the company's business to another company which he controlled, and convened a general meeting at which he ensured that a resolution giving himself a large bonus and large pension

---

[25a] [1986] 1 W.L.R. 281.
[25b] [1958] 3 All E.R. 689, [1989] 1 W.L.R. 62.

contributions was passed. When the minority shareholder started proceedings under section 459 the majority shareholder convened a meeting to pass a resolution for a rights issue which he knew the minority shareholder could not afford to take up—or if the minority shareholder had taken it up, it would have deprived him of funds with which to continue the section 459 action. The minority shareholder successfully obtained an order preventing the implementation of the large bonus, the pension contributions and the rights issue.[26]

However, the minority shareholders do not always triumph.

11.31   In a publicly quoted plc, any informal arrangements between certain shareholders will be ignored by the courts in the context of a section 459 petition.

> *Re Tottenham Hotspur plc*[26a]
> As part of the dispute between Terry Venables (the minority shareholder) and Alan Sugar, Venables petitioned for relief under section 459 on the grounds that there had been an understanding between him and Sugar that they would share control and that Venables would be chief executive of the football club. It was held that even if there had been some understanding between Venables and Sugar, this was a private matter between the two of them which was not specifically about his rights as a shareholder and did not affect any other shareholders' rights. Furthermore it would be a misuse of the company's money to have it involved in what was essentially a private dispute. Relief was not therefore available under section 459. The court was clearly reluctant to use section 459 as a remedy for all private disputes between shareholders in publicly quoted companies—which should not be entertaining such private arrangements anyway.

11.32   Shareholders cannot necessarily use section 459 petitions to force the hand of the majority shareholders if they have not necessarily suffered any unfairly prejudicial conduct.

> *Re Astec BSR plc*[26b]
> Astec BSR plc was listed on the London Stock Exchange but its registered office was in Hong Kong. Most of the shares in the company were held by a large shareholder, Emerson, and the minority shareholders hoped that in accordance with the normal listing rules Emerson would buy out them out at a substantial premium. However, it is not obligatory or a legal requirement to

---

[26] For a Scottish example of a majority allotting shares in an improper manner see *Pettie v. Thomson Pettie Tube Products Ltd*, 2001 S.L.T. 473.
[26a] [1994] BCLC 655.
[26b] [1998] 2 BCLC 556.

follow the listing rules, although failure to do so may attract criticism from the London Stock Exchange.

When Emerson failed to buy the minority as expected, the minority claimed that they had suffered unfairly prejudicial conduct as a result of being denied what they had thought should take place. However it was held that desirable as adherence to the listing rules might be, the rules were not binding on the company. The company's articles in Hong Kong did not require that buy-outs should take place merely because the majority were expected to do so or because the minority would like them to do so, and the listing rules were not part of the articles. The minority shareholders had been aware of this (or at least should have been) when they became shareholders. A section 459 petition was not a method for forcing majority shareholders to buy out minority shareholders who perfectly well knew the risks of being minority shareholders.

As can be seen from the above examples of cases heard under the CA 1985 section 459, section 459 has been used extensively by minority shareholders seeking redress. Although the tide is now turning against this, at one stage a section 459 petition was seen as a panacea for all corporate ills, even when it was hardly cost-effective to do so.[27] A further use of a section 459 petition is as a bargaining tool against directors and/or majority shareholders in the knowledge that it would be expensive and time-consuming for them to defend the action—better to settle the matter on the petitioner's terms, however outrageous, than waste time in court.

Because of cases such as this, and particularly because of the costs **11.33** and time involved,[28] the courts have in the last few years become anxious not to widen the gates of litigation to litigants unless section 459 genuinely is the appropriate remedy, and there has genuinely been unfairly prejudicial conduct. Unfairly prejudicial conduct seems now to require a degree of deliberate intention to make life difficult for the minority, or a lack of consideration for the minority, and in the absence of this, a section 459 petition may fail.

Re Saul Harrison & Sons plc[28a]

The petitioner held special shares which did not permit her any votes but which did instead enable her to receive high dividends and a capital distribution on a winding-up. The company had run at a loss for some time but had substantial assets. The directors, who were also the majority shareholders, having taken professional

---

[27] As in *Re Elgindata Ltd* [1991] BCLC 959 where £320,000 was spent arguing over shares which finally were decided to be worth £24,600.

[28] One of the issues the courts felt was a particular waste of time and effort was the rehearsal at length of all the instances of alleged prejudicial conduct.

[28a] [1994] BCLC 475.

advice, moved their business premises, paid themselves greater (though not unreasonably so) salaries, and attempted to improve the business generally. By contrast the petitioner believed that the directors should have had the company wound up and a return of capital made to all the members. She sought a petition under section 459 to obtain redress for what she saw as unfairly prejudicial conduct towards herself. In the light of the evidence it became apparent that the directors' actions were unexceptionable. They had taken commercial decisions which the petitioner might not have liked, but were still properly arrived at. It was true that there had been some trivial and technical breaches of their duties under the articles, but none of those breaches was serious enough to constitute unfairly prejudicial conduct towards the petitioner. The important issue was that the directors had not breached their fiduciary duties in the management of the company, and that they had overall conducted themselves in accordance with the articles of association. There was no element of "self-serving" by the directors/majority shareholders as is found in other minority protection cases, such as *Re Bird Precision Bellows Ltd*, nor any suggestion of ill-will towards the petitioner. Lord Hoffman in his judgment introduced the term "legitimate expectations" to describe what the shareholder might have hoped to receive in her capacity as a shareholder. She was not entitled to expect more than that the directors had abided by their fiduciary duties and managed the company within the rights and powers given to them under the company's memorandum and articles. Furthermore, as a shareholder she had known what she was entitled to in terms of the rights attaching to her shares and what the directors had been entitled to do in terms of the memorandum and articles, and she had consented to their management of the company within those parameters. She could not have legitimately expected that they should have taken any further consideration of her particular wishes. As it was apparent that the majority shareholders/directors had not breached their duties, they were entitled to take such commercial decisions as they saw fit, and her petition was refused.

11.34   The concept of "legitimate expectation" was reviewed in the first important House of Lords case on minority protection for many years, *O'Neill v. Phillips*.[29]

O'Neill, the petitioner, had been given 25 per cent of the shares of a company for which he worked as a foreman. The majority shareholder in the company, and therefore the effective controller

[29] [1999] 2 All E.R. 961, [1999] 1 W.L.R. 1092, (HL), and also known as *Re a Company (No. 00709 of 1992)*.

of the company, Phillips, indicated that in due course a further 25 per cent of the company's shares would be made available to O'Neill, in the expectation that O'Neill would permanently take over the management of the company. O'Neill was also to receive 50 per cent of the company's profits. Phillips did not, however, put this indication in writing, and subsequently decided in the light of a turn-down in the company's business neither to give O'Neill any more shares nor let him take over the management of the company. O'Neill then alleged that he had been prejudiced as a minority shareholder. When the case reached the House of Lords, Lord Hoffman held that O'Neill had not been treated unfairly. This was mainly because there had never been any binding agreement on Phillips to grant O'Neill the extra shares[30] and so O'Neill was not in a position to say that he had been treated unfairly in his position as shareholder.

In the course of the judgment, Lord Hoffman took the opportunity to lay down various guidelines which should be used in connection with section 459 petitions. The first of these is that fairness alone is not a matter for the judge at first instance to decide upon at his own discretion,[31] there must be "rational principles"[32] on which to make any decision as to fairness, and these rational principles should establish a degree of certainty which will enable professional advisers to tell their clients whether or not their petition is likely to succeed. One of these principles is that the constitution of the company is paramount (as suggested in *Re Astec BSR plc*[33]). This is because members of a company must be assumed to be aware of the contents of the memorandum and articles of association of the company of which they are members,[34] and are free to take legal advice as to the implications of the terms of those documents. Having become a member of a company on such terms, the member must live with those terms (as in *Re Saul Harrison and Sons plc*[35]) or seek to have them changed by special resolution. Shareholders' agreements or other contractual agreements are equally important; and in either case rights or expectations clearly

---

[30] Both O'Neill and Phillips had taken professional advice and had agreed that the shares would not be transferred until a formal document had been signed. At no stage did Phillips give O'Neill any legal rights, although O'Neill may well have believed that his own actings were sufficient to be equivalent to an entitlement to the transfer of the shares. However unhappy O'Neill may have been with Phillips's actions, it was difficult for him to deny that Phillips had at all times reserved to himself the right to take back the management of the company and not to transfer the shares.

[31] Lord Hoffman was at pains to point out that fairness is a concept that varies according to its context, and that what might be seen as unfair in, say, a family or a game of cricket, is not necessarily unfair in business.

[32] At 1098.

[33] [1998] 2 BCLC 556.

[34] As in the terms of CA 1985, s.14.

[35] [1995] 1 BCLC 14.

contracted for and subsequently ignored by a majority might give rise to a claim for breach of contract or possibly a petition under section 459. However, there may be occasions where the majority shareholders might not be technically transgressing the terms of the memorandum, articles, shareholders' agreement or other contractual agreement but still not be treating the minority fairly, as for example, where the majority is exercising its rights in bad faith. On such an occasion there would be an equitable restraint[36] on the strict application of the terms of the memorandum, articles or shareholders' agreement. As an example of an equitable restraint, Lord Hoffman referred to the case of *Ebrahimi v. Westbourne Galleries Ltd*[37–39] where the petitioner was given the remedy he sought because the respondents, although apparently acting within the letter of the law, had used their rights under the law in bad faith. As further examples he referred to promises which it would be unjust not to enforce because the majority and minority shareholders had actually agreed them at the time of making them, (in which case it would be unjust of the majority to break them) or to the situation where both the majority and minority shareholders had agreed to a course of action which subsequently could not be carried out because of an unforeseen change in circumstances. If the majority insisted that the course of action should still take place notwithstanding the change of circumstances, despite the fact that it would be prejudicial to the minority shareholders, an equitable restraint would apply.

11.35   Lord Hoffman, clearly unhappy at the potential direction of his former idea of "legitimate expectation", also indicated that a legitimate expectation could only arise out of an equitable restraint, and that he was anxious not to let the concept of a "legitimate expectation" have a life of its own[40] thereby widening the opportunities for minority protection. Indeed, Lord Hoffman indicated a restrictive view of section 459 by saying that merely because a member is dismissed as a director or otherwise excluded from management, and has difficulty withdrawing his capital, he is not automatically entitled to a remedy under section 459. Just because the minority has lost trust or confidence in the majority it cannot demand that its shares be bought by the majority or the company; or as Lord Hoffman put it, there is no system of "no-fault

---

[36] An equitable remedy is one given by the courts when although the strict letter of the law denies a claimant his remedy, it would be contrary to justice and fairness to deny him it, usually because the respondent has acted in bad faith or taken unfair advantage of some rule of law. An equitable restraint is therefore an occasion when some legal rule is not followed because of the dubious conduct of the party seeking to enforce the rule.

[37–39] [1973] A.C. 360, [1972] 2 All E.R. 492. In this case the petitioner was forced out of his directorship by the majority shareholders and the majority shareholders also refused to buy his shares, both actions being technically permissible under the articles, though not quite in the spirit under which the company had originally been set up by the petitioner and his former partner.

[40] At 1104.

divorce" operating. "Unfairly prejudicial conduct" thus becomes something more demanding than mere dissatisfaction with the majority.

Lord Hoffman also suggested how a majority shareholder may protect himself. The normal order granted following a section 459 petition is for the majority (or the company) to buy the petitioner's shares. If the majority offers:

- to buy the minority's shares,
- at a fair value,
- with no discount for being a minority shareholding,
- with the value if necessary being established by independent valuers acting as experts not as arbiters, and
- with both parties being entitled to equal access to all relevant financial information

it will be difficult for the minority to complain that he is the victim of unfairly prejudicial conduct.

Although this may seem harsh for minority shareholders, Lord Hoffman was in effect (albeit in a part of his judgment that is obiter) reining in the rights of the minority shareholders who, in some quarters at least, had been seen to be making life unreasonably difficult for majority shareholders. **11.36**

At the same time it is recognised that section 459 fills a need. Some majority shareholders do behave in a blatantly oppressive way, and the great virtue of section 459 is that gradually it has educated majority shareholders to think twice before treating minority shareholders unfairly.

Proposals for reform

Although Lord Hoffman's proposals for majority shareholders' buyouts of minority shareholders in *O'Neill v. Phillips*[41] have gone some way towards satisfying some immediate difficulties with the operation of section 459, the Law Commission report[42] and the DTI Review[43] have also been addressing the issue of reform. Various suggestions have been made, such as the requirement that where directors refuse to allow minority shareholders to transfer their shares, the reasons for the refusal by the directors to permit the transfer should be given. It is also suggested that when the members of a company ratify a wrong on the **11.37**

---

[41] [1999] 2 All E.R. 961, [1999] 1 W.L.R. 1092 (HL). It is perhaps worth observing that following the DTI consultations the majority of views was in favour of reversing this case and extending the range of remedies available to minority shareholders. Nonetheless the Steering group came to the view that *O'Neill v. Phillips* should not be reversed.

[42] *Shareholder Remedies*, Law Commission Report, No. 246, 1997.

[43] *Modern Company Law for a Competitive Economy—the Final Report*, DTI, July 2001, paras. 7.33–7.62.

company or by the board not to pursue a wrong, the validity of the
ratification should depend on whether or not the wrongdoers' votes
enabled the requisite majority to be obtained; or to put it another way,
ideally the wrongdoers' votes should not be counted. It remains to be
seen which, if any, of these reforms will be implemented.

A further suggestion in the White Paper is that Alternative Dispute
Resolution avenues should be explored as a way of saving unnecessary
and expensive litigation in shareholder disputes.

WINDING UP ON THE "JUST AND EQUITABLE GROUNDS"

11.38 Before the existence of the CA 1985, section 459 an unhappy minority
shareholder had either to obtain redress through the limited exceptions
to *Foss v. Harbottle* or, in desperation, have the company wound up.
Having the company wound up might ensure the return of the shareholder's capital, but in many cases, was a drastic remedy for the
particular problem. It could also be unfair on other shareholders who
were not involved in the unfairly prejudicial conduct, either as perpetrators or as victims.

The remedy of winding up where there has been prejudice to a
minority is available under the Insolvency Act 1986, section 122(1)(g)
where it is stated that the court may wind up the company if the court
is of the opinion that it is just and equitable that the company should be
wound up. Windings-up are not lightly entered upon, and the courts will
need to be satisfied that no better remedy (such as the use of a section
459 petition) is available and that the petitioner is acting reasonably in
seeking a winding up order.[44] Winding up is dealt with in Chapter
16.

JUDICIAL FACTORS IN SCOTLAND

11.39 This remedy for an aggrieved minority is only available in Scotland. If
the directors are at loggerheads or have all resigned, or for any other
good reason which is acceptable to the court, it is possible for any
shareholder to petition the court for the appointment of a judicial factor
to the company. A judicial factor is a court-appointed accountant (usually) or lawyer who in these circumstances is given the task of acting as
a temporary company caretaker and protecting the interests of the
shareholders.[45]

---

[44] IA 1986, s.125(2).
[45] *Weir v. Rees*, 1991 S.L.T. 345.

DTI INVESTIGATIONS

11.40 The DTI has extensive powers to investigate the affairs of a company. This can be one more weapon in the minority shareholders' armoury although in practice the use of inspectors by the DTI for minority protection purposes appears to be slender. Investigations are carried out by one or more inspectors, usually a lawyer and an accountant working together, and are appointed by the Secretary of State. DTI-appointed inspectors can be asked specifically to investigate majority shareholders' abuse of their majority voting power. DTI investigations are also sometimes used to investigate alleged insider dealing or other nefarious activity within a company.

The present law on DTI investigations is contained in the CA 1985, Part XIV.

Who may apply to have a company investigated?

11.41 A company with a share capital, 200 or more members, or members holding in total more than one-tenth of the shares issued, may apply,[46] or the company itself may apply.[47]

In a company without a share capital, a minimum of one-fifth of the members on the company's register of members can apply.[48] The application must be supported by evidence showing that there is good reason for requiring the investigation.[49] In order to deter frivolous applications, the Secretary of State may require the applicant to provide security for the costs of the investigation.[50]

If a court by order declares that its affairs ought to be investigated, the Secretary of State must appoint inspectors for the investigation.[51]

When may a company be investigated?

11.42 In addition to investigation following an application by the company or the members as detailed above, the Secretary of State may appoint inspectors on the following grounds under the CA 1985, section 432(2), if it appears to him that:

(a) the company's affairs are being or have been conducted with intent to defraud its creditors or the creditors of any other person, or otherwise for a fraudulent or unlawful purpose, or in a manner which is unfairly prejudicial to some part of its members; or

---

[46] CA 1985, s.431(2)(a).
[47] CA 1985, s.341(2)(c).
[48] CA 1985, s.421(2)(b).
[49] CA 1985, s.431(3).
[50] CA 1985, s.431(4).
[51] CA 1985, s.432(1).

(b) any actual or proposed act or omission of the company (including an act or omission on its behalf) is or would be so prejudicial, or that the company was formed for any fraudulent or unlawful purpose; or

(c) persons concerned with the company's formation or the management of its affairs have in connection therewith been guilty of fraud, misfeasance or other misconduct towards it or towards its members; or

(d) the company's members have not been given all the information with respect to its affairs which they might reasonably expect.

While normally the inspectors publish a report on their investigations, if the inspectors are appointed on any of the above four grounds they may be appointed on the basis that any report they prepare is not for publication.[52]

11.43   Even if a company is in voluntary liquidation, under the CA 1985, section 432(3) inspectors may be appointed if the court requires it under the CA 1985, section 432(1) or if the Secretary of State considers it appropriate under section 432(2). Where the Secretary of State has ordered the appointment of inspectors, he is not obliged to give his reasons for the appointment provided he has not ordered the investigation for an improper purpose or in the absence of good faith.[53]

The inspectors have wide powers to interview directors and employees and anyone else connected with the company—including its solicitors, bankers and auditors—under investigation. All such persons have to provide such assistance as they reasonably can, and to produce any relevant documents in their care[54] except where in the case of solicitors they can justifiably claim that they hold privileged information which they would be entitled to refuse to disclose in the Court of Session or the High Court.[55]

11.44   Bankers have a similar privilege except where the bankers' client is the company being investigated, where the company itself consents to disclosure or where the Secretary of State orders the privilege to be overruled.[56] The inspectors can demand that the interviewees can be put on oath,[57] and refusal by the interviewees to comply with the inspectors' requests may result in the matter being reported to the court. Any statements thus obtained may be used in civil matters, as for example, disqualifying a person from being a director[58] but it was held that it was

---

[52] CA 1985, s.432(2A).
[53] *Norwest Holst Ltd v. Secretary of State for Trade* [1978] Ch. 201.
[54] CA 1985, s.4343(1) and (2).
[55] CA 1985, s.452(1).
[56] CA 1985, s.452(1A).
[57] CA 1985, s.434(3).
[58] *R. v. Secretary of State for Trade and Industry, ex p. McCormick* [1998] 2 BCLC 18.

a breach of Article 6(1) of the European Convention on Human Rights to use those statements in criminal matters.[59] As a result there are now statutory limits on the use to which the statements may be put in criminal trials in order to prevent self-incrimination.[60]

The inspectors are required to act fairly while remembering that they are not a court of law. This was established by the cases raised by the late Robert Maxwell in *Re Pergamon Press Ltd*[61] and *Maxwell v. Department of Trade and Industry*,[62] where he attempted to deter or delay the publication of the report into his questionable business practices.

The inspectors' report

The inspectors compile a report within the terms of the remit given to **11.45** them by the Secretary of State. If the court had ordered the report to be produced, the courts must be given a copy.[63] If it appears from the report that in the public interest civil proceedings ought to be instituted on the company's behalf, perhaps against errant directors or majority share-holders, the Secretary of State has power to order this to be done.[64] The report is itself admissible evidence to be used if necessary against any director under the Company Directors Disqualification Act 1986[65] or in any criminal proceedings.[66] The report may also be used as evidence in any petition brought by the Secretary of State to have the company wound up under the Insolvency Act 1986 ("IA 1986"), section 124A, or to obtain a remedy for conduct unfairly prejudicial to the company's members.[67]

Other powers of investigation

The inspectors may be appointed to report on the membership of the **11.46** company, and in particular the ownership of its shares and debentures, and to ascertain who truly controls the company.[68] Under the CA 1985, section 442(3) the Secretary of State must appoint inspectors to ascer-tain the true ownership where requested to do so by the minorities referred to in CA 1985, section 431(2)(a) and (b), unless he considers that the members' application is vexatious or where it is unreasonable

---

[59] *Saunders v. U.K.* [1998] 1 BCLC 362. It was not disputed that Ernest Saunders committed criminal acts, but the use of statements of his, obtained from the inspectors, was held to be unjust.
[60] CA 1985, s.434(5A), (5B).
[61] [1971] Ch. 388.
[62] [1974] Q.B. 523.
[63] CA 1985, s.437(2).
[64] CA 1985, s.438.
[65] CA 1985, s.441.
[66] CA 1985, s.441.
[67] CA 1985, s.460.
[68] CA 1985, s.442

that any or part of the matters to which the minorities are objecting should be investigated.[69]

If the Secretary of State wishes he may investigate the ownership of shares or debentures in the company or its members using inspectors.[70] To refuse to give information or to give false information is an offence.

11.47 If members are being obstructive about providing the information to the inspectors or to the Secretary of State, the Secretary of State, under CA 1985, sections 454–457, may prohibit all or any of the following:

- the transfer of any shares;
- the transfer of the right to be issued with new shares and any subsequent issue of those new shares;
- the exercise of any voting rights in respect of shares whose ownership is being investigated;
- the issue of any further shares arising out of the existing owner-ship of shares (*i.e.* a bonus issue or the exercise of pre-emption rights);
- the repayment of capital or payment of dividends, except in the case of a liquidation.

Investigation of share dealings

11.48 Under CA 1985, section 446 inspectors may be appointed to inves-tigate whether or not directors and their families have been contravening the rules on share options in listed companies under CA 1985, section 323, or failing to disclose their interests in their companies' securities under CA 1985, section 324.

Requisition and seizure of books and papers

11.49 Appointing inspectors is a public process and may do the company and innocent shareholders more harm than good. There is a more discreet option available to the Secretary of State in order to establish whether or not a full-scale investigation is necessary. This is the requisi-tion and seizure of the company's books by personnel within the DTI. Compared to a full-scale investigation, this type of investigation is cheap, and is by far the commonest response by the DTI to any requests for an investigation. Any statements obtained in the process may again be used in civil matters,[71] but in criminal matters there are restrictions on the use of these statements without evidence.[72]

---

[69] CA 1985, s.442(3A).
[70] CA 1985, s.444.
[71] CA 1985, s.447(8).
[72] CA 1985, s.447(8A), (8B).

The Secretary of State may require documents to be brought to him.[73] He may obtain warrants to permit the police to search premises to prevent the destruction or concealment of such documents.[74] He is only allowed to disclose what information he finds within certain defined circumstances, these being mostly in connection with criminal matters, disciplinary proceedings, or disqualification of company directors.

Further Reading

Davies, *Introduction to Company Law* (Oxford University Press, 2002), Chap. 8

Clark "Unfairly prejudicial conduct: a pathway through the maze" (2001) 22(6) *Company Lawyer* 170–177

DTI investigations, see: www.dti.gov.uk/cld/comp_inv.htm

---

[73] CA 1985, s.447.
[74] CA 1985, s.448.

CHAPTER 12

INSIDER DEALING

12.01   Insider dealing is the use for gain of secret information about publicly traded investments by those who are privy to that information and who should not be taking advantage of their knowledge of that information.

The victimless crime

12.02   Insider dealing is described sometimes as a victimless crime, because, while it is easy to see who benefits from it, it is harder to see who loses by the crime. Nevertheless the victims are those investors who are denied the same opportunities as the insider dealers to make profits or avoid losses because they do not have access to the information which the insider dealers have.

The need for immediate access to information

12.03   In order to minimise the opportunities for insider dealing or misleading the financial markets, the Stock Exchange requires that in the United Kingdom all relevant information about securities is made public as soon as possible.[1-2] In the gap between the price-sensitive event taking place and its release to the market the opportunity for insider dealing arises: the smaller the gap, the less opportunity for insider dealing. When insider dealing takes place, it causes investors to lose confidence in the stock market because those "not in the know" feel that not all investors are being treated equally. They feel that the market is rigged in favour of the insider dealer. The market will not be seen to be running smoothly and fairly. "Clean" investors may then go to another stock market abroad, where the market is seen to operate more fairly and share prices more truly reflect the value of stock.

Arguments in favour of insider dealing

12.04   Although few would now openly approve of insider dealing, there are those who claim that as it has always existed, and always will, it is as

---

[1-2] Admission of securities to listing, Chap. 9, ss.1–10.

well to accept the fact of its existence.[3] Some see insider dealing as a reward for managers for their entrepreneurial ability.[4] However, there are other fairer and more accountable methods of ensuring that managers are rewarded for their entrepreneurial skills. Managers allowed to reward themselves by means of insider dealing will forget their wider duties to act for the overall body of shareholders, let alone impress the employees. Insider dealing may also be a breach of the fiduciary duty of the managers to act in the best interests of the company as a whole, and at least in the United Kingdom it would be a breach of Stock Exchange rules for directors of listed companies for directors to acquire or sell securities outside of the few permitted occasions.[5]

Those who support the argument that insider dealing is a fair return for managers' entrepreneurial ability struggle to justify managers' sales of securities in advance of price-sensitive bad news about the company. It is one thing to reward managers by letting them take advantage of good results arising from their hard work or good ideas when the share price rises: it is another to let those same managers be rewarded for knowing about bad news sooner than anyone else—and making a profit out of the fall in their company's share price.

Insider dealing helps relay information into the market and thereby makes it efficient

It is said that insider dealers, by their moving before anyone else, **12.05** ensure that price-sensitive information about the company is not withheld by the company. If a company had poor end of year results, it might wish to delay publishing them for as long as it could get away with it. But the insider dealer would sell his shares while he could. Because he would sell them, other investors would wonder what was behind the inside dealer's move, and raise questions about the Company's finances —thus flushing out the unwelcome news about the accounts. Thus to a certain extent, this argument is valid. However, even if it is valid, it does not mean that it serves as a justification for unfair treatment of shareholders not "in the know".

CRIMINAL JUSTICE ACT 1993 SECTIONS 52–64

The above legislation contains most of the current law on insider **12.06** dealing because insider dealing is a criminal offence, not a civil offence. The offence of insider dealing is defined in terms of the actual dealing by insider dealers within the context of a regulated market. Any act within those parameters is an offence unless it comes within the various

---

[3] Harry McVea "What's wrong with Insider Dealing?" (1985) 15(3) LKS 390.
[4] Manne "In Defense of Insider Dealing" (1996) 44 (6) *Harvard Law Review* 113.
[5] Admission of securities to listing, Chap. 16, (Appendix).

permitted defences. What is meant by insider dealing, insider dealers, and regulated markets is carefully explained. Insider dealing, depending on the severity of the offence, can be prosecuted either at summary level (*i.e.* before one judge with a maximum penalty of two years' imprisonment and/or a fine) or on indictment (*i.e.* before a judge and jury, with a maximum penalty of seven years' imprisonment and/or a much greater fine). As an additional penalty, a company director may be disqualified from being a director under the Company Directors Disqualification Act 1986 ("CDDA 1986").[6]

The offence of insider dealing

12.07   The offence of insider dealing takes place when an individual (but not a corporate entity) who has insider information (from an inside source) as an insider deals in securities whose price will be affected by that information if and when the information is made public. The dealing must take place on a regulated market, and must be done by the insider or through a professional intermediary or by an insider acting in his capacity as a professional intermediary.[7] In addition, the legislation catches an insider who encourages some other person to deal in securities which are price-affected—irrespective of whether or not the other person knows they are price-affected—while knowing or expecting that dealing would take place on a regulated market, through a professional intermediary, or through the insider acting as a professional intermediary.[8]

It is also insider dealing to disclose information which a person has as an insider to any other person except in the proper performance of his employment, office, or profession.[9]

Inside information

12.08   This is information about particular securities, or a particular issuer of securities, which is specific to the securities in question. The information must not have been made public, but if it were to be made public it would have a "significant" effect on the price or value of the securities.[10] "Significant" is not defined in the Criminal Justice Act 1993 ("CJA 1993"), but presumably means non-marginal. "Public" is discussed shortly.

---

[6] *R. v. Goodman* [1993] 2 All E.R. 789.
[7] Criminal Justice Act 1993 ("CJA 1993"), s.52(1), (3).
[8] CJA 1993, s.52(2)(a). This is designed to prevent insider dealers either using unsuspecting friends or relations to do their insider dealing for them or trying to give their friends and relatives the benefit of secret "tips" even if the original insider dealer himself does not benefit.
[9] CJA 1993, s.52(2)(b).
[10] CJA 1993, s.56(1).

Insider

Under the CJA 1993, section 57(1) an insider is someone who: **12.09**

(1) has inside information (as opposed to information which he thinks is inside information but actually is public knowledge);
(2) knows that the information he has is inside information;
(3) has information which he has obtained from an inside source (as opposed to obtaining it from some other method, such as an intelligent guess or by deduction from observing the previous business practice of the company and its directors); and
(4) knows that it came from an inside source (as opposed to obtaining it from someone who he did not realise was an inside source).

So if an accused can prove that he genuinely did not know his information was inside information and that he did not know it came from an inside source (neither of which would be easy to prove unless the accused was very naïve) he should be able to raise a defence.

Insider source

Under CJA 1993, section 57(2) a person has information from an **12.10** inside source if he has that information:

(1) because he is a director, employee or shareholder of an issuer of securities, or
(2) because he has access to the information through his employment, office or profession, or
(3) because the direct or indirect source of his information was from someone in (1) or (2) above.

This provision is designed to widen the range of persons to whom the legislation applies, and in particular to professional and others persons not just in the employment of the company but also working for the company as consultants, as professional advisers or by having the company as a client.

Securities

Securities is defined in Schedule 2 to Part V of the CJA 1993 and **12.11** covers:

- shares;
- debt securities, being debentures, bonds, deposit certificates, local authority bonds, and treasury bonds ("gilts");

- warrants to subscribe for shares or debt securities;
- depositary receipts[11];
- options to acquire any of the items in Schedule 2;
- futures[12] in respect of shares, debt securities, or depository receipts;
- contracts for differences[13] in respect of the same items as futures.

For the definition of shares, debentures, warrants and options, see Chapter 6.

Public

12.12 The CJA 1993 clearly did not wish to limit the many potential ways by which information can be made public. It therefore stated that information is made public under the CJA 1993, section 58(2) if:

- it is published in accordance with the rules of the market in which the securities are being traded for the purpose of informing investors and their professional advisers;
- it is to be found in records which under statute are open to the public;
- it can be readily acquired by those likely to deal either in the securities to which the information relates or of an issuer to which the information relates;
- it derived from information which has been made public.

Information is still deemed to be public even if it can only be acquired by persons exercising "diligence or expertise", is limited to a few recipients, can only be obtained by observation or requires to be paid for, or is published outside the United Kingdom.[14] This particular exemption is designed to protect investment analysts who study company results and happen to be very well informed relative to other investors. It would be iniquitous if perspicacious analysts were to be classed as insider dealers just because they happened to be more perceptive or astute than others. These rules are not exhaustive,[15] and other

---

[11] Depositary receipts are a form of investment comprising a package of securities issued by a particular issuer and deposited with a bank. The bank then issues further securities which can be traded but whose underlying value is secured by the deposited securities.

[12] A future is a contract which provides for securities to be bought or sold and delivered at a future date at a predetermined price.

[13] A contract for differences is similar to a future except that in general the investor is betting not on securities but on the price movements of such things as shares indices (like the FTSE 100) or interest rates.

[14] CJA 1993, s.58(3).

[15] CJA 1993, s.58(1).

methods of becoming public, such as publication in a newspaper, will be deemed to be public.

Dealing

Dealing is any buying or selling, or agreeing to buy or sell, securities **12.13** as principal or as agent, or the procuring of any buying or selling of any securities by an agent or nominee or someone acting under the dealer's directions.[16] Holding shares without buying or selling, even if the price rises as a result of insider information that the insider knows about, is not insider dealing.

Regulated market

A regulated market at present means the London Stock Exchange **12.14** (both the Official List and the Alternative Investment Market) and such other markets as the Treasury approves from time to time.[17]

Professional intermediary

A professional intermediary means, in effect, a stockbroker or other **12.15** broker of securities acting in the course of his regular business. Occasional broking transactions are not deemed to be carrying on a business.[18]

Price-affected and price-sensitive

In relation to securities and information respectively, the information **12.16** about the securities must be likely to have an effect on the price of the securities if the inside information about the securities were made public.[19]

Issuer

An issuer is a company, public sector body or individual which or **12.17** who issues securities. A public sector body includes the Government, local authorities, international organisations which include the United Kingdom or other EC members, the Bank of England or the central bank of any sovereign state.[20]

To whom does the Criminal Justice Act 1993 apply?

Clearly the CJA 1993 applies to insider dealers, but as a matter of **12.18** practice certain people are more likely to have to be aware of the reach of the CJA 1993 than others. These include:

---

[16] CJA 1993, s.55.
[17] CJA 1993, s.60(1).
[18] CJA 1993, s.59.
[19] CJA 1993, s.56(2).
[20] CJA 1993, s.60.

- directors and employees of quoted companies;
- professionals, such as lawyers and accountants, acting for such companies;
- those providing services to such companies, such as bankers or stockbrokers;
- those working in certain Government departments which have access to confidential matters in connection with such companies, such as the Inland Revenue, Customs and Excise, the DTI, the Monopolies Commission;
- those working for the Stock Exchange itself.

This list is not exhaustive. It is now common for bank employees and other persons working in the financial industry to have to report their personal dealings in any investments to an official known as a compliance officer (frequently the same person as the company secretary) whose task is to monitor those dealings and thereby to ensure that no employee is taking advantage of any inside information.

Investigations into insider dealing

12.19   In order to prosecute an insider dealer, it is necessary to detect instances of insider dealing and, if necessary, to investigate those instances. Under the Financial Services Act 1986 ("FSA 1986"), sections 177–178 the Secretary of State can appoint inspectors to investigate any insider dealing and make a report to him.[21] The team of inspectors, who usually comprise an accountant and lawyer, can require anyone who knows about the insider dealing to hand over documents (whether in written or computer form) to them, to be examined by them, on oath if necessary, and to assist in the investigation.[22] It is the duty of that person to comply with these requirements. Any evidence supplied by that person may later be used in evidence against him[23] in criminal or civil proceedings subject to provisions to prevent self-incrimination.[24] Exemptions to this also arise where legal privilege or banking confidentiality arises.[25] If, as a result of any subsequent proceedings arising out of the report by the investigation the accused is convicted, he also has to pay the expense of the investigation.[26]

Since anyone involved in insider dealing would be understandably reluctant to volunteer information to the inspectors, the FSA 1986, section 178 provides means of enforcing compliance. If someone refuses to co-operate or answer questions put to him, the matter can be referred to court. If there is no reasonable excuse for his lack of

---

[21] FSA 1986, s.177(4).
[22] FSA 1986, s.177(3).
[23] FSA 1986, s.177(6).
[24] FSA 1986, s.177(6A).
[25] FSA 1986, s.177(7) and (8).
[26] FSA 1986, s.177(11).

co-operation or refusal to answer questions he can be punished as if for contempt of court even though he is not technically before a court of law when he is being questioned by the inspectors.[27] The Secretary of State is also empowered to cancel any authorisation that person may have to carry on investment business.[28]

The permitted defences

Normally in a criminal trial, the burden of proving that the accused committed a crime lies upon the prosecution. If the prosecution cannot prove beyond reasonable doubt that the accused committed the crime, the accused is acquitted. However, in a trial for insider dealing, the burden of proof lies upon the accused to show that his defence comes within the terms of one or more of the permitted defences stated in CJA 1993, section 53 and Schedule 1. But because the wording of the CJA 1993, section 53 and Schedule 1 specifically uses "shows", as opposed to "proves", the accused does not have to prove beyond all reasonable doubt that his actions fell within the terms of the permitted defences.

12.20

Specific defences

Some of the defences involve the lack of a deliberate intention to commit an insider deal. So if someone was unaware that certain information was inside information, although in reality it was, and he made a profit because the information turned out to be price-sensitive, he would not be committing a crime.[29] Likewise if someone had reasonable grounds for believing that his information was sufficiently well known to ensure that no other investors were prejudiced, although in reality it was inside information, he would have committed no crime.[30] If someone would have dealt anyway even if he had not had the information, again no crime is committed[31] as might happen when someone is forced to sell all his securities to pay a debt.

12.21

There are similar defences for those who encourage others to deal in securities.[32]

For those who disclose inside information, and would normally be guilty of insider dealing under CJA 1993, section 52(2)(b) (disclosing information other than in the proper course of their business), there are two defences. The first is that they did not expect those who received the information to use it to deal in securities on a regulated market,[33] and

---

[27] FSA 1986, s.178(2).
[28] FSA 1986, s.178(3).
[29] CJA 1993, s.53(1)(a).
[30] CJA 1993, s.53(1)(b).
[31] CJA 1993, s.53(1)(c).
[32] CJA 1993, s.53(2).
[33] CJA 1993, s.53(3)(a).

the second is that while they did expect the recipients of the information to deal on a regulated market, they did not expect that dealing to result in profit because the information turned out to be price-sensitive.[34]

In all these defences, making a profit means both making a profit and avoiding making a loss.[35]

12.22   In addition to the above defences, there is another set of defences, known as "Special Defences", to which the same shifting of the burden of proof applies as above. The special defences are to be found in Schedule 1.

The first of them protects market-makers who are acting in good faith in the course of business.[36] The second defence is that the insider dealer (or the person encouraged to deal on his behalf) was using "market information" and that it was reasonable for him to have used it as he did. "Market information" is information about the buying or selling of securities, their prices and the identity of the buyers and sellers[37] and the sort of person who might be in possession of it without being categorised as an insider dealer might be, for example, a liquidator winding up the assets of a company which happens to have investments in another company which that liquidator, in another capacity, might happen to have inside information about, or someone, say, working in a merchant bank, involved on his client's behalf in mounting a takeover bid, and being instructed to acquire more securities in the target company. The third defence is that the accused was acting in conformity with the price stabilisation rules under the Financial Services Act 1986, section 48(2)(i). These are rules which an authorised body can draw up for the purpose of preventing the price of investments fluctuating wildly. Acting in accordance with the regulations will be a valid defence.

12.23   There are further possible defences. Under CJA 1993, section 62 the legislation only applies within the United Kingdom, so insider dealing carried out from abroad will be difficult to prosecute. Insider dealing on another country's stock market is also not a crime justiciable in the United Kingdom.[38]

A further defence arose in the Scottish case of *H.M.Advocate v. Mackie*,[39] where the panel was acquitted because of the failure on the part of the prosecution to establish corroboration of the evidence from two independent sources.

---

[34] CJA 1993, s.53(3)(b).

[35] CJA 1993, s.53(6).

[36] CJA 1993, Sched. 1, para. 1.

[37] CJA 1993, Sched. 1, para. 2.4.

[38] CJA 1993, s.62(1)(b).

[39] 1994 SCCR 277. Allegedly, when Mackie was being held in Edinburgh's Gayfield Square police station after his arrest, a fellow inmate in the cells asked him what he was in for. Mackie replied that he was accused of insider dealing. The other inmate apparently then asked if that was some form of sexual offence.

Should insider dealing give rise to civil penalties?

At present insider dealing does not gives rise to civil penalties **12.24** (although market abuse, as defined later, does). Some would say that it should, on the grounds that having to repay, by way of damages, the amount that others have lost, or failed to gain, might, it is thought, concentrate the insider dealer's mind towards honesty. On the other hand there are various practical difficulties with the idea of having to pay damages to such victims. This is because it is difficult to establish who suffered loss as a result of the insider deal, how great the loss was, and sometimes, who the insider dealer actually was. The insider dealer who buys in the stock market does not generally know who held the shares before he did, and any former shareholder might have been quite happy to sell anyway irrespective of the fact that the purchaser had the benefit of insider information. The insider dealer who sells shares while they are still high before the announcement of bad news will not generally know who buys his shares once he sells them. A purchaser might have been quite happy to buy at the insider dealer's price anyway. It is thus difficult precisely to identify the aggrieved shareholders who could be the pursuers in any action for civil damages against an insider dealer.[40]

It is also difficult to devise a scheme whereby compensation was payable to those who were truly the victims of an insider deal (which might be hard to establish), but not to those who would have been dealing anyway. In any event for some smaller shareholders the amount of compensation might be minimal—far less than the administrative cost of giving each shareholder his proportional share of the compensation.

If it is difficult to identify the pursuer, it can be difficult to identify the **12.25** defender. Although the Stock Exchange Surveillance Unit may notice insider dealing, the astute inside dealer spreads his insider deals through a number of different brokers, through different pseudonyms or nominee companies, and makes sure that as much as possible of his activity is based off-shore.

The quantification of loss is also a difficult issue: it is not easy to establish how much a victim of insider dealing lost as a result of insider deals taking place.

Market abuse

This is a term introduced by the Financial Services and Markets Act **12.26** 2000, Part VIII, which prohibits the sort of behaviour, primarily involving the use of insider information,[41] which has the effect of creating a

---

[40] This leaves aside the further vexed issue of jurisdiction, and the fact that an offshore company carrying out insider deals might apparently have no assets. Enforcement of any decree might be pointless.

[41] Financial Services and Markets Act 2000 ("FSMA 2000"), s.118(2)(a).

false market in securities. One type of market abuse is deliberately driving down the price of a security by spreading rumours about either its management or its prospects. It is also possible to indulge in market abuse by giving the impression that the securities are more desirable than they actually are. The Financial Services Authority is required to produce a Code that helps clarify what is or is not market abuse.[42] This may tie in with the City Code on Takeovers and Mergers.[43] In addition market abuse is explained as behaviour which is likely to be regarded by a regular user of the market as "a failure ... to observe the standard of behaviour reasonably expected of a person in his or their position in the market",[44] which gives a false or misleading impression as to the value of the investments in question[45] and which would be seen by a regular user of the market as likely to distort the market in investment of that kind.[46]

Such behaviour must take place within the United Kingdom.[47] Penalties may be imposed by the Financial Services Authority[48] or the courts[49] where market abuse has taken place. The penalties are not used to compensate those who suffer from market abuse, but will be paid to the FSA itself,[50] no doubt to enable it to carry on its good work. An equivalent of an appeal may be made to the Financial Services and Markets Tribunal[51] and appeals on points of law may be made to the courts.[52]

As the legislation is very new, the details of the operation of the new Code still remain to be worked out and will be promulgated in due course.

Is the criminalisation of insider dealing an effective sanction?

12.27   Although there is a certain amount of identification of suspected insider dealing, the prosecution rate has not been high. In Scotland there has only been a handful of reported cases. Nonetheless the legislation has been effective in that:

> (1) it serves as a deterrent to insider dealing, and
> (2) it changes people's attitudes to something which to a certain extent had formerly been seen as one of the prerequisites of working in the City of London or in a stockbroker's office;

---

[42] FSMA 2000, s.119.
[43] FSMA 2000, s.120(4).
[44] FSMA 2000, s.118(2)(a).
[45] FSMA 2000, s.118(2)(b).
[46] FSMA 2000, s.118(2)(c).
[47] FSMA 2000, s.118(5).
[48] FSMA 2000, s.123.
[49] FSMA 2000, s.129.
[50] FSMA 2000, s.206(3).
[51] FSMA 2000, ss.132–136.
[52] FSMA 2000, s.137.

(3) it has encouraged reputable businesses to have compliance officers and to set up systems to limit the opportunities for self-seeking behaviour,

(4) it has forced businesses to remember that they should consider the interests of their clients as paramount.[53]

However, there are several reasons why the legislation to date has not been very effective:

(1) the financial world is highly complex and inhabited by some very sophisticated and secretive investors, most of whom are and always will be well versed in methods of avoiding being caught by any insider dealing laws;

(2) in some countries, banking secrecy laws are strictly enforced. Any inquiries from the Surveillance Unit will be ignored. British police warrants may not be recognised. Some countries have uncertain and anomalous international recognition. Some countries have no extradition treaties with the United Kingdom.

(3) in Scotland, as stated above, there is a requirement of corroboration. When there are two people in the room, and two differing accounts of the same conversation, whom do you believe?

On the other hand, the criminalisation of insider dealing has made **12.28** those who work in the financial services industry a great deal more cautious and professional in their research. It is no longer widely acceptable to be taking advantage of investors in such a manner, and the management of a merchant bank whose employees have a reputation for insider dealing will probably in the long run suffer a loss of credibility. Insider dealing will inevitably always take place, and where a miscreant is caught, not only is he likely to lose his job, but he will also have trouble getting another thereafter.

Further Reading

Insider Dealing

Grier, *UK Company Law* (Wiley, 1998), Chap. 12.
Rider, Alexander and Linklater, *Market Abuse and Insider Dealing* (Butterworths, 2002)

---

[53] In the USA in 2002, recovered emails indicated that analysts at various well known merchant banks were puffing securities which they knew perfectly well were poor investments because they gained from the commission on recommending purchases. In the financial world, conflicts of interest abound, and the insider dealing rules at their best should force managerial minds to remember their duties to their clients.

Brazier, *Insider Dealing Law and Regulation* (Cavendish, 1996)
David Hume Institute, *Hume Occasional Paper No. 41 on Insider Dealing* (1993)

Market Abuse

Alcock "Market Abuse" (2002) 23(5) *Company Lawyer* 142–150

CHAPTER 13

MEETINGS AND RESOLUTIONS

There are two main reasons that meetings are held. The first is that **13.01**
meetings are an opportunity to hold the directors accountable to the
members for the directors' use of the members' money. On the whole,
members will be content to let the directors carry on the management of
the company in terms of the powers delegated to them under the
Articles, but from time to time members like to be reassured that the
directors are making the best use of the funds entrusted to them.
Directors must justify to the members the use of the company's
resources, and on the basis of what the directors tell the members about
the company's past performance and future prospects the members will
decide whether or not to continue investing in the company. If the
members, who after all are the ones who actually own the company and
so should have some say in how their investment is spent, are not happy
with what the directors are doing, they may impose restrictions upon the
directors' behaviour and actions by means of special resolution (which
is tantamount to rewriting the articles of association) or *in extremis*
dismiss the directors under Companies Act 1985 ("CA 1985"), section
303.

There is a human side to this issue. Few people like to be exposed to **13.02**
public criticism, and a general meeting where the directors have made
a poor return on their investors' funds and where the members are
baying for the directors' blood can be a humiliating experience for
conscientious directors. On the other hand, there are high-handed directors whose hides are so thick that only the public scrutiny of a general
meeting, sometimes with journalists present, will cause the directors to
reconsider their actions. Directors tend to associate with their own kind,
and may from time to time lose sight of the impact of their decisions
—and a general meeting is an opportunity to remedy this.

Furthermore, an indifferent performance by the directors at a general **13.03**
meeting, where it can be assumed that the directors ought to be primed on
all aspects of the company's activities, says much about the quality of the
management—a view that may swiftly be reflected in the share price.

The second reason that meetings are necessary is that (with certain
exceptions for private companies) company law and companies' articles

of association require that certain acts can only be performed following
the members' approval obtained in general meeting.

13.04   Although general meetings are designed primarily for these two
purposes, they have one further significant feature. This is that meetings
are a form of democracy within the microcosm of the company, save
that (except in companies limited by guarantee) instead of each member
having only one vote, each member has the number of votes represented
by the number of shares that he owns.[1] Those who have most shares
have most votes. Even so, every shareholder is entitled to a copy of the
accounts and directors' report, and entitled to attend and speak at
general meetings: it is for that reason that sometimes environmental
protestors and other lobby groups will buy one share in a company, thus
entitling them to attend general meetings and protest at the company's
policies—often to the directors' and other shareholders' irritation. However, it is possible to subvert the effects of shareholder democracy by
such means as having shares with weighted voting rights,[2] having
articles that require a named individual to be present to make the
meeting quorate, having articles that permit classes of shares to have a
veto on certain actions, or having a shareholders' agreement.

TYPES OF MEETING

13.05 There are four main types of meeting:

- Annual general meeting ("AGM")
- Extraordinary general meeting ("EGM")
- Class meeting
- Board meeting

Annual general meetings

13.06   AGMs must be held once a year[3] by all companies with the exception
of private companies that have previously passed an elective resolution
not to hold them. By convention at an AGM it is common to discuss the
following:

- tabling and approval of the accounts and directors' report on the
  company's activities for the year;
- declaration of a dividend;
- re-appointment of auditors;
- directing the directors to fix the auditors' remuneration;
- (sometimes) appointment of directors.

---

[1] Unless the shares are non-voting shares, or the shares have weighted voting rights.
[2] *Bushell v. Faith* [1970] A.C. 1099.
[3] CA 1985, s.366.

In larger companies it is common to deal with many other matters as well. For example, quoted companies, with effect from August 1, 2002, must allow members to vote on their directors' remuneration.

There is no requirement that a company has to deal with these matters at an AGM unless the articles say so: these matters could equally well be dealt with at an EGM. Private companies, as will be seen later, may be able to dispense with the tabling of accounts and the re-appointment of auditors if they have passed elective resolutions to that effect. Under Table A one third of the directors are required to retire each year and to put themselves forward for re-election at the next annual general meeting, which is why it is common for directors to be appointed at AGMs; but as was seen in Chapter 8, directors may be appointed by whatever means are provided in the articles.

AGMs require 21 days notice,[4] originally so that members could **13.07** consult their professional advisers. The notice of an AGM has to make it clear that it is an AGM.[5] AGMs may be held at short notice, provided all voting members agree to this.[6] Private companies may dispense with AGMs by means of an elective resolution.[7] Where AGMs have been dispensed with by elective resolution, an AGM may be requisitioned by any member by notice, either in paper or electronic form, to the company within three months before the end of the year in question.[8] Although it is good practice to hold AGMs at much the same time each year, AGMs may be held up to 15 months apart,[9] provided that one is held each year. However the very first AGM need not take place within the year of the company's incorporation provided that it does take place within 18 months of incorporation.[10]

AGMs are usually called by the company secretary on the instruction of the board of directors, but may also be called by the Secretary of State[11] on the application of a member, or by the court on the application of a director, a member or by the court itself.[12]

Extraordinary general meetings

An EGM is any general meeting that is not an AGM, and may be **13.08** called whenever the directors wish, or by the Secretary of State or the court as above.

---

[4] CA 1985, s.369. It is now possible to use electronic communications to call meetings and to post notices of meetings on a website (CA 1985, s.369(4A)–(4G)).
[5] CA 1985, s.366(1).
[6] CA 1985, s.366(3)(a). This means that provided each member has signed a paper indicating his consent to holding the meeting without the normal 21 day period of notice, the meeting could take place immediately.
[7] CA 1985, s.366A(1).
[8] CA 1985, s.366A(3), (3A).
[9] CA 1985, s.366(3).
[10] CA 1985, s.366(2).
[11] CA 1985, s.367.
[12] CA 1985, s.371.

Members' requisition of an EGM

13.09   The members may also requisition an EGM providing the requisitionists hold at least 10 per cent of the issued voting share capital or 10 per cent of a class thereof, or in the case of a company without share capital, 10 per cent of the voting rights.[13] The requisitionists must state the objects of the meeting. Directors must then within 21 days of the date of deposit of the requisition convene a meeting to be held within three months.[14] Failure to do this entitles the members to organise the meetings themselves (also within three months) and to seek reimbursement of their expenses from the company. The company then is reimbursed out of the directors' salaries.[15] The directors are deemed not to have convened a meeting properly (thus entitling the members to do it instead) if they convene a meeting for a date more than 28 days after the date of the notice convening the meeting.[16]

Auditors' requisition of an EGM

13.10   If the auditors believe there is something that should be brought to the attention of the members they too may requisition a meeting in the same manner as above,[17] with the meeting being held within 28 days of the date of the notice convening the meeting[18] (section 392A(5)).

EGM for a plc suffering a fall in net asset value

13.11   Under CA 1985, section 142 the directors must convene an EGM for a plc if the net asset value of the company falls to half or less than the value of the paid up share capital. However, the legislation is silent as to what should be done at that EGM other than consider what steps the directors should take to deal with the loss of assets.

Notice of an EGM

13.12   EGMs normally require 14 days notice,[19] unless one of the matters to be discussed is a special resolution, in which case 21 days notice is required.[20] If the company is an unlimited company, seven days notice is required.[21]

---

[13] CA 1985, s.368(2). This is to prevent trivial or unsupported requisitions.
[14] CA 1985, s.368(4).
[15] CA 1985, s.368(6).
[16] CA 1985, s.388(8).
[17] CA 1985, s.392A(2).
[18] CA 1985, s.392A(5).
[19] CA 1985, s.369(1)(b)(ii). This too may be done by electronic means or posted on a website.
[20] CA 1985, s.369(1)(b).
[21] CA 1985, s.369(1)(b)(i) and (2)(b)(i).

It is possible to have short notice of an EGM provided 95 per cent of the voting members have agreed to it.[22] If the company is private and has passed an elective resolution to that effect the figure of 95 per cent may be reduced to 90 per cent.[23]

The information contained in notices of general meetings

Under Table A, regulation 38 a notice of an AGM or EGM will state **13.13** the date, place and time of the meeting, plus sufficient information to the members to enable them to understand what will be discussed at the meeting and to enable them to decide whether to attend in person or in proxy. The notice will also give the full text of any special or extraordinary resolutions,[24] together with instructions on how to arrange for a proxy[25] to vote on the member's behalf.[26] The notice must state if the meeting is an AGM.[27] Normally the company secretary acts "by order of the board of directors", and signs and dates the notice. He sends it from the registered office. Any accidental failure to send a member the notice will not invalidate the meeting.[28] There is authority in Scotland to the effect that the "clear days notice" of 14 or 21 days, as the case may be, may, if the articles provide for it, include the day of the meeting itself within the period of notice.[29] In practice most companies adopt Table A's version which does not include the day of the meeting itself.

In addition to the normal special, extraordinary and ordinary resolutions (of which more later) and elective resolutions in private companies (of which again more later), there may be ordinary resolutions with "special notice", and requisitioned resolutions.

Resolutions requiring special notice

"Special notice" means that in the notice of the general meeting there **13.14** will be a statement that the company has received special notice of a

---

[22] CA 1985, s.369(4).

[23] CA 1985, s.369(4).

[24] CA 1985, s.378(2) and (1). Curiously there appears to be no requirement to provide the text of ordinary resolutions, but it would be very odd not to do so, and most notices of AGMs and EGMs will automatically do so.

[25] CA 1985, s.372. A proxy is a person (already a member) who is asked by the member to vote on his behalf, either in accordance with the member's instructions, or in accordance with the proxy's own views. Proxy forms normally allow the member to select his own proxy, or if he cannot think of anyone to be his proxy, to select the chairman to be his proxy, again either voting according to the member's direction or at the chairman's discretion. See Table A, regs. 60 and 61A, a company is not allowed to make life difficult for members by insisting that proxy forms will be deemed to be invalid unless they are lodged more than 48 hours before the actual meeting (CA 1985, s.372(5).

[26] CA 1985, s.372(3).

[27] Table A, reg. 38.

[28] Table A, reg. 39.

[29] *Aberdeen Combworks Ltd, Petitioners* (1902)10 S.L.T. 210.

particular resolution, such special notice being required to be given to the company at least 28 days before the meeting at which the resolution is to be moved. This is because the matters that require special notice, being

- the dismissal of a director at a general meeting[30];
- the filling of a casual vacancy in the office of auditor[31];
- the re-appointment of a retiring auditor who was appointed to fill a casual vacancy[32];
- the removal of an auditor before the expiry of his term of office[33];
- the appointment of an auditor other than the retiring auditor[34] or
- the appointment to a directorship of a plc of a person over the age of 70.[35]

all are matters which the legislation deems to be sufficiently important that members should be told that the matter is "special"—though of the few members who actually bother to read the notice of a general meeting even fewer probably will be aware of the significance of the word "special".

It is open to companies to provide in their articles that certain other matters will need special notice too.

Requisitioned resolutions

13.15   A requisitioned resolution is one that members wish to have included in the next AGM. In order for a resolution to be requisitioned at least five per cent of the members with voting rights, or not less than 100 members holding shares in the company, on which there has been paid up an average sum per member of not less than £100, must have signed up to the resolution.[36] This is to deter frivolous applications. The company, on the receipt of the requisition, but at the requisitioning members' expense, must then send to the members notice of the resolution together with a statement from the requisitionists, up to 1,000 words in length, concerning the matter referred to in the requisitioned resolution.[37] It is in practice normal to include the requisitioned resolution in the notice of the next AGM and to send out the statement at the same time. The requisitionists must also deposit at the company's

---

[30] CA 1985, s.303.
[31] CA 1985, s.388(3)(a).
[32] CA 1985, s.388(3)(b).
[33] CA 1985, s.391A(1)(a).
[34] CA 1985, s.391A(1)(b).
[35] CA 1985, s.293(5).
[36] CA 1985, s.376(2).
[37] CA 1985, s.376(1).

registered office a copy or copies of the requisitioned resolution not less than six weeks before the meeting at which the resolution is to be moved.[38] If they wish to have their statement circulated it must lodged at least a week before the meeting. In both cases, the requisitionists must also tender the reasonably anticipated expenses of sending out the documents.[39] If the company then brings the date of the meeting forward, the time limit is still deemed to have been complied with.[40] The company is not obliged to disseminate the statement if on an application to the court by the company or anyone aggrieved by the statement the court holds that the right to produce the statement is being abused to secure needless publicity for defamatory matter.[41]

These various procedures are designed to prevent vexatious share- **13.16** holders making a nuisance of themselves and wasting everyone's time at general meetings, but equally they have the effect of making it expensive and inconvenient for shareholders with a justified grievance to raise their concerns. The requirement to pay the expenses is particularly onerous in a listed company and ensures that only the very wealthy can afford to requisition a resolution[42]: how much easier just to sell the shares and walk away from the problem.

The White Paper proposes that the company should bear the expenses of requisitioned resolutions.

The practice of the meeting

Assuming the meeting has been properly summoned, and is taking **13.17** place with sufficient notice or consent to short notice, the meeting, if quorate,[43] will be duly convened. Table A, regulations 40–63 provide standard rules for the conduct of the meeting. The chairman chairs the meeting,[44] usually assisted by the company secretary who will be

---

[38] CA 1985, s.377(1)(a).

[39] CA 1985, s.377(1)(b).

[40] CA 1985, s.377(2).

[41] CA 1985, s.377(3).

[42] Requisitioning a resolution for the general meeting of a major Scottish listed company a few years ago cost the brave shareholder who requisitioned it £300,000, and even so his resolution was not approved.

[43] CA 1985, s.370(4). The point of a quorum is to show that decisions have been considered by at least a modicum of members rather than the sole dictat of one member. The quorum for companies other than single member companies is two, though companies' articles may provide for more to be present if necessary. If a meeting is inquorate, technically no resolutions may be passed, though resolutions may be taken on an interim basis and ratified at a later quorate meeting. If a company takes a decision at an inquorate meeting and acts upon it in a transaction with a third party, unless the third party is aware of the inquoracy, he will normally be protected by the operation of CA 1985, ss.35A and 35B. Under certain circumstances the company might also be personally barred from founding on its own inquorate decisions.

[44] The chairman will normally be the chairman of the board of directors, but the members may if they wish (and provided the articles do not say otherwise) elect some other member to be chairman (CA 1985, s.370(5)).

guiding the chairman on any points of order, and with his fellow directors beside him. Normally there will be a note of those present (*i.e.* members), those attending (such as auditors or other experts in a professional capacity) and apologies. After the approval of minutes of the previous meeting, and the insertion of any corrections (or instructions to rewrite the minutes as necessary) and the discussion of any business arising from those minutes and not already on the agenda for later in the meeting, the chairman will go through each item on the agenda, taking the mood of the meeting and allowing some discussion of each item before proceeding to a vote, unless the item is one merely to be noted for the record, adjourned pending further information or withdrawn perhaps because of a change of circumstances.

Voting

13.18   Voting is normally done on a show of hands, but if necessary, and assuming Table A is being used, a poll may be demanded by the chairman, by any two voting members, by a member or members representing one-tenth of the voting rights, or by voting members whose paid-up capital in the company collectively is equal to one-tenth of the company's issued share capital.[45] It is not possible to build in provisions in the articles that effectively make it difficult for members to demand a poll by insisting on at least five members asking for a poll, or insisting that members have more than the above voting rights or capital in the company[46] except on the matter of the election of the chairman or the adjournment of the meeting.[47] A proxy is entitled to demand a poll[48] though a proxy in a plc may not speak otherwise.[49] Normally a proxy may not vote on a show of hands[50] but should do so on a poll. Companies and other corporations, which are physically unable to represent themselves, may send "corporate representatives" to speak and vote on their behalf.[51] Normally the chairman will have a casting vote.[52]

Any other business

13.19   After each item on the agenda has been duly considered and voted on or adjourned or otherwise dealt with, the chairman will commonly invite questions from the audience (sometimes known as "any other business"). This is the opportunity for the members to put the directors "on

---

[45] Table A, reg. 46.
[46] CA 1985, s.373(1)(b).
[47] CA 1985, s.373(1)(a).
[48] CA 1985, s.373(2).
[49] CA 1985, s.372(1). This was apparently to prevent plc shareholders hiring people to speak on their behalf.
[50] Unless the articles say otherwise—CA 1985, s.372(2)(c).
[51] CA 1985, s.375.
[52] Table A, reg. 50.

the spot" on any matters on which the directors or their company may not have fared well. Some directors are known to be so alarmed by this process that they arrange for stooges in the audience to set up gentle questions for them to answer, or insist that they will only answer questions of which they have had prior notice—thereby confirming other members' worst suspicions. As it is well known that chairmen only will ask for questions from respectable-looking people, environmental or other protestors have been known to go to Oxfam beforehand to buy suits and ties in order to pass themselves off as investment analysts or chartered accountants before asking their awkward questions on environmental or ethical matters.[53] Most questions need not be asked at all, since a careful reading of well drafted accounts and directors' reports will generally contain all the information investors could want.

After dealing with any other business, the meeting is drawn to a close and the company secretary goes off to write up the minutes.

Class meetings

Class meetings are run as a smaller version of general meetings, save **13.20** that only the members of the class are entitled to be present at the meeting. If a class of shareholders wishes to change certain matters relating to its class of shares, it will need to pass a resolution itself.[54] As a matter of practice, a class of shares is unlikely to be allowed to change any rights attaching to its own class of shares without consent from the other classes of shares beforehand.

Board meetings

How the directors run their board meetings is a matter for the **13.21** directors alone unless the articles say otherwise, or unless the board members devise their own standing orders. Table A, regulations 88–98 lay down standard rules which many companies adopt. It is common for larger companies to have board meetings every month, where the board deals with the commercial and administrative matters of the company and any business of the company that does not require shareholders' approval. The company secretary will normally take the minutes of the meetings. Members are not entitled to see board minutes, though auditors are. Companies are expected to give board members reasonable notice and there is normally a quorum of two directors.[55] There are

---

[53] As happened to Robert Wilson, chairman of the controversial mining group, Rio Tinto Zinc, at its AGM on May 12, 1999.

[54] Normally this will be an extraordinary resolution.

[55] Except in single member companies with a sole director. Even so, single member companies are expected to hold board meetings for such matters as require board approval, as evidenced by board minutes, preferably recorded by the company secretary. A director who has an interest in a matter on which he is not supposed to be voting may not be part of the quorum (Table A, reg. 95).

provisions to permit the validity of decisions if it turns out that a director voting at a board meeting should not technically have been there because unwittingly he had not been properly appointed or because his appointment had expired.[56] It is permissible to have written resolutions of board meetings, whereby all the directors sign a resolution to save the inconvenience of actually meeting in a room together.[57]

A board member who has a material interest in a matter being discussed should not, unless the articles say otherwise, vote on that matter.[58] The members of the company may, however, decide that they are willing to release the director in question from this prohibition[59] or the directors may refer the matter to the chairman for his decision.[60]

13.22 If they wish, directors may delegate certain matters to a committee, and that committee may have such powers as the articles provide or as the directors may decide.[61]

TYPES OF RESOLUTION

13.23 There are five main types of resolution. They are:

- ordinary resolutions
- special resolutions
- extraordinary resolutions
- elective resolutions
- written resolutions

In addition some ordinary resolutions require special notice (see above under Information contained in Notices of General Meetings).

Where a resolution needs to be registered, it must be registered within 15 days of its being passed.[62]

Ordinary resolutions

13.24 Ordinary resolutions need 14 days notice and a simple majority of those voting and entitled to vote in person or by proxy. They are used for the less contentious matters though dismissing a director, which one would normally consider contentious, only requires an ordinary resolution, albeit with special notice. Most ordinary resolutions do not need to be registered with the Registrar of Companies within the normal 15 day

---

[56] Table A, reg. 92.
[57] Table A, reg. 93.
[58] Table A, reg. 94.
[59] Table A, reg. 95.
[60] Table A, reg. 96.
[61] Table A, reg. 72.
[62] CA 1985, s.380.

period, but a few, such as a notice of increase in authorised capital, do.[63]

Special resolutions

Special resolutions need 21 days notice and a 75 per cent majority of **13.25** those voting and entitled to vote in person or in proxy.[64] Special resolutions are generally used for contentious and significant matters, such as the alteration of the company's constitution or issued capital. The high percentage approval is to ensure that a significant number of the members really approve of the resolution. All special resolutions must be registered with the Registrar of Companies.[65]

The White Paper recommends reducing the number of days' notice to 14.

Extraordinary resolutions

Extraordinary resolutions require 14 days notice and 75 per cent **13.26** approval.[66] They are normally used when a class of shareholders wishes to vary the rights attaching to its class of shares,[67] when a liquidator proposes to pay out to the members the company's assets by way of a dividend[68] or when the members resolve that their company cannot continue in existence because of its liabilities and that it is advisable to wind up the company.[69] All extraordinary resolutions must be registered with the Registrar of Companies.[70]

The White Paper recommends abolishing extraordinary resolutions.

Elective resolutions

Elective resolutions were designed in order to make life easier for **13.27** private companies. The DTI carried out research on how companies, and in particular private companies, held meetings, and discovered that the rules about meetings and resolutions were widely ignored, little understood and much of the time unnecessary anyway. However, rather than abolish the rules entirely, some new rules were invented, including the creation of elective resolutions.[71]

Elective resolutions are only available to private companies, and are only used in five circumstances:

---

[63] CA 1985, s.122.
[64] CA 1985, s.378(2).
[65] CA 1985, s.380(4)(a).
[66] CA 1985, s.380(1).
[67] CA 1985, s.125(2)(b).
[68] Table A, reg. 117.
[69] Insolvency Act 1986 ("IA 1986"), s.84(1)(c).
[70] CA 1985, s.380(4)(b).
[71] CA 1985, s.379A. Elective resolutions were introduced in 1996 by Neil Hamilton, the later disgraced MP for Tatton and the then DTI Minister for State.

- to give the directors authority to allot shares for a period in excess of five years[72];
- to dispense with the requirement to table the annual accounts at a general meeting[73];
- to dispense with the need to hold AGMs[74];
- to reduce the majority for short notice of an EGM from 95 per cent to 90 per cent[75];
- to dispense with the annual appointment of auditors.[76]

In order to pass an elective resolution there must be:

- 21 days notice of the resolution[77];
- unanimous approval in person or by proxy of all members entitled to vote[78];
- registration of the resolution with the Registrar of Companies within 15 days.[79]

13.28 The notice of the meeting at which the resolution is to be passed may be intimated electronically or on the company's website.[80] The resolution may be passed by way of written resolution.[81]

An elective resolution may be revoked by the company by an ordinary resolution,[82] though it should be noted that, as stated above under *annual general meetings*, only one member is needed to requisition an AGM where an elective resolution has been passed to dispense with holding AGMs,[83] any member or the auditor can requisition the holding of a general meeting at which to lay the accounts[84] and any member can deposit a notice at the company's registered office proposing that the annual re-appointment of the auditor should be brought to an end.[85] Although in these circumstances only one member or the auditor is needed to propose the revocation, the passing of the resolution for revocation must still be an ordinary resolution.

---

[72] CA 1985, s.80A.
[73] CA 1985, s.252(1).
[74] CA 1985, s.366A.
[75] CA 1985, ss.369(4) and 378(3).
[76] CA 1985, s.386.
[77] CA 1985, s.379A(2)(a). Unless there has been consent to short notice (CA 1985, s.379A(2A)).
[78] CA 1985, s.379A(2)(b).
[79] CA 1985, s.380(4)(bb).
[80] CA 1985, s.379A(2B) and (2C).
[81] CA 1985, s.381A(6).
[82] CA 1985, s.379A(3).
[83] CA 1985, s.366A(3).
[84] CA 1985, s.253(2).
[85] CA 1985, s.393(1).

All elective resolutions, and their revocations, must be registered within 15 days of their being passed[86].

Elective resolutions as a reform have been successful although the reduction of the majority required for short notice of an EGM makes very little difference in practice.

Written resolutions

Written resolutions were introduced at the same time and for the same **13.29** purpose as elective resolutions, as part of an attempt to make life easier for private companies. It was also to legitimise a practice that had been unofficially been going on for some years of members all signing a resolution and claiming that that was equivalent to a passed resolution.

Written resolutions have the following features:

- they are only available to private companies;
- they can be used for almost any type of resolution[87] except dismissal of auditors and directors, because of their right of protest[88];
- they must be signed by all members entitled to vote and voting in person or in proxy;
- they must be intimated to the auditors beforehand.[89]

The point of the intimation to the auditors is that the auditors will, it is hoped, warn the company if it is about to pass by way of written resolution something that cannot be done by written resolution, such as dismissing a director, or something that actually requires more procedure than the directors might be aware of, such as a company reducing its capital by written resolution.

Written resolutions must be registered within 15 days in the normal **13.30** manner provided that the resolution itself was one that if it were passed at a meeting would need to be registered.[90]

Written resolutions have been very successful and have saved many unnecessary meetings and much unnecessary travel. It is not necessary that all the members' signatures be on the one sheet of paper attached to the resolution: it is possible to send a copy of the resolution to each member who may then sign it.

---

[86] CA 1985, s.380(1).
[87] CA 1985, s.381A(1).
[88] CA 1985, s.381A(7), in turn referring to CA 1985, Sched. 15A, Pt 1.
[89] CA 1985, s.381B. The sanction for failure to do this is a fine, but if the company passes a written resolution without telling the auditors first the resolution is not invalid (CA 1985, s.381B(4)).
[90] CA 1985, s.380(4).

A well organised private company, provided nothing contentious arises, can effectively avoid having general meetings all together by the judicious use of elective and written resolutions.

The White Paper proposes having written resolutions with 75 per cent approval rather than 100 per cent approval, which is undoubtedly a sensible suggestion.

SHAREHOLDER DEMOCRACY

13.31 Although meetings are ostensibly about the democratic right of members to vote on matters that affect their shareholdings, it is well recognised that they are failing to do what they are supposed to do. This is for various reasons, amongst them being:

- the fact that in larger companies, the major investors will be reluctant to air grievances with the company's management in open forum when quieter more effective results can be obtained round the boardroom table;
- the major investors in larger companies are usually insurance companies and pension fund companies (the "institutions") who can command far more clout than private investors;
- most private investors cannot be bothered to read the directors' report, cannot understand the accounts, only look at the dividend figure, and certainly cannot be bothered to turn up to an AGM;
- AGMs are often held at a time when most working people are at work anyway, so those who attend are often corporate representatives of major investors appearing for form's sake, the retired or pensioners, employees' representatives, and those with axes to grind;
- there is little point in having meetings for small companies where all the members are related or see and work with each other every day;
- the perception that many companies' managements are not very interested in shareholders' views anyway.

It is noticeable that the most popular AGMs are those of companies, particularly food and drinks companies, that provide free samples of their products after the meeting is over.

13.32 In the forthcoming White Paper it is suggested that private companies need not have AGMs at all, but that they may have them if they wish or if the members insist; at the same time plcs (though probably not quoted ones) can opt out of having AGMs. This is probably very realistic since, as indicated above, most AGMs are a waste of time anyway.

However, at least in the United Kingdom we do not suffer, so far, the problem suffered by Japanese listed companies. So far as possible they all try to have their AGMs on the same day in order to limit the opportunities for the Yakuza (the Japanese equivalent of the Mafia) from disrupting proceedings. Normally the Yakuza have to be paid off to keep them out of the way, but even the members of the Yakuza cannot be at all the major meetings at once.

Further Reading

Davies, *Gower's Principles of Modern Company Law* (6th ed., Sweet and Maxwell, 1997), Chap. 21

CHAPTER 14

TAKEOVERS AND MERGERS

TAKEOVERS[1]

14.01 Strictly speaking a takeover of a company occurs when one company buys either all or the greater part of the share capital of the other. The company carrying out the takeover is sometimes called the acquiring company, the bidder, the offeror, or in the case of an unwelcome takeover bid, the "predator". The company whose shares are being bought by the acquiring company is sometimes known as the "target" company, or in extreme cases, the "victim". In the circumstances of a takeover bid, the acquiring company will wish to buy sufficient of the share capital of the target to be able either to control its board of directors and to pass ordinary resolutions. The acquiring company will give the shareholders of the target company either cash, assets, shares or other securities in the acquiring company in exchange for their shares in the target company. Takeovers are usually agreed between the directors of the two companies, who will draw up a large contract outlining the terms on which the acquisition will proceed, but in quoted companies, it is possible to have a hostile takeover, which is where the target company resists the approach of the predator company, on the grounds that the offer being made to the target company shareholders is not high enough or that the predators are unprincipled rogues who will destroy a good business. Sometimes, in what is known as the Pacman[2] defence, the target turns round and starts bidding for the predator. With a hostile takeover there is no contract: the predator merely has to acquire a majority of shares in the target, and having done so is in control and may do with it, up to a point, as it pleases. At the same time, because there is no contract, the predator may not necessarily know exactly what the target company's assets and liabilities are until it is in possession of the

---

[1] In a book of this length there is not space to devote to the greater issues of this subject, but for an informed and thoughtful discussion of the underlying issues see Lowry and Watson, *Company Law*, (Butterworths, 2001), Chap. 15.

[2] Pacman was one of the first computer games, featuring a small gobbling mouth which scurried about in a labyrinth while trying to avoid being gobbled by various monsters. From time to time it would turn round and gobble its attackers.

shares and in a position to find out.[3] With an agreed takeover, the acquiring company and the selling company will have tried to iron out any surprises. With a hostile takeover, both predator directors and target directors are appealing directly to the shareholders of the target in a bid to convince the shareholders either to sell or to hang on to their shares.

A takeover can be contrasted with a merger, also sometimes known as an amalgamation. In a merger two companies unite to become one company, which may be a brand new company designed to absorb both businesses. The controllers of both original businesses become controllers of the new combined business and are given shares in the new merged company in exchange for their shares in the two old companies. One way of doing this is by a scheme of arrangement under the Companies Act 1985 ("CA 1985"), section 425 (described later).

The law relating to takeovers

There is very little law relating to the above, though sometimes there **14.02** are legal implications arising out of the practice of the takeover: for example, a company fearing a takeover might try to buy back its own shares to drive the predator away by the rising share price; takeover bids attract furtive insider dealers; or there might be illegal financial assistance, as arose in the Guinness takeover of Distillers. Another area where there is also difficulty relates to directors: the directors should above all consider the interests of the company as a whole, and if the directors receive an offer that in their view is the best price the members are likely to get for their shares, they should be mindful of their fiduciary duty to their members collectively and recommend it—but by so doing, the directors may well be doing themselves out of their jobs. The Companies Act 1985, sections 312–316 were designed to prevent directors receiving secret blandishments to encourage their shareholders to accept takeover offers.

The bid documentation inviting the target company's shareholders to sell their shares to the bidder must be accurate and informative in conformity with the requirements of the Financial Services and Markets Act 2000 and the Stock Exchange Listing requirements.

The commercial significance of the takeover market

Takeovers and mergers matter not just to companies and their share- **14.03** holders themselves, but also to the public generally, because of the

---

[3] When the Royal Bank of Scotland bought the National Westminster Bank, its executives did not necessarily know very much about all the various businesses and interests National Westminster had, nor how its systems and computers operated. Having managed the takeover, the Royal Bank was pleasantly surprised with what it found, though as one executive allegedly put it, three months after the acquisition: "We're still unwrapping the package".

dangers of industrial giants "cornering the market" in particular products. Takeovers and mergers also matter to the economy of the United Kingdom as a whole, because of the enormous sums of money involved, most of it being dealt with in the City of London. The City of London, with all its financial markets and resources, generates enormous invisible earnings for the United Kingdom, but it can only do so while the City is seen to be a place where honest businessmen can practise. Should the conduct of takeovers and mergers in Britain attract a reputation for dishonesty and sharp practice, the City would cease to attract foreign capital, resulting in diminished opportunities for all who work there. It is therefore in the City's interest that takeovers and mergers are properly policed to ensure that shareholders are treated properly and that there is a fair and established set of rules for takeovers and mergers. This set of rules is known as the City Code.

The City Code

14.04 The City Code is administered by the Panel on Takeovers and Mergers. The Panel is self-regulated[4] and controlled by members of the leading accountancy bodies and representatives from banking, insurance, stockbroking, industry and various financial regulatory authorities. It applies to all those involved in takeovers and mergers of major companies, whether as directors or in any other capacity in connection with the company, such as its corporate advisers, lawyers, bankers or accountants. Companies mounting takeovers and mergers, and those connected with such companies are expected to abide by the regulations promulgated by the Panel, but the regulations have no statutory authority. The principle behind the 10 general principles and 38 regulations is that the spirit rather than the letter of the regulations should be followed, and furthermore the regulations are deemed to apply even in circumstances not specifically mentioned in the regulations. The regulations are in effect a set of best commercial practices which directors and their advisers in the context of takeovers and mergers are expected to follow. The advantage of having regulations drafted in this way is their commendable flexibility and adaptability, as well as their appeal to the integrity of the participants. Although there are no legal sanctions for non-compliance, the non-legal sanctions are not without effect: delisting and the denial of access to the securities markets would have a serious effect on a company, and those working in the financial services industry might find that they ceased to be authorised by their appropriate self-regulatory authority to carry on their business.

---

[4] Cynics will say that self-regulation means that the City closes ranks round those who do not play by the rules; but equally the City collectively has much to lose by being seen to be overly protective or failing to maintain the highest standards of corporate probity.

The City Code is drawn up on the basis of:

- providing all shareholders with equal, sufficient and accurate and independent information to enable them to decide whether or not to accept the bid;
- treating all shareholders fairly, so that none receives a better price for his shares than others, and each shareholder is offered an equal chance to sell his shares;
- treating all shareholders within a class of shareholders equally;
- making directors of the target company obtain approval of the members before disposing of any assets that could prejudice the desirability of the takeover bid;
- making directors, when advising the members on the terms of any takeover, disregard their own personal interest in the company,[5] and concentrate on what in their view would be best for the members generally;
- daily disclosure of any dealings in securities of the companies involved by anyone connected with the takeover;
- preserving the strictest confidentiality in relation to price-sensitive information (to prevent insider dealing and market abuse);
- preventing the operation of a false market in shares on the basis on inadequate or inaccurate information;
- ensuring that offers for takeovers should only be made when the acquiring company believes he can indeed implement the takeover;
- "testing the water" being unacceptable;
- making it difficult for takeover bids to be withdrawn without the consent of the Panel; and
- making all parties conform to strict guidelines and time-limits failing which the bid will lapse unless it has been withdrawn.

Those involved in takeovers and mergers are expected to consult the executive of the Panel on Takeovers and Mergers where they are unsure of their proposed course of conduct. Where there has been a breach of the City Code there is a disciplinary hearing which may be appealed if necessary. Where decisions have not been well received by the protagonists, the Panel's decision has from time to time been challenged in the courts by means of judicial review, though not always to the satisfaction of the challengers.[6]

---

[5] This in particular means that self-seeking defensive tactics are unacceptable. This is in contrast to what is permitted elsewhere in other jurisdictions, where sometimes local legislation or local politics intrude on the otherwise freemarket approach to takeovers.

[6] *R. v. Panel on Takeovers and Mergers, ex p. Guinness plc* [1990] Q.B. 147, CA; *R. v. Panel on Takeovers and Mergers, ex p. Datafin* [1987] Q.B. 815; *R. v. Panel on Takeovers and Mergers, ex p. Fayed* [1992] BCLC 938.

14.05   The City Code is well regarded because every honest businessman stands to gain by adhering to sensible common standards of integrity and fair play. In addition, the City Code tells foreign investors that the British capital markets are well regulated and reasonably free from market manipulation. The City Code to a certain extent is the basis for the proposed 13th Company Law Directive on Takeovers promulgated by the EC Commission and which was rejected in 2001, much to the irritation of the Commissioners.

The Legal Status of the City Code

14.06   The City Code is slightly like the Highway Code. If a motorist did not adhere to the Highway Code it would not be well regarded, but it might not make his transgression a criminal offence—though it might have some bearing on his credibility. Equally the City Code is well regarded and is seen as an example of good commercial practice—and as ever with good commercial practice, it is difficult for the company not conforming to good commercial practice to explain why its behaviour should therefore be acceptable.[7] However, in the minority protection case of *Re Astec (BSR) plc*[8] it was held that while adherence to the City Code was desirable, it was not obligatory. This should however be understood in the context that the minority shareholders in this case were actively abusing the spirit of the City Code in an attempt to be bought out at a premium, so that the balance of equity was not entirely in their favour.

The Competition Commission and the Office of Fair Trading

14.07   It is not usually in the public interest to have companies operating cartels or monopolies, and accordingly there is extensive legislation, both at a national and at a European level, to limit the opportunity for cartels or monopolies to arise. Inevitably some cartels and monopolies do arise, either because without them the business in question may disappear or may lower its standards to a level injurious to the common good, or because the Government has given the cartel or monopoly its blessing—as initially happened with the privatised utilities. In such circumstances the cartel or monopoly may be allowed to continue in existence.

   If, however, there is a possibility of a cartel or monopoly arising through a takeover or a merger, and where such a cartel or monopoly might adversely affect the public interest, under the Monopolies and Mergers Act 1965 and the Fair Trading Act 1973, the Secretary of State for Trade and Industry can refer a takeover or merger to the Competition Commission. While the reference takes place, the takeover bid is deemed to lapse in terms of the City Code and cannot be renewed during

---

[7] *Re St Piran Ltd* [1981] 3 All E.R. 270.
[8] [1998] 2 BCLC 556.

the period of the reference. When the Secretary of State makes the reference to the Commission, he may also receive advice from the Director-General of Fair Trading although there is no obligation on the Secretary of State to accept the Director General's advice. Equally the Secretary of State is not obliged to accept the Commission's recommendation, but if he does accept it, he has various powers under the Fair Trading Act 1973 to prohibit or limit mergers or takeovers. Another options is that the Director-General of Fair Trading can negotiate voluntary undertakings from the parties concerned, on the basis of which he may let a merger or takeover proceed.[9] Failure to adhere to the undertaking could entitle a third party to obtain an injunction or interdict to compel the company to perform its undertaking.[10]

Approval for proposed takeovers and mergers

14.08 As the prospect of a takeover or a merger being refused would be highly significant for the companies involved, it is possible to refer the proposed takeover or merger in advance to the Commission. Alternatively the Secretary of State can make a reference in connection with a proposed takeover or merger.[11] While the reference takes place the companies either agree to defer the takeover or merger, or if necessary, under the Fair Trading Act 1973, section 74, may be forced to defer the takeover or merger while the Commission deliberates.

The implications of takeovers have traditionally been seen as highly political since takeovers may affect issues of national sovereignty and loss of employment. It is for that reason that the Secretary of State has been involved. However, the current Enterprise Bill proposes that the politics should be taken out of competition issues and should be left to the Office of Fair Trading and the Competition Commission on the grounds that politicians only muddy the water. There are residual powers left to the Secretary of State to intervene,[12] but generally only after other avenues have been explored and found unsatisfactory. The primary interest of the Competition Commission will be the public weal as opposed to political expediency.

Substantial Acquisition Rules

14.09 Should an acquiring company acquire 30 per cent of the voting rights of a listed company, it is required to make a mandatory bid for the company. Up to the 30 per cent limit, however, the acquisition of shares by a potential acquiring company is covered by the Substantial Acquisition Rules ("SAR"), issued by the Panel on Takeovers and Mergers. These Rules are published as part of the City Code.

---

[9] Fair Trading Act 1975, s.75G–K.
[10] Fair Trading Act 1975, s.137(5).
[11] Fair Trading Act 1975, s.75.
[12] This is for such matters as national security.

The SAR do not apply to acquiring companies which have announced their intention to make an offer, because in that case the City Code applies to their offer. Nor do the SAR apply to those who have 30 per cent or more of the voting rights in a listed company, because they are covered by the Mandatory Bid Rules. The SAR state that in general a purchaser may not within a seven-day period acquire shares representing 10 per cent or more of the voting rights if he already holds shares representing between 15 per cent and 30 per cent of the voting rights, though where a tender offer is made (*i.e.* a firm offer to buy a specified number of shares for cash at a fixed price or up to a maximum price) or if the acquisition precedes a formal offer the rule may be varied. The SAR also state that a purchase of shares entitling the member to control 15 per cent or more of the voting rights, and every subsequent percentage point thereafter, must be disclosed to the Stock Exchange. Contravention of the SAR is contrary to the City Code and attracts the same penalties as other contraventions of the City Code.

Mandatory bids

14.10   Where a shareholder has, either on his own account or in conjunction with others, acquired 30 per cent or more of the voting rights of the company, and subsequently acquires more than one per cent more of the voting rights within a 12–month period, he is obliged to make a mandatory bid for the company. This must be addressed to all the members, and must be for cash or for a cash alternative such as shares. Any shares issued for this purpose will need to comply with the normal rules for allotment of shares and the rules relating to the issue of shares following a prospectus.[13]

Share for assets offers

14.11   Sometimes the acquiring company purchases, not the shares of the target company, but the assets and undertaking of the target company. The consideration for the assets and undertaking is shares in the acquiring company, or as the case may be, cash. If so, the procedure should follow the terms of the CA 1985, Schedule 15A. This Schedule, broadly speaking, requires there to be disclosure of all relevant information to the members of both companies, together with experts' reports and draft documentation for the members' approval prior to the court's approval. In effect, as much information is presented to the members as would be presented in a prospectus. The above set of rules, enacting the terms of the Sixth Company Law Directive[14] is not in practice much used in the United Kingdom, partly because of its complexity, but mainly because it is more usual in the United Kingdom to effect takeovers and mergers by way of purchases and sales of shares rather than of assets.

---

[13] See Chap. 5.
[14] Directive 1978/855.

The above set of rules also applies when public companies split off and transfer their assets and undertaking to another company by means of a demerger and a scheme of arrangement.

Buying out the minority

Once an acquiring company owns 30 per cent of the target company, **14.12** under the City Code it is obliged to make an offer in the form or an offer document. Once the acquiring company has obtained acceptances from over 50 per cent of the members it has effective control of the company as it can then control the board of directors. However, although the acquiring company could state that its offer was binding even with a bare majority shareholding, it is common for the acquiring company to state that the offer will only be unconditional and binding once it has acceptances from 90 per cent of the target company's shareholders. From the point of view of the acquiring company, it may wish to have at least 90 per cent or complete control of the company if it is going to invest substantial sums in the company. Furthermore, the acquiring company may not wish to trouble itself with the problem of possibly dissentient minorities.

If the acquiring company is able to obtain 90 per cent of the target company's shares, there are statutory provisions to enable it to acquire the remaining shares. In order to obtain the benefit of the provisions under statute, the acquiring company must have made a takeover offer under the CA 1985, section 428(1). A takeover offer is one where the acquiring company undertakes to buy all the shares of a target company, or all the shares of a class of shares in the target company, other than those already held by the acquiring company, on terms that apply equally to all the shares to which the offer relates.

Where the offer is accepted by 90 per cent of the shareholders within **14.13** four months from the beginning of the offer,[15] the acquiring company can serve a notice on the remaining shareholders stating that it proposes to buy their shares.[16] A copy must also be sent to the company along with a statutory declaration confirming that the grounds under which the notice can be given have been satisfied.[17]

The notice will state that the acquiring company can buy the remaining shares at a price the same as that offered to all the other shareholders. If the remaining shareholders are dissatisfied with this for a valid reason they can apply within six weeks of the date of the notice to the courts for an order[18] that the acquiring company may not buy their shares or may only do so on different terms. If the complaint is that the offer is not high enough, it is for the complainers to explain why it was

---

[15] CA 1985, s.429(3).
[16] CA 1985, s.429(1).
[17] CA 1985, s.429(4).
[18] CA 1985, s.430C(1).

clearly good enough for 90 per cent of the other shareholders to accept it. The complaint may succeed where, as in *Re Bugle Press Limited*,[19]

(1) those 90 per cent shareholders were the instigators of the offer, and
(2) there were very few or no other shareholders available to provide a different view as to the fairness of the price the majority shareholders were offering.

14.14   Assuming there is no objection, the purchase of the outstanding shares may take place after the expiry of the six-week period.[20] The acquiring company sends the target company the consideration for the purchased shares and the target company holds the consideration monies (or shares, as the case may be) in trust for the target company's shareholders.[21] If after 12 years some untraced shareholders have still not emerged, the funds held to their account are paid into court.[22]

Just as the acquiring company may buy out a 10 per cent minority, so may the 10 per cent minority ask to be bought out. A minority shareholder may write to the acquiring company requiring it to purchase his shares.[23] It then has one month in which to tell the shareholder of his rights under the takeover offer, and it must give the shareholder a period of at least three months after the expiry of the takeover offer in which to take up the offer[24] after which the offer may lapse. If the acquiring company chooses to buy the minority shareholder's shares, he may do so in terms of the offer or under any other terms as may be agreed.[25]

It should be pointed out that the above methods of buying out the 10 per cent minority apply in respect both of public and private companies.

SCHEMES OF ARRANGEMENT

14.15   The problems with an Insolvency Act 1986 ("IA 1986"), section 110 reconstruction as described in Chapter 16 are that the company has to be in liquidation, shareholders' rights have to be strictly adhered to, creditors' rights cannot be altered and its only options are sales or amalgamations. A more flexible method had to be found which could accommodate such matters as the continuation of the company's trade, and variations to shareholders' and creditors' rights. Indeed so inflexible

---

[19] [1961] Ch. 270.
[20] CA 1985, s.430(2).
[21] CA 1985, s.430(5).
[22] CA 1985, s.430(13).
[23] CA 1985, s.430A.
[24] CA 1985, s.430A(4).
[25] CA 1985, s.430b(2).

is the section 110 method that it is very rarely used nowadays. A more satisfactory method is to be found in what is known as a section 425 compromise or, more commonly, section 425 scheme of arrangement.

The word "compromise" is, however, apt. The essence of a scheme of arrangement is that all interested parties are fully aware of what is being suggested. The court gives approval to various rearrangements of a company's or companies' debts and shareholdings which reconcile various differing interests and effect a compromise between those interests. There must be an element of give and take for a compromise, and without some give and take between all or most of the interests the courts will not sanction the arrangement. Once the courts have given their approval to the scheme of arrangement it is binding on all the parties, even though there may be some objectors. Unlike a section 110 voluntary arrangement neither the objecting shareholders nor creditors can prevent the scheme of arrangement taking place once the court has given its approval.

The procedure for a section 425 scheme of arrangement is as follows:

If a company is proposing to have a section 425 scheme of arrange- **14.16** ment, the company, a member, a creditor, the administrator or the liquidator may apply to the court for an order for meetings of the creditors, classes of creditors, members, or any classes of members to be called.[26] At each meeting the terms of the arrangement are explained and those present can vote on it. In order for the scheme of arrangement to take place, at each meeting those in favour of the scheme of arrangement must:

- in each meeting be at least a majority in number, and
- in the case of a creditors' meeting, hold at least 75 per cent of the debt due to all the creditors collectively, or
- in the case of a meeting of a class of creditors, hold 75 per cent of the debt due to the collective debt of that class of creditors, or,
- in the case of members, hold 75 per cent in value of the issued share capital or,
- for a class of members, have 75 per cent of the capital relating to that class of shares.[27]

Voting will be in person or by proxy in the normal manner.[28]

The notice calling the various meetings must be accompanied by an **14.17** explanatory note detailing what the scheme of arrangement proposes and in particular how it may affect the material interests of the directors, either in their capacity as directors or in their capacity as members or in

---

[26] CA 1985, s.425(1).
[27] CA 1985, s.425(2).
[28] CA 1985, s.435(2).

any other capacity such as a lender to the company.[29] In the case of trustees for debenture trust deeds, a similar disclosure must be made.[30]

Assuming the meetings approve the scheme of arrangement, the scheme of arrangement and confirmation of the approval from the relevant meetings are sent to the court. The court can then sanction the arrangement[31] and the scheme of arrangement becomes binding on the company, the members and the creditors.[32] A copy of the scheme of arrangement must be sent to the Registrar of Companies and the court's order is ineffective until this has been done.[33]

14.18   The court has wide powers under the CA 1985, section 427 to implement whatever the scheme of arrangement proposes, to transfer property, to allot shares, debentures or other interests, to institute legal proceedings, to dissolve any unwanted companies, to deal with dissentient members or creditors or to carry out whatever else needs to be done.

The main advantage of a scheme or arrangement is that only a majority in number and 75 per cent in value of the members and creditors need approve the scheme. This can be compared with the requirement that 90 per cent of the shares in a takeover or merger be acquired before the remaining 10 per cent can be compulsorily bought out. The main disadvantage is that the whole procedure is extremely expensive, as there have to be two applications to court, meetings need to be convened, and extensive negotiations between all the interested parties have to take place before the meetings take place. On the other hand, once the court's sanction has been given, the scheme of arrangement can be fully implemented without reference to any other authority.

Further Reading

Davies, *Gower's Principles of Modern Company Law* (6th ed., Sweet and Maxwell, 1997), Chap. 29

The City Code on Takeovers and Mergers (updated regularly, Panel on Takeovers and Mergers)

Policing of takeovers by FSA, see: www.fsa.gov.uk/pubs/other/market_conduct

---

[29] CA 1985, s.426(2).
[30] CA 1985, s.426(4).
[31] CA 1985, s.425(2).
[32] CA 1985, s.425(2).
[33] CA 1985, s.425(3).

Chapter 15

CHARGES AND RECEIVERSHIP

The concept of the charge

The concept of a charge is simple. If a borrower borrows money, there **15.01** is always the risk that he will not repay it. If the borrower physically deposits one of his assets with the lender as security for the loan, he must repay the loan and any interest if he wants the asset back. If the borrower never reclaims the asset, the lender has the right either to sell the asset or keep it. The leaving of the asset with the lender effectively creates a charge over the asset.

The practice of a charge is not so simple. In the example above, the asset is moveable and so can be placed in the lender's hands, but while the lender has it the borrower cannot use it.[1] This means that he cannot use the asset to generate the funds to repay the lender. The lender also has to look after it, which may be inconvenient if it is large.

Suppose the lender agrees that he will lend against the value of an **15.02** asset, but that the borrower, whom he trusts to some extent, may use the asset in the meantime. What would prevent the borrower selling the asset and disappearing with the funds, or charging the asset to some other lender who might insist on the asset being lodged with him? As far as companies are concerned, some of those concerns are dealt with by having a registration system, whereby a charge is not valid to confer rights on the secured creditor unless the charge is properly registered in accordance with the required methods.

Registration, to a limited extent, also alerts other creditors and potential investors to the extent to which the company's assets are secured in favour of the secured creditor, and it provides a degree of reassurance to the creditor that the charge is valid. Registration is performed by lodging the required form and a copy of the charging document with the Registrar of Companies. If the procedure is correctly carried out, the Registrar issues a certificate of registration which is evidence, not as to the actual viability of every aspect of the charge, but as to the fact that the charge was properly registered.

---

[1] This form of charge is known as a pledge.

15.03   It is not a perfect system, and the whole business of charges and registration of charges leaves much to be desired. At the time of writing, a consultation exercise is taking place on the registration of charges in the United Kingdom, initiated by an (English) Law Commission Consultation Paper[2] in the light of which the current law on charges may well be drastically revamped.

Fixed charges

15.04   There are two main categories of company charges: fixed charges and floating charges. A fixed charge is one that is secured over an asset and which prevents the disposal of the asset by the owner without the consent of the chargeholder. The easiest example is the standard security.[3] The owner of heritage may not sell his house subject to a standard security without the consent of the standard security holder, who will only give his consent to sale following repayment of the loan. If a purchaser bought the house without the standard security being discharged, apart from the fact that this would be impossible in terms of conveyancing practice, the standard security-holder could still enforce his right to repossess the house and sell it. A fixed charge is the best charge there is from the security-holder's point of view, because the security holder has the right if necessary to enter in possession of the asset, and the charge runs with the asset,[4] not with the person who granted it.[5] So if the grantor becomes insolvent, the charge is still valid over the asset, the asset can be sold, and the security holder gets his money back, plus interest and expenses. A fixed chargeholder does not have to worry about preferential creditors or other imposts.

In return for granting a fixed charge, a fixed chargeholder may grant a lower interest rate for the loan than he might otherwise do.

15.05   As indicated above, the problem with the fixed charge is that the lender has to look after the asset, unless there is some means otherwise, such as the use of a standard security, and the borrower cannot (usually) use the asset, or sell it, without the lender's consent. In addition, Scots law cannot cope with the idea of a fixed charge which is not in the hands of the lender, in accordance with its Roman law origins, summed up in the Latin maxim, *Traditionibus, non nudis pactis, dominia rerum transferuntur.*[6] This means that apart from heritage, for which there are special rules, it is impossible in Scotland to give a fixed charge over a moveable asset without handing the asset over to the lender.[7] This leads

---

[2] No. 164. A similar one taking place in Scotland.

[3] The equivalent of a land mortage in England.

[4] What is known as a *ius in rem* (a right in the thing).

[5] What is known as a *ius in personam* (a right against the person).

[6] By delivery, rather than by mere agreement, are the titles to things transferred.

[7] In England to get round this problem, bills of sale were invented. A charge over a person's moveable assets can be registered in a special registry, but the procedure is little used.

to ingenious practices. Casks of whisky used as security for a loan have to be stored in a special part of the bonded warehouse, carefully partitioned off, with the key being under the control of a stockkeeper who reports to the lender and not to the actual owner of the whisky.

The floating charge

These difficulties are not unique to Scots law, but in England a **15.06** solution to the difficulty of the inaccessibility of goods secured by a fixed charge led to the invention of the floating charge. A floating charge can be likened to an imaginary net suspended from the chargeholder's hand over the assets of the company.[8] In return for the loan of money by the lender/chargeholder to the borrowing company, the borrower agrees to repay the loan on a predetermined date, to pay the interest on the loan and to fulfil all other necessary requirements of the loan. The loan, however, is not secured on any one item belonging to the company: it is secured collectively over the assets of the company, whatever they may happen to be from time to time, usually provided that the total value of the assets is no less than the loan. While the interest on the loan continues to be paid on time, the net/charge remains suspended over the assets of the company, and the company may change those assets in the course of business. If the company defaults on the loan, the charge is said to crystallise or attach to the assets of the company, or to continue the simile, the net is released by the chargeholder and traps all the assets of the company not already subject to a prior-ranking security (or otherwise unavailable). At that point a receiver is appointed, as will be discussed shortly. The receiver then exercises the powers open to him to recover the sums due to the chargeholder.

A particular issue with regards to floating charges is the extent to which the company can exercise its rights to use the assets that are subject to the floating charge. It is not such an issue in Scotland, where, because of the requirement of delivery, an asset is either subject to a fixed charge or it is not, but in England, in their quest for ever more ingenious wording to allow maximum flexibility for both lender and borrower alike,[9] there is a long line of cases trying to establish whether or not a particular charge is fixed or floating, irrespective of the label given to the charge. The best-known definition of a floating charge was given by Romer L.J. in *Re Yorkshire Woolcombers Association Ltd*[10]:

---

[8] Floating charges are in general only available to companies and limited liability partnerships though they do also exist for farming businesses under the Agricultural Credits Act 1928.

[9] It is possible to have a charge that is both fixed and floating under English law, so that it can convert from being a fixed charge to a floating charge (though there might be difficulty in appointing an administrative receiver because of the operation of the IA 1986, s.29(2)(a)), or a floating charge to a fixed charge, and despite the possible adverse effect on creditors, there is no requirement for the conversion to be made apparent to other creditors.

[10] [1903] 2 Ch. 284 at 295.

"I certainly think that if a charge has three characteristics that I am about the mention it is a floating charge. (1) If it is a charge on a class of assets of a company present and future; (2) if that class is one, which, in the ordinary course of business, would be changing from time to time; and (3) if you find that by the charge it is contemplated that, until some future step is taken by or on behalf of those interested in the charge, the company may carry on its business in the usual way as far as concerns the particular class of assets I am dealing with."

15.07   Despite some bizarre decisions on the way,[11] the current position as regards the distinction between a fixed and a floating charge, particularly in connection with book debts, is encapsulated within the case of *Agnew v. Inland Revenue Commissioners*, better known as *Re Brumark Investments Ltd*,[12] a New Zealand Privy Council case which Lord Millett specifically indicated would be of interest to English lawyers.[13] This case restated the previous view that where book debts are paid into an account and once there may be drawn on by the borrower, the book debts are subject to the floating charge; but if the book debts, once paid into an account, may not be drawn upon and are under the control of the lender, they are subject to a fixed charge. The important issue is that of control: if the borrowing company controls the asset, it is a floating charge; if the lender controls the asset, it is a fixed charge.

In terms of priority, a fixed charge always ranks ahead of a floating charge unless there is some agreement to the contrary.[14] If a company grants a floating charge, the floating chargeholder must be aware that unless there is a term in the charging documentation to the contrary (as there usually will be, such a term being known as a negative pledge clause), it is open to the company to grant a fixed charge which will take priority over the floating charge.

15.08   Once a receiver has been appointed under the terms of the floating charge, he is not allowed to disburse to the floating chargeholder the sums he gathers in until he has paid the preferential creditors.[15] In the forthcoming Enterprise Bill it is proposed to abolish the Crown preference in the preferential debts,[16] but it is well known that unpaid taxes and VAT normally form a large portion of the sums the receiver realises

---

[11] For example, *Re New Bullas Trading Ltd* [1994] 1 BCLC 485, CA.

[12] [2001] UKPC 28, [2001] 3 W.L.R. 454 (PC) (NZ)).

[13] At the time of writing, there has not been an English case confirming this Privy Council case, and so technically the previous cases still apply. Many administrative receiverships and other insolvency disputes are being held "in limbo" until such time as an English case confirming the Privy Council case is decided.

[14] Companies Act 1985 ("CA 1985"), s.464(4)(a). This is also true if the fixed charge arises by operation of law, as in, for example, a landlord's hypothec or a hotelier's lien.

[15] IA 1986, s.59. See also IA 1986, s.386 and Sched. 6.

[16] The Crown preference was for VAT, PAYE, etc.

—thus diminishing the amount due to the floating chargeholder, and forcing the receiver to act as a tax gatherer for the Government. As the preferential creditors' sums may be large, there is again an incentive for a chargeholder to seek a fixed charge (free from preferential creditors' claims) rather than a floating charge from the company.

Floating charges in Scotland

A particular difficulty for floating charges in Scotland is that floating **15.09** charges do not sit easily with the way that Scots law sees property. Floating charges were only introduced into Scotland with the Companies (Floating Charges) (Scotland) Act 1961 and receivers were introduced by the Companies (Floating Charges and Receivers) (Scotland) Act 1972. Until then a company could only be put into liquidation and receivership was not possible.

An advantage of being such a late admission to the law was that it was introduced by statute, which has the virtue of simplifying the Scottish law of floating charges. The entire procedure for appointing a receiver is outlined in statute and while the legislation has its faults, it is at least accessible and relatively public. The major difference between English floating charges and Scottish ones is that the Scottish procedure and attitude is generally more unsecured creditor-friendly. Broadly speaking it is easier to know what terms apply to the floating charge in Scotland,[17] whereas in England there is a greater emphasis on commercial secrecy.

A particular issue is that when a company grants a floating charge **15.10** over all its assets, it will not be apparent from the property registers, being the Land Register and the Register of Sasines, that a floating charge is in existence,[18] and that a floating chargeholder could have rights in heritage owned by the company, though one might have thought that the whole point of a property registration system is to show the world at large who has what rights in the property.[19] It is extraordinary that in these days of networking of computers there is still no method of showing on the property registers in the entry for each property that the company that owns that property has granted a floating

---

[17] For example, negative pledge clauses are shown on the Scottish Form 410 but are not required to be shown on the English Form 395 and so technically there is no requirement to pay attention to them (though to ignore them in practice would be contrary to good business practice and possibly good faith).

[18] CA 1985, s.462(5).

[19] The fact that the property registers do not show the interests of floating chargeholders is probably (a) because statute does not require it at present, (b) because when the legislation was drafted, it would have physically very difficult to note on every property title that the company that owned it had granted a floating charge, since someone would physically have had to check all properties owned by U.K. companies. Before computers this would not have been feasible.

charge and that therefore there is a possibility that the floating charge-holder may appoint a receiver.[20] The current practice is that when it is apparent that the seller is a company it should also be ascertained whether or not that company has granted a floating charge. The seller will show to the purchaser a letter of non-crystallisation from the floating chargeholder confirming that the company will not be put into receivership within a designated number of days and permitting the transaction to take place. In return the purchaser's agent must register/record the disposition and any other documents within a specified period of days.

The case of *Sharp v. Thomson*[21] also highlighted difficulties with the law of receivership, whereby a new category of ownership, known as beneficial ownership, which can defeat a receiver, was introduced to the law of Scotland. This is discussed later in the context of receivership.

Confusingly, what in Scotland is called a receiver, is called in England an administrative receiver. A receiver in English law is a manager or factor appointed by a creditor and does not necessarily have rights over all the property of a company, but an administrative receiver does usually have rights over all or most of the property of a company. A Scottish receiver has rights over that part of the property of a company which is subject to the floating charge.

The practice of registering charges

15.11   The practice of registering a charge depends on what type of charge it is. If the charge is over heritage, the company executes the standard security and sends the top copy to the Keeper of the Land Register or the Register of Sasines, while retaining a certified copy in the office. On confirmation from the Keeper of the registration or recording of the standard security, which is what gives the company a real right in the heritage, the company, or the standard security holder must send the certified copy standard security, the Keeper's confirmation and the Form 410 to the Registrar of Companies within 21 days of the date of registration or recording of the standard security.[22] If a Scottish company is granting a charge over English property it must still use a Form 410 while complying with the English mortgage registration requirements. An English company registering a charge over property in Scotland completes a Form 395 on the same basis. Although there is no statutory basis for it, if an oversea company is registering a charge over

---

[20] At the same time, desirable as some form of notification would be, it would probably only be possible with registration of title, and something would have to be done about the 21 day blind period during which a charge is being registered. To prevent confusion there would probably also need to be some form of compulsory notification of discharge of charges.

[21] 1997 S.C. (HL) 66, 1997 S.L.T. 636, 1997 SCLR 328 (HL), [1997] 1 BCLC 603, [1998] B.C.C. 115, also known as *Sharp v. Woolwich Building Society.*

[22] CA 1985, s.410(5)(b).

property in Scotland, the charge can be entered into a special Scottish Slavenburg register.[23]

If the charge is a floating charge, the 21 day period runs from the date of execution of the floating charge. It is again permissible to send a certified copy charge while retaining the principle copy in the office.

Although standard securities and floating charges are the main **15.12** charges that are registered, charges over the following must also be registered within 21 days and using the Form 410 to be valid:

- the uncalled capital of the company;
- the book debts of the company;
- calls made but unpaid;
- goodwill;
- a patent or a licence under a patent;
- a trademark;
- a copyright or a licence under a copyright;
- a registered design or a licence in respect of such a design;
- a design or licence under a design right;
- a security over a ship or aircraft or any share in a ship.[24]

Securities over a ship or aircraft need also to be registered in specialist shipping[25] and aircraft mortgage[26] registries.

It is possible to register a charge over land outside the United Kingdom, in which case the 21 day period runs from the date that the copy of the charging instrument could have been received in the United Kingdom.[27] It is not necessary that all the proceedings in the other country be completed at the time of registering the charge in Scotland.[28]

If a cheque or bill of exchange is given as security for payment of **15.13** book debts, in order to obtain an advance pending receipt of those book debts, there is no requirement to register a charge.[29] There are further provisions in statute for the registration of charges associated with a series of debentures[30] and *ex facie* dispositions,[31] although these are almost unheard of nowadays. Statute does not indicate who should

---

[23] The Slavenburg register is not referred in CA 1985, but is the register maintained by the Registrar of Companies for overseas companies charging property in England and Wales under CA 1985, s.409.

[24] CA 1985, s.410(4).

[25] The Shipping Register is expressly designed to keep a record of ships and mortgages granted over ships.

[26] Mortgaging of Aircraft Order 1972 (S.I. 1972 No. 1268).

[27] CA 1985, s.411(1).

[28] CA 1985, s.411(2).

[29] CA 1985, s.412.

[30] CA 1985, s.413.

[31] CA 1985, s.414.

lodge the charge[32]: it may be the chargeholder, the company, the chargeholder's agents or the company's agents, though the company may be
fined if the charge is not registered. The charging document, once
registered, is not shown at the Registrar of Companies, although the
Form 410 in each case should reveal enough details to encourage a
prospective creditor or investor to find out more from the company
itself.

Some charges are not registrable with the Registrar of Companies.
These include charges on shares,[33] charges on the proceeds of life
insurance policies and charges arising by operation of law, such as a
landlord's hypothec. For many years there were questions as to whether
or not a retention of title clause was a registrable charge, but following
the case of *Armour v. Thyssen Edelstahlwerke*[34] it was established that
such a clause was neither a charge nor registrable.

Failure to register in time

15.14   If this is not done, the only remedies are to apply, expensively and
embarrassingly, to the court for late registration,[35] or to start again.
Failure to register in time renders the charge void against a liquidator,
creditor or administrator[36] and while the debt still stands and is immediately repayable, the priority relative to other creditors is lost. This
means that where a bank advanced funds to a company in the expectation that it would be placed at the top of the list of creditors as a secured
creditor, it could find that it was merely an unsecured creditor, and any
loss it suffered would have to be recovered from the agents who were
supposed to be lodging the charge.

The company's own register of charges

15.15   Each company is supposed to keep a register of the charges it creates,
whether registrable with the Registrar of Companies or not, and creditors and members may inspect it.[37] Apparently in practice many companies ignore this rule and very few creditors or members ever take
advantage of the rule anyway. Future creditors may not inspect it, which
means that it is not much use to those trying to find out whether or not
it is wise to deal with the company.

---

[32] CA 1985, s.415(1).
[33] See Chap. 5.
[34] [1991] 2 A.C. 339, [1990] 3 W.L.R. 810, [1990] 3 All E.R. 481, 1990 S.L.T. 891, [1991]
    BCLC 28, 1990 B.C.C. 925.
[35] CA 1985, s.420. Late registration will only be permitted where the courts consider it
    just and equitable and no creditors or shareholders would be prejudiced thereby.
[36] CA 1985, s.410(2).
[37] CA 1985, ss.421–423.

The certificate of registration

Assuming all the procedure has been correctly carried out, the Registrar will issue a certificate of registration, which is conclusive evidence that all the requirements of Chapter II of Part XII of the Companies Act 1985 have been complied with.[38] The Registrar does not vouch that the charge is a good charge: he merely states that all the procedure has been dealt with. **15.16**

Entries of satisfaction and relief

It is best practice whenever a charge is discharged to send in a Form 419 proving that the charge is discharged. This clears the searches as well as putting paid to any arguments as to whether or not a charge is still in existence. **15.17**

Ranking agreements

Ranking agreements are complex and frequently unintelligible documents that are used when a company borrows funds from a number of different lenders, secured over heritage by standard securities and over the rest of the company's assets by floating charges. In the absence of a ranking agreement, fixed charges rank in priority to floating charges,[39] floating charges rank in date order of registration[40] and where floating charges arrive in the same post they are deemed to rank with each other equally.[41] But with a ranking agreement it is possible to re-arrange the pecking order of the charges, so that in the event of the liquidation of the company it is possible to ascertain who gets what and in what order, usually so that the company's assets are divided up proportionally instead of the first lender getting all the assets.[42] But if there is an existing registered floating charge and the company grants a second floating charge, the first chargeholder is only entitled to his present advances, any future advances which he had contracted to make, interest due on all such advances, expenses reasonably incurred by the holder, and the value of any contingent liability for the charge had been granted.[43] **15.18**

A floating charge may, and indeed commonly does, on creation contain provisions restricting the grant of any charge ranking in priority

---

[38] CA 1985, s.418.
[39] CA 1985, s.464(4)(a).
[40] CA 1985, s.464(4)(b).
[41] CA 1985, s.464(4)(c).
[42] If the first lender stood to get everything, the company would never be able to get further loans, and the lender would have no opportunities to limit its exposure short of causing the company to collapse.
[43] CA 1985, s.464(5). These rules could be disapplied, if necessary, by a ranking agreement.

to the floating charge (the "negative pledge"), or may contain provisions allowing another charge to rank ahead of it. These will normally be indicated on the Form 410, and it is generally agreed that this is useful, as no later creditor can claim he was unaware of these provisions. However, whenever an existing floating charge is varied, a Form 466 needs to be completed and sent to the Registrar of Companies in respect of each floating charge to be varied.[44] This can mean that for a complex transaction with several lenders, each of whose advance is secured by a floating charge, there will need to be a Form 466 in respect of each floating charge. The Form 466 will normally be accompanied by and refer to the ranking agreement, although this will not be shown on the register.[45]

Invalidity of charges generally

15.19   Provided the charge is registered properly within 21 days of its creation, a charge is likely to be valid, but there can be occasions when a charge is not valid. A charge may also be invalid if it is held to be an unfair preference[46] in an insolvent winding up.

This only arises in the context of a liquidation, but if a company has granted a charge to a creditor within six months of the company's winding up or administration, the floating charge may be reduced by the courts in the application of a creditor, the liquidator or the administrator under the Insolvency Act 1986 ("IA 1986"), section 243(5) unless it was:

(1) a transaction in the ordinary course of business[47];
(2) a payment in cash for a debt which was due and payable, unless the payment had been collusively set up between the company and the creditor in order to prejudice other creditors[48];
(3) part of some reciprocal obligations (not necessarily contemporaneous) between the company and the preferred creditor, unless it was collusive as in (2)[49];
(4) the grant of instructions or mandate to a third party to pay out arrested funds to an arrester[50] (section 243(2)(d)).

---

[44] Alternatively an existing charge could be discharged and a new one lodged, but there might then be a hiatus during which a lender's advance might be at risk.
[45] This results in a plethora of registered documents filed with the Registrar of Companies, making it even more confusing for any outside creditor researching the company to work out the extent of its indebtedness.
[46] IA 1986, s.243. Fraudulent preferences exist at common law as well, but they are very rarely used nowadays.
[47] IA 1986, s.243(2)(a).
[48] IA 1986, s.243(2)(b). *R. Gaffney and Son Ltd v. Davidson*, 1996 S.L.T. (Sh.Ct) 36.
[49] IA 1986, s.243(2)(c). *Nicoll v. Steel Press (Supplies) Ltd*, 1992 S.C. 119.
[50] IA 1986, s.243(2)(d).

The point of this provision is that it might be tempting for a company **15.20**
to arrange for a favoured creditor to receive a charge which allows him
rights over the company's assets at the expense of all the other creditors—especially if the creditor had not supplied full consideration to
the company in exchange for the charge.

Invalidity of floating charges

A floating charge will be invalid if **15.21**

    (a) it is granted to a connected person within 2 years of the onset
        of the company's insolvency[51]; or
    (b) it is granted to any person at any time between the presenta-
        tion of a petition for the making of an administration order
        and the making of that order.[52]

A "connected" person is a director or shadow director of the company, an associate of the company, or an associate of a director or
shadow director.[53] An associate is extensively defined in IA 1986,
section 435, but in essence is a close relative or spouse of a director, a
partner of the director, an employer or employee either of the director or
the company.[54]

Where the charge is granted within 12 months to someone not
connected with the company, the charge will be invalid if:

    (c) at the time of granting the security the company was unable
        to pay its debts in terms of IA 1986, section 123[55]; or
    (d) the company became unable to pay its debts because of the
        transaction for which the charge was granted.[56]

Despite the above, a charge in favour of either a connected person or **15.22**
an unconnected person will still be valid if the charge was granted in
respect of

    (e) monies paid, or good or services supplied at the same time or
        after the creation of the charge[57]; or
    (f) the value of any reduction or discharge of debt of the company
        in exchange for which the charge was granted[58]; or

---

[51] IA 1986, s.245(3)(a). The "onset of insolvency" means the commencement of the
winding up or the date of the presentation of the petition on which an administration
order was made (IA 1986, s.245(5)).
[52] IA 1986, s.245(3)(c).
[53] IA 1986, s.249.
[54] This is not a full definition: reference should be made to the actual section.
[55] IA 1986, s.245(4)(a).
[56] IA 1986, s.245(4)(b).
[57] IA 1986, s.245(2)(a).
[58] IA 1986, s.245(2)(b).

(c) any interest payable in respect of (e) or (f) above.[59]

What in practice all this is designed to achieve is that creditors do not try to get the benefit of a new charge for an old loan. If the lender had wanted a charge for the old loan, he should have taken it out at the beginning of his loan. The point of the legislation is to prevent the granting of retrospective charges at the expense of other creditors.

In more detail what it means is that if the company is insolvent at the time an *unconnected* person gets the floating charge (or becomes so as a result of the transaction involving the floating charge) (and provided the charge was granted within the 12 month period prior to the onset of insolvency) the unconnected person does not get the benefit of the floating charge except to the extent of (e), (f) and (g) above. If the company was solvent at the time of granting the floating charge, even if it was within the 12 month period, an unconnected person can have the entire benefit of the floating charge, including money lent before the granting of the charge, as well as the sums under (e), (f) and (g).

15.23   On the other hand, it makes no difference whether the company is solvent or not as far as the granting of a floating charge to a *connected* person is concerned: within the two year period the connected person can only get the benefit of the floating charge to the extent of (e), (f) or (g).

Outside the time periods above the charges will be valid.

Problems with charges

15.24   For some years there has been disquiet about the whole method of registering charges, not least because the United Kingdom is out of step with most other common law systems in having its 21 day registration period during which other creditors have no way of knowing whether a charge is being registered or not. There are other problems with charges: at present priority can be determined, at least in England, not by the date of registration, as one might expect, but by the date of execution; some charges are not registrable and perhaps should be; the sanctions for late registration are onerous; there are difficulties with regards to cross-border matters relating to both charges and receiverships, within the United Kingdom and outside the United Kingdom; the published details in the Forms 395 and 410 do not usefully reveal the extent of the borrowing company's obligations to the chargeholder,[60] the registered particulars are not helpful to creditors and investors alike; the provisions for the registration of charges for oversea companies are unsatisfactory;

---

[59] IA 1986, s.245(2)(c).

[60] Most charges just say "All sums due and that may become due, together with interest and expense"—not least because the sums may vary according to the extent to which the company may be reborrowing.

the list of registrable charges is now very out of date; and so on,[61] It is suggested that what should be adopted is a new form of notice-filing so that a notice of a charge can be lodged even before the charge is in place, and which serves to tell the world at large that the company's assets are charged or about to be charged. It would appear that this procedure is used in North America with some success. Were it, or any other new system, to be adopted here, however, there would be considerable learning costs while business and the law came to terms with the new methods. Any new system will undoubtedly fall foul of the Law of Unintended Consequences whereby the practice of any new legislation throws up issues that never were considered by the nation's legislators, as well as creating unexpected winners and losers. There are even suggestions that Scotland may have to continue with its present system or a variation of it,[62] even though England and Wales might be adopting a new system. In a small island, with much in common it seems odd to have a security registration system markedly different depending on which side of the Tweed one happens to be. In a world where business law and company law are increasingly being conducted in much the same manner, and often in the same language (usually English) it makes sense to use what works elsewhere and which investors and creditors can feel comfortable with. What is not in doubt is that reform of the law relating to charges is necessary; but in fairness to the Law Commissioners, what should replace the current procedure is by no means easy to establish.

RECEIVERSHIP

A receiver is an insolvency practitioner appointed under the terms of a **15.25** floating charge granted by a company to a floating chargeholder. It is the receiver's task to ingather the assets caught by the attached floating charge and to use the proceeds thereof to repay the loan from the floating-chargeholder.

The rules relating to receivership in Scotland are to be found in IA 1986, sections 50–71 and the Insolvency (Scotland) Regulations 1986.[63] The official receiver does not exist in Scots law.

Under IA 1986, section 52 a receiver is appointed on the occurrence of any of the following events:

---

[61] See *Registration of Security Interests: Company Charges and Property other than Land*, Law Commission Consultation Paper No. 164 (2002).
[62] See *Registration of Security Interests: Company Charges and Property other than Land*, English Law Commission Consultation Paper No. 164, paras 5.107–5.112.
[63] S.I. 1986 No. 1915.

(1) the expiry of a period of 21 days after a demand for payment of the whole of part of the principal sum secured by a charge without payment having been made[64];

(2) the expiry of a period of two months during which interest has been unpaid and is in arrears[65];

(3) the making of an order or the passing of a resolution to wind up the company[66];

(4) the appointment of a receiver by virtue of any other floating charge created by the company (IA 1986, section 52(1)(d)).

A floating charge may specify other grounds as well, such as the failure to keep the assets insured up to a certain level, or a failure to adhere to certain covenants in a debenture.

15.26 Normally there is some warning by the floating chargeholder first, but this is not necessary unless the charging documentation provides for it.

Although it is possible to appoint a receiver by application to the court[67] this would normally only be used where there was some defect which precluded the normal method of appointment by the chargeholder.

The chargeholder completes an instrument of appointment which is sent to the nominated receiver. The receiver must accept his appointment the day after appointment[68] and the Registrar of Companies must be informed of his appointment within seven days[69] and an entry made in the company's register of charges.[70] On the appointment of the receiver the floating charge attaches to the company's assets and becomes a fixed charge over those assets.[71] All creditors must be informed of the receivership by post[72] and by publication.[73]

15.27 Following appointment the receiver:

(1) ascertains what assets are caught by the floating charge;

---

[64] IA 1986, s.52(1)(a).

[65] IA 1986, s.52(1)(b).

[66] IA 1986, s.52(1)(c).

[67] IA 1986, s.52(2) and s.54. Receivership by application to court would also be an expensive method.

[68] As evidenced by a docquet which the receiver completes (IA 1986, s.53(6)(a) and (b)).

[69] IA 1986, s.53(1). The seven day gap is an issue for unsecured creditors who may unwittingly be supplying goods to the company in receivership without knowing of the receivership.

[70] IA 1986, s.53(5).

[71] IA 1986, s.53(7).

[72] IA 1986, s.65(1)(b).

[73] IA 1986, s.65(1)(a). Publication will normally be in the newspapers and may also be in the Edinburgh Gazette. But there is no method of alerting the Register of Sasines or Land Register of the receivership.

(2) tries to realise them as advantageously as possible from the point of view of the charge-holder[74];

(3) uses the proceeds to pay the preferential debts exigible under IA 1986, section 59;

(4) remits the sums due to the charge-holder; and

(5) if there is anything left over (which is unlikely), returns it to the company.

The receiver has extensive powers under IA 1986, Schedule 2 to carry out the above and he can apply to the courts for further powers if necessary. As part of this process he requires the officers and employees to supply to him affidavits which will make up a statement of affairs about the company's assets, debts, liabilities and the grant of any securities.[75] Within three months of appointment the receiver must prepare a report for the benefit of the floating chargeholder and the creditors about the events leading up to his appointment, about his disposal of the company's assets or his continuation of the company's business, the amounts due to the floating chargeholder and preferential creditors and the amount likely to be left over for the unsecured creditors.[76] The report will contain a summary of the statement of affairs.[77] If the company has gone into liquidation, the liquidator will need to receive a copy too.[78] A committee of unsecured creditors may be set up,[79] consisting of between three to five persons, in order to advise the receiver of the concerns of the unsecured creditors.

During the receivership the directors lose their management rights in **15.28** respect of the assets caught by the receivership, though if the floating charge is only partial, they may maintain their management roles in respect of the unsecured parts of the company. There is conflicting caselaw on the extent to which directors may exercise rights over the company's assets.[80] However, where the receiver is failing in his duties, it is open to the directors to act against him if they think he is not overall

---

[74] This can be done either by holding a sale of the assets, by hiving off the better assets to a subsidiary which is then sold, or by continuing to trade the company out of difficulty until the debt, interest and expenses are repaid and the company can be handed back to the directors.

[75] IA 1986, s.66.

[76] IA 1986, s.67.

[77] IA 1986, s.67(5).

[78] IA 1986, s.67(4).

[79] IA 1986, ss.67(2) and 68, Insolvency (Scotland) Rules, Pt 3, Chap. 3.

[80] *Imperial Hotel (Aberdeen) Ltd v. Vaux Breweries Ltd*, 1978 S.L.T. 113, suggests that directors have no rights, while *Shanks v. Central Regional Council*, 1987 S.L.T. 113 allows directors very limited rights. For the English position, see *Newhart Developments Ltd v. Co-operative Commercial Bank Ltd* [1978] 1 Q.B. 814 (which did allow the directors some rights) and *Tudor Grange Holdings Ltd v. Citibank NA* [1991] BCLC 1009 (which did not).

acting in the best interests of the company,[81] or if the receiver had either
failed to make a claim for assets which he should have claimed or been
involved in a conflict of interest between him and the company.[82] There
is English authority to the effect that a receiver may be liable for his
incompetence in running the business which has been handed over to
him[83] but this was in the context of a farming receivership and it will not
necessarily apply in respect of company law.

The receiver as agent

15.29   The receiver acts as agent for the company in relation to such
property of the company as is attached by the floating charge.[84] In
general, unless he is acting on his own account and/or breaching his
fiduciary duty to the company,[85] he will not be at risk personally in
respect of that property. If he were not an agent, he would be liable for
whatever he did, which would serve as little incentive to act as receiver.
However, he is personally liable for any contract entered into by him,
except to the extent that the contract provides otherwise.[86] Not surprisingly, a receiver, wherever possible, will state in the terms of any new
contract with a third party that he will not personally be liable under the
terms of that contract. The third party may resist this, but even so, where
the receiver is personally liable, he is still entitled to be indemnified out
of the company's assets to the extent of his liability.[87] If the company's
funds are unlikely to cover this indemnity, the receiver may need an
indemnity from the floating chargeholder before he enters into the
contract.

As regards contracts in existence before the receiver was appointed,
they may continue in existence[88] but the receiver will not be liable in
respect of those contracts.[89] This means that if the receiver chooses to
make the company break those contracts he will not be liable, and it will
probably not be worthwhile for the other party to the contract to sue the
company in receivership. However, there have been cases in England
where the other party to the contract has attempted to take out an
injunction to prevent the receiver making the company dishonour a

---

[81] *Standard Chartered Bank v. Walker* [1982] 3 All E.R. 938.
[82] *Independent Pension Trustee Ltd v. Law Construction Co. Ltd*, 1996 G.W.D.
33–1956.
[83] *Medforth v. Blake* [1999] B.C.C. 771.
[84] IA 1986, s.57(1).
[85] Technically he would also be liable if he acted *ultra vires* the company's objects clause,
but this is not likely to be an issue nowadays.
[86] IA 1986, s.57(2).
[87] IA 1986, s.57(3).
[88] In practice many contracts will have a clause that automatically terminates the contract
in the event of the appointment of a receiver.
[89] IA 1986, s.57(4).

contract.[90] The general view is that if honouring the contract would not make any difference to the receiver's ability to realise the company's assets at the best price, the contract should be allowed to continue. In one recent Scottish case, what the other party wanted the company in receivership to do was an impossibility, and so no interdict could force the company to do it.[91]

There are special provisions with regard to the employees of a company in receivership. Following the Insolvency Act 1994, a receiver is only the agent of the company in relation to the adoption of any employment contracts in the carrying out of his functions as a receiver and is therefore not personally liable for the employment contracts of employees whose contracts were in existence prior to the receivership,[92] but he does become personally liable to the extent of a "qualifying liability" for the employment contracts of those employees whose contracts he adopts after the onset of receivership either formally or after a period of 14 days, during which time the receiver can make up his mind whether or not to adopt the contracts.[93] A qualifying liability is a liability to pay wages, salary or contributions to a pension scheme, is incurred while the receiver is in office, and is in respect of services rendered wholly or partly after the adoption of the contract by the receiver.[94] In *Lindop v. Stewart Noble & Sons Ltd and Henderson and Russell as receivers of Stewart Noble & Sons Ltd and as individuals,*[95] Lindop, the former managing director of the company in receivership, was dismissed despite having had his contract adopted. He claimed that the damages for his dismissal should entitle him to a higher claim than his mere qualifying liability, but it was held that though he was entitled to his qualifying liability, he was not entitled to any more except as an unsecured creditor.

15.30

Where the receiver does become personally liable for an employment contract, he is able to indemnify himself out of the company's assets.[96]

---

[90] *Airline Airspares Ltd v. Handley Page Ltd* [1970] 1 All E.R. 29; *Freevale Ltd v. Metrostore Ltd* [1984] 1 All E.R. 495; *Ash & Newman Ltd v. Creative Devices Research Ltd* [1991] BCLC 403.

[91] *Macleod v. Alexander Sutherland Ltd,* 1977 S.L.T. (Notes) 44.

[92] IA 1986, s.57(1A).

[93] IA 1986, s.57(2) and (5). The point of the legislation was that if receivers became liable for all employment claims from the original date of commencement of the employee's employment, as opposed to those claims with effect from the dates that receivers adopted the employee's contract, receivers would not be in a position to rescue companies as all their efforts would end up being diverted into satisfying employees' claims. Accordingly the 14 day rule was adopted, which is perhaps unfortunate for some employees, but equally gives a chance for the rest of the business (and its employees) to survive.

[94] IA 1986, s.57(2A).

[95] 1999 SCLR 889. See also Lewis "Lindop is back" (1999) 7 *Insolvency Lawyer* 303–305.

[96] IA 1986, s.57(3).

The receiver as tax collector

15.31   Out of the assets gathered in by the receiver in satisfaction of the debenture or bond connected with the floating charge, he must pay himself and his expenses, and the preferential creditors, thus giving himself and them a prior right to funds before the floating-chargeholder. Preferential debts can be found at IA 1986, section 386(1) and Schedule 6. The main ones are PAYE on employees' wages for the last six months, VAT for the last six months, various other taxes, social security and pension contributions, and wages to employees of up to £800 for the last four months. If there are insufficient funds to go round, each of the preferential creditors abate their claims proportionally, though the receiver gets his fees and expenses first—otherwise he would not do the work.[97]

The disbursal of the sums gathered in by the receiver

15.32   Of the sums the receiver gathers in, he must first pay his own creditors' fees and expenses, and then his own fees and expenses. After that he pays the preferential creditors as above. Once these have all been paid, the floating chargeholder gets what he is due.[98] If there are other postponed receivers, they have what is left over,[99] in accordance with their ranking agreement, if there is one. If there is a surplus, it is handed back to the company so that it may keep on trading with it if the company is still solvent and not in liquidation. If the company is in liquidation, it is handed to the liquidator. If there is a shortfall in the sums due to the floating chargeholder, the floating chargeholder is an unsecured creditor to that extent in the liquidation.

The receiver will not generally have any dealing with assets secured by prior-ranking fixed securities and so will not receive any sums in respect of those assets, unless those fixed securities have been ranked behind the floating charge in a ranking agreement or otherwise. When a company goes into receivership, the fixed security holders are entitled to enter into possession and sell their secured assets, usually with the co-operation of the receiver. The receiver will receive any surplus on the sale of the assets.

15.33   As regards the unsecured, non-preferential creditors, they are usually unable to obtain much satisfaction from a receivership and have to write off their losses. The receiver may not needlessly dissipate the company's assets, but he is not obliged to do much more than keep the unsecured creditors informed[1] though as indicated above a failure to exercise a duty of care may be actionable.[2] Unsecured creditors should

---

[97] Unless the chargeholder guaranteed his fees.
[98] IA 1986, s.60.
[99] IA 1986, s.60(2).
[1] IA 1986, ss.66, 67.
[2] *Standard Chartered Bank v. Walker* [1982] 3 All E.R. 938.

therefore, wherever possible, try to protect their position by means of retention of title clauses, hire purchase agreements and other mechanisms whereby title does not pass to the company.[3] Unsecured creditors can always put the company into liquidation, which may well wreck the receiver's ability to trade the company out of any difficulties.

A receiver is entitled to any assets recovered from directors by a liquidator under IA 1986, section 212 (the misfeasance provision) since the assets were originally part of the company's assets and thus subject to the floating charge[4] assuming the charge was properly drafted to that effect.

Cross-border receiverships

A Scottish receiver can exercise his powers over English property and **15.34** an English one over Scottish property, subject to the requirement that *lex situs* will apply to the disposal of any property.[5] In *Norfolk House plc (in receivership) v. Repsol Petroleum Ltd*[6] the company had granted a fixed and floating charge which duly converted to a fixed charge, such conversion not being recognised in Scotland. The question arose as to whether the conversion amounted to a fixed charge over heritage in Scotland. It did not, but it was also held that the appointment of a receiver did cause the floating charge to attach to heritage, and by that method the receiver was able to sell heritage in Scotland.

Methods of defeating receivership

Apart from the invalid charges referred to above, there are some **15.35** methods of defeating a receivership.

Retention of title

A supplier may be able to rely on a retention of title clause, which **15.36** ensures that goods never leave the suppliers' ownership until the purchaser pays the full price. As the goods are not part of the purchasing company's assets, the receiver has no rights in the goods. Provided the goods are significantly the same, the retention of title will still apply.[7]

Goods subject to hire-purchase agreements and other conditional sale agreements, where title does not pass to the user of the goods, also cannot be caught by the receiver.

---

[3] This is particularly unfortunate for unsecured creditors supplying services to the company—such as electricians, plumbers, and so on—who by the nature of their work are not able to impose retention of title clauses.
[4] *Re Anglo-Austrian Printing and Publishing Union* [1895] 2 Ch. 891.
[5] IA 1986, s.72.
[6] 1992 S.L.T. 235.
[7] *Kinloch Damph Ltd v. Nordvik Salmon Farms Ltd*, 1999 S.L.T. 106, 1998 SCLR 496.

Effectually executed diligence

15.37 A receiver has no rights over assets of the company that are subject to effectually executed diligence prior to the appointment of the receiver.[8] Sadly, the words "effectually executed diligence" are not satisfactorily explained, and insofar as it is possible to understand what was meant by this, it seems to mean that where a diligence process has several steps, which have been completed, the diligence has priority over the attachment of the floating charge; and equally if the procedure is not complete, as in the failure to have an action of furthcoming before the appointment of a receiver, despite there being an initial arrestment, the diligence is not effectually executed[9] and the receivership has priority. As regards inhibitions, property inhibited before the attachment of the charge is not available to the receiver.[10] At the time of writing the Scottish Law Commission is considering new and more coherent forms of diligence generally, and against land in particular, and it is to be hoped that a workable and intelligible system will ultimately be devised.[11]

Prior-ranking fixed charges arising by operation of law

15.38 Apart from various possessory liens, the best known prior ranking fixed charge arising by operation of law is the landlord's hypothec, which entitles the landlord to a right in security over *invecta et illata* in the tenant's possession, even if they are not owned by the tenant.[12] It only applies in respect of the current year's rent. It also only applies to certain urban property and agricultural subjects smaller than two acres, and must be followed up by a sequestration for rent. But it does defeat the receiver. It is, however, little used and its continued existence is being considered by Scottish Law Commission as above.

The new form of "beneficial interest"

15.39 The case of *Sharp v. Thomson*,[13] referred to above, introduced a new form of ownership to Scots property law, this being beneficial interest. Due to incompetent conveyancing practice on the part of the Thomsons' lawyers, the Thomsons were allowed into a new house on the missives alone, without a recorded title, but having paid the purchase price. There has been no satisfactory explanation of why the disposition was not

[8] IA 1986, s.55(3)(a).
[9] *Lord Advocate v. Royal Bank of Scotland*, 1977 S.C. 155.
[10] *Armour & Mycroft, Ptns*, 1983 S.L.T. 354.
[11] Scottish Law Commission Discussion Paper on Diligence against Land, 1998 No. 107.
[12] In *Grampian Regional Council v. Drill Stem (Inspection Services) Ltd (in receivership)*, 1994 SCLR 36, even a sub-tenant's assets were caught by the landlord's hypothec.
[13] 1997 S.C. (HL) 66, 1997 S.L.T. 636, 1997 SCLR 328 (HL), [1997] 1 BCLC 603, [1998] B.C.C. 115, also known as *Sharp v. Woolwich Building Society*.

properly recorded in the normal manner, but before it should have been recorded, the selling company went into receivership, and the Thomsons found themselves in the unhappy position of having paid for a house that now apparently belonged to the receiver. In the normal course of events the Thomsons would have been thrown out of the house and sued their solicitors.[14] The House of Lords, taking pity on the innocent Thomsons, and possibly mindful of the potential for a roar of abuse from consumer rights organisations, said that the Thomsons had a "beneficial interest" in their home by virtue of having paid for it, and that equally the company no longer had their former interest in the house by virtue of having received payment for it. This decision effectively destroyed the integrity of the property registers,[15] since the whole point of the property registers is to provide confirmation by registration of ownership. It also reduced the scope of the receivership. The Scottish Law Commission, in order to resolve the impasse, proposes that title to land ownership should continue to be entered conclusively on the registers, but that there should be a statutory priority in favour of a purchaser of 14 days within which period the disposition may be registered irrespective of the solvency of the seller.[16] The Law Society of Scotland has also issued practice notes which effectively make the failure to register the disposition timeously a breach of professional practice. In practice the issue may not arise again; but there still needs to be legislation to tidy the matter up completely.

Problems with receivership

The major problem with receivership is that it is unduly unfavourable **15.40** for unsecured creditors, and too easily leads to the death of a company and employment losses. The United Kingdom is seen as a very secured-creditor-friendly environment, and it is out of step with most other European countries where more is done to save the company if possible. On the other hand, if banks were not allowed to have receivership as it stands at the moment, they would either have to charge higher interest rates or seek more personal guarantees to compensate for the loss of security.

Notwithstanding the above, the Enterprise Bill before Parliament at the time of writing proposes to do away with receivers, though retaining the right of existing floating chargeholders to appoint receivers, and instead to increase the powers of administrators. Administrators will be required to do their best to keep the company as a going concern, to

---

[14] What probably ought to have happened, and which would have saved the bank that appointed the receiver being accused of greed, is that the Thomsons would have been allowed to buy the house from the receiver, the entire cost thereof being borne by the solicitors. To the solicitors' considerable relief, this did not happen.

[15] See Gretton "The integrity of the property law and the property registers" 2001 S.L.T. (Notes) 135.

[16] Scottish Law Commission Consultation Paper No. 114, 2001.

consider the interests of all creditors generally, and only then to worry about the secured creditors. While the administrator is in place he can give the company a breathing space during which it is insulated from its creditors who still preserve their rights. If the proposed legislation is enacted over a period of time receiverships will become less significant, and perhaps unsecured creditors will receive less unfavourable treatment.

Further Reading

Mackenzie-Skene, *Insolvency Law in Scotland* (Butterworths, 1999)

Greene and Fletcher, *The Law and Practice of Receivership in Scotland* (Butterworths, 2002)

Belcher "*Sharp v. Thomson*: the SLC discussion paper" (2002) 3 *Insolvency Lawyer* 83–89

For more information on the Enterprise Bill, see: www.parliament.the-stationery-office.co.uk

CHAPTER 16

WINDING UP

The purpose of winding up is to ensure a fair distribution of a **16.01** company's assets to those who are entitled to them, in the first place to the creditors and in the second place to the members in accordance with the terms of the articles. The official carrying out this task is a liquidator who is an insolvency practitioner. Once a company is in liquidation it cannot carry on any further business except through the liquidator, no shares may be transferred and the directors cease to manage the company. The liquidator is like a director in that he is in a fiduciary relationship with the company. He also has various public duties such as reporting to the Secretary of State if there are matters concerning the directors' conduct which may be significant.

If the process of winding up did not exist, the keener and fiercer creditors would seize all the company's assets at the expense of other creditors, and there would be no opportunity for directors to have a second chance. Winding up also enables unresolved company business to be terminated in everyone's interests.

Summary of winding up procedure

In essence, when a company is wound up by whichever means: **16.02**

(1) the company is put into liquidation;
(2) an interim liquidator is appointed;
(3) creditors are invited to submit their claims;
(4) a liquidator is appointed at a meeting of the members and creditors;
(5) the liquidator gathers in the company's assets in all the permissible ways;
(6) the liquidator then pays out funds to the creditors, in full if possible, otherwise in proportion to their claims;
(7) if there are still funds, the shareholders are repaid their capital, in full if possible, otherwise in proportion to their shareholding;
(8) the liquidator applies to have the company struck off if necessary.

(9) Occasionally companies may be revived if undiscovered assets or liabilities emerge later.

The distinction between a liquidator and a receiver

16.03 The liquidator can be contrasted with the receiver. The receiver is primarily interested in the assets subject to the floating charge and in satisfying the floating-chargeholder. He is not unduly concerned about the claims of other creditors, though he should not take them lightly. The liquidator is interested in all the assets of the company, in the first place for the creditors' benefit and thereafter for the members', though he has no rights in assets subject to the prior claims of secured creditors such as standard securityholders, floating chargeholders or preferential creditors. The secured and preferential creditors take what they are entitled to, and the liquidator gets the rest.

Liquidation triggers the appointment of a receiver where there is a floating charge and entitles fixed chargeholders (such as standard securityholders) to exercise their rights too. Where there are no charges, the liquidator can deal with all the company's assets himself.

16.04 Liquidation ensures the death of the company, though the liquidator may sell on the business itself. This can have severe effects on employees and suppliers. Receivership is not necessarily the death of the company, since a good receiver may be able to turn the company around, repay the floating chargeholder and return the operational company to the directors again.

A liquidator has the right to challenge antecedent transactions and make the directors compensate the company. A receiver does not have this right.

The distinction between a liquidator and an administrator

16.05 As indicated above, liquidation kills the company, whereas the whole point of administration is to salvage some of the company and where possible keep it going. An administrator once appointed is able to insulate the company from its creditors, to give it a breathing space while the administrator sorts itself out, and if done well, can ensure the survival of a good deal of the company in a way that is not feasible in a liquidation, and in a way that does not purely benefit the floating chargeholder, as in a receivership.

An administrator has the right to challenge antecedent transactions[1] but not to make the directors compensate the company unless he specifically asks the court for permission to do so.

[1] IA 1986, ss.242–245.

Methods of winding up

There are three types of winding up: 16.06

- members' voluntary winding up
- creditors' voluntary winding up
- compulsory winding up by the court

VOLUNTARY WINDING UP

Provisions applicable to both types of voluntary winding up

Winding up is voluntary where the members choose to wind up the   16.07
company, by ordinary resolution if the company has reached its expiry
event or expiry date in terms of its articles,[2] by special resolution[3] or by
extraordinary resolution if the company cannot continue its business by
reason of its liabilities and it is advisable to wind up the company.[4] In
each event, the company must send a copy of the resolution to the
Registrar of Companies with 15 days[5] of the passing of the resolution,
and send a copy to the Edinburgh Gazette within 14 days.[6] The winding
up is deemed to commence on the time of the passing of the resolution.[7]
The appointment of the liquidator must be intimated to the Registrar of
Companies and the Edinburgh Gazette within 14 days of his appointment.[8]

Once the resolution has been passed, the business of the company
ceases except to the extent required to wind the company up,[9] but the
company still stays in existence until it is dissolved.[10] There may be no
more share transfers.[11] If the directors believe that the company will be
able to pay its debts in full within the succeeding 12 months, the
directors may make a statutory declaration of solvency to that effect.[12]
The declaration must be made no more than five weeks before the
resolution to wind up the company[13] and forwarded to the Registrar of

---

[2] IA 1986, s.84(1)(a).

[3] IA 1986, s.84(1)(b). The disadvantage of this is that unless consent is given or a written
resolution is used in a private company, the company will need to wait 21 days before
the meeting for the resolution can be held.

[4] IA 1986, s.84(1)(c). This resolution only requires 14 days notice.

[5] IA 1986, s.84(3).

[6] IA 1986, s.85(1).

[7] IA 1986, s.86. This may be significant when it comes to calculating the periods for the
adjustment of antecedent transactions.

[8] IA 1986, s.109. The time of appointment varies according to the type of winding up.

[9] IA 1986, s.87(1).

[10] IA 1986, s.87(2).

[11] IA 1986, s.88.

[12] IA 1986, s.89(1). If the company is insolvent, the directors will not make the declaration.

[13] IA 1986, s.89(2)(a).

Companies within 15 days of the resolution. If it turns out that the statement was unjustified, and the directors had no reasonable grounds for making it and the company's debts were not paid within in the succeeding 12 months, the directors may be fined, though they will not be personally liable.[14-15]

16.08   If for some reason no liquidator is appointed or nominated by the company the company must take steps to dispose of the company's perishable assets and safeguard the rest.[16]

The liquidator's fees will always be paid out of the company's assets in priority to all other claims.[17]

It should be noted that voluntary winding up does not terminate the employees' contracts of employment, although the liquidator may terminate contracts of employment if he wished to do so.[18]

16.09   On the completion of the voluntary winding up by either method, the liquidator may write to the Registrar of Companies with the final accounts and three months later the company will be dissolved.[19]

Members' voluntary winding up

16.10   A members' voluntary winding up means that the company is believed to be solvent at the time of winding up and so there should be funds repayable to the members after payment in full first to the preferential creditors and then to the other creditors.[20] The winding up is therefore for the members' benefit. As the creditors will be paid in full, creditors will not be anxious about the procedure. The directors, as indicated above, must have made a statutory declaration as to the company's solvency.

At the resolution for the members' voluntary winding up, the members will appoint one or more liquidators.[21] The directors' powers all cease[22] and the liquidator will then gather in the company's assets,[23] pay all the creditors out of them, repay the members and having prepared final accounts, call a final meeting of the members to explain what he

---

[14-15] IA 1986, s.89(4) and (5).

[16] IA 1986, s.114.

[17] IA 1986, s.115.

[18] This is different from a compulsory winding up where the employees lose their jobs unless the liquidator keeps them on: *Laing v. Gowans* (1902) 10 S.L.T. 461 (OH).

[19] IA 1986, s.201.

[20] IA 1986, s.107.

[21] IA 1986, s.91(1). The director must inform the Registrar of Companies and the Edinburgh Gazette of his appointment (IA 1986, s.109(1)).

[22] Except insofar as the liquidator or the members collectively permit otherwise (IA 1986, s.91(2)).

[23] In order to do this, he is given powers under IA 1986, s.165 and Sched. 4, Pts I, II and III. Part I powers require him to seek the approval of the members first, since he may be compromising their rights or otherwise reducing the amount of money available to them. Parts II and III do not require the sanction of the members and allow the liquidator to carry on the business of the company, defend or raise actions, etc.

has done.[24] He will then send in his final account to the Registrar of Companies[25] and apply for the company's dissolution as above.

Creditors' voluntary winding up

A creditors' voluntary winding up means that although the members **16.11** still choose to put the company into liquidation there will be no funds repayable to the members but there should be some for the creditors. Consequently a creditors' voluntary winding up is for the creditors' benefit and the creditors have the major say in the conduct of the liquidation.[26]

In a creditors' voluntary winding up the company must convene a meeting of all its creditors to take place within 14 days of the resolution to wind up the company having advertised the meeting in the local newspapers and the Edinburgh Gazette.[27] The notice of the meeting will contain the name and address of an insolvency practitioner who will supply the creditors with information about the company in liquidation. Meanwhile, the directors will prepare a statement about the accounts of the company, its creditors and securities,[28] which will be laid before the meeting of the creditors under the chairmanship of one of the directors.[29]

Both the members, at their initial meeting at which they resolve to **16.12** wind up the company, and the creditors at their initial meeting, may appoint a liquidator,[30] but unless the creditors do not choose a liquidator[31] or the courts decide otherwise,[32] the creditors' choice prevails.[33] The creditors may decide to appoint a committee of not more than five persons to advise the liquidator.[34] The company members may also decide that they wish to appoint five of their members to the liquidation committee,[35] but the creditors may object to the members' choices unless the court decides otherwise.[36]

---

[24] IA 1986, s.94(1).
[25] IA 1986, s.94(3).
[26] Historically, a liquidator could usually be appointed by the members and some liquidators were well known to be particularly member-friendly, which is why the creditors were allowed to have their choice of liquidator. Nowadays, with the rise of the profession of insolvency practitioner, insolvency practitioners are supposed to be more professional and indeed more neutral in their task, though as a matter of practice liquidators are usually unwilling to risk many actions that will incur excessive cost or potentially land them personally with any liability.
[27] IA 1986, s.98.
[28] IA 1986, s.99(2).
[29] IA 1986, s.99(1).
[30] IA 1986, s.100(1).
[31] IA 1986, s.100(2).
[32] IA 1986, s.100(3).
[33] IA 1986, s.100(2).
[34] IA 1986, s.101(1).
[35] IA 1986, s.101(2).
[36] IA 1986, s.101(3).

Once the liquidator has been appointed by the relevant committee, the directors' powers cease[37] and the notice of the appointment of the liquidator is forwarded to the Registrar of Companies for publication in the Gazette.[38]

16.13   The liquidator will then manage the liquidation in terms of the Insolvency Act 1986 ("IA 1986"), sections 165 and 167,[39] and have regular annual meetings to explain the conduct of the liquidation.[40] At the end of the liquidation, there will be a final meeting[41] before the liquidator applies to have the company dissolved.

Voluntary winding up as a method of disposing of a company's property[42]

16.14   Although it is a slightly cumbersome method of selling a company's property to another business, it is possible, following a voluntary winding up of the company (either members' or creditors') for the liquidator to transfer the company's assets to another company (or limited liability partnership)[43] in exchange for shares in (or membership of) the purchasing company (or limited liability partnership). In the case of a members' voluntary winding up, a special resolution will be required to approve this,[44] in the case of a creditors' voluntary winding up, the court's or the creditors' committee's approval is needed.[45] The shares or memberships will then be paid as a dividend to the members of the company just wound up. This can be used either to merge companies, or equally to demerge companies (as for example, where a liquidated holding company sells off its assets to various little companies and the shareholders of the holding company receive shares in all the little companies). There is protection built in for shareholders who dissent from the arrangement,[46] but this dissent mechanism is precisely why it is not much used by companies except where everyone is agreed.

---

[37] IA 1986, s.103 .

[38] IA 1986, s.109.

[39] This enables the liquidator to get in all the company's assets in much the same manner as a members' voluntary winding up, with slight variations to take account of the fact that the creditors' meeting may wish to choose its own liquidator and so only no disposals or dealings with the company's assets (except where they might disappear or perish) may be taken by any liquidator until after the creditors' meeting (IA 1986, s.167).

[40] IA 1986, s.105. The longest known liquidation apparently lasted over 100 years and saw two liquidators die in office.

[41] IA 1986, s.105.

[42] Also known as a reconstruction in the course of a voluntary winding up.

[43] IA 1986, s.110(1).

[44] IA 1986, s.110(3)(a).

[45] IA 1986, s.110(3)(b). The creditors' approval is very important: without it a creditor could petition for the liquidation of the company and collapse the reconstruction.

[46] IA 1986, s.111.

COMPULSORY WINDING UP BY THE COURT

Jurisdiction

In Scotland, a company may be wound up compulsorily in the Court **16.15**
of Session or, if the company's share capital is less than £120,000, in the
sheriff court in which the company's registered office is situated.[47]

Grounds under which a company may be wound up compulsorily

A company may be wound up by the courts if: **16.16**

- the company has resolved by special resolution to be wound up
  by the court[48];
- it was registered as a plc on incorporation, and has not obtained
  a section 117 trading certificate within a year of registration[49];
- the company does not commence its business within a year of
  incorporation or suspends its business for a year[50];
- its members drop below two in number unless it is a private
  company limited by shares or by guarantee[51];
- the company is unable to pay its debts;[52] or
- the court is of the opinion that it is just and equitable that the
  company should be wound up.[53]

Of these grounds only the last two are in practice ever used.

Although it too is very unlikely to be used, as a remnant of the old
provisions whereby a floating chargeholder in Scotland could not
appoint a receiver, but have the company wound up, section 122(2)
preserves a Scottish floating chargeholder's right to wind up the company.

The company's inability to pay its debts

The company's inability to pay its debts is defined in section 123 (1) **16.17**
as:

- a failure to pay a debt of £750 or more, either in cash or by
  granting a security, when given three weeks notice to do so

---

[47] IA 1986, s.120.
[48] IA 1986, s.122(1)(a). This would be an expensive way of being wound up.
[49] IA 1986, s.122(1)(b). This is very rare indeed.
[50] IA 1986, s.122 (1)(d). This too is rare, and would need a member to feel strongly
  enough about the matter to incur the expense of going to court.
[51] IA 1986, s.122(1)(e). This effectively therefore only applies to plcs.
[52] IA 1986, s.122(1)(f).
[53] IA 1986, s.122(1)(g).

following delivery of prescribed written demand (known as a section 122 letter)[54]; or

- in England and Wales, execution issued on a judgment, decree or order of any court is returned unsatisfied in whole or in part[55]; or
- a failure to pay within the *induciae* of a charge (15 days) following an extract decree, extract registered bond or extract protested bill[56]; or
- the company's inability to pay its debts as they fall due.[57] This means that the company cannot pay its bills when they should be paid even though technically it may be solvent—it is just that it has a cash flow problem; or
- that the company's assets are less than its liabilities taking into account all its contingent and prospective liabilities.[58]

As regards the failure to pay a debt of £750 or more, it is possible for various creditors to combine together to demand payment provided that the total is at least £750, but where there is a demand for £750 or more, that demand must be justified. If a company's terms of trade were that it did not pay its bills for 45 days, and the creditor accepted those terms, the creditor would be premature if he petitioned under section 122(1)(f) a mere 10 days after the account was rendered. Equally, if the debt is genuinely disputed, a petition for liquidation will be unjustified.[59] Furthermore, if a creditor is acting in bad faith, or there is evidence that the other creditors are unhappy about the prospect of the company being wound up, the court may ascertain the other creditors' and contributories' views,[60] though the courts are not bound to pay any attention to employees' interests or the public interest.[61] Just because a company's assets are all secured in favour of creditors or the company has no assets

---

[54] IA 1986, s.123(1)(a). Technically it is a Form 4.1.

[55] IA 1986, s.123(1)(b).

[56] IA 1986, s.123(1)(c). The *induciae* of a charge are the number of days between a sheriff officer's serving of a charge (a demand for payment) on the debtor company during which the debtor must pay or face the first steps in the public sale of his goods. An "extract" decree is a form of certified copy decree from the courts. A registered bond is a bond or debt instrument that has been registered in the Books of Council and Session or the Sheriff Court Books and a certified copy thereof is an "extract". An extract registered protest is a certified copy of a document proving that a bill of exchange was not honoured by the person on whom the bill was drawn when it should have been, the process of the bill not being honoured and a public record being made of this being known as a protest. It is very rare nowadays.

[57] IA 1986, s.123(1)(e).

[58] IA 1986, s.123(2). A contingent liability is a liability that is dependent on something else happening and so may not necessarily take place; a prospective liability is one that probably will arise but it is not known when it may do so.

[59] *Cunninghame v. Walkingshaw Oil Co. Ltd* (1886) 14 R. 87.

[60] IA 1986, s.195.

[61] *Re Craven Insurance Co. Ltd* [1968] 1 All E.R. 1140.

does not mean that the company cannot be wound up.[62] Nevertheless, where the debt is due, courts in general have no compunction about putting companies in liquidation if they are not paying their creditors when they required to do so.[63]

The just and equitable grounds for winding up a company

The "just and equitable" grounds are used by the courts when in the **16.18** light of the circumstances surrounding the company the fairest thing to do with it is to wind it up. The just and equitable grounds are entirely separate from issues of the company's solvency, and indeed, there is no virtue in winding up the company on the just and equitable grounds unless the company is solvent, since the members would not get money back.[64] The courts will also have to be satisfied that the members of the company seeking the winding up order are not acting unreasonably in not seeking a better remedy.[65]

Occasions where the courts have wound up companies on the just and equitable grounds include the following:

- loss of substratum of the company[66];
- illegality of the company's activities[67];
- deadlock in the management of the company[68];

---

[62] IA 1986, s.125(1).

[63] See also the Late Payment of Commercial Debts (Interest) Act 1998 which requires the payment of interest on outstanding debts.

[64] Students in particular often mistakenly believe that winding up on the just and equitable grounds is a form of insolvency—which it is not!

[65] IA 1986, s.125(2). If the company were insolvent, a cheaper method than winding up through the courts would be to put the company into a creditors' voluntary winding up.

[66] The substratum is the primary purpose for which the company was set up, as shown in the objects clause: *Re German Date Coffee Company Ltd* (1882) 20 Ch. D. 169. With the decline in significance of the objects clause, this particular ground is very unlikely to be used now, but it has never technically been overruled, though nowadays the matter would almost certainly be remitted to the shareholders for their decision rather than a winding up order being granted.

[67] *Re Thomas Brinsmead & Sons Ltd* [1897] 1 Ch. 45. Again, this is very unlikely nowadays, since a company set up as a fraud would generally be wound up on the grounds of public interest under IA 1986, s.124A. Nevertheless, this case is still good law.

[68] *Re Yenidje Tobacco Co. Ltd* [1935] Ch. 693. In this case two traders sold their businesses to a company in which they each had 50 per cent of the shares. The two traders started bickering and were unable to work together despite the profitability of their company. As the poorly drafted articles of association of their company had no arbitration clause, their only remedy was to have the company wound up. Nowadays special articles, known as deadlock articles, prevent this type of situation arising. Nonetheless, the principle of winding up where there is no other resolution of conflict is still valid.

- quasi-partnership cases[69];
- oppressive conduct by the majority shareholders or directors.[70]

Who may petition to wind up the company?

16.19   Those who may petition to wind up the company on other than public interest grounds are:

- the company itself[71];
- the directors[72];
- creditors[73];
- contributories[74];
- the Secretary of State, on public interest grounds,[75] or where a plc incorporated as such, does not have a trading certificate and has been in existence for over a year[76];
- an administrator[77];
- a receiver in Scotland[78];
- an administrative receiver in England[79];
- the Lord Advocate if the company is a charitable company[80];

and certain others if the company is a bank or insurance company.

Creditors are likely to be the ones who petition on the grounds of the company's inability to pay its debts, but under certain circumstances, as contributory may petition as well. A contributory—broadly

---

[69] *Ebrahimi v. Westbourne Galleries Ltd* [1973] A.C. 360; *Virdi v. Abbey Leisure Ltd* [1990] BCLC 342; *Jesner v. Jarrad Properties Ltd*, 1993 S.C. 34, [1993] BCLC 1032. A quasi-partnership is a company which before its business was incorporated was run as a partnership, and a sense of the partnership ethos and mutual trust has been carried forward to the company. Where this has been lost by taking legal but unfair advantage of some rule applicable to companies, it is appropriate to have the company wound up on the grounds that the trust that used to be maintained by the partners towards each other, and which should be maintained by the directors to the members, has been lost. The courts will not rush to grant a winding up order on these grounds since there may be other members of the company who are not involved in the issue of loss of trust, and the court will wish to be sure that their concerns are not ignored.
[70] *Loch v. John Blackwood Ltd* [1924] A.C. 783. In this case the majority shareholders deliberately made it difficult for the minority to find out what was happening in the company and how much the company was worth, in the hope that the minority would become fed up and sell their shares to the majority. Were such a situation to arise nowadays, the minority would almost certainly use a s.459 minority protection petition instead.
[71] IA 1986, s.124(1).
[72] IA 1986, s.124(1).
[73] IA 1986, s.124(1).
[74] IA 1986, s.124(1).
[75] IA 1986, s.124A(1).
[76] IA 1986, s.124(4)(a).
[77] IA 1986, s.14(1).
[78] IA 1986, s.55(2) and Sched. 2.21.
[79] IA 1986, s.42(1) and Sched. 1.21.
[80] Law Reform (Miscellaneous Provisions) (Scotland) Act 1990, s.14.

speaking—is a member or very occasionally past member of a company who holds or used to hold partly paid shares,[81] or in the case of a guarantee company has not paid his guarantee to the liquidator.[82] In addition, directors, who within a year of the winding up authorised payments out of capital on the redemption or repurchase of shares in a private company, may be contributories to the extent of the company's loss if the company's funds turn out to be insufficient.[83] Past or present members who received payments out of capital as indicated above will also be contributories[84] to the same extent together with those directors. Past or present directors who have unlimited liability may be contributories under limited circumstances[85]. Past members of an unlimited company which converted to a limited company or a plc may also be contributories and liable if the new limited company or plc went into insolvent liquidation within three years of the conversion.[86]

A director who is found liable for wrongful trading under IA 1986, section 214, or any officer or member found liable for fraudulent trading under IA 1986, section 213, is not deemed to be a contributory.[87]

If the contributory is a member, past member or director involved in the purchase or redemption of shares in a private company out of capital,[88] he may petition on either the grounds of inability to pay debts (*i.e.* IA 1986, section 122(1)(f)) or the just and equitable grounds (*i.e.* IA 1986, section 122(1)(g)) without any further qualification; but if the contributory is not a member, past member or director involved in a purchase or redemption of shares out of capital as above, the contributory may only petition on the grounds of inability to pay debts or the just and equitable grounds if the number of members in a plc has dropped below two,[89] or he was allotted the shares or inherited the shares and thereby held the shares for at least six out of the preceding 18 months before the commencement of the winding up.[90] **16.20**

The Secretary of State regularly petitions to wind up companies in the public interest under IA 1986, section 124A, common examples being illegal lotteries[91] and dodgy pyramid trading ventures.

---

[81] There is an extensive definition under IA 1986, s.76, of which this is a brief summary. A past member may be liable where he transferred partly paid shares within 12 months before the winding up of the company, but he will only be liable in respect of debts contracted by the company while he was still a member, and he can only be found liable when the other members' funds are inadequate.

[82] IA 1986, s.79(1).

[83] IA 1986, s.76(2)(b).

[84] IA 1986, s.76(2)(a).

[85] IA 1986, s.75.

[86] IA 1986, s.77.

[87] IA 1986, s.79(1).

[88] IA 1986, s.124(3).

[89] IA 1986, s.124(2(a).

[90] IA 1986, s.124(2)(b).

[91] *Secretary of State for Trade and Industry v. Hasta International Ltd*, 1998 S.L.T. 73 (OH).

The procedure for the petition

16.21   The details of the procedure may be found in the Insolvency (Scotland) Rules 1986.[92] Assuming the petition has been properly served by a suitable petitioner, and there has been advertisement in the newspapers and the Gazette of the forthcoming hearting, the courts will entertain the petition. In cases of emergency, it may be possible to obtain a provisional liquidator at any time after the presentation of the petition[93] but before the granting of the order for winding up. A provisional liquidator will be used where there is a danger of the company's assets disappearing. If the winding up petition is ultimately dismissed he demits office. Again, during the time between the presentation of the petition and the granting of the order for winding up, the company, any creditor or contributory may apply for a stay of proceedings if there is action being taken against the company elsewhere in the United Kingdom.[94] On the hearing of the actual petition for winding up, the court may make such decision as it sees fit[95] but as indicated above, the courts will not grant to members or contributories a winding up order if there is some better, more reasonable remedy.[96]

Where the petition is granted, the time of commencement of the winding up is deemed to be the time of the presentation of the petition for winding up[97] unless the company has passed an extraordinary resolution for winding up beforehand, in which case (in the absence of fraud or mistake) the time of commencement of the winding up is the time of the passing of the resolution.[98] With effect from the commencement of the winding up any dispositions of the company's property or transfers of shares are void.[99]

Once a winding up order has been given, the Registrar of Companies and Accountant in Bankruptcy must be informed within seven days[1] and thereafter no-one can raise an action against the company except with leave of the court.[2] Within 28 days of appointment notices are sent to the creditors and/or put in the newspapers and the Edinburgh Gazette intimating the winding up and indicating who the interim liquidator[3] is.

---

[92] S.I. 1986 No. 1915, rr. 4.1–82.
[93] IA 1986, s.135. Quite often the provisional liquidator becomes the liquidator.
[94] IA 1986, s.126.
[95] IA 1986, s.125(1).
[96] IA 1986, s.125(2).
[97] IA 1986, s.129(2).
[98] IA 1986, s.129(1).
[99] IA 1986, s.127.
[1] IA 1986, s.130(1), and Insolvency (Scotland) Rules 1986, rr. 4.18, 4.19.
[2] IA 1986, s.130(2).
[3] The interim liquidator is the one appointed by the court at the court hearing. At the creditors' or contributories' meeting a different insolvency practitioner may be appointed as the liquidator (as opposed to interim liquidator) though in practice it may be the same person.

Once the liquidator (or indeed provisional liquidator) is appointed, he **16.22**
may obtain statements of affairs from the officers, promoters, employees
and recent past employees of the company concerning the company's
assets and liabilities, creditors and their securities, and any other useful
information.[4] The liquidator may apply to the court for a public examination of any officer, receiver, manager, liquidator, administrator or
promoter of the company[5]; and if anyone summoned to appear for a
public examination absconds, he may be arrested and his papers and
records seized.[6]

The interim liquidator will within 42 days[7] of the winding up order
summon separate meetings of the creditors and contributories (if there
are any, which is unusual) in order to choose who the liquidator will be.[8]
If there is disparity between the two meetings' choice, the creditors'
choice will prevail unless the court can be persuaded otherwise.[9] If the
company has been in administration or a company voluntary arrangement the court may appoint the administrator or the supervisor to be the
liquidator.[10]

The liquidator may set up a liquidation committee to advise him.[11]

Once appointed and in office, the liquidator proceeds to get in the **16.23**
company's property. He takes control of it all,[12] makes inventories of
it[13] and it is vested in him so that he may dispose of it or raise
proceedings to recover it.[14] He may obtain payment from any contributories[15] and make creditors prove their debts.[16] The liquidator has
extensive powers under IA 1986, Schedule 4, Parts I, II and III to deal
with the company's assets, most without the sanction of the court, but
some, being the more problematic issues that may affect members' or
creditors' rights, needing the approval of the court. There is no specific
provision, as there is in England, entitling the liquidator to repudiate
contracts, though by doing so the insolvent company may be liable in
damages to the other party. The liquidator must make regular returns to
the registrar of Companies and Accountant in Bankruptcy, as well as
keeping the creditors and contributories informed.[17]

---

[4] Insolvency (Scotland) Rules 1986, Chap. 2 (referring to IA 1986, s.131).
[5] IA 1986, s.133.
[6] IA 1986, s.134.
[7] Insolvency (Scotland) Rules 1986, r.4.12(2A).
[8] IA 1986, s.138.
[9] IA 1986, s.139.
[10] IA 1986, s.140.
[11] IA 1986, s.142.
[12] IA 1986, s.144.
[13] Insolvency (Scotland) Rules 1986, r.4.22.
[14] IA 1986, s.145.
[15] IA 1986, ss.148, 149.
[16] Insolvency (Scotland) Rules 1986, r.4.15.
[17] IA 1986, s.170.

There are extensive provisions relating to the replacement of liquidators and the proper conduct of the liquidation.

16.24   If an order for winding up has been made by the court, but it is
apparent to the liquidator that the company's assets are insufficient to
justify the expenses of the winding up, the liquidator may apply to the
court to have the company dissolved.[18]

"Getting in" or gathering in the insolvent company's estate

16.25   The liquidator assesses what assets the company still has, and then
tries to get in all the debts the company is due. Having done that, he has
further means of swelling the company's estate. In particular he can:

> (1)   have certain forms of diligence against the company's assets
>   set aside under the "equalisation of diligence rules"[19]
>   whereby any poindings or arrestments within a period of 60
>   days prior to the appointment of the liquidator are all treated
>   as taking place at the same time: the creditors then have to
>   hand back what they have received from the company and
>   then can reclaim as ordinary creditors later though they are
>   entitled to their expenses of poinding, arrestment, etc.;
>
> (2)   set aside certain antecedent transactions if they are *gratuitous
>   alienations* or *unfair preferences*:
>
>> (a)   a gratuitous alienation[20] is a gift or transfer at less than
>>   full value of an asset of the company's within a period of
>>   five years of the commencement of the winding up if the
>>   recipient is an associate[21] or within a period of two years
>>   for any other person; any such recipient will have to
>>   restore the asset to the company (or other redress as may
>>   be appropriate) unless he can prove:
>>
>>> (i)   the company's assets were greater than its liabilities
>>>   at the time of the alienation[22];

---

[18] IA 1986, s.204.

[19] IA 1986, s.185, referring to the Bankruptcy (Scotland) Act 1985, s.37. It is worth noting
that poindings and arrestments may disappear in due course if the Scottish Parliament
can ever decide what exactly to put in their place in terms of the Abolition of Poindings
and Warrant Sales Act 2001 (asp 1).

[20] IA 1986, s.242. There is also a common law form of gratuitous alienation but it is very
rarely used. It has the advantage that the two year rule does not apply but the
disadvantage that the challenger to the transaction has to prove that the company was
both insolvent at the time of the gratuitous alienation, which in practice may be difficult
to establish, and at the time of the challenge as well (*Stuart Eves (in liquidation) v.
Smiths Gore*, 1993 S.L.T. 1274 (OH)).

[21] In terms of the Bankruptcy (Scotland) Act 1985. An associate is very similar to a
"connected" person referred to above., being close family, employer, employee, fellow
partners or companies with which the company is connected.

[22] IA 1986, s.242(4)(a).

(ii) the alienation was made for adequate consideration[23];

(iii) the alienation was a birthday, Christmas or other
conventional gift, or a charitable gift which in either
case it was reasonable for the company to make[24];

In England the equivalent rule is know as a "transaction
at an undervalue".[25]

(b) an unfair preference[26] is the early repayment of a loan or
payment of a creditor which has the effect of prejudicing
other creditors. Any such early repayments within six
months of the liquidation may be recalled. An unfair
preference can be the granting of a floating charge. The
following are not unfair preferences:

(i) transactions in the ordinary course of business[27];

(ii) transactions in cash when the debt was due and
payable, with no collusive purpose[28];

(iii) reciprocal transactions unless collusive[29];

(iv) the grant of a mandate authorising an arrestee to pay
over sums to the arresting creditor[30]

Unfair preferences can be challenged by a creditor or the
liquidator and the recipient required to repay the loan. He
then claims for the value of his loan as an ordinary
creditor.[31]

In England a similar rule is known as a "preference"[32].

(3) set aside certain extortionate credit transactions[33] (IA 1986,
section 244);

(4) A floating charge will be invalid[34] if:

(a) it is granted to a connected person within two years of the
onset of the company's insolvency[35]; or

---

[23] IA 1986, s.242(4)(b). For the meaning of "adequate" see *Lafferty Construction Ltd v. McCombe*, 1994 S.L.T. 858 and *Rankin v. Meek*, 1995 S.L.T. 526(OH).
[24] IA 1986, s.242(4)(c).
[25] IA 1986, s.238.
[26] IA 1986, s.243.
[27] IA 1986, s.243(2)(a).
[28] IA 1986, s.243(2)(b). *R. Gaffney and Sons Ltd v. Davidson*, 1996 S.L.T. (Sh.Ct) 36.
[29] IA 1986, s.243(2)(c). *Nicoll v. Steel Press (Supplies) Ltd*, 1993 S.L.T. 119.
[30] IA 1986, s.243(2)(d).
[31] IA 1986, s.243(4).
[32] IA 1986, s.239.
[33] IA 1986, s.244.
[34] The following passage on the invalidity of certain floating charges may also be found in Chap. 15.
[35] IA 1986, s.245(3)(a). The "onset of insolvency" means the commencement of the winding up or the date of the presentation of the petition on which an administration order was made (IA 1986, s.245(5)).

(b) it is granted to any person at any time between the presentation of a petition for the making of an administration order and the making of that order.[36]
    A "connected" person is a director or shadow director of the company, an associate of the company, or an associate of a director or shadow director[37]. An associate is extensively defined in IA 1986, section 435, but in essence is a close relative or spouse of a director, a partner of the director, an employer or employee either of the director or the company.[38]

Where the charge is granted within 12 months to someone not connected with the company, the charge will be invalid if:

(c) at the time of granting the security the company was unable to pay its debts in terms of IA 1986, section 123[39]; or
(d) the company became unable to pay its debts because of the transaction for which the charge was granted.[40]

Despite the above, a charge in favour of either a connected person or an unconnected person will still be valid if the charge was granted in respect of:

(e) monies paid, or good or services supplied at the same time or after the creation of the charge[41]; or
(f) the value of any reduction or discharge of debt of the company in exchange for which the charge was granted[42]; or
(g) any interest payable in respect of (e) or (f) above.[43]

16.26   What in practice all this is designed to achieve is that creditors do not try to get the benefit of a new charge for an old loan. If the lender had wanted a charge for the old loan, he should have taken it out at the beginning of his loan. The point of the legislation is to prevent the granting of retrospective charges at the expense of other creditors.

In more detail what it means is that if the company is insolvent at the time an *unconnected* person gets the floating charge (or becomes so as a result of the transaction involving the floating charge) (and provided the charge was granted within the 12 month period prior to the onset of insolvency) the unconnected person does not get the benefit of the

---

[36] IA 1986, s.245(3)(c).
[37] IA 1986, s.249.
[38] This is not a full definition: reference should be made to the actual section.
[39] IA 1986, s.245(4)(a).
[40] IA 1986, s.245(4)(b).
[41] IA 1986, s.245(2)(a).
[42] IA 1986, s.245(2)(b).
[43] IA 1986, s.245(2)(c).

floating charge except to the extent of (e), (f) and (g) above. If the company was solvent at the time of granting the floating charge, even if it was within the 12 month period, an unconnected person can have the entire benefit of the floating charge, including money lent before the granting of the charge, as well as the sums under (e), (f) and (g).

On the other hand, it makes no difference whether the company is **16.27** solvent or not as far as the granting of a floating charge to a *connected* person is concerned: within the two year period the connected person can only get the benefit of the floating charge to the extent of (e),(f) or (g).

Outside the time periods above the charges will be valid.

Liability of directors on insolvent liquidation[44]

Directorial liability can extend to: **16.28**

(1) make directors repay or return to the company in liquidation such sums of money or other assets as they may have misappropriated or been otherwise liable for under the misfeasance provisions of IA 1986 s.212[45];

(2) make anyone involved in fraudulent trading re-imburse the company in liquidation[46];

(3) make any officer of the company who had caused the company to trade wrongfully to contribute to the company's assets[47];

(4) make any director involved in the management of a phoenix company contribute to the company in liquidation.[48]

Although all these methods are open to liquidators, they are not much used in practice because of the cost of raising the actions against the directors.[48a] The creditors generally will probably wish to be convinced that they are not throwing good money after bad in pursuing directors who in many cases will not be worth suing after the collapse of their companies.

Scots corporate insolvency law does not have certain useful mecha- **16.29** nisms available to English law, such as the Official Receiver, or a specific statutory provisions dealing with transactions by subsequently

[44] Reference should be made to Chap. 9 where directors' liability on insolvency is explored in much greater depth.
[45] *Re DKG Contractors Ltd* [1990] B.C.C. 903; *Re Barton Manufacturing Co Ltd* [199] 1 BCLC 741.
[46] IA 1986, s.213. Actual dishonesty must be proved: *Re Patrick and Lyon Ltd* [1933] Ch. 786.
[47] IA 1986, s.214. *Re Produce Marketing Consortium Ltd (No. 2)* [1989] BCLC 520.
[48] IA 1986, s.216.
[48a] Under the terms of the Enterprise Bill, actions such as these may only be brought if the sanction of the court or the creditors' committee is sought beforehand.

insolvent companies defrauding creditors.[49] However, it is submitted that it would be possible for the court to use the *nobile officium* if no other remedy were available to trace money that had been fraudulently removed from the company.

Liquidators may report directors of insolvent companies to the Secretary of State who may then apply for the disqualification of those directors if the directors' behaviour justifies it.[50]

Distribution of the company's assets

16.30   Once the liquidator has amassed as much as he is able to, he may begin the distribution, though he may also pay interim distributions as funds arrive. The order of payment to the creditors (on the assumption that there are no fixed creditors) is as follows[51]:

> (1) the expenses of the liquidation, being the liquidator's own fees and expenses[52];
>
> (2) if at the time when a winding up order was granted there was in situ already a company voluntary arrangement, the expense of the company voluntary arrangement;
>
> (3) preferential debts in terms of IA 1986, section 386 and Schedule 6;
>
> (4) ordinary (unsecured) debts;
>
> (5) interest on the preferential debts;
>
> (6) interest on the ordinary debts;
>
> (7) postponed debts, being debts due to the recipient of a gratuitous alienation which has been reduced or restored to the company's assets.

In the event of the company being solvent, the members are repaid what they are due in terms of their shareholding and the articles.

In the event of the company having granted securities to chargeholders, on the liquidation of the company standard securityholders and other fixed chargeholders would be able to exercise their rights over the secured assets, recouping their loans, interest and expenses, but if the sums realised were insufficient, the fixed chargeholders would rank as unsecured creditors for the unpaid amounts. Equally, should the fixed chargeholders make a surplus, the surplus is handed to any receiver, whom failing the liquidator.

16.31   The same principle applies where the company has granted a floating charge: the receiver takes such of the company's assets as he entitled to take, pays himself and the preferential creditors (thus relieving the

---

[49] IA 1986, ss.423–425.

[50] Company Directors Disqualification Act 1986, s.7.

[51] Insolvency (Scotland) Rules 1986, r.4.66.

[52] Rule 4.67, details these rules, and includes the provisional liquidator's fees and expenses, and the petitioning creditor's or member's expenses.

liquidator of the duty to pay the preferential creditors) and pays what the floating chargeholder is due. Any shortfall is an unsecured debt; any surplus is handed to the liquidator.

There are cross-border provisions to ensure that orders for winding up made in one part of the United Kingdom are enforceable in other parts[53] subject to the *lex situs* in respect of any property. The courts are required to assist one another where possible. Rules to improve the cross border provisions are being drawn up in terms of the Insolvency Act 2000, section 14.

The liquidator is able to insist on delivery of any papers, books or other records of the company in liquidation notwithstanding any lien over those papers unless they happen to be documents giving a title to property.[54]

Methods of defeating a liquidator

As indicated in the previous chapter on receivership, the liquidator's reach will not extend to all assets being used by the company. Goods subject to retention of title, to hire purchase or conditional sale agreements may not be seized by the liquidator.[55] Goods held on trust for someone unconnected with the company, or goods borrowed from another person are not goods owned by the company and must be returned to their true owners. **16.32**

Dissolution of the company

Although the ability of the liquidator to have the company dissolved has already been mentioned, it should be noted that the liquidator, or any other interested person may apply to the court to have the dissolution declared void.[56] However, this may only be done within two years of the dissolution unless the application is for the purpose of bringing proceedings against the company in respect of a claim for damages for personal injury or for damages under the Fatal Accidents Act 1976 or the Damages (Scotland) Act 1976.[57] **16.33**

The Registrar's dissolution of a company

The Registrar of Companies may strike a defunct company[58] off the register if it fails to reply to correspondence from him, and appears not **16.34**

---

[53] IA 1986, s.426.
[54] IA 1986, s.246.
[55] *Armour v. Thyssen Edelstahlwerke*, 1990 S.L.T. 891; *Vale Sewing Machines v. Robb*, 1997 SCLR 797.
[56] IA 1986, s.651(1).
[57] IA 1986, s.651(5).
[58] Or a company in liquidation of which the liquidation may have been abandoned as not being worth continuing.

to be carrying on any business.[59] Eventually, usually after about six months, the company's name will be struck from the register and publication of the company's demise will be published in the Edinburgh Gazette. The directors may still be liable for any claims against them until the five year period of prescription expires.

Dissolution on application

16.35   The company itself may apply to the Registrar for its own dissolution under CA 1985, section 652A, provided the appropriate documentation is supplied. However the company must genuinely have ceased trading except to the extent of paying any liabilities, must not have changed its name recently, and providing there are no insolvency proceedings taking place against the company or section 425 schemes of arrangement being presented to the court. Once the company has been struck off, the company, any creditor or member may apply within 20 years of the dissolution to have the company restored to the register if it would be just that it should be restored.[60]

Bona vacantia

16.36   If no-one can be found who should be entitled to the assets of the company, the company's goods can be seized by the Crown as *bona vacantia* and the Lord Treasurer's Remembrancer will take them over.[61] That official may disclaim those goods should someone appear later who is entitled to the goods.[62]

Further Reading

Mackenzie-Skene, *Insolvency Law in Scotland* (Butterworths, 1999)
St Clair and Drummond Young, *The Law of Corporate Insolvency in Scotland* (Butterworths 1992)

---

[59] IA 1986, s.652.
[60] IA 1986, s.653.
[61] IA 1986, s.654.
[62] IA 1986, ss.656, 657.

CHAPTER 17

ADMINISTRATION AND COMPANY VOLUNTARY ARRANGEMENTS

ADMINISTRATION

The need for administration

One of the problems afflicting companies in financial difficulties is **17.01** that there is no easy method of ensuring fairness for all those involved in the company. Receivership is very advantageous for the secured creditor, but of little help to employees; liquidation often kills the company, leaves unsecured creditors stranded, members empty-handed, and allows the defunct company to dump all its responsibilities on those least able to cope with them or on those who never anticipated having to deal with them—such as the environment, local councils or the taxpayer.

What is also true of companies in financial difficulties is that sometimes what they need is some skilled management to take over from directors who may not have been up to the task. A skilled insolvency practitioner, parachuted in, can take an overview of what needs to be done, and can restore a company to health or at least keep it going as a viable enterprise with minimal loss to its custom and employees. This is what administration aims to do. By way of example, readers in Edinburgh will recall that the well-known bookshop, Thins, found itself in financial difficulties following expansion into England and higher than anticipated costs arising out of their ventures there. Because the underlying business of Thins was clearly worth preserving, the company was put into administration, and in due course some of the business was sold, but overall, continuity was maintained and most employees were retained.

An administration order is accordingly designed to provide a breath- **17.02** ing space for a company and to be an alternative to receivership and to liquidation. It insulates the company from its creditors temporarily while preserving the creditors' entitlements though denying the creditors, for the time being, the opportunity to enforce their rights. Administration is designed to produce a better return for everybody than the alternatives.[1] It is a court procedure, so unlike receivership it is recognised abroad.[2] The concept of administration is based on receivership but it has one fundamental point, which is that once an administration order is in place, it can defeat all other creditors, but until it is in place, a receiver and/or floating chargeholder has a right of veto over an administration. Accordingly floating chargeholders are still in a strong position. Under the forthcoming Enterprise Bill this will change.

The process of administration

17.03   Assuming the company is not already in receivership or liquidation,[3] the court, on the application by petition of the company, the directors, any creditor or creditors, or any combination of the above, may apply for an administration order.[4] The court will grant an administration order if the court is satisfied that the company is not or is unlikely to be able to pay its debts and considers that the making of the order will be likely to achieve one or more of the following[5]:

(1) The survival of the company as a going concern
(2) The approval of a voluntary arrangement
(3) The sanctioning of a scheme of arrangement under CA 1985 s.425
(4) A more advantageous realisation of the company's assets than would be effected by a company's winding up.

The first and the last are the commonest reasons, though they obviously are inapplicable if the company is already in liquidation.

17.04   An administrator must be an insolvency practitioner and he is subject to the fiduciary and other rules applicable to company officers.

On applying for an administration order, floating chargeholders must be told,[6] in which event those floating chargeholders may appoint a receiver, thus frustrating the appointment of an administrator. If the court is satisfied that notwithstanding the floating chargeholder's right to appoint a receiver, he is not going to do so, or that the charge which might have allowed the floating chargeholder to appoint a receiver would in any event have been struck down as an unfair preference,[7]

[1] If a company goes into liquidation, no creditor may get much; if it goes into receivership, the floating chargeholder may get some of its funds back but may lose much goodwill in the process. It is usually a matter of judgement whether the return on a receivership will be better than the return on an administration.
[2] It is true that it is possible to have a court-based receivership, but this is rare.
[3] Insolvency Act 1986 ("IA 1986"), s.8(4).
[4] IA 1986, s.9.
[5] IA 1986, s.8(3).
[6] IA 1986, s.9(2).
[7] IA 1986, s.242.

gratuitous alienation[8] or an avoidable floating charge,[9] the order will be granted or the court will make such other decision as it sees fit.[10]

From the moment of the presentation of the petition, creditors lose their rights to enforce any securities they may have or any other rights, such as retention of title, which they may have.[11] A creditor can still present a petition to have the company wound up, but the petition will not be granted unless the administration order petition is refused, whereupon the creditor's petition will be entertained.[12]

Once an administration order has been granted, the company may not **17.05** be put into liquidation or receivership and any existing receiver demits office.[13] Creditors lose their rights of enforcement of any decrees or rights against the company though not their rights to what they are owed. Any documentation coming from the company must make it clear that it is in administration[14] and the utilities are not allowed to use administration as a excuse to cut off supplies.[15]

The administrator has extensive powers under Schedule 1 to the Insolvency Act 1986 ("IA 1986") to deal with the company's assets and he may seek court advice on his powers if necessary.[16] He may override existing securities or retention of title clauses[17] and sell assets otherwise subject to a charge—though the chargeholder's entitlement to the value of the charged asset remains protected. He must prepare a statement of the company's assets and liabilities and order a meeting of the company's creditors if 10 per cent of the company's creditors request it or the court so orders.[18] He has extensive duties as well and must adhere to them, and so must look after the company's assets properly.[19] Within three months of his appointment he must present to the Registrar of Companies, all creditors and in due course all members of the company a statement of proposals for achieving the purposes of the administration.[20] The creditors may then vote on his proposals according to the value of their claims against the company.[21] If the creditors suggest modifications to his plan he is not obliged to accept them.[22] The administrator must make a report to the court[23] and indicate if the

---

[8] IA 1986, s.243.
[9] IA 1986, s.245.
[10] IA 1986, s.9(4).
[11] IA 1986, s.10.
[12] IA 1986, s.10.
[13] IA 1986, s.11.
[14] IA 1986, s.12.
[15] IA 1986, s.233.
[16] IA 1986, s.14.
[17] IA 1986, s.15.
[18] IA 1986, s.17(3).
[19] IA 1986 ,s.17(2).
[20] IA 1986, s.23(1), (2).
[21] IA 1986, s.23.
[22] IA 1986, s.24(2).
[23] IA 1986, s.24(4).

proposals were accepted, on which occasion the courts may if necessary discharge or otherwise vary that administration order.[24]

If the creditors or members have good grounds for complaining about the management of the administration they may apply to court for relief.[25]

17.06 As with a receiver, an administrator is only liable to the extent of a qualifying liability in respect of employees' wages with effect from his adoption of their contracts, and he has 14 days from the date of his appointment during which to decide whether or not to adopt their contracts without incurring liability.[26] The qualifying liability is a charge to be ranked ahead even of the administrator's own fees and expenses which otherwise form a first charge on the company's assets.[27]

As with a liquidation, an administrator may make the company's officers and employees provide him with a statement of affairs about the company's affairs.[28] Assuming the proposals are accepted, commonly the administrator does what he can and fulfils his plan or proposals. He may sell off or close down parts of the company and what is left is often put into liquidation. When his purposes are fulfilled, he is discharged from his office, and the company either is saved for another day, in which case the directors would resume office, or what is left after the administration is left to be wound up[29] if that is worthwhile doing.

Proposals under the Enterprise Bill

17.07 As indicated in Chapter 15, receivership is now seen to be too secured-creditor-friendly, and the Enterprise Bill will reduce the opportunities for a floating chargeholder to get the lion's share of the company's assets. However, it would appear that existing floating charges, up to the point of enactment of the Bill, will preserve the right to appoint receivers, but for floating charges after that date, it will not be possible to appoint a receiver, and instead the floating chargeholder will have to apply for administration. It will be possible to do this informally without recourse to court. The primary task of the administrator will be to rescue the company, failing which to obtain a better return than a winding up, only upon failing which may he realise property in order to make a distribution to the secured or preferential creditors, but in so doing he may not "unnecessarily harm" the interest of the creditors as a whole.

---

[24] IA 1986, s.24(5).
[25] IA 1986, s.27.
[26] IA 1986, s.19(6).
[27] IA 1986, s.19(4).
[28] IA 1986, s.22.
[29] It would also be possible to have the remnant of the company dealt with by a company voluntary arrangement.

Following his appointment there will also be a moratorium against any legal process against the company with the exception of the public interest provisions of IA 1986, section 124A and certain petitions by the Financial Services Authority in respect of businesses in the financial world.[30]

These proposals are under consideration at the time of writing.

COMPANY VOLUNTARY ARRANGEMENTS

Voluntary arrangements are the unloved poor relations of the insolvency **17.08** methods. They are unloved because insolvency practitioners are not generally familiar with them, and in turn insolvency practitioners are not as familiar with them as the Government might wish because voluntary arrangements are not as glamorous or as financially rewarding as receiverships and liquidations where the insolvency practitioner's fees will usually be met out of the company's assets. The advantages of a voluntary arrangement are that it need not be expensive; it is relatively informal; it binds even those who have not voted in favour of it; and it may keep the company going, particularly in the light of the moratorium provisions to be discussed shortly. Compared to the use of IA 1986, section 110 it is useful in that not every member need consent to it; compared to a section 425 scheme of arrangement it is cheap. However, it has one significant disadvantage: the secured creditors can effectively veto it and so can the preferential creditors, though this latter may change in the light of the proposals to remove the Crown preferences under the Enterprise Bill.[31]

The practice of the voluntary arrangement

The directors[32] of a company in financial difficulty may suggest to the **17.09** creditors that they wish to make a "proposal" for the payment of its debts. The proposal will effectively be a rescheduling of the company's debts, in the hope that by rearranging the debts and marshalling the payments in a coherent manner all the creditors will either get more than they would otherwise, or will actually get something as opposed to getting nothing. The proposal may not, however, propose anything which may affect the right of a secured creditor to enforce his security without his consent[33] or a preferential creditor to lose his preferential right without his consent.[34] As part of the proposal a "nominee" will be put in charge of it. The nominee used to have to be an insolvency practitioner but now other professional bodies involved in recovery of

---

[30] Financial Services and Markets Act 2000, s.367.
[31] The other preferential non-Crown debts would still remain as preferences.
[32] Or indeed the liquidator or administrator (IA 1986, s.1(3)).
[33] IA 1896, s.4(3).
[34] IA 1986, s.4(5).

companies may be eligible.[35] If the nominee is not already the liquidator or administrator (as is permitted[36]) but has been appointed by the directors, he is required within 28 days after he has been given notice of the proposal, and having received a suitable report from the directors outlining the state of the company's finances[37] to give to the court a report indicating whether the members and the creditors should be invited to separate meetings to consider the proposal.[38] The report effectively is a statement saying whether or not the proposal is viable. If the nominee makes the report to the court and indicates that the meeting should be summoned, the meetings should be convened.[39] If the nominee is the liquidator or administrator, he may summon the meetings anyway.[40] The two meetings may approve the report or suggest modifications. Approval is indicated by three quarters of the creditors voting at their meeting doing so in favour of the resolution[41] and a bare majority for the members.[42] The creditors and members may both suggest modifications, but among the modifications that are not permitted are those that would affect the rights of a secured creditor without the consent of that creditor,[43] or that would affect the rights of any preferential creditor without the consent of that creditor.[44] The results of the meetings will be reported to the court. If both meetings approve, the proposal takes effect and is deemed to bind every person who was entitled to appear at the meetings[45] and if the court is in liquidation or administration at the time of the approvals, the courts may sist the liquidation or administration in order to allow the proposal to be implemented.[46] The proposal may still be challenged in the court, by a member, creditor or contributory if such a person may be unfairly prejudiced by the proposal or there has been some irregularity at the meeting[47] in which case the court may revoke the proposal or arrange further meetings to resolve the difficulty.

Once the proposal has been approved, the nominee is known as the supervisor and he implements the proposal.[48] The proposal, which by

---

[35] IA 2000, s.4.
[36] If the nominee is the liquidator or administrator, it is assumed that he is sufficiently cognisant of the company's affairs not to need to have to present a report to the court.
[37] IA 1986, s.2(3).
[38] IA 1986, s.2(2).
[39] IA 1986, s.3(1).
[40] IA 1986, s.3(2).
[41] Insolvency (Scotland) Rules 1986, r.7.12(2).
[42] Insolvency (Scotland) Rules 1986, r.7.12(1).
[43] IA 1986, s.4(3).
[44] IA 1986, s.4(4).
[45] IA 1986, s.5(2).
[46] IA 1986, s.5(3).
[47] IA 1986, s.6. The challenge must be brought within 28 days of the arrival of the first report with the court: *IRC v. Adams and Partners Ltd* [1999] 2 BCLC 730.
[48] IA 1986, s.7.

then is known as a scheme, binds all creditors[49] including those who may not have voted in its favour or not turned up to the meetings to vote.

Proposed—Moratorium for small companies

As part of the Government's attempts to introduce a rescue culture for small businesses, if the Insolvency Act 2000 is brought into force, it will be open to small private companies[50] to apply for a moratorium of 28 days (though it may be extended) from its debts, during which time the directors may put forward their proposal to a nominee for a company voluntary arrangement.[51] Certain companies in the financial world are banned from applying for the moratorium, as is any company already subject to insolvency proceedings.   **17.10**

The directors prepare a document outlining why they believe a moratorium in conjunction with the company voluntary arrangement would be useful, and the nominee gives his opinion on both the voluntary arrangement and the on the continued viability of the company during the proposed moratorium.[52] If his opinion is favourable, the directors lodge with the court all the supporting documentation for their request for a moratorium, the nominee's written consent to being the supervisor, the nominee's approval of the company voluntary arrangement and moratorium, and his opinion that members' and creditors' meetings should be summoned to approve the proposed voluntary arrangement.[53] On filing all these documents with the court the moratorium will come into place[54] and lasts for 28 days, though the Secretary of State may choose to extend or shorten it if necessary[55] and the members and creditors may choose to make it last two further months.[56] The moratorium may be brought to an end by the expiry of the 28 day period, the decision of the creditors or members, by the nominee's withdrawal from acting or by the court.[57] Creditors, the court and the Registrar of Companies must all be kept informed of these extensions or cessations of the moratorium.[58]

During the moratorium, without the consent of the court no creditor can touch the company's assets, nor take any steps to enforce any rights against the company. All actions against the company are stayed.[59] The   **17.11**

---

[49] With the except of the secured creditors and preferential creditors, who are still entitled to their respective rights unless they consent to waive or reduce them.
[50] In terms of CA 1985, s.247(3).
[51] IA 1986, Sched. A1.
[52] IA 1986, Sched. A1, para. 6.
[53] IA 1986, Sched. A1, para.7.
[54] IA 1986, Sched. A1, para.8(1).
[55] IA 1986, Sched. A1, para. 8(8).
[56] IA 1986, Sched. A1, para. 32.
[57] IA 1986, Sched. A1, para. 8(6).
[58] IA 1986, Sched. A1, para. 11.
[59] IA 1986, Sched. A1, paras 12–14.

company may continue to trade in the ordinary course of business.[60]
During the moratorium the nominee will continue to assess whether or
not the proposed voluntary arrangement is still viable[61] and he may
withdraw from acting if he thinks that it is no longer viable.[62] If it is in
his view viable, he may summon meetings of the members and creditors
to approve the voluntary arrangement as in a normal company voluntary
arrangement as described above.[63]

It should be stressed, however, that at the time of writing these
proposals have not been brought into force.

Further Reading

Mackenzie-Skene, *Insolvency Law in Scotland* (Butterworths, 1999)
St Clair and Drummond Young, *The Law of Corporate Insolvency in
    Scotland* (Butterworths 1992)

---

[60] IA 1986, Sched. A1, para. 18, but any disposals must be of benefit to the company and
    receive approval by a specially set up moratorium committee.
[61] IA 1986, Sched. A1, para. 24.
[62] IA 1986, Sched. A1, para. 25.
[63] IA 1986, Sched. A1, para. 29–31.

INDEX

[all references are to paragraph number]

Access to information
  insider dealing, 12.03
Accounting disclosure rules
  European legislation, and, 1.14
Accounting records
  auditors' reports, 7.32–7.33
  directors' reports, 7.35
  introduction, 7.27
  preparation of
    accounting reference date, 7.30
    auditors, 7.32–7.33
    charities, 7.34
    directors report, 7.35
    general, 7.28
    lodging, time of, 7.36–7.37
    subsequent financial years, 7.31
    summary accounts, 7.39
    true and fair view, 7.29
    unlimited companies, 7.38
  publication of
    accounting reference date, 7.30
    auditors, 7.32–7.33
    charities, 7.34
    directors report, 7.35
    general, 7.28
    lodging, time of, 7.36–7.37
    subsequent financial years, 7.31
    summary accounts, 7.39
    true and fair view, 7.29
    unlimited companies, 7.38
Accounting reference date
  accounts, 7.30
  company incorporation, 3.04
Accounts
  accounting records
    auditors' reports, 7.28–7.39
    directors' reports, 7.28–7.39
    introduction, 7.27
    preparation of, 7.28–7.39
    publication of, 7.28–7.39
  accumulated, 7.03

Accounts—*cont.*
  capitalisation, 7.09
    distributable profits
    accounts, 7.19–7.21
    development expenditure, 7.15–7.18
    dividends, non-cash, 7.14
    expenditure, development, 7.15–7.18
    introduction, 7.13
    non-cash dividends, 7.14
    non-cash revaluation, 7.14
    revaluation, non-cash, 714
  consolidation
    European legislation, and, 1.14
  distribution, 7.02
  distribution rules for public limited
      companies
    directors' liability for improper
        dividend, 7.25
    dividends, payment of, 7.23
    improper distribution, members'
        liability, 7.24
    improper dividend, directors'
        liability, 7.25
    introduction, 7.21–7.22
    members liability for improper
        distribution, 7.24
    payment of dividends, 7.23
    reform, 7.26
  failure to publish, 1.07
  introduction, 7.01
  losses, realised, 7.04–7.08
  private companies
    accounts, defective, revision of, 7.49
    audit, exemption from, 7.43–7.44
    defective accounts, revision, 7.49
    defective reports, revision, 7.49
    dormant, 7.48
    group companies, 7.45–7.47
    introduction, 7.40–7.42
    reform proposals, 7.50
    reports, defective, revision , 7.49
  profits, realised, 7.04–7.08

Accounts—*cont.*
realised losses, 7.04–7.08
realised profits, 7.04–7.08
reduction, 7.11
reorganisation, 7.12
written off, 7.10
Accounts, defective
revision of, 7.49
Accumulated
dividends and accounts, 7.03
Acquisition of existing business
company incorporation, 3.37
Acquisition rules
takeovers and mergers, 14.09
Acting in good faith
directors' fiduciary duties, 9.10
Administration
introduction, 17.01–17.02
process, 17.03–17.06
reform proposals, 17.07
Administration order
administration, and, 17.02
Administrative receiver
charges, 15.10
Administrator
winding up, and, 16.05
Agency
corporate veil, 2.19
Agent
receiver, 15.29–15.30
Allotment of shares
authorised share capital, 5.11
borrow, 5.08–5.09
directors' authority, 5.12–5.13
increase share capital, 5.08–5.09
intimation of, 5.19–5.21
members pre-emption rights, 5.14–5.15
payment for, 5.16–5.18
procedure, 5.10
registration of new shares, 5.19–5.21
share capital, authorised, 5.11
Alternate director
generally, 8.11
Alternative dispute resolution
minority protection, 11.37
Alternative Investment Market
company incorporation, 3.15
Alternative remedies
corporate veil, 2.21–2.23
Annual general meeting
generally, 13.06–13.07
Appointment
auditors, 10.08
directors and, 8.16
Approval
mergers, 14.08
takeovers, 14.08

Articles of association
function of, 4.21–4.22
introduction, 4.01
shareholders' agreements, 4.24–4.25
shares, class of, 4.23
Assets offers, share for
takeovers and mergers, 14.11
Assignment of right to purchase
capital maintenance, 6.30
Audit, exemption from
dividends and accounts, 7.43–7.44
Auditors
appointment, 10.08
introduction, 10.01–10.02, 10.07
liability, 10.18–10.19
qualifications, 1.14
reform proposals, 10.20
removal, 10.13–10.16
reports, 7.32–7.33
resignation, 10.13–10.16
role, 10.17
Auditor's certificate
dividends, 7.20
Auditors' report
capital maintenance, 6.21
dividends and accounts, 7.32–7.33
Authorised capital
company incorporation, 3.11
memorandum, 4.02
Authorised share capital
company incorporation, 3.11
securities, 5.11

Bankrupts
directors, 8.27
Beneficial interest
receivership, 15.38
Best interests of the company
directors' fiduciary duties, 9.11
Board meeting
generally, 13.21–13.22
Bona vacantia
winding up, and, 16.36
Bonus rights
securities, 5.23
Bonus shares
dividends, 7.09
Breach
directors' fiduciary duties, 9.12–9.13
Breach of disqualification order
directors, 8.34–8.35
Burden of proof
insider dealing, 12.20
Business judgement rule
directors, 9.17

Buying out the minority
takeovers and mergers, 14.12–14.14

Capital
company
account, types of, 6.04
alteration of, 6.05
rules, 6.03
theory, 6.01–6.02
financial assistance
generally, 6.13–6.16
purpose, 6.17–6.19
whitewash procedure, 6.20–6.22
loss of, 6.43
reduction
introduction, 6.06
procedure, 6.11–6.12
reasons for, 6.07–6.09
types, 6.10
share premium account, 6.44–6.45
shares, purchase of
assignment of right to purchase, 6.30
capital redemption reserve,
6.35–6.36
contingent purchases, 6.31
disclosure, 6.32
failure to, 6.42
introduction, 6.23–6.24
own shares out of capital in private
companies, 6.37–6.41
payment, 6.33–6.34
process, 6.27–6.29
reasons, 6.25
redemption, 6.26
redemption reserve, 6.35–6.36
right to purchase, assignment of,
6.30
shares, redemption of
assignment of right to purchase, 6.30
capital redemption reserve,
6.35–6.36
contingent purchases, 6.31
disclosure, 6.32
failure to, 6.42
introduction, 6.23–6.24
own shares out of capital in private
companies, 6.37–6.41
payment, 6.33–6.34
process, 6.27–6.29
reasons, 6.25
redemption, 6.26
redemption reserve, 6.35–6.36
right to purchase, assignment of,
6.30
Capital maintenance rule
company incorporation, 3.11

Capital redemption reserve
capital maintenance, 6.04, 6.35–6.36
securities, 5.23
Capitalisation
dividends and accounts, 7.09
Case law
corporate veil, 2.20
Certificate of registration
charges, 15.16
company incorporation, 3.04
Chairman of the board
generally, 8.09
Charges
concept, 15.01–15.03
fixed, 15.04–15.05
floating
generally, 15.06–15.08
Scotland, and, 15.09–15.10
invalidity
floating charges, 15.21–15.23
generally, 15.19–15.20
problems, 15.24
registering
certificate of registration, 15.16
discharge, 15.17
failure to register in time, 15.14
generally, 15.11–15.13
ranking agreements, 15.18
register of charges, 15,15
Charities
company incorporation, 3.11
dividends and accounts, 7.34
memorandum and articles of
association, 4.16
City Code on Takeovers and Mergers
European legislation, and, 1.14
generally, 14.04–14.05
insider dealing, 12.26
legal status, 14.06
Civil penalties
insider dealing, 12.24–12.25
Civil proceedings
dti investigations, 11.45
Civil sanctions
directors' liability, 9.41
Class meeting
generally, 13.20
Combined Code
directors, 8.02
directors' duties, 9.50
Commerce, promotion of
companies, 1.06
Commercial company clause
memorandum and articles of
association, 4.08–4.11
Common law
agency, 2.19

Common law—*cont.*
alternative remedies, 2.21–2.23
case law, 2.20
crime, and, 2.25–2.28
evasion of responsibilities, 2.14
group entity theory, 2.17–2.18
introduction, 2.13
moral issue, 2.29
public policy, 2.15–2.16
problematic areas, 2.24
remedies
alternative, 2.21–2.23
minority protection, and,
11.13–11.14
Companies
features
commerce, promotion of, 1.06
disclosure principle, 1.07
European legislation, 1.14–1.17
fraud, 1.09
existence, 1.01
incorporation, 1.02–1.03
legislation, 1.12–1.13, 1.14–1.17
limited liability, 1.04–1.05, 1.11
personal wealth, 1.10
professional standards, 1.08
United Kingdom legislation,
1.12–1.13
foreign
European legislation, and, 1.14
jurisprudence, and, 1.28
Scottish law, comparison with, 1.27
trading organisations, other
limited liability partnership,
1.21–1.23
limited partnership, 1.24
partnerships, 1.19–1.20
registered companies, 1.25–1.26
sole traders, 1.18
types
dormant, 3.24
introduction, 3.09
overseas, 3.28
private limited company, 3.20–3.23
public limited company, 3.10–3.19
subsidiaries, 3.25–3.27
**Company approval for property
transfer**
directors' statutory duties, 9.21
Company approval for share transfer
directors' statutory duties, 9.21
Company capital
account, types of, 6.04
alteration of, 6.05
rules, 6.03
theory, 6.01–6.02

Company, dissolution of
application, 16.35
bona vacantia, 16.36
generally, 16.33
Registrar's, 16.34
Company incorporation
conversion
introduction, 3.29
limited to unlimited, 3.31
private to public, 3.30
public to private, 3.33
unlimited to limited, 3.32
documents, 3.01–3.04
name, 3.05–3.07
newly formed company
acquisition of existing business, 3.37
introduction, 3.35
off the shelf companies, 3.36
passing off, 3.08
promoters, 3.39–3.41
types of company
dormant, 3.24
introduction, 3.09
overseas, 3.28
private limited company, 3.20–3.23
public limited company, 3.10–3.19
subsidiaries, 3.25–3.27
Company name
company incorporation, 3.05–3.07
inaccurate
corporate veil, 2.08–2.09
memorandum, 4.02
Company secretary
company incorporation, 3.03, 3.14,
3.23
duties, 10.05–10.06
introduction, 10.01–10.02
role, 10.03–10.04
Company voluntary arrangements
introduction, 17.08
moratorium for small companies,
17.10–17.11
practice of, 17.09
Company's assets, distribution of
winding up, and, 16.30–16.31
Company's property, disposal of
winding up, 16.14
Compensation
insider trading, 12.24
Competition Commission
takeovers and mergers, 14.07
Compulsory winding up
getting in the estate, 16.25–16.27
grounds
eligibility to petition, 16.19–16.20
generally, 16.16
inability to pay debts, 16.17

Compulsory winding up—*cont.*
grounds—*cont.*
"just and equitable" grounds, 16.18
insolvent company's estate, getting in, 16.25–16.27
jurisdiction, 16.15
liability of directors, 16.28–16.29
petition, procedure, 16.21–16.24
procedure, 16.21–16.24
Concert party
securities, 5.29
Confidentiality
insider dealing, 12.19
Conflicts interest
directors' fiduciary duties, 9.07–9.09
Contingent purchases
capital maintenance, 6.31
Contract of employment
winding up, 16.08
Contracts with sole directors
directors' statutory duties, 9.27
Contracts with sole members
directors' statutory duties, 9.27
Conversion
introduction, 3.29
limited to unlimited, 3.31
private to public, 3.30
public to private, 3.33
unlimited to limited, 3.32
Convertible shares
securities, 5.07
Corporate criminal responsibility
corporate veil, 2.27
Corporate Homicide Bill
corporate veil, 2.26
Corporate veil
generally, 2.04
lifting the veil
common law, 2.13–2.29
statute, 2.05–2.12
separate legal identity, 2.01–2.03
Corroborative evidence
insider trading, 12.23
Credit transaction
directors, 9.30
Creditors
directors' duty, 9.34–9.35
Creditors' buffer
capital maintenance, 6.01
Creditors' voluntary winding up
generally, 16.11–16.13
CREST
securities, 5.20–5.21
Crime
corporate veil, and, 2.25–2.28
Criminal offences
directors' liability, 9.41

Criminal offence of insider trading
definition, 12.07
generally, 12.06
interpretation
dealing, 12.13
inside information, 12.08
insider, 12.09
insider source, 12.10
issuer, 12.17
price-affected securities, 12.16
price-sensitive information, 12.16
professional intermediary, 12.15
public, 12.12
regulated market, 12.14
securities, 12.11
Criminal proceedings
dti investigations, 11.45
Criminalisation of insider trading
insider dealing, 12.27–12.28
Cross-border receivership
generally, 15.34
Crown preference
charges, 15.08

De facto director
generally, 8.12
Dealing
insider dealing, 12.13
Debentures
securities, 5.32
Debts, inability to pay
compulsory winding up, 16.17
Declaration of interest
directors' statutory duties, 9.22
Deemed notice
memorandum, 4.06
Default share
securities, 5.04
Defeating receivership, methods
beneficial interest, 15.38
effectually executed diligence, 15.37
introduction, 15.35
prior ranking fixed charge, 15.37
retention of title, 15.36
Defective accounts, revision
dividends and accounts, 7.49
Defective reports, revision
dividends and accounts, 7.49
Defences
insider dealing
generally, 12.20
specific, 12.21–12.23
Defiant Directors' Hotline
directors, 8.24
Demergers
European legislation, and, 1.14

Development expenditure
dividends and accounts, 7.15–7.18
Diligence
winding up, 16.25
Directing mind
corporate veil, 2.25
Directors
appointment, 8.16
disclosure of information
interest in contracts entered into by
company, 8.20
interest in securities, 8.19
registrar of companies, 8.18
disqualification
breach of, 8.34–8.35
general, 8.24
grounds for order, 8.26–8.27
human rights, and, 8.36
length of, 8.32–8.33
order, 8.25
unfit director, insolvent company
and, 8.28–8.31
generally, 8.01–8.03
ineligible, 8.15
meetings, and, 13.03
remuneration, 8.17
responsibilities, 8.04
termination
dismissal, 8.23
methods, 8.22
unsatisfactory director, 8.21
types
alternate, 8.11
chairman of the board, 8.09
de facto director, 8.12
executive director, 8.07
introduction, 8.05
managing director, 8.06
nominee, 8.10
non-executive, 8.08
senior executives, 8.14
shadow director, 8.13
Directors acting in own interest
memorandum and articles of
association, 4.17
Directors' duty
creditors, 9.34–9.35
employees, 9.36
fiduciary
acting in good faith, 9.10
best interests of the company, 9.11
breach, 9.12–9.13
conflicts interest, 9.07–9.09
introduction, 9.05–9.06
personal interests, 9.07–9.09
remedies for breach, 9.12

Directors' duty—*cont.*
insolvency practitioners, cooperation
with, 9.39
introduction, 9.03–9.04
members, 9.37–9.38
skill and care, 9.14–9.17
statutory duties
company approval for property
transfer, 9.21
company approval for share transfer,
9.21
contracts with sole directors, 9.27
contracts with sole members, 9.27
declaration of interest, 9.22
introduction, 9.18
loans, 9.29–9.32
loss of office, payment for, 9.20
payments for loss of office, 9.20
political donations, 9.33
property transactions, 9.25
property transfer, company approval,
9.21
service contracts, 9.23–9.24
share transfer, company approval,
9.21
sole directors, 9.27
sole members, 9.27
tax free payments, 9.19
traded options, 9.28
ultra vires contracts, 9.26
Directors' liability
improper dividend, 7.25
insolvency
duty, breach of, 9.43–9.44
fraudulent trading, 9.45
introduction, 9.41–9.42
phoenix trading, 9.49
wrongful trading, 9.46–9.48
introduction, 9.40
**Directors' liability for improper
dividend**
dividends and accounts, 7.25
Directors' remuneration
meetings, and, 13.06
Directors' reports
dividends and accounts, 7.28–7.39
Discharge of charges
generally, 15.17
Disclosure
capital maintenance, 6.32
**Disclosure of information, directors
and**
interest in contracts entered into by
company, 8.20
interest in securities, 8.19
registrar of companies, 8.18

Disclosure of interests
securities, 5.29
Disclosure principle
companies, 1.07
Disclosure rules, accounting
European legislation, and, 1.14
Dismissal
directors, and, 8.23
Disqualification, directors and
breach of, 8.34–8.35
general, 8.24
grounds for order, 8.26–8.27
human rights, and, 8.36
length of, 8.32–8.33
order, 8.25
unfit director, insolvent company and,
8.28–8.31
Disqualification order
directors, 8.25
grounds, 8.26–8.27
human rights, 8.36
length of, 8.32–8.33
Dissolution of the company
application, 16.35
bona vacantia, 16.36
generally, 16.33
Registrar's, 16.34
Distributable profits
accounts, 7.19–7.21
development expenditure, 7.15–7.18
dividends, non-cash, 7.14
expenditure, development, 7.15–7.18
introduction, 7.13
non-cash dividends, 7.14
non-cash revaluation, 7.14
revaluation, non-cash, 714
Distribution
dividends and accounts, 7.02
Distribution, improper
members' liability, 7.24
**Distribution rules for public limited
companies**
directors' liability for improper
dividend, 7.25
dividends, payment of, 7.23
improper distribution, members'
liability, 7.24
improper dividend, directors' liability,
7.25
introduction, 7.21–7.22
members liability for improper
distribution, 7.24
payment of dividends, 7.23
reform, 7.26
Dividends
accounting records
auditors' reports, 7.28–7.39

Dividends—*cont.*
accounting records—*cont.*
directors' reports, 7.28–7.39
introduction, 7.27
preparation of, 7.28–7.39
publication of, 7.28–7.39
accumulated, 7.03
capitalisation, 7.09
distributable profits
accounts, 7.19–7.21
development expenditure, 7.15–7.18
dividends, non-cash, 7.14
expenditure, development, 7.15–7.18
introduction, 7.13
non-cash dividends, 7.14
non-cash revaluation, 7.14
revaluation, non-cash, 714
distribution, 7.02
distribution rules for public limited
companies
directors' liability for improper
dividend, 7.25
dividends, payment of, 7.23
improper distribution, members'
liability, 7.24
improper dividend, directors'
liability, 7.25
introduction, 7.21–7.22
members liability for improper
distribution, 7.24
payment of dividends, 7.23
reform, 7.26
introduction, 7.01
losses, realised, 7.04–7.08
private companies
accounts, defective, revision of, 7.49
audit, exemption from, 7.43–7.44
defective accounts, revision, 7.49
defective reports, revision, 7.49
dormant, 7.48
group companies, 7.45–7.47
introduction, 7.40–7.42
reform proposals, 7.50
reports, defective, revision , 7.49
profits, realised, 7.04–7.08
realised losses, 7.04–7.08
realised profits, 7.04–7.08
reduction, 7.11
reorganisation, 7.12
written off, 7.10
Divorce
corporate veil, 2.24
Documents
company incorporation, 3.01–3.04
Dormant company
company incorporation, 3.24
dividends and accounts, 7.48

Dormant company—*cont.*
memorandum, 4.10
DTI inspection
directors, and, 8.36
DTI investigations
application for, 11.41
generally, 11.40
grounds for, 11.42–11.44
inspectors report, 11.45
powers, 11.45–11.47
report, inspectors, 11.45
requisition of books and papers, 11.49
seizure of books and papers, 11.49
share dealing, 11.48
Duty, breach of
directors' liability, 9.43–9.44

Effectually executed diligence
receivership, 15.37
Electronic record
securities, 5.20–5.21
Eligibility to petition
compulsory winding up, 16.19–16.20
Employee
directors' duty, 9.36
protection
European legislation, and, 1.14
share scheme, 5.12, 5.15
Employment, contract of
winding up, 16.08
European community
accounts, and, 7.45
European legislation
companies, 1.14–1.17
Evasion of responsibilities
corporate veil, 2.14
Evidence, corroborative
insider trading
Ex shareholders
minority protection
liability, 11.28
Executive director
generally, 8.07
Existence
companies, 1.01
External policy rule
memorandum and articles of
association, 4.18–4.19
Extraordinary general meetings
generally, 13.08–13.12

Failure to register charge in time
charges, 15.14
Fair trial
directors, 8.36
Fiduciary duty
acting in good faith, 9.10

Fiduciary duty—*cont.*
best interests of the company, 9.11
breach, 9.12–9.13
conflicts interest, 9.07–9.09
insider dealing, and, 12.04
introduction, 9.05–9.06
personal interests, 9.07–9.09
remedies for breach, 9.12
Financial assistance
generally, 6.13–6.16
purpose, 6.17–6.19
whitewash procedure, 6.20–6.22
Financial Reporting Standards
dividends, 7.05
Financial Services Authority
insider dealing, 12.26
**Financial Services and Market
Tribunal**
insider dealing, 12.26
Fixed asset
dividends, 7.07
Fixed charges
generally, 15.04–15.05
prior ranking, 15.37
Fixed chargeholders
winding up, 16.03
Floating-chargeholder
winding up, 16.03
Floating charges
generally, 15.06–15.08
invalidity of, 15.21–15.23
Scotland, and, 15.09–15.10
securities, 5.30
winding up, 16.03
Foreign companies
European legislation, and, 1.14
Foreign subsidiary
capital maintenance, 6.15
Forfeiture
securities, 5.31
Foss v Harbottle, **rules in**
exceptions
failure to follow proper procedure,
11.08–11.09
fraud, 11.11–11.12
illegal transaction, 11.07
introduction, 11.06
procedure, failure to follow,
11.08–11.09
shareholder, infringement of
personal rights, 11.10
ultra vires, 11.07
generally, 11.04–11.05
Fraud
companies, 1.09
company secretary, and, 10.19
minority protection, 11.11–11.12

Fraudulent directors
company secretary, 10.19
Fraudulent trading
directors' liability, 9.45
Freestanding legal personality
companies, 1.01
Funds, disbursal of
receiver and, 15.32–15.33

General meetings, purpose of
generally, 13.01–13.04
"getting in" the estate
winding up, and, 16.25–16.27
Good faith
memorandum, 4.18
Gratuitous alienation
winding up, 16.25
Grounds for disqualification order
directors, 8.26–8.27
Group companies
dividends and accounts, 7.45–7.47
Group entity theory
corporate veil, 2.17–2.18

Health and safety legislation
directors, 9.36
Human rights
directors
disqualification order, and, 8.36
dti investigation, 11.44

Illegal transaction
minority protection, 11.07
Improper distribution
members' liability, 7.24
Improper dividend
directors' liability, 7.25
Inability to pay debts
compulsory winding up, 16.17
Incorporation
generally, 1.02,
registration, 1.03
Ineligibility
directors and, 8.15
Information, immediate access
insider dealing, 12.03
Insanity
directors, 8.22
Inside information
insider dealing, 12.08
Insider
insider dealing, 12.09
Insider dealing
access to information, 12.03
civil penalties, 12.24–12.25
criminal offence
definition, 12.07

Insider dealing—*cont.*
criminal offence—*cont.*
generally, 12.06
interpretation, 12.08–12.18
criminalisation of, 12.27–12.28
defences
generally, 12.20
specific, 12.21–12.23
generally, 12.04
information, immediate access, 12.03
introduction, 12.01
investigations, 12.19
market abuse, 12.26
price-sensitive information, exposure
of, 12.05
victimless crime, 12.02
Insider source
insider dealing, 12.10
Insolvency
duty, breach of, 9.43–9.44
fraudulent trading, 9.45
introduction, 9.41–9.42
phoenix trading, 9.49
wrongful trading, 9.46–9.48
Insolvency practitioners
administration, and, 17.04
cooperation with
directors' duties, 9.39
Insolvent company's estate
gathering in, 16.25–16.27
Inspectors report
dti investigations, 11.45
Intention
insider dealing, 12.21
Inter-group liability
European legislation, and, 1.15
**Interest in contracts entered into by
company**
directors and, 8.20
Interest in securities
directors and, 8.19
Internal policy rule
memorandum and articles of
association, 4.14
Invalidity of charges
floating charges, 15.21–15.23
generally, 15.19–15.20
Invitation to treat
securities, 5.25
Issued share capital
capital maintenance, 6.04
Issuer
insider dealing, 12.17
Issues
bonus, 5.23
rights, 5.22
scrip, 5.24

Issuer
insider dealing, 12.17

Judicial factors
minority protection, 11.39
Jurisdiction
compulsory winding up, 16.15
Jurisprudence
companies, and, 1.28
"just and equitable" grounds
compulsory winding up, 16.18

Legalities
takeovers and mergers, 14.02
Legislation
companies, 1.12–1.13, 1.14–1.17
memorandum and articles of
association
internal policy rule, 4.14
introduction, 4.12
over-riding statute, 4.13
Legitimate expectation
minority protection, 11.34
Liability
disqualification, and, 2.11
insolvency, and, 2.10
inter-group
European legislation, and, 1.15
Liability for ex-shareholders
minority protection, 11.28
Liability of auditors
generally, 10.18–10.19
Liability of directors
insolvent liquidation, and, 16.28–16.29
Lien
securities, 5.31
Lifting the veil
common law
agency, 2.19
alternative remedies, 2.21–2.23
case law, 2.20
crime, and, 2.25–2.28
evasion of responsibilities, 2.14
group entity theory, 2.17–2.18
introduction, 2.13
moral issue, 2.29
public policy, 2.15–2.16
problematic areas, 2.24
remedies, alternative, 2.21–2.23
statute, and
company name, inaccurate,
2.08–2.09
introduction, 2.05
liability, 2.10–2.11
personal liability, 2.12
plcs trading with one shareholder,
2.06

Lifting the veil—*cont.*
statute, and—*cont.*
trading certificate, absence of,
2.07–2.12
Limited liability
company, 1.11
general, 1.04–1.05
partnership, 1.21–1.23
memorandum, 4.02
Limited partnership
companies, 1.24
Liquidation
administration, and, 17.01
winding up, 16.03–16.05
Liquidator
defeating, 16.32
generally, 16.03–16.04
Loans
directors' statutory duties, 9.29–9.32
securities, 5.32
London Stock Exchange
company incorporation, 3.15
Loss of capital
capital maintenance, 6.43
Loss of office, payment for
directors' statutory duties, 9.20
Losses, realised
dividends and accounts, 7.04–7.08

Majority shareholders
corporate veil, and, 2.02
minority protection, 11.30–11.36
Managing director
generally, 8.06
Mandatory bids
takeovers and mergers, 14.10
Mandatory bid rule
takeover and mergers, 14.09
Market
takeovers and mergers, 14.03
Market abuse
insider dealing, 12.26
Market information
insider dealing, 12.22
Market purchase
capital maintenance, 6.29
Matrimonial settlement
corporate veil, 2.24
Maxims
minority protection, 11.26
Meetings
board meeting, 13.21–13.22
class meeting, 13.20
general meetings, purpose of,
13.01–13.04
notices
necessary information, 13.13

Meetings—*cont.*
notices—*cont.*
special, 13.14
procedure
any other business, 13.19
introduction, 13.17
voting, 13.18
requisitioned resolutions, 13.15
resolutions requiring special notice,
13.14
types
annual general meeting, 13.06–13.07
extraordinary general meetings,
13.08–13.12
introduction, 13.05
Member
minority protection, 11.16
Members
directors' duty, 9.37–9.38
Members' interests
minority protection, 11.20
Members' liability
improper distribution, 7.24
Members pre-emption rights
securities, 5.14–5.15
Members' voluntary winding up
generally, 16.10
Memorandum of association
capital maintenance, 6.12
introduction, 4.01
objects clause
charities, 4.16
commercial company clause,
4.08–4.11
directors acting in own interest, 4.17
external policy rule, 4.18–4.19
generally, 4.04–4.06, 4.20
legislation, 4.12–4.15
reform, 4.07
purpose of memorandum, 4.02–4.03
shareholders' agreements, 4.24–4.25
Mergers
approval, 14.08
acquisition rules, 14.09
buying out the minority, 14.12–14.14
City Code
generally, 14.04–14.05
legal status, 14.06
Competition Commission, 14.07
European legislation, and, 1.14
introduction, 14.01
legalities, 14.02
mandatory bids, 14.10
market, 14.03
Office of Fair Trading, 14.07
scheme of arrangement, 14.15–14.18
share for assets offers, 14.11

Minority protection
capital maintenance, 6.06
common law remedies, 11.13–11.14
generally, 11.01–11.03
Foss v Harbottle, rules in
exceptions, 11.06–11.12
generally, 11.04–11.05
Scotland
judicial factors, 11.39
statutory protection
actual conduct, 11.21
conducted, 11.18
introduction, 11.15
liability for ex-shareholders, 11.28
majority shareholders, use of
position, 11.30–11.36
maxims and, 11.26
member, 11.16
members' interests, 11.20
minority shareholder, maxims and,
11.26
minority shareholding, purchase of
by majority at fair value, 11.25
order, 11.17
prejudice, 11.19
proposed conduct, 11.21
reform proposals, 11.37
remedies, 11.23, 11.29
Secretary of state, 11.22
unfairness, 11.19
unreasonable act, 11.27
winding up
just and equitable grounds, 11.38
Minority shareholder, maxims and
minority protection, 11.26
**Minority shareholding, purchase of by
majority at fair value**
minority protection, 11.25
Moral issue
corporate veil, 2.29
Moratorium for small companies
company voluntary arrangements,
17.10–17.11

Name, company
company incorporation, 3.05–3.07
Negligence
minority protection, 11.11
Negotiable instruments
inaccurate company name, 2.08
Net asset rule
company incorporation, 3.11
dividends, 7.21
Newly formed company
acquisition of existing business, 3.37
introduction, 3.35
off the shelf companies, 3.36

Nominee director
  generally, 8.10
Non-cash dividends
  dividends and accounts, 7.14
Non-cash revaluation
  dividends and accounts, 7.14
Non-corporate interest
  directors' statutory duties, 9.51
Non-executive director
  generally, 8.08
Non-statutory duties
  generally, 9.50
  non-corporate interest, 9.51
Non-trading company
  memorandum, 410
Notices
  necessary information, 13.13
  special, 13.14

Objects clause
  capital maintenance, 6.06
  charities, 4.16
  commercial company clause, 4.08–4.11
  directors acting in own interest, 4.17
  external policy rule, 4.18–4.19
  generally, 4.04–4.06, 4.20
  legislation
    internal policy rule, 4.14
    introduction, 4.12
    over-riding statute, 4.13
  reform, 4.07
Off market purchase
  capital maintenance, 6.28
Off the shelf companies
  company incorporation, 3.36
Office of Fair Trading
  takeovers and mergers, 14.07
Option
  securities, 5.01
Order
  minority protection, 11.17
Ordinary resolution
  company incorporation, 3.14
Ordinary shares
  securities, 5.04
Over-riding statute
  memorandum and articles of
    association, 4.13
Overseas companies
  company incorporation, 3.28

Pacman defence
  takeovers and mergers, 14.01
Parent undertaking
  company incorporation, 3.26
Partnerships
  companies, 1.19–1.20

Passing off
  company incorporation, 3.08
Payment of dividends
  dividends and accounts, 7.23
Payments for loss of office
  directors' statutory duties, 9.20
Permissible capital payment
  capital maintenance, 6.37–6.41
Personal interests
  directors' fiduciary duties, 9.07–9.09
Personal liability
  corporate veil, 2.12
Personal wealth
  companies, 1.10
Petition, procedure
  compulsory winding up, and,
    16.21–16.24
Phoenix trading
  company incorporation, 3.06
  directors' liability, 9.49
Plcs trading with one shareholder
  corporate veil, 2.06
Political donations
  directors' statutory duties, 9.33
Pre-emption rights
  company incorporation, 3.37
  securities, 5.08
  waiver, 5.14
Preference
  winding up, 16.25
Preference shares
  securities, 5.05
Preferential creditors
  charges, 15.08
Preferential debts
  charges, 15.08
Prejudice
  minority protection, 11.19
Preparation of accounting records
  accounting reference date, 7.30
  auditors, 7.32–7.33
  charities, 7.34
  directors report, 7.35
  general, 7.28
  lodging, time of, 7.36–7.37
  subsequent financial years, 7.31
  summary accounts, 7.39
  true and fair view, 7.29
  unlimited companies, 7.38
Price-affected securities
  insider dealing, 12.16
Price-sensitive information
  insider dealing and
    exposure of, 12.05
    interpretation, 12.16
Prior ranking fixed charge
  receivership, 15.06, 15.37

Private companies
accounts, defective, revision of, 7.49
audit exemption from, 7.43–7.44
defective accounts, revision, 7.49
defective reports, revision, 7.49
dormant, 7.48
group companies, 7.45–7.47
introduction, 7.40–7.42
reform proposals, 7.50
reports, defective, revision , 7.49
**Private companies, purchase of own
    shares**
capital maintenance, 6.37–6.41
Private limited company
guarantee, limited by, 3.22
shares, limited by, 3.20–3.23
single member, 3.23
Privilege
insider dealing, 12.19
Procedure
failure to follow
    minority protection, 11.08–11.09
meeting
    any other business, 13.19
    introduction, 13.17
    voting, 13.18
Professional intermediary
insider dealing, 12.15
Professional liability insurance
professional standards, 1.08
Professional standards
companies, 1.08
Profit, distributable
dividends, 7.01
Profits, realised
dividends and accounts, 7.04–7.08
Promoters
company incorporation, 3.39–3.41
Proper plaintiff rule
minority protection, 11.06
Property transactions
directors' statutory duties, 9.25
Property transfer, company approval
directors' statutory duties, 9.21
Proposed conduct
minority protection, 11.21
Prospectuses
securities, 5.25–5.26
Public
insider dealing, 12.12
Public examination
winding up, 16.22
Public interest
takeover and mergers, 14.07
Public limited company
accounting requirements, 3.17
advantages of, 3.18

Public limited company—*cont.*
capital of, 3.11
European legislation, and, 1.14
general meetings, 3.16
introduction, 3.10
officers, 3.14
private company, and, 3.19
shares
    issue to public, 3.15
    non cash consideration for, 3.13
trading certificate, and, 3.12
Public policy
corporate veil, 2.15–2.16
Publication of accounting records
accounting reference date, 7.30
auditors, 7.32–7.33
charities, 7.34
directors report, 7.35
general, 7.28
lodging, time of, 7.36–7.37
subsequent financial years, 7.31
summary accounts, 7.39
true and fair view, 7.29
unlimited companies, 7.38
Purchase of shares
assignment of right to purchase, 6.30
capital redemption reserve, 6.35–6.36
contingent purchases, 6.31
disclosure, 6.32
failure to, 6.42
introduction, 6.23–6.24
own shares out of capital in private
    companies, 6.37–6.41
payment, 6.33–6.34
process
    introduction, 6.27
    market purchase, 6.29
    off market purchase, 6.28
reasons, 6.25
redemption, 6.26
redemption reserve, 6.35–6.36
right to purchase, assignment of, 6.30
Purple book
company incorporation, 3.15
– directors, 8.02
securities, 5.26

Quorum
company incorporation, 3.23

Ranking agreements
charges, 15.18
Realised losses
dividends and accounts, 7.04–7.08
Realised profits
dividends and accounts, 7.04–7.08

Receiver
  agent, 15.29–15.30
  funds, disbursal of, 15.32–15.33
  tax collector, 15.31
  winding up, and, 16.03–16.04
Receivership
  administration, 17.01
  cross-border, 15.34
  defeating
    beneficial interest, 15.38
    effectually executed diligence, 15.37
    introduction, 15.35
    prior ranking fixed charge, 15.37
    retention of title, 15.36
  generally, 15.25–15.28
  problems, 15.39
  receiver
    agent, 15.29–15.30
    funds, disbursal of, 15.32–15.33
    tax collector, 15.31
Recklessness
  corporate, 2.25
Recognised investment exchange
  company incorporation, 3.15
Redeemable shares
  securities, 5.06
Redemption of shares
  assignment of right to purchase, 6.30
  capital redemption reserve, 6.35–6.36
  contingent purchases, 6.31
  disclosure, 6.32
  failure to, 6.42
  introduction, 6.23–6.24
  own shares out of capital in private
    companies, 6.37–6.41
  payment, 6.33–6.34
  process
    introduction, 6.27
    market purchase, 6.29
    off market purchase, 6.28
  reasons, 6.25
  redemption, 6.26
  redemption reserve, 6.35–6.36
  right to purchase, assignment of, 6.30
Redemption reserve
  capital maintenance, 6.35–6.36
Redemption shares
  capital maintenance, 6.23
Reduction
  dividends and accounts, 7.11
Reduction of capital
  introduction, 6.06
  procedure, 6.11–6.12
  reasons for, 6.07–6.09
  types, 6.10
Reform proposals
  directors, 9.52

Reform proposals—*cont.*
  minority protection, 11.37
Register of charges
  generally, 15,15
Register of directors
  directors, 8.18
Register of disqualified directors
  directors, 8.24
Register of secretaries
  directors, 8.18
Registered companies
  companies, 1.25–1.26
Registering charges
  certificate of registration, 15.16
  discharge, 15.17
  failure to register in time, 15.14
  generally, 15.11–15.13
  ranking agreements, 15.18
  register of charges, 15,15
Registrar of companies
  disclosure to
    directors, 8.18
Registrar's dissolution of a company
  winding up, and, 16.34
Registration
  incorporation, 1.03
Registration of new shares
  securities, 5.19–5.21
Regulated market
  insider dealing, 12.14
Remedies, alternative
  corporate veil, 2.21–2.23
Remedies
  breach directors' fiduciary duties, 9.12
  minority protection , 11.23, 11.29
Removal of auditors
  generally, 10.13–10.16
Remuneration
  directors and, 8.17
Reorganisation
  dividends and accounts, 7.12
Report, inspectors
  dti investigation, 11.45
Reports
  dividends and accounts, 7.49
Requisitioned resolutions
  generally, 13.15
Requisition of books and papers
  dti investigation, 11.49
Resignation of auditors
  generally, 10.13–10.16
Resolution
  requiring special notice, 13.14
  types of
    elective, 13.27–13.28
    extraordinary, 13.26
    introduction, 13.23

Resolution—*cont.*
  types of—*cont.*
    ordinary, 13.24
    special, 13.25
    written, 13.29–13.30
Responsibilities
  directors and, 8.04
Retained profit
  dividends, 7.13
Retention of title
  receivership, and, 15.36
Retirement
  directors, 8.22
Revaluation reserve
  capital maintenance, 6.04
Rights issues
  securities, 5.22
Right to purchase, assignment of
  capital maintenance, 6.30

Sale and purchase agreement
  company incorporation, 3.37
Scheme of arrangement
  takeovers and mergers, 14.15–14.18
Scission
  European legislation, and, 1.14
Scottish law
  companies, 1.27
  minority protection
    judicial factors, 11.39
Scrip issues
  securities, 5.24
Secretary of state
  minority protection, 11.22
Securities
  allotment of shares
    authorised share capital, 5.11
    borrow, 5.08–5.09
    directors' authority, 5.12–5.13
    increase share capital, 5.08–5.09
    intimation of, 5.19–5.21
    members pre-emption rights,
      5.14–5.15
    payment for, 5.16–5.18
    procedure, 5.10
    registration of new shares, 5.19–5.21
    share capital, authorised, 5.11
  debentures, 5.32
  definition, 5.01
  insider dealing, 12.11
  issues
    bonus, 5.23
    rights, 5.22
    scrip, 5.24
  prospectuses, 5.25–5.26
  shares
    convertible, 5.07

Securities—*cont.*
  shares—*cont.*
    generally, 5.02–5.03
    ordinary, 5.04
    preference, 5.05
    redeemable, 5.06
  transfer of shares
    charges, 5.30
    concert party, 5.29
    disclosure of interests, 5.29
    forfeiture, 5.31
    generally, 5.27–5.28
    lien, 5.31
Seizure of books and papers
  dti investigation, 11.49
Self-incrimination
  directors, 8.36
  insider trading, 12.19
Senior executives
  generally, 8.14
Separate legal identity
  corporate veil, 2.01–2.03
Sequestration
  directors, 8.22
Service contracts
  directors' statutory duties, 9.23–9.24
Shadow director
  company secretary, and, 10.04
  generally, 8.13
Share
  securities, 5,01
Share capital, authorised
  securities, 5.11
Share dealing
  dti investigation, 11.48
Share for assets offer
  takeovers and mergers, 14.11
Share premium account
  capital maintenance, 6.44–6.45
  securities, 5.23
Share support scheme
  capital maintenance, 6.14
Share transfer, company approval
  directors' statutory duties, 9.21
Shareholder democracy
  generally, 13.31–13.32
**Shareholder, infringement of personal
  rights**
  minority protection, 11.10
Shareholders' agreements
  memorandum and articles of
    association, 4.24–4.25
Shareholders, ex
  minority protection
    liability, 11.28
Shares
  convertible, 5.07

Shares—*cont.*
  generally, 5.02–5.03
  ordinary, 5.04
  preference, 5.05
  redeemable, 5.06
Shares, class of
  memorandum and articles of
    association, 4.23
Shares, purchase of
  assignment of right to purchase, 6.30
  capital redemption reserve, 6.35–6.36
  contingent purchases, 6.31
  disclosure, 6.32
  failure to, 6.42
  introduction, 6.23–6.24
  own shares out of capital in private
    companies, 6.37–6.41
  payment, 6.33–6.34
  process
    introduction, 6.27
    market purchase, 6.29
    off market purchase, 6.28
  reasons, 6.25
  redemption, 6.26
  redemption reserve, 6.35–6.36
  right to purchase, assignment of, 6.30
Shares, redemption of
  assignment of right to purchase, 6.30
  capital redemption reserve, 6.35–6.36
  contingent purchases, 6.31
  disclosure, 6.32
  failure to, 6.42
  introduction, 6.23–6.24
  own shares out of capital in private
    companies, 6.37–6.41
  payment, 6.33–6.34
  process
    introduction, 6.27
    market purchase, 6.29
    off market purchase, 6.28
  reasons, 6.25
  redemption, 6.26
  redemption reserve, 6.35–6.36
  right to purchase, assignment of, 6.30
Single member companies
  company incorporation, 3.04
  corporate veil, and, 2.06
  European legislation, and, 1.14
  sole traders, and, 1.18
Skill and care
  directors' duty, 9.14–9.17
Sole directors
  directors' statutory duties, 9.27
Sole members
  directors' statutory duties, 9.27
Sole traders
  companies, 1.18

Sole traders—*cont.*
  company incorporation, 3.23
South Sea Bubble
  company incorporation, 1.02
Special notice
  company incorporation, 3.11
  meetings, 13.14
Special resolution
  company incorporation, 3.06
  memorandum, 4.03
Stamp duty
  company incorporation, 3.37
  securities, 5.19
Standard of care
  directors, 9.15
**Statement of Standard Accounting
  Practice**
  dividends, 7.05
Statute, and
  company name, inaccurate, 2.08–2.09
  introduction, 2.05
  liability, 2.10–2.11
  personal liability, 2.12
  plcs trading with one shareholder, 2.06
  trading certificate, absence of,
    2.07–2.12
Statutory duties
  company approval for property
    transfer, 9.21
  company approval for share transfer,
    9.21
  contracts with sole directors, 9.27
  contracts with sole members, 9.27
  declaration of interest, 9.22
  introduction, 9.18
  loans, 9.29–9.32
  loss of office, payment for, 9.20
  payments for loss of office, 9.20
  political donations, 9.33
  property transactions, 9.25
  property transfer, company approval,
    9.21
  service contracts, 9.23–9.24
  share transfer, company approval, 9.21
  sole directors, 9.27
  sole members, 9.27
  tax free payments, 9.19
  traded options, 9.28
  ultra vires contracts, 9.26
Statutory protection
  actual conduct, 11.21
  conducted
    interpretation, 11.18
  introduction, 11.15
  liability for ex-shareholders, 11.28
  majority shareholders, use of position,
    11.30–11.36

Statutory protection—*cont.*
maxims and, 11.26
member, 11.16
members' interests, 11.20
minority shareholder, maxims and, 11.26
minority shareholding, purchase of by majority at fair value, 11.25
order, 11.17
prejudice, 11.19
proposed conduct, 11.21
reform proposals, 11.37
remedies, 11.23, 11.29
Secretary of state, 11.22
unfairness, 11.19
unreasonable act, 11.27
Stock Exchange Surveillance Unit
insider dealing, 12.25
Stock-watering
securities, 5.08
Strict liability
crimes
corporate veil, 2.25
offences
company incorporation, 3.06
Subsequent financial years
dividends and accounts, 7.31
Subsidiaries companies
company incorporation, 3.25–3.27
Subsidiary undertaking
company incorporation, 3.26
Summary accounts
dividends and accounts, 7.39

Table A
articles of association, 4.21–4.22
directors, 9.01
meetings, and, 13.06, 13.13, 13.17–13.18, 13.21
Takeover
approval, 14.08
acquisition rules, 14.09
buying out the minority, 14.12–14.14
City Code
generally, 14.04–14.05
legal status, 14.06
Competition Commission, 14.07
introduction, 14.01
legalities, 14.02
mandatory bids, 14.10
market, 14.03
Office of Fair Trading, 14.07
scheme of arrangement, 14.15–14.18
share for assets offers, 14.11
Tax collector
receiver, 15.31

Tax free payments
directors' statutory duties, 9.19
Termination of directorship
dismissal, 8.23
methods, 8.22
unsatisfactory director, 8.21
Traded options
directors' statutory duties, 9.28
Trading certificate
absence of
company incorporation, 3.12
corporate veil, 2.07
securities, 5.18
Trading organisations, other
limited liability partnership, 1.21–1.23
limited partnership, 1.24
partnerships, 1.19–1.20
registered companies, 1.25–1.26
sole traders, 1.18
Transaction at an undervalue
winding up, 16.25
Transfer of shares
charges, 5.30
concert party, 5.29
disclosure of interests, 5.29
forfeiture, 5.31
generally, 5.27–5.28
lien, 5.31
True and fair view
dividends and accounts, 7.29
Types of director
alternate, 8.11
chairman of the board, 8.09
de facto director, 8.12
executive director, 8.07
introduction, 8.05
managing director, 8.06
nominee, 8.10
non-executive, 8.08
senior executives, 8.14
shadow director, 8.13

Ultra vires
European legislation, and, 1.14
minority protection, 11.07
Ultra vires contracts
directors' statutory duties, 9.26
Unfair preferences
winding up, 16.25
Unfairness
minority protection, 11.19
Unfit director
insolvent company and disqualification, 8.28–8.31
United Kingdom legislation
companies, 1.12–1.13

Unlimited companies
dividends and accounts, 7.38
Unreasonable act
minority protection, 11.27
Unsatisfactory director
termination of directorship, and, 8.21

Valuation report
securities, 5.17
Victimless crime
insider dealing, 12.02
Voluntary liquidation
dti investigation, 11.43
Voluntary winding up
company's property, disposal of, 16.14
creditors', 16.11–16.13
generally, 16.07–16.09
members', 16.10
Voting
generally, 13.18
takeovers and mergers, 14.16
Voting rights
takeover and mergers, 14.10

Warrant
securities, 5,01
Whitewash procedure
capital maintenance, 6.20–6.22
Winding up
administrator, 16.05
company, dissolution of
application, 16.35
bona vacantia, 16.36
generally, 16.33
Registrar's, 16.34
company's assets, distribution of,
16.30–16.31

Winding up—*cont.*
compulsory
getting in the estate, 16.25–16.27
grounds, 16.16–16.20
insolvent company's estate, getting
in, 16.25–16.27
jurisdiction, 16.15
liability of directors, 16.28–16.29
petition, procedure, 16.21–16.24
procedure, 16.21–16.24
dissolution of the company
application, 16.35
bona vacantia, 16.36
generally, 16.33
Registrar's, 16.34
just and equitable grounds, 11.38
liquidator
defeating, 16.32
generally, 16.03–16.04
methods, 16.06
procedure, 16.02
purpose, 16.01
receiver, 16.03–16.04
voluntary
company's property, disposal of,
16.14
creditors', 16.11–16.13
generally, 16.07–16.09
members', 16.10
Written off
dividends and accounts, 7.10
Wrongful trading
directors' liability, 9.46–9.48